ENDANGERED SPECIES

PROTECTING BIODIVERSITY

ISSN 1930-3319

ENDANGERED SPECIES

PROTECTING BIODIVERSITY

Kim Masters Evans

INFORMATION PLUS® REFERENCE SERIES
Formerly Published by Information Plus, Wylie, Texas

THOMSON

GALE

Detroit • New York • San Francisco • New Haven, Conn. • Waterville, Maine • London

Endangered Species: Protecting Biodiversity

Kim Masters Evans
Paula Kepos, Series Editor

Project Editor
John McCoy

Permissions
Shalice Caldwell-Shah, Emma Hull,
Edna Hedblad

Composition and Electronic Prepress
Evi Seoud

Manufacturing
Drew Kalasky

ISBN-13 978-0-7876-5103-9 (set)
ISBN-10 0-7876-5103-6 (set)
ISBN-13 978-1-4144-0412-7
ISBN-10 1-4144-0412-3
ISSN 1930-3319

This title is also available as an e-book.
ISBN-13 978-1-4144-1045-6 (set)
ISBN-10 1-4144-1045-X (set)
Contact your Thomson Gale sales representative for ordering information.

Printed in the United States of America
10 9 8 7 6 5 4 3 2 1

TABLE OF CONTENTS

PREFACE

Endangered Species: Protecting Biodiversity is part of the *Information Plus Reference Series*. The purpose of each volume of the series is to present the latest facts on a topic of pressing concern in modern American life. These topics include today's most controversial and most studied social issues: abortion, capital punishment, care for the elderly, crime, health care, the environment, immigration, minorities, social welfare, women, youth, and many more. Although written especially for the high school and undergraduate student, this series is an excellent resource for anyone in need of factual information on current affairs.

By presenting the facts, it is Thomson Gale's intention to provide its readers with everything they need to reach an informed opinion on current issues. To that end, there is a particular emphasis in this series on the presentation of scientific studies, surveys, and statistics. These data are generally presented in the form of tables, charts, and other graphics placed within the text of each book. Every graphic is directly referred to and carefully explained in the text. The source of each graphic is presented within the graphic itself. The data used in these graphics are drawn from the most reputable and reliable sources, in particular from the various branches of the U.S. government and from major independent polling organizations. Every effort has been made to secure the most recent information available. The reader should bear in mind that many major studies take years to conduct, and that additional years often pass before the data from these studies are made available to the public. Therefore, in many cases the most recent information available in 2006 dated from 2003 or 2004. Older statistics are sometimes presented as well, if they are of particular interest and no more recent nformation exists.

Although statistics are a major focus of the *Information Plus Reference Series*, they are by no means its only content. Each book also presents the widely held positions and important ideas that shape how the book's subject is discussed in the United States. These positions are explained in detail and, where possible, in the words of their proponents. Some of the other material to be found in these books includes: historical background; descriptions of major events related to the subject; relevant laws and court cases; and examples of how these issues play out in American life. Some books also feature primary documents, or have pro and con debate sections giving the words and opinions of prominent Americans on both sides of a controversial topic. All material is presented in an even-handed and unbiased manner; the reader will never be encouraged to accept one view of an issue over another.

HOW TO USE THIS BOOK

The status of endangered species is an issue of concern both for many Americans and for people around the world. In particular, balancing biodiversity with economics has led to much controversy. This book looks at what has been done to protect endangered species in America and around the world, and examines the debate over what future actions are warranted.

Endangered Species: Protecting Biodiversity consists of eleven chapters and three appendices. Each chapter is devoted to a particular aspect of endangered species. For a summary of the information covered in each chapter, please see the synopses provided in the Table of Contents at the front of the book. Chapters generally begin with an overview of the basic facts and background information on the chapter's topic, then proceed to examine subtopics of particular interest. For example, Chapter 5: Marine Mammals begins by describing the laws and regulations enacted in the United States specifically to protect marine mammals, as well as the role the Endangered Species Act plays in protecting these animals. The status of different classes of marine mammals are then examined, with sections on whales, dolphins, seals, sea otters, manatees, and others. Both U.S. and foreign species are covered. Threats to different types of marine mammals, species that are especially endangered, and plans for recovery are all discussed in detail. Readers can find their way through a chapter by looking for the section and subsection headings, which are clearly set off from the text. Or, they can refer to the book's extensive index if they already know what they are looking for.

Statistical Information

The tables and figures featured throughout *Endangered Species: Protecting Biodiversity* will be of particular use to the reader in learning about this issue. The tables and figures represent an extensive collection of the most recent and important statistics on endangered species, as well as related issues—for example, graphics in the book cover the number of endangered species and the reasons for their endangerment; the locations of National Parks; pesticide runoff threats; and medically useful plant species. The photographs illustrate some of the most threatened species on earth, including the Asian box turtle, the Texas horned lizard, and the red wolf. Thomson Gale believes that making this information available to the reader is the most important way in which we fulfill the goal of this book: to help readers understand the issues and controversies surrounding endangered species and reach their own conclusions about them.

Each table or figure has a unique identifier appearing above it, for ease of identification and reference. Titles for the tables and figures explain their purpose. At the end of each table or figure, the original source of the data is provided.

In order to help readers understand these often complicated statistics, all tables and figures are explained in the text. References in the text direct the reader to the relevant statistics. Furthermore, the contents of all tables and figures are fully indexed. Please see the opening section of the Index at the back of this volume for a description of how to find tables and figures within it.

Appendices

In addition to the main body text and images, *Endangered Species: Protecting Biodiversity* has three appendices. The first is the Important Names and Addresses directory. Here the reader will find contact information for a number of government and private organizations that can provide further information on aspects of endangered species. The second appendix is the Resources section, which can also assist the reader in conducting his or her own research. In this section the author and editors of *Endangered Species: Protecting Biodiversity* describe some of the sources that were most useful during the compilation of this book. The final appendix is the Index.

ADVISORY BOARD CONTRIBUTIONS

The staff of Information Plus would like to extend its heartfelt appreciation to the Information Plus Advisory Board. This dedicated group of media professionals provides feedback on the series on an ongoing basis. Their comments allow the editorial staff who work on the project to continually make the series better and more user-friendly. Our top priorities are to produce the highest-quality and most useful books possible, and the Advisory Board's contributions to this process are invaluable.

The members of the Information Plus Advisory Board are:

- Kathleen R. Bonn, Librarian, Newbury Park High School, Newbury Park, California
- Madelyn Garner, Librarian, San Jacinto College— North Campus, Houston, Texas
- Anne Oxenrider, Media Specialist, Dundee High School, Dundee, Michigan
- Charles R. Rodgers, Director of Libraries, Pasco-Hernando Community College, Dade City, Florida
- James N. Zitzelsberger, Library Media Department Chairman, Oshkosh West High School, Oshkosh, Wisconsin

COMMENTS AND SUGGESTIONS

The editors of the *Information Plus Reference Series* welcome your feedback on *Endangered Species: Protecting Biodiversity*. Please direct all correspondence to:

Editors
Information Plus Reference Series
27500 Drake Rd.
Farmington Hills, MI 48331-3535

CHAPTER 1
EXTINCTION AND ENDANGERED SPECIES

Earth is richly supplied with different types of living organisms, including animals, plants, fungi, and bacteria. Various living organisms co-exist in their environments, forming complex, interrelated communities. Living organisms depend on one another for nutrients, shelter, and other benefits. The extinction of any one species can set off a chain reaction that affects many other species, particularly if the loss occurs near the bottom of the food chain. For example, the extinction of a particular insect or plant might seem inconsequential. However, there may be fish or small animals that depend on that resource for foodstuff. The loss can threaten the survival of these creatures, and larger predators that prey upon them. Extinction can have a ripple effect that spreads throughout nature.

In addition to its biological consequences, extinction poses a moral dilemma for humans, the only species capable of saving the others. The presence of humans on the planet has affected all other life forms, particularly plants and animals. Human lifestyles have proven to be incompatible with the survival of some other species. Purposeful efforts have been made to eliminate animals that prey on people, livestock, crops, or pose any threat to human livelihoods. Some wild animals have been decimated by human desire for meat, hides, fur, or other body parts with commercial value. Likewise demand for land, water, timber, and other natural resources has left many wild plants and animals with little to no suitable habitat. Humans have also affected nature by introducing nonnative species to local areas and producing pollutants that have a negative impact on the environment. The combination of these anthropogenic (human-related) effects with natural obstacles that limit survival, such as disease or low birthrates, have proven to be too much for some species to overcome. They have no chance of survival without human help.

As a result, societies have difficult choices to make about the amount of effort and money they are willing to spend to keep imperiled species from becoming extinct. Will people accept limits on their property rights, recreational activities, and means of livelihood to save a plant or animal? Should saving such popular species as whales and dolphins take priority over saving obscure, annoying, or feared species? Is it the responsibility of humans to save every kind of life form from disappearing, or is extinction an inevitable part of nature, in which the strong survive and the weak perish? These are some of the difficult questions that people face as they ponder the fate of other species living on this planet.

DEFINING AND NAMING LIFE ON EARTH

Living organisms are named and categorized according to a taxonomy, a hierarchical system of order based on the natural relationships among all types of life. For example, Table 1.1 shows the taxonomic chart for blue whales, the largest creatures on Earth. Blue whales are described by eight taxonomic levels ending with "species." A species is a term assigned to a group of organisms that are considered capable of interbreeding with one another. There is another category called "subspecies," that ranks immediately below species. A subspecies (abbreviated ssp.) is a population of a particular geographical region that is genetically different from other populations of the same species, but can still interbreed with them.

Animals and plants are identified by their common names and by unique scientific names. Some organisms have more than one common name. The animal known as the mountain lion is also called a puma or a cougar. To avoid confusion, scientific bodies have established systems of nomenclature (naming) for animals and plants. These systems are based on the example set by Carolus Linnaeus (1707–78), a Swiss botanist who published classifications for thousands of plants and animals. Linnaeus popularized the use of a binary naming system in

TABLE 1.1

Taxonomic chart for blue whales

Classification	Blue whale example	Explanation
Kingdom	Animalia	Whales belong to the kingdom Animalia because whales, have many cells, ingest food, and are formed from a "blastula" (from a fertilized egg).
Phylum	Chordata	An animal from the phylum Chordata has a spinal cord and gill pouches.
Class	Mammalia	Whales and other mammals are warm blooded, have glands to provide milk for their off-spring, and have a four-chambered heart.
Order	Cetacea	Cetaceans are mammals live completely in the water.
[Suborder]	Mysticeti	Whales that belong to the suborder Mysticeti have baleen plates (big filters in their mouths) rather than teeth.
Family	Balaenidae	The family Balaenidae, also called rorqual whales. They have pleats around their throat that allow them to hold lots of water (which contains their food).
Genus	*Balaenoptera*	A genus is a group of species that are more closely related to one another than any group in the family. *Balaenoptera* refers to the genus.
Species	*Musculus*	A species is a grouping of individuals that interbreed successfully. The blue whale species name is *musculus*.

SOURCE: "The Chart Below Is a Sample Taxonomic Chart for Blue Whales," in *Scientific Classification*, U.S. Department of Commerce, National Oceanic and Atmospheric Administration, National Marine Mammal Laboratory, March 3, 2004, http://nmml.afsc.noaa.gov/education/taxonomy .htm (accessed February 7, 2006)

which the first word names the genus of the organism. The genus, which identifies a group of closely related species, is followed by a specific epithet (a descriptive word or phrase) that differentiates one species from another. Linnaeus used Latin words in his nomenclature because Latin was the preferred language for scientific publications during the eighteenth century.

Since the time of Linnaeus many thousands of additional plants and animals have been discovered or intentionally bred. Modern convention dictates that the scientist who first describes an organism in a scholarly publication chooses the scientific name for that organism. The scientific name must be in Latin or contain words that have been "Latinized" (rendered to appear Latin). During the 1800s the American researcher Frank Higgins discovered a new species of mussel (clam) in the Mississippi River. He called it Higgins' Eye. The scientific name is *Lampsilis higginsii*. In this case the specific epithet reflects the common name of the organism, but it is not required to do; it can be any descriptive term.

Scientific names are either italicized or underlined in print to distinguish them from surrounding text. The genus is capitalized, while the specific epithet is not capitalized.

Subspecies are indicated in scientific nomenclature with an additional term. For example, the scientific name of the blue whale is *Balaenoptera musculus*. A subspecies, the pygmy blue whale, is called *Balaenoptera musculus brevicauda*. Genus reassignments are indicated with the "=" sign in a scientific name. When the royal snail was discovered in 1977 it was assigned to the genus *Marstonia*. Ten years later biologists decided the snail was more properly a member of the genus *Pyrgulopsis*. Thus, the scientific name of the royal snail is written as *Pyrgulopsis (=Marstonia) ogmorhaphe*. When the species is not known for an organism of known genus, the scientific name is written with sp. (indicating a single species) or spp. (indicating multiple species) as the specific epithet. The latter format is also used when referring to all species in a genus. For example, *Pyrgulopsis spp.*, refers to all species within the genus *Pyrgulopsis*.

The rules governing scientific names for animals are overseen by the International Commission on Zoological Nomenclature, headquartered in London, England. The International Code of Botanical Nomenclature for plants is set by the International Botanical Congress (IBC), a meeting of botanists from around the world held every six years. The most recent IBC took place in Vienna, Austria, in 2005.

BIODIVERSITY

Biodiversity is short for biological diversity. It refers to the richness and variety of living organisms across the planet. Biodiversity is important at levels within the taxonomic table and at the genetic level. For example, all humans are members of one species—*Homo sapiens*—but humans can vary widely in their personal characteristics, such as race, hair color, and eye color. These differences are due to slight variations in genetic material from person to person. Genetic biodiversity results in different individual properties within a species. It also helps ensure that deformities or disorders in genetic material do not become concentrated in a population.

Inbreeding is mating between closely related individuals with extremely similar genetic material. It is almost certain that if one of these individuals has any kind of gene disorder, the other individual will also have it. This disorder might not cause any notable problems in the parents, but could become concentrated in the offspring and cause serious health problems for them. This explains why there is a certain lower limit to the population of some species, particularly those that are isolated in a specific location. If the population falls too low, the remaining individuals will be so closely related that any inherent gene problems can kill off the resulting offspring and ultimately wipe out the entire species.

WHAT ARE ENDANGERED SPECIES?

A species is described as extinct when no living members remain. Scientists know from the study of fossils that dinosaurs, mammoths, saber-toothed cats, and countless other animal and plant species that once lived on Earth no longer exist. These species have "died out", or become extinct. Once a species is extinct, there is no way to bring it back.

The U.S. government defines endangered species as those that are at risk of extinction through all or a significant portion of their natural habitats. Threatened species are defined as those likely to become endangered in the foreseeable future. The management at the federal level of endangered and threatened species is handled by two agencies, the U.S. Fish and Wildlife Service (FWS) and the National Marine Fisheries Service (NMFS). The FWS is an agency of the Department of the Interior and oversees the terrestrial (land-based) and freshwater species. The NMFS is an agency of the National Oceanic and Atmospheric Administration (NOAA) under the U.S. Department of Commerce. The NMFS is responsible for marine (ocean-dwelling) species and those that are anadromous (migrate between the ocean and freshwater).

The U.S. Fish and Wildlife Service maintains a list of species that are endangered or threatened in the United States and abroad. Both endangered and threatened species are protected by laws intended to save them from extinction. In many cases, recovery plans for endangered species have also been developed and implemented. These include measures designed to protect endangered and threatened species and to help their populations grow.

MASS EXTINCTION

In the billions of years since life began on Earth, species have formed, existed, and then become extinct. Scientists call the natural extinction of a few species per million years a background, or normal, rate. When the extinction rate doubles for many different groups of plants and animals at the same time, this is described as a mass extinction. Mass extinctions have occurred infrequently in Earth's history and, in general, have been attributed to major cataclysmic geological or astronomical events. Five mass extinctions have occurred in the last 600 million years. These episodes, known as the Big Five, occurred at the end of five geologic periods:

- Ordovician (505–440 million years ago)
- Devonian (410–360 million years ago)
- Permian (286–245 million years ago)
- Triassic (245–208 million years ago)
- Cretaceous (146–65 million years ago)

After each mass extinction the floral (plant) and faunal (animal) composition of the Earth changed drastically. The largest mass extinction on record occurred at the end of the Permian, when an estimated 90% to 95% of all species became extinct. The Cretaceous extinction is perhaps the most familiar—it was at the end of the Cretaceous that many species of dinosaurs became extinct. The Cretaceous extinction is hypothesized to have resulted from the collision of an asteroid with the Earth.

The Sixth Mass Extinction?

Scientists estimate that hundreds, or even thousands, of species are being lost around the world each year. This suggests that we are currently in the midst of another mass extinction. Unlike previous mass extinctions, however, the current extinction does not appear to be associated with a cataclysmic physical event. Rather, the heightened extinction rate has coincided with the success and spread of human beings. Researchers predict that as humans continue to alter natural ecosystems through destruction of natural habitats, pollution, introduction of nonnative species, and global climate change, the extinction rate may eventually approach several hundred species per day. This would be a rate millions of times higher than normal background levels. The United Nations, in *Global Biodiversity Outlook 2* (March 2006), concluded that without immediate intervention, more species of flora and fauna may disappear than were lost in the mass extinction that wiped out the dinosaurs sixty-five million years ago.

In 1948 an international conference on conservation resulted in formation of the International Union for the Protection of Nature. In 1956 the name was changed to the International Union for the Conservation of Nature and Natural Resources (IUCN; now the World Conservation Union). The IUCN is based in Gland, Switzerland, and is the world's largest conservation organization. As of 2006 more than eighty nations and 800 nongovernmental organizations are members. The IUCN reports that in the last 500 years, at least 816 species are known to have become extinct as a result of human activity. The actual number is probably much higher.

U.S. HISTORY—SOME EXTINCTIONS AND SOME CLOSE CALLS

Colonization of the New World by European settlers severely depleted the ranks of some native wild species. The introduction of livestock brought new animal diseases that devastated some native animals. Widespread hunting and trapping led to the demise of other species. During the early 1800s the United States was home to millions, perhaps billions, of passenger pigeons. These migratory birds traveled in enormous flocks and were extremely popular with hunters. By the beginning of the twentieth century the species was virtually exterminated. The last known passenger pigeon died in the Cincinnati Zoo in 1914. The heath hen, a small wild fowl native to the United States and once very abundant, was wiped out of existence by 1932. Stocks of other animals—beaver, elk, and bison (American buffalo)—were driven to the brink of extinction, but saved by conservation efforts.

Bison Comeback

The bison is the largest terrestrial animal in North America. It has short, pointed horns and a hump over the front shoulders. The head, neck, and front parts of the body are covered by a thick, dark coat of long, curly hair; the rear has shorter, lighter hair. Adult males weigh as much as 1,800 to 2,400 pounds; females are smaller. Adult males also have black "beards" about a foot long. Bison are social animals and travel in herds. Considering their size and weight, bison are remarkably light on their hooves—unlike cattle, they love to run and are surprisingly fast. Bison were central to the existence of Plains Native Americans, who used them for food and made clothing from their hides and tools from their bones. The dried dung, called buffalo chips, was used for fuel.

Sixty million bison—or buffalo—once roamed the grasslands of America. (See Figure 1.1.) Historical accounts describe herds stretching as far as the eye could see. Although Native Americans hunted bison, it was not until European settlers came with firearms that their numbers fell drastically. Many people shot the animals for fun, while others sold the hides. Bison numbers were eventually reduced to fewer than one thousand.

Bison first received protection from the U.S. government in 1872, with the establishment of Yellowstone National Park in Wyoming and Montana. However, the welfare of the small herd of bison in the park was largely ignored until 1901, when it was discovered that only twenty-five individuals remained. The herd was restored to 1,000 by 1930 with bison imported from the Great Plains. As the Yellowstone herd multiplied, the park service shot animals to keep the population under control. This practice was unnecessary, however, because harsh winters caused the herd to dwindle naturally. The park service stopped shooting bison in the 1960s, and by 1994 the population of the Yellowstone herd had reached a peak of 4,200 animals. According to the National Park Service there are more than 150,000 bison on public and private lands across the United States, including approximately 4,000 at Yellowstone National Park.

Today some populations of bison are managed as livestock because they have become a food source for humans. Bison are a source of high-protein, low-fat, low-cholesterol meat. According to the National Bison Association, more than 35,000 bison were slaughtered for food during 2005.

FIGURE 1.1

Bison (or American buffaloes) are the largest terrestrial animals in North America. (Field Mark Publications.)

HOW MANY SPECIES ARE ENDANGERED?

Since 1960 the International Union for the Conservation of Nature and Natural Resources has compiled the *IUCN Red List of Threatened Species*, which aims to examine the status of biological species across the globe. The so-called "Red List" categorizes species based on the level of risk of their extinction in the wild, as follows:

- Critically endangered—extremely high risk

- Endangered—very high risk

- Vulnerable—high risk

- Near threatened—likely to qualify for a risk category in the near future

The IUCN refers to species in all of these categories as "threatened" species.

Determining how many species of plants and animals are threatened or endangered is difficult. In fact, only a small fraction of the species in existence have even been identified and named, let alone studied in detail. Various estimates of the total number of threatened/endangered species on Earth range from five million to 100 million with most estimates figuring around ten million species worldwide. Of these, about 1.5 million species have been named and described. Mammals, which are probably the best-studied group—and the one that includes humans—make up less than 1% of all known organisms. Insects are a particularly rich biological group—over 900,000 insect species have been identified, with countless more to be described.

Worldwide, in the IUCN's 2004 Red List, a total of 15,503 species were listed as threatened. Just over 38,000 species were examined out of the 1.5 million species that the IUCN considers "described species." Thus, only 2.5% of all known species were evaluated by the IUCN.

The listed species were as follows:

- 1,101 of 4,853 mammal species evaluated (23%)
- 1,213 of 9,917 bird species evaluated (12%)
- 304 of 499 reptile species evaluated (61%)
- 1,770 of 5,743 amphibian species evaluated (31%)
- 800 of 1,721 fish species evaluated (46%)
- 559 of 771 insect species evaluated (73%)
- 974 of 2,163 mollusk species evaluated (45%)
- 429 of 498 crustacean species evaluated (86%)
- 30 of 55 other species evaluated (55%)

In addition, the IUCN listed 8,321 plant species as threatened in 2004 out of 11,824 species evaluated. More than 280,000 plant species are known to the IUCN.

According to the IUCN nearly all described bird, amphibian, and mammal species were evaluated during 2004. The other species have not yet been thoroughly assessed. Further study will likely result in many more species being added to the Red List.

Table 1.2 lists the number of species identified as threatened or endangered under the Endangered Species Act (ESA) as of February 1, 2006. Of the 1,090 animal species listed, 527 are found in the United States. Among these, 398 are endangered and 129 are threatened. Among animals, the greatest numbers of listed species occur among fish, birds, and mammals. Of the 748 plant species listed, 745 are found in the United States. Among these, 599 are endangered, and 146 are threatened. Nearly all of the endangered plants are flowering plants.

Figure 1.2 shows the number of listed U.S. species per calendar year from 1980 through 2005. Table 1.3 shows the breakdown by species group and year. The number of listed species increased dramatically between 1980 and the mid-1990s. The plateau in listings during the late 1990s and early 2000s reflects, in part, budgetary constraints on listing activity at the U.S. Fish and Wildlife Service.

Within the United States, endangered and threatened species are not evenly distributed but are clustered in specific geographical areas. Figure 1.3 shows the number of federally listed endangered and threatened species in each state on February 1, 2006. Regions where the number of listed species is particularly high include southern Appalachia, Florida, the Southwest, California, and Hawaii. Hawaii harbors more threatened and endangered species than any other state, despite its small size. This is due largely to the fact that a significant proportion of Hawaiian plant and animal life is endemic—that is, found nowhere else on Earth. Endemism is very dangerous for imperiled species for a variety of reasons. A single calamitous event, such as a hurricane, earthquake, or disease epidemic, could wipe out the entire population at one time. The likelihood of interbreeding and resulting genetic problems is also higher for a species that is so geographically limited

SPECIES LOSS—CRISIS OR FALSE ALARM?

Environmental issues, which have a tendency to pit conservation against business or economic development, are often hotly debated. With respect to current threats to biodiversity, some critics argue that the scale of loss is not as great as we imagine. They point to uncertainty regarding the total number of species, as well as the geographic distributions of species. Other challengers claim that loss of habitat and disruption by human activity are not powerful enough to cause the massive extinction being documented. Still other challengers contend that extinction is inevitable, and that the Earth has experienced, and recovered from, mass extinctions before. They conclude that the current biodiversity loss, while huge, is not disastrous.

In addition, opponents of conservation frequently argue that "green" policies such as the U.S. Endangered Species Act place the needs of wildlife before those of humans. This was the central issue in one of the bitterest battles over an endangered species, that concerning protection of northern spotted owl habitat. (See Figure 1.4.) In 1990 declining populations resulted in the listing of the northern spotted owl as a threatened species. In 1992 the Fish and Wildlife Service set aside seven million acres of forestland in the Pacific Northwest—both private and public—as critical habitat for the species. Logging was banned on federal lands within these areas. Loggers protested this ban, arguing that jobs would be lost. Supporters of the ban, on the other hand, claimed that the logging industry in the area was already in decline and that continued logging would preserve existing jobs only for a short time. Eventually, a compromise was reached in which logging was limited to trees under a certain size, leaving the mature growth for owl habitat. By early 1993 almost all old-growth logging on federal lands had been stopped by court action.

TABLE 1.2

Count of endangered and threatened species and U.S. species with recovery plans, February 2006

Group	Endangered U.S.	Endangered Foreign	Threatened U.S.	Threatened Foreign	Total species	U.S. species with recovery plans[b]
Mammals	68	254	11	20	353	55
Birds	77	175	13	6	271	78
Reptiles	14	64	22	16	116	33
Amphibians	12	8	9	1	30	16
Fishes	74	11	42	1	128	98
Clams	62	2	8	0	72	69
Snails	24	1	12	0	37	29
Insects	36	4	9	0	49	32
Arachnids	12	0	0	0	12	5
Crustaceans	19	0	3	0	22	13
Animal subtotal	398	519	129	44	1090	428
Flowering plants	571	1	143	0	715	584
Conifers and cycads	2	0	1	2	5	3
Ferns and allies	24	0	2	0	26	26
Lichens	2	0	0	0	2	2
Plant subtotal	599	1	146	2	748	615
Grand total	997	520	275	46	1838[a]	1,043

Total U.S. endangered—997 (398 animals, 599 plants)
Total U.S. threatened—275 (129 animals, 146 plants)
Total U.S. species—1,272 (527 animals[c], 745 plants)

[a]There are 1,868 total listings (1,300 U.S.). A listing is an E (endangered) or a T (threatened) in the "status" column of 50 CFR 17.11 or 17.12 (the Lists of Endangered and Threatened Wildlife and Plants). The following types of listings are combined as single counts in the table above: species listed both as threatened and endangered (dual status), and subunits of a single species listed as distinct population segments. Only the endangered population is tallied for dual status populations (except for the following: Olive ridley sea turtle; for which only the threatened U.S. population is tallied). The dual status U.S. species that are tallied as endangered are: California tiger salamander, chinook salmon, Coho salmon, gray wolf, green sea turtle, piping plover, Roseate tern, sockeye salmon, steelhead, steller sea-lion. The dual status foreign species that are tallied as endangered are: argali, chimpanzee, leopard, saltwater crocodile. Distinct population segments tallied as one include: California tiger salamander, chinook salmon, chum salmon, Coho salmon, Dugong, steelhead. Entries that represent entire genera or families include: Alabama lampmussel, Anthony's riversnail, argali, birdwing pearlymussel, black-footed ferret, bog (=Muhlenberg) turtle, Boulder darter, brown pelican, Cactus ferruginous pygmy-owl, California condor, California tiger salamander, catspaw (=purple cat's paw pearlymussel), chimpanzee, chinook salmon, Chum salmon, clubshell, Coho salmon, Colorado pikeminnow (=squawfish), Columbian white-tailed deer, copperbelly water snake, cracking pearlymussel, Cumberland bean (pearlymussel), Cumberland monkeyface (pearlymussel), Cumberlandian combshell, Delmarva Peninsula fox squirrel, desert tortoise, Dromedary pearlymussel, Dugong, duskytail darter, finerayed pigtoe, gopher tortoise, gray whale, gray wolf, green sea turtle, grizzly bear, Guam rail, leopard, marbled murrelet, Mariana fruit bat (=Mariana flying fox), mountain yellow-legged frog, olive ridley sea turtle, oyster mussel, piping plover, red wolf, Roseate tern, saltwater crocodile, shiny pigtoe, smoky madtom, sockeye salmon, Southern sea otter, spotfin chub, steelhead, steller sea-lion, straight-horned markhor, tidewater goby, Tubercled blossom (pearlymussel), turgid blossom (pearlymussel), Western snowy plover, whooping crane, winged mapleleaf, woodland caribou, woundfin, yellow blossom (pearlymussel), yellowfin madtom.
[b]There are 553 distinct approved recovery plans. Some recovery plans cover more than one species, and a few species have separate plans covering different parts of their ranges. This count include only plans generated by the United States Fish and Wildlife Service (USFWS) or jointly by the USFWS and National Marine Fisheries Service (NMFS), and includes only listed species that occur in the United States.
[c]11 animal species have dual status in the U.S.

SOURCE: "Summary of Listed Species: Species and Recovery Plans as of 02/01/2006," in *Threatened and Endangered Species System (TESS)*, U.S. Fish and Wildlife Service, 2006, http://ecos.fws.gov/tess_public/Boxscore.do (accessed February 1, 2006)

In 1994 a group of federal agencies adopted the *Northwest Forest Plan* for management of old-growth forests in the Pacific Northwest. The plan has three goals:

- Manage federal forests so that sustainable timber production and biological diversity are achieved

- Coordinate actions by various federal agencies involved in forest management and ensure that they receive input from nonfederal parties

- Provide economic assistance and job retraining for displaced timber workers and other parties adversely affected by reduced timber harvesting

FIGURE 1.2

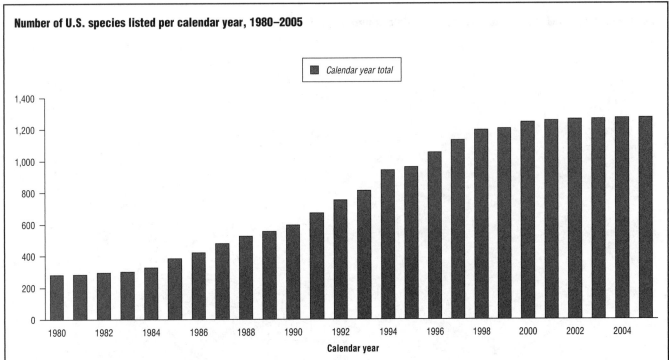

Number of U.S. species listed per calendar year, 1980–2005

Calendar year total

Calendar year

SOURCE: "Number of U.S. Listed Species Per Calendar Year, 1980–2005," in *Threatened and Endangered Species System (TESS)*, U.S. Fish and Wildlife Service, 2006, http://www.fws.gov/endangered/stats/cy%20count_2005.pdf (accessed February 1, 2006)

TABLE 1.3

Number of U.S. species listed per calendar year, by category, 1980–2005

[Total listed (endangered & threatened)]

Calendar year	Mammals	Birds	Reptiles	Amphibians	Fish	Crustaceans	Snails	Insects	Arachnids	Clams	Plants	Calendar year total*
1980	36	61	25	8	47	1	7	14	0	23	59	281
1981	36	61	25	8	47	1	8	13	0	23	61	283
1982	36	61	26	8	49	3	8	13	0	23	67	294
1983	39	61	26	8	49	4	8	13	0	23	69	300
1984	42	69	26	8	51	4	8	13	0	23	82	326
1985	48	72	26	8	64	4	8	13	0	23	118	384
1986	49	75	28	8	70	5	8	15	0	23	141	422
1987	52	82	32	9	74	6	8	15	0	28	174	480
1988	56	81	32	9	77	9	8	18	4	31	201	526
1989	58	81	32	11	82	9	9	19	4	34	217	556
1990	61	83	32	11	86	10	9	21	4	39	240	596
1991	64	83	32	11	88	10	13	23	4	42	302	672
1992	65	84	33	11	91	11	18	25	4	42	369	753
1993	65	88	33	11	98	13	19	26	4	53	403	813
1994	66	90	33	12	105	17	22	28	4	54	510	941
1995	66	91	33	12	105	17	22	29	5	57	525	962
1996	66	90	33	13	107	17	22	29	5	57	614	1,053
1997	66	93	36	16	108	19	22	37	5	62	668	1,132
1998	69	93	36	16	119	20	28	37	5	69	702	1,194
1999	69	89	38	17	112	20	28	37	5	69	721	1,205
2000	72	93	36	18	114	21	31	42	12	69	736	1,244
2001	73	92	36	19	115	21	32	44	12	70	740	1,254
2002	74	92	36	22	115	21	32	44	12	70	745	1,263
2003	74	92	36	22	115	21	32	44	12	70	746	1,264
2004	78	93	36	22	115	21	32	44	12	70	748	1,271
2005	79	90	36	21	116	22	36	45	12	70	745	1,272

*Totals are not additive. Number of species listed fluctuate between years because of new listings, reclassifications, delistings, new information on taxonomy, and other reasons. For the 11 species that have dual status, only the endangered population is tallied except for one species for which only the threatened population is tallied.

SOURCE: "Number of Endangered and Threatened U.S. Listed Species Per Calendar Year," in *Threatened and Endangered Species System (TESS)*, U.S. Fish and Wildlife Service, 2006, http://www.fws.gov/endangered/stats/cy%20count_2005.pdf (accessed February 1, 2006)

FIGURE 1.3

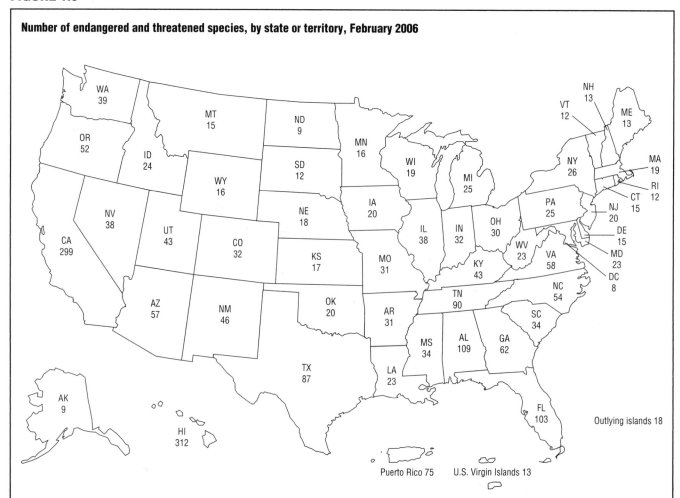

Number of endangered and threatened species, by state or territory, February 2006

Note: Total U.S. species is 1,272. Numbers are not additive, a species often occurs in multiple states. Omits "similarity of appearance" and experimental populations. Does not map whales and non-nesting sea turtles in state coastal waters. The species counted include listed pinnipeds (seals, etc.) and anadromous fishes under the sole jurisdiction of the National Marine Fisheries Service that use land or fresh waters within the states and territories of the United States. Species are not broken up into listing entities as they are in the state list reports. Species not listed in a state are not counted, although these may occur there in a non-protected population.

SOURCE: "Listed Species Range by State/Territory as of Wed Feb 1 01:00:04 MST 2006," in *Threatened and Endangered Species System*, U.S. Department of the Interior, U.S. Fish and Wildlife Service, February 1, 2006, http://www.fws.gov/endangered/wildlife.html#maps (accessed February 1, 2006)

The compromise worked out in the *Plan* did not fully please either side in the controversy. In 2002 organizations representing the timber industry sued the U.S. Fish and Wildlife Service claiming that northern spotted owl populations had recovered enough to remove the bird from the list of threatened species. The FWS conducted a status review and concluded in 2004 that the threatened listing should remain in place. The agency noted that the *Northwest Forest Plan* has successfully minimized habitat loss on federal lands. However, populations of northern spotted owls in Washington, Oregon, and California have continued to decline due to a combination of threats, including forest fires, bird and tree diseases, and competition for habitat from barred owls.

WHY SAVE ENDANGERED SPECIES?

Proponents of conservation believe that saving species from extinction is important for many reasons.

Species have both aesthetic and recreational value, as the tremendous popularity of zoos, wildlife safaris, recreational hiking, and wildlife watching (bird watching, whale watching, etc.) indicate. Wildlife also has educational and scientific value. In addition, because all species depend on other species for resources, the impact of a single lost species is difficult to predict and could potentially be immense. Scientists have shown that habitats with greater biodiversity are more stable—that is, they are better able to adjust to and recover from disturbances. This is because different species may perform overlapping functions in a biologically diverse ecosystem. Habitats with less diversity are more vulnerable, because a disturbance affecting one species may cause the entire network of interactions to collapse. Furthermore, many species have great economic value to human beings. Plants provide the genetic diversity used to breed new strains of agricultural crops, and many have been used to develop pharmaceutical

FIGURE 1.4

The northern spotted owl, which inhabits old-growth forests in the Pacific Northwest, was the subject of a lengthy battle pitting environmentalists against logging interests. (U.S. Fish and Wildlife Service.)

FIGURE 1.5

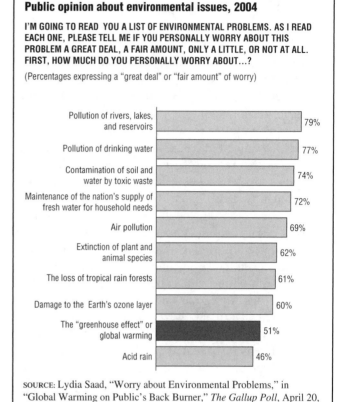

Public opinion about environmental issues, 2004

I'M GOING TO READ YOU A LIST OF ENVIRONMENTAL PROBLEMS. AS I READ EACH ONE, PLEASE TELL ME IF YOU PERSONALLY WORRY ABOUT THIS PROBLEM A GREAT DEAL, A FAIR AMOUNT, ONLY A LITTLE, OR NOT AT ALL. FIRST, HOW MUCH DO YOU PERSONALLY WORRY ABOUT...?

(Percentages expressing a "great deal" or "fair amount" of worry)

Pollution of rivers, lakes, and reservoirs	79%
Pollution of drinking water	77%
Contamination of soil and water by toxic waste	74%
Maintenance of the nation's supply of fresh water for household needs	72%
Air pollution	69%
Extinction of plant and animal species	62%
The loss of tropical rain forests	61%
Damage to the Earth's ozone layer	60%
The "greenhouse effect" or global warming	51%
Acid rain	46%

SOURCE: Lydia Saad, "Worry about Environmental Problems," in "Global Warming on Public's Back Burner," *The Gallup Poll*, April 20, 2004, http://poll.gallup.com/content/default.aspx?ci=11398 (accessed March 10, 2006). Copyright © 2004 by The Gallup Organization. Reproduced by permission of the Gallup Organization.

products. Aside from the economic or utilitarian reasons for preserving species, however, many people think that humankind has a moral responsibility to maintain the Earth's biodiversity. When species are lost, the quality of all life is diminished.

The Gallup Organization conducts an annual poll on environmental issues. In 2004 Gallup pollsters asked participants to express their level of worry about various environmental problems. As shown in Figure 1.5, more than 60% of those asked expressed a "great deal" or "fair amount" of concern regarding the extinction of plant and animal species. This placed extinction sixth in the listing of environmental problems in terms of amount of worry. Extinction was considered less pressing a problem than water and air pollution, but more worrisome than damage to the Earth's ozone layer, global warming, or acid rain. Sixty-one percent of those surveyed were also concerned about the loss of tropical rain forests—home to many of the world's imperiled species.

Are Some Species More Important than Others?

In general, the public places high value on some endangered species and not others. For example, whales and seals are popular animals for which protection measures receive widespread support. On the other hand, there are several species listed under the Endangered Species Act that are considered pests or predators, because they pose a threat to human livelihoods or safety. Utah prairie dogs are burrowing animals that produce networks of underground tunnels. The resulting holes and dirt mounds can ruin cropland and trip and injure livestock. The protection of Utah prairie dogs and other imperiled rodents is a source of contention for people who believe that the Endangered Species Act puts animal interests above human interests. The same debate rages over such predators as wolves and mountain lions that may prey upon livestock, pets, and even people.

From a scientific standpoint some species are more valued because they are the last remnants of biological groups that once flourished. Examples of these include the coelacanth, one of the few species (along with lungfish) that help to document the transition from aquatic to terrestrial life in vertebrates, and the tuatara, a highly endangered reptile found only in New Zealand. The extinction of species that have no closely related species left on Earth represent particularly significant losses to the genetic diversity of the planet.

Biological Indicator Species.

The rapid rate of species loss should also concern human beings because many are dying out due to pollution and environmental degradation, problems that affect human health and well-being as well. Species that are particularly useful in reporting on the health of ecosystems are called biological indicator species. Environmental scientists rely on sensitive indicator species just as coal miners once relied on canaries to check air safety in underground tunnels, where dangerous gases frequently became concentrated enough to be poisonous. Miners carried a canary into the mineshaft, knowing that the air was safe to breathe as long as the canary lived. If the bird started to sicken, however, miners evacuated the tunnel. In the same way, the sudden deaths of large numbers of bald eagles and peregrine falcons warned people about the dangers of DDT, a powerful pesticide in wide use at the time. The disappearance of fish from various rivers, lakes, and seas also alerted people to the presence of dangerous chemicals in waters.

During the final decades of the twentieth century, many scientists became concerned about the sudden disappearance of many amphibians, particularly frogs, all over the world. Most troubling was the fact that many species disappeared from protected parks and wildlife refuges, areas that appeared relatively pristine and undisturbed. Amphibians are believed to be particularly sensitive to environmental disturbances such as pollution because their skins readily absorb substances from the environment. Their decline is a suggestion that all may not be well.

FACTORS THAT CONTRIBUTE TO SPECIES ENDANGERMENT

Experts believe that the increasing loss and decline of species cannot be attributed to natural processes, but results instead from the destructive effect of human activities. People hunt and collect wildlife. They destroy natural habitats by clearing trees and filling swamps for development. Aquatic habitats are altered or destroyed by the building of dams. Humans also poison habitats with polluting chemicals and industrial waste. Indeed, human activity may be causing changes in climate patterns on a global scale.

With each passing day, humans require more space and resources. According to the U.S. Census Bureau in *Global Population at a Glance: 2002 and Beyond* (March 2004), the human population totaled about one billion at the beginning of the nineteenth century. It surpassed the two billion mark in 1922 and began a period of rapid increase that saw the world population triple to six billion by the turn of the twenty-first century. According to the Census Bureau, the world population as of May 2006 was more than 6.5 billion people, and the population of the United States was expected to reach 300 million during October 2006. The large numbers of human beings puts tremendous pressure on other species.

Habitat Destruction

Habitat destruction is probably the single most important factor leading to the endangerment of species. It plays a role in the decline of nearly all listed species and has had an impact on nearly every type of habitat and ecosystem.

Many types of human activity result in habitat destruction. Agriculture is a leading cause, with nearly half of the total land area in the United States used for farming. Besides causing the direct replacement of natural habitat with fields, agricultural activity also results in soil erosion, pollution from pesticides and fertilizers, and runoff into aquatic habitats. Agriculture has compromised forest, prairie, and wetland habitats in particular. Nearly 90% of wetland losses have resulted from drainage for agriculture. According to a study by Brian Czech, Paul R. Krausman, and Patrick K. Devers ("Economic Associations among Causes of Species Endangerment in the United States," *Bioscience*, vol. 50, no. 7, 2000), the role of agriculture in the endangerment of species is greatest in the Southeast and California. However, agriculture impacts threatened and endangered species throughout the country, contributing to endangerment in thirty-five states.

Urban expansion has destroyed wild habitat areas as well, and is a primary factor in the endangerment of many plant species. As with agriculture, urbanization leads to the direct replacement of natural habitat. It also results in the depletion of local resources, such as water, which are important to many species. According to Czech and his colleagues, urbanization contributes to the endangerment of species in thirty-one states. The greatest impact is in California, Florida, and Texas, the three states that are urbanizing most rapidly. In contrast, only two species are endangered by urbanization in Utah, Nevada, and Idaho. The authors argue that this is because a large proportion of land in these states is public land and therefore not available for private development.

Logging, particularly the practice of clear-cutting forests (removal of all trees in a designated area), destroys important habitat for numerous species. Clear-cutting or extensive logging can also lead to significant erosion, harming both soils and aquatic habitats, which become blocked with soil.

Numerous other forms of human activity result in habitat destruction and degradation. Grazing by domestic livestock has a direct impact on numerous plant species, as well as animal species that compete with livestock. Mining destroys vegetation and soil, and also degrades habitat through pollution. Dams destroy aquatic habitats in rivers and streams. Finally, human recreational activity, particularly the use of off-road vehicles, results in the destruction of natural habitat. Czech, Krausman, and Devers reported that recreational activity has a particularly detrimental effect on species in California, Hawaii, Florida, as well as species in the Mojave Desert, which includes portions of Arizona, California, Nevada, and Utah.

Habitat Fragmentation

Human land-use patterns often result in the fragmentation of natural habitat areas that are available to species. Studies have shown that habitat fragmentation is occurring in most habitat types. Habitat fragmentation can have significant effects on species. Small populations can become isolated, so that dispersal from one habitat patch to another is impossible. Smaller populations are also more likely to become extinct. Finally, because there are more "edges" when habitats are fragmented, there can be increased exposure to predators and increased vulnerability to disturbances associated with human activity.

Global Warming

Global warming is a phenomenon associated with the enhanced greenhouse effect. Gases such as carbon dioxide and methane in the atmosphere absorb and maintain heat in the same way that glass traps heat in a greenhouse. This natural greenhouse effect keeps Earth warm and habitable for life. (See Figure 1.6.)

An enhanced greenhouse effect refers to the possible increase in the temperature of Earth's surface due to the release of excessive amounts of greenhouse gases from the burning of fossil fuels. Figure 1.7 shows that the global average of carbon dioxide in the atmosphere has increased dramatically since the early 1980s. A global temperature increase has also been compellingly documented, as shown in Figure 1.8, and has already had important effects on ecosystems worldwide.

According to ecologist Chris D. Thomas in "Extinction Risk from Climate Change," (*Nature*, no. 427, January 2004), a study of habitats comprising 20% of the Earth's surface suggested that 15% to 37% of the world's species may be extinct by 2050 if recent warming trends continue. Summarizing his findings, Thomas said, "The midrange estimate is that 24% percent of plants and animals will be committed to extinction by 2050. We're not talking about the occasional extinction—we're talking about 1.25 million species. It's a massive number."

FIGURE 1.6

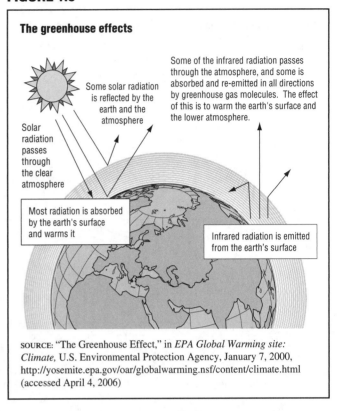

The greenhouse effects

Some solar radiation is reflected by the earth and the atmosphere

Some of the infrared radiation passes through the atmosphere, and some is absorbed and re-emitted in all directions by greenhouse gas molecules. The effect of this is to warm the earth's surface and the lower atmosphere.

Solar radiation passes through the clear atmosphere

Most radiation is absorbed by the earth's surface and warms it

Infrared radiation is emitted from the earth's surface

SOURCE: "The Greenhouse Effect," in *EPA Global Warming site: Climate*, U.S. Environmental Protection Agency, January 7, 2000, http://yosemite.epa.gov/oar/globalwarming.nsf/content/climate.html (accessed April 4, 2006)

Continued warming of the Earth would alter habitats drastically, with serious consequences for numerous species. In places like Siberia and the northernmost regions of Canada, habitats such as tundra—permanently frozen land supporting only low-growing plant life such as mosses and lichens—and taiga—expanses of evergreen forests located immediately south of the tundra—are shrinking. Deserts are expanding. Forests and grasslands are beginning to shift towards more appropriate climate regimes. Animal and plant species that cannot shift their ranges quickly enough, or have no habitat to shift into, are dying out. Some plants and animals that are found in precise, narrow bands of temperature and humidity, such as monarch butterflies or edelweiss, are likely to find their habitats wiped out entirely. Global warming is already endangering some of the most diverse ecosystems on Earth, such as coral reefs and tropical cloud forests. The impact on endangered species, which are already in a fragile state, may be particularly great.

Pollution

Pollution is caused by the release of industrial and chemical wastes into the land, air, and water. It can damage habitats and kill or sicken animals and plants. Pollution comes from a wide variety of sources, including industrial operations, mining, automobiles, and agricultural products such as pesticides and fertilizers. Even animals that are not directly exposed to pollution can be affected, if other species they rely on die out. According to Czech and his colleagues, pollution currently affects a

FIGURE 1.7

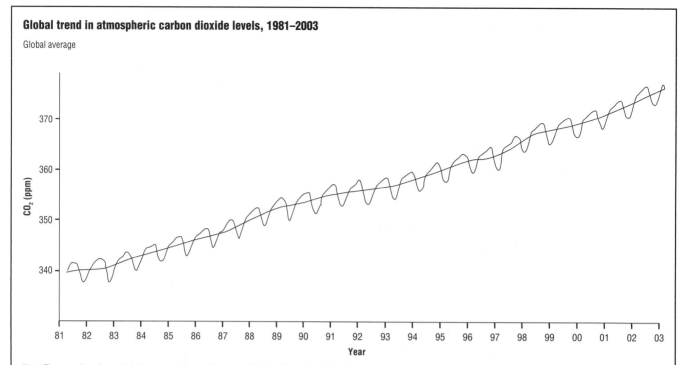

Global trend in atmospheric carbon dioxide levels, 1981–2003

Note: The wavy line shows global average atmospheric carbon dioxide mixing ratios determined using measurements from the National Oceanic and Atmospheric Administration (NOAA) Climate Monitoring and Diagnostics Laboratory (CMDL) cooperative air sampling network. The smooth line represents the long-term trend.

SOURCE: Adapted from "Carbon Dioxide Measurements," in *Carbon Cycle Greenhouse Gases Figures*, U.S. Department of Commerce, National Oceanic and Atmospheric Administration, Climate Monitoring and Diagnostics Laboratory, 2006, http://www.cmdl.noaa.gov/gallery/ccgg_figures/co2trend_global (accessed March 8, 2006)

large number of species in the Southeast, particularly aquatic species such as fish or mussels.

Hunting and Trade

Humans have hunted numerous animal species to extinction, and hunting continues to be a major threat to some species. In the United States, gray wolves were nearly wiped out because they were considered a threat to livestock. The Caribbean monk seal was viewed as a competitor for fish, and exterminated. Other animals are hunted for the value of their hides, tusks, or horns, including elephants and rhinoceroses. Many exotic species, such as parrots and other tropical birds, are taken from their natural habitats for the pet trade.

Invasive Species

Invasive species are those that have been introduced from their native habitat into a new, nonnative habitat, and which cause environmental harm. Most introductions of invasive species are accidental, resulting from "stowaways" on ships and planes. Invasive species harm native life forms by competing with them for food and other resources, or by preying on them or parasitizing them. As of 2005 approximately 50,000 species were believed to have been introduced into the United States alone. While there are sometimes beneficial

effects from introducing nonnative species, most of the effects are harmful.

The introduction of invasive species can lead to genetic swamping. This is a condition that arises when large numbers of one species breed with a much smaller population of another related species. The genetic material of the invasive species becomes overwhelming, causing the resulting generations to lose many of the characteristics that made the smaller population a unique species in the first place.

Many species in peril are endangered partly or entirely because of invasive species. Similarly, the *IUCN Red List* suggested in 2000 that invasive species affect hundreds of species of threatened birds and plants. In fact, the International Union for the Conservation of Nature and Natural Resources found that the majority of bird extinctions since 1800 have been due to invasive species such as rats and snakes. In 2003 the IUCN reported that the unique flora and fauna of islands such as the Galapagos Islands, Hawaii, the Seychelles, the Falkland Islands, and the British Virgin Islands, have been devastated by invasive species. Human commensals—species that are used by and associated with humans—can be among the most destructive introduced species. In Hawaii, for example, grazing by feral pigs,

FIGURE 1.8

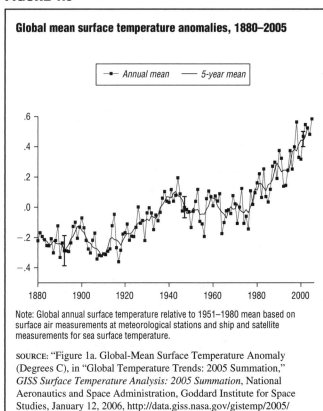

Global mean surface temperature anomalies, 1880–2005

Note: Global annual surface temperature relative to 1951–1980 mean based on surface air measurements at meteorological stations and ship and satellite measurements for sea surface temperature.

SOURCE: "Figure 1a. Global-Mean Surface Temperature Anomaly (Degrees C), in "Global Temperature Trends: 2005 Summation," *GISS Surface Temperature Analysis: 2005 Summation*, National Aeronautics and Space Administration, Goddard Institute for Space Studies, January 12, 2006, http://data.giss.nasa.gov/gistemp/2005/2005cal_fig1.pdf (accessed March 10, 2006)

goats, cattle, and sheep is responsible for the endangerment of numerous plants and birds.

The introduction of invasive species by humans has also taken a toll on mammalian wildlife. Australia is overrun with domestic cats whose ancestors were brought by settlers to the island continent 200 years ago. Stray domestic cats have driven indigenous species such as bandicoots, bettongs, numbats, wallabies, and dozens of other bird and mammal species, most of which are found nowhere else on Earth, towards extinction. Richard Evans, a member of the Australian Parliament, claims the feral cats are responsible for the extinction of at least thirty-nine species in Australia. He has called for total eradication of cats from the island by 2020, to be achieved by neutering pets and spreading feline diseases in the wild. The Australian National Parks and Wildlife Service reports that each house cat kills twenty-five native animals each year on average, and feral domestic cats kill as many as 1,000 per year.

Recognizing the threat posed by invasive species, President Bill Clinton signed Executive Order 13112 on Invasive Species in 1999. This order requires federal agencies to make every possible effort to control the spread of invasive species, and resulted in the formation of the Invasive Species Council, which drafted the first National Invasive Species Management Plan in January 2001. The plan emphasizes prevention of introduction of alien species, early detection of invasions, rapid response to them, and coordination of national and international efforts in management and control of these species.

In "Update on the Environmental and Economic Costs Associated with Alien-Invasive Species in the United States" (*Ecological Economics*, vol. 52, no. 3, February 15, 2005), researchers at Cornell University, including David Pimentel, reported that invasive species cause environmental damages and losses that cost the country nearly $120 billion per year. Invasive species are blamed, in part, for imperiling approximately 42% of the species on the list of threatened and endangered species in the United States.

CHAPTER 2
THE ENDANGERED SPECIES ACT

The Endangered Species Act of 1973 (ESA) is generally considered one of the most far-reaching laws ever enacted by any nation for the preservation of wildlife. The passage of the ESA resulted from alarm at the decline of numerous species worldwide, as well as from recognition of the importance of preserving species diversity. The purpose of the ESA is to identify species that are either endangered—at risk of extinction throughout all or a significant portion of their range—or threatened—likely to become endangered in the foreseeable future. With the exception of recognized insect pests, all animals and plants are eligible for listing under the ESA. Listed species are protected without regard to either commercial or sport value.

For its supporters, the Endangered Species Act has proved to be one of the most effective conservation laws ever enacted. Many Americans believe that the ESA has saved numerous species from extinction. However, critics charge that the ESA puts too many restrictions on land and water development projects and is too expensive for the results that it achieves.

HISTORY OF SPECIES PROTECTION

Conservation has a long history. One of the oldest examples dates from 242 BCE, when the Indian emperor Asoka created nature reserves in Asia. Marco Polo reported that the Asian ruler Kublai Khan (1215–94) helped conserve bird and mammal species valued for hunting by banning hunting during their reproductive periods. He also helped to increase their numbers by planting food and providing protected cover areas. In South America, during the reign of the Inca kings, many species of seabirds were protected.

By the mid-nineteenth century many governments had developed an interest in wildlife conservation and an awareness of the need to protect natural habitats. In 1861 painters of the Barbizon school established the first French nature reserve, which covered nearly 3,458 acres of forest at Fontainebleau near Paris. Three years later the American government set aside the Yosemite Valley in California as a National Reserve. This became Yosemite National Park in 1890. Wyoming's Yellowstone Park was created in 1872 and became the first U.S. National Park.

Organizations and laws dedicated to the protection of species soon followed. In 1895 the first international meeting for the protection of birds was held in Paris, and resulted in new laws protecting species in several countries. The first international conference for the protection of nature was held in 1913. The International Whaling Commission was established in 1946, and two years later, the World Conservation Union was founded as the International Union for the Protection of Nature. In 1956 that organization became the International Union for Conservation of Nature and Natural Resources, or IUCN. In 1990 the name became IUCN—The World Conservation Union.

In 1961 a private conservation organization, the World Wildlife Fund (WWF), was founded. The Chinese giant panda was selected as the WWF symbol, not only because of the animal's great popularity, but also to reaffirm the international character of nature conservation, and to emphasize the independence of wildlife conservation from political differences. The Convention on International Trade in Endangered Species (CITES), an international treaty established to regulate commerce in wildlife, was first ratified in 1975 in an attempt to block both the import and export of endangered species and to regulate international trade in threatened species.

In the United States, Congress passed the Endangered Species Preservation Act in 1966, and the first species were listed in 1967. (See Table 2.1.) This established a process for listing species as endangered and provided some measure of protection. The Endangered

TABLE 2.1

First list of endangered species, 1967

In accordance with section 1(c) of the Endangered Species Preservation Act of October 15, 1966 (80 Stat. 926; 16 U.S.C. 668aa(c) I [the Secretary of the Interior] find after consulting the states, interested organizations, and individual scientists, that the following listed native fish and wildlife are threatened with extinction.

Mammals
- Indiana bat—*Myotis sodalis*
- Delmarva Peninsula fox squirrel—*Sciurus niger cinereus*
- Timber wolf—*Canis lupus lycaon*
- Red wolf—*Canis niger*
- San Joaquin kit fox—*Vulpes macrotis mutica*
- Grizzly bear—*Ursus horribilis*
- Black-footed ferret—*Mustela nigripes*
- Florida panther —*Felis concolor coryi*
- Caribbean monk seal—*Monachus tropicalis*
- Guadalupe fur seal—*Arctocephalus philippi townsendi*
- Florida manatee or Florida sea cow—*Trichechus manatus latirostris*
- Key deer—*Odocoileus virginianus clavium*
- Sonoran pronghorn—*Antilocapra americana sonoriensis*

Birds
- Hawaiian dark-rumped petrel—*Pterodroma phaeopygia sandwichensis*
- Hawaiian goose (nene)—*Branta sandvicensis*
- Aleutian Canada goose—*Branta canadensis leucopareia*
- Tule white-fronted goose—*Anser albifrons gambelli*
- Laysan duck—*Anas laysanensis*
- Hawaiian duck (or koloa)—*Anas wyvilliana*
- Mexican duck—*Anas diazi*
- California condor—*Gymnogyps californianus*
- Florida Everglade kite (Florida Snail Kite)—*Rostrhamus sociabilis plumbeus*
- Hawaiian hawk (or ii)—*Buteo solitarius*
- Southern bald eagle—*Haliaeetus t. leucocephalus*
- Attwater's greater prairie chicken—*Tympanuchus cupido attwateri*
- Masked bobwhite—*Colinus virginianus ridgwayi*
- Whooping crane —*Grus americana*
- Yuma clapper rail—*Rallus longirostris yumanensis*
- Hawaiian common gallinule—*Gallinula chloropus sandvicensis*
- Eskimo curlew —*Numenius borealis*
- Puerto Rican parrot—*Amazona vittata*
- American ivory-billed woodpecker—*Campephilus p. principalis*
- Hawaiian crow (or alala)—*Corvus hawaiiensis*
- Small Kauai thrush (puaiohi)—*Phaeornia pulmeri*
- Nihoa millerbird—*Acrocephalus kingi*
- Kauai oo (or oo aa)—*Moho braccatus*
- Crested honeycreeper (or akohekohe)—*Palmeria dolei*
- Akiapolaau—*Hemignathus wilsoni*
- Kauai akialoa—*Hemignathus procerus*
- Kauai nukupuu —*Hemignathus lucidus hanapepe*

- Laysan finchbill (Laysan Finch)—*Psittirostra c. cantans*
- Nihoa finchbill (Nihoa Finch)—*Psittirostra cantans ultima*
- Ou—*Psittirostra psittacea*
- Palila—*Psittirostra bailleui*
- Maui parrotbill—*Pseudonestor xanthophyrys*
- Bachman's warbler—*Vermivora bachmanii*
- Kirtland's warbler—*Dendroica kirtlandii*
- Dusky seaside sparrow—*Ammospiza nigrescens*
- Cape Sable sparrow—*Ammospiza mirabilis*

Reptiles and Amphibians
- American alligator—*Alligator mississippiensis*
- Blunt-nosed leopard lizard—*Crotaphytus wislizenii silus*
- San Francisco garter snake—*Thamnophis sirtalis tetrataenia*
- Santa Cruz long-toed salamander—*Ambystoma macrodactylum croceum*
- Texas blind salamander—*Typhlomolge rathbuni*
- Black toad, Inyo County toad—*Bufo exsul*

Fishes
- Shortnose sturgeon—*Acipenser brevirostrum*
- Longjaw Cisco—*Coregonus alpenae*
- Paiute cutthroat trout—*Salmo clarki seleniris*
- Greenback cutthroat trout—*Salmo clarki stomias*
- Montana Westslope cutthroat trout—*Salmo clarki*
- Gila trout—*Salmo gilae*
- Arizona (*Apache*) trout—*Salmo sp.*
- Desert dace—*Eremichthys acros*
- Humpback chub—*Gila cypha*
- Little Colorado spinedace—*Lepidomeda vittata*
- Moapa dace—*Moapa coriacea*
- Colorado River squawfish—*Ptychocheilus lucius*
- Cui-ui—*Chasmistes cujus*
- Devils Hole pupfish—*Cyprinodon diabolis*
- Commanche Springs pupfish—*Cyprinodon elegans*
- Owens River pupfish —*Cyprinodon radiosus*
- Pahrump killifish—*Empetrichythys latos*
- Big Bend gambusia—*Gambusia gaigei*
- Clear Creek gambusia—*Gambusia heterochir*
- Gila topminnow—*Poeciliopsis occidentalis*
- Maryland darter—*Etheostoma sellare*
- Blue pike—*Stizostedion vitreum glaucum*

SOURCE: Stewart L. Udall, "Native Fish and Wildlife Endangered Species," in *Federal Register*, vol. 32, no. 48, March 11, 1967

Species Conservation Act of 1969 provided protection to species facing worldwide extinction, prohibiting their import and sale within the United States.

THE ENDANGERED SPECIES ACT OF 1973 (ESA)—A LANDMARK PROTECTION

Passed by the U.S. Congress in 1973, the Endangered Species Act was substantially amended in 1978, 1982, and 1987. The ESA is administered by the U.S. Department of the Interior through the U.S. Fish and Wildlife Service (FWS). The U.S. Department of Commerce, through the National Marine Fisheries Service (NMFS), is responsible for most marine (ocean-based) species and those that are anadromous (migrate between fresh waters and marine waters). The Biological Resources Division of the U.S. Geological Survey (USGS) conducts research on species for which the Fish and Wildlife Service has management authority.

It should be noted that the original Endangered Species Act defined the word "species" to include species, subspecies, or "smaller taxa." Taxa is the plural of taxon, which is a grouping on the taxonomic table. In 1978 the ESA was amended to define a smaller taxon for vertebrates (animals with a backbone) as a "distinct population segment" (DPS). A DPS is a distinct population of vertebrates capable of interbreeding with each other that live in a specific geographical area. A DPS is usually described using geographical terms, such as northern or southern, or by a given latitude or longitude. In 1991 the National Marine Fisheries Service developed a policy defining the DPS for Pacific salmon populations. Salmon are anadromous, meaning they migrate between the ocean and inland fresh waters. Most salmon migrate in groups at particular times of the year. Each of these groups is called a stock. The NMFS developed a new term, the evolutionarily significant unit (ESU), to refer to a distinct stock of Pacific salmon.

In summary, the word "species" as used in the Endangered Species Act can mean a species, a subspecies, a DPS (vertebrates only), or an ESU (Pacific salmon only).

LISTING UNDER THE ENDANGERED SPECIES ACT

Under the Endangered Species Act there are five criteria that must be evaluated before a decision is made to list a species:

- The present or threatened destruction, modification, or curtailment of the species' habitat or range

- Overutilization for commercial, recreational, scientific, or educational purposes

- Disease or predation

- The inadequacy of existing regulatory mechanisms

- Other natural or manmade factors affecting the species' survival

The primary status codes assigned to listed species are E for endangered and T for threatened. However, there are numerous other status codes for specific types of listings as shown in Table 2.2. Details of these listing actions are provided in the sections below.

In February 2006 there were 997 U.S. species (398 animals and 599 plants) and 520 foreign species (519 animals and one plant) listed as endangered, and 275 U.S. species (129 animals and 146 plants) and forty-six foreign species (forty-four animals and two plants) listed as threatened under the ESA. Thousands of other species are being studied to see if they need to be added to the list. (See Table 1.2 in Chapter 1.)

The Listing Process

The process by which a species becomes listed under the Endangered Species Act is a legal process with specifically defined steps. Successful listing results in regulations that are legally enforceable within all U.S. jurisdictions. At various stages of the listing process the U.S. Fish and Wildlife Service or the National Marine Fisheries Service publishes their actions in the *Federal Register*, an official document published daily by the National Archives and Records Administration in Washington, D.C. The *Federal Register* details specific legal actions of the federal government, such as rules, proposed rules, notices from federal agencies, executive orders, and miscellaneous presidential documents. Online access to the *Federal Register* is available at http://www.gpoaccess.gov/fr/index.html.

There are three ways for the listing process to be initiated:

TABLE 2.2

Endangered Species Act status codes

E	Endangered
T	Threatened
EmE	Emergency listing, endangered
EmT	Emergency listing, threatened
EXPE, XE	Experimental population, essential
EXPN, XN	Experimental population, non-essential
SAE, E(S/A)	Similarity of appearance to an endangered taxon
SAT, T(S/A)	Similarity of appearance to a threatened taxon
PE	Proposed endangered
PT	Proposed threatened
PEXPE, PXE	Proposed experimental population, essential
PEXPN, PXN	Proposed experimental population, non-essential
PSAE, PE(S/A)	Proposed similarity of appearance to an endangered taxon
PSAT, PT(S/A)	Proposed similarity of appearance to a threatened taxon
C	Candidate taxon, ready for proposal
D3A	Delisted taxon, evidently extinct
D3B	Delisted taxon, invalid name in current scientific opinion
D3C	Delisted taxon, recovered
DA	Delisted taxon, amendment of the act
DM	Delisted taxon, recovered, being monitored first five years
DO	Delisted taxon, original commercial data erroneous
DP	Delisted taxon, discovered previously unknown additional populations and/or habitat
DR	Delisted taxon, taxonomic revision (improved understanding)
AD	Proposed delisting
AE	Proposed reclassification to endangered
AT	Proposed reclassification to threatened

SOURCE: Adapted from "Endangered Species Act Status Codes," in *Species List Help File*, U.S. Department of the Interior, U.S. Fish and Wildlife Service, Undated, http://www.fws.gov/ifw2es/EndangeredSpecies/lists/help.cfm (accessed February 23, 2006)

- Submittal of a petition to the U.S. Fish and Wildlife Service or the National Marine Fisheries Service (hereafter called the "Agencies")

- Initiative of the Agencies

- Emergency designation by the Agencies

Figure 2.1 diagrams the most common listing process under the ESA, one that begins with a petition submittal.

PETITION SUBMITTAL. The process for listing a new species as endangered or threatened begins with a formal petition from a person, organization, or government agency. This petition is submitted to the U.S. Fish and Wildlife Service for terrestrial and freshwater species or to the National Marine Fisheries Service for marine and anadromous species. All petitions must be backed by published scientific data supporting the need for listing. Within ninety days, the FWS or NMFS determines whether there is "substantial information" to suggest that a species requires listing under the Endangered Species Act.

STATUS REVIEW. A status review is triggered when a petition is found to suggest that listing may be necessary or upon the initiative of the U.S. Fish and Wildlife Service or the National Marine Fisheries Service. The

FIGURE 2.1

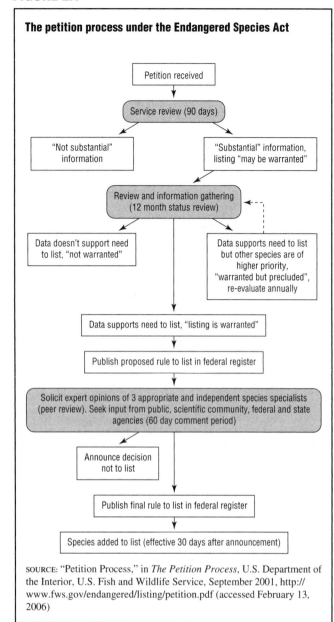

The petition process under the Endangered Species Act

Petition received

Service review (90 days)

"Not substantial" information

"Substantial" information, listing "may be warranted"

Review and information gathering (12 month status review)

Data doesn't support need to list, "not warranted"

Data supports need to list but other species are of higher priority, "warranted but precluded", re-evaluate annually

Data supports need to list, "listing is warranted"

Publish proposed rule to list in federal register

Solicit expert opinions of 3 appropriate and independent species specialists (peer review). Seek input from public, scientific community, federal and state agencies (60 day comment period)

Announce decision not to list

Publish final rule to list in federal register

Species added to list (effective 30 days after announcement)

SOURCE: "Petition Process," in *The Petition Process*, U.S. Department of the Interior, U.S. Fish and Wildlife Service, September 2001, http://www.fws.gov/endangered/listing/petition.pdf (accessed February 13, 2006)

purpose of a status review is to determine whether or not a listing is warranted and what that listing should be.

The FWS defines a status review as follows: "the act of reviewing all the available information on a species to determine if it should be provided protection under the ESA. A status review should also use the knowledge of experts; the greater the extent to which Service biologists can build an external consensus using the expertise of various parties (e.g., Federal, State, Tribal, University, Heritage programs), the better." Comments and information are also requested from the general public through publication of a notice in the *Federal Register*.

The Status Review must be completed within twelve months. There are three possible determinations from the status review:

- Listing is not warranted
- Listing is warranted but precluded
- Listing is warranted

LISTING IS NOT WARRANTED. A finding that listing is not warranted must be accompanied by information explaining why the data presented do not support the petitioned action or why there are not enough data to make an appropriate determination.

LISTING IS WARRANTED BUT PRECLUDED—CANDIDATE SPECIES. In some cases it may be decided that a species should be proposed for listing, but development of the listing regulation is precluded by other listing activities with higher priorities. In other words, the Agency acknowledges that a species deserves protection under the ESA, but the Agency has other priorities that it believes must come first. The species is designated a "candidate species."

Candidate species are assigned a listing priority number ranging from 1 to 12 with lower numbers (1–3) indicating greater priority compared to other candidates. Priority is determined based on three considerations:

- The magnitude of the threats facing the species
- The immediacy of the threats facing the species
- The taxonomic uniqueness of the species

The ratings table is shown in Table 2.3. The National Marine Fisheries Service has a different definition for candidate species. That agency calls them "species of concern" and does not propose them for listing on the basis that available information is inadequate to justify doing so.

Candidate species are re-evaluated annually to confirm that listing continues to be appropriate. These re-evaluations continue until the species is proposed for listing or until its status improves sufficiently to remove it from consideration for listing. The Agencies work with state wildlife agencies and other groups to help preserve and improve the status of candidate species, hoping that populations may recover enough that species will not require listing.

In February 2006 there were 282 candidate species designated under the ESA, and distributed as shown in Figure 2.2. Just over half the candidates were plant species.

LISTING IS WARRANTED. A determination that listing is warranted means that a species is officially proposed for listing through the publication of this action in the *Federal Register*. At this point, the Agency asks at least three independent biological experts to verify that the petitioned species requires listing under either threatened or endangered status. After that, input from the public, from other federal and state agencies, and from the scientific community is welcomed. This period of public comment typically

TABLE 2.3

Basis for listing priority for candidate species

Threat			
Magnitude	Immediacy	Taxonomy	Priority
High	Imminent	Monotypic genus	1
		Species	2
		Subspecies/population	3
	Non-imminent	Monotypic genus	4
		Species	5
		Subspecies/population	6
Moderate to low	Imminent	Monotypic genus	7
		Species	8
		Subspecies/population	9
	Non-imminent	Monotypic genus	10
		Species	11
		Subspecies/population	12

SOURCE: "Listing Priority Guidance Number," in "Table 1—Candidate Notice of Review (Animals and Plants)," in *Threatened and Endangered Species System (TESS)*, U.S. Department of the Interior, U.S. Fish and Wildlife Service, February 17, 2006, http://ecos.fws.gov/tess_public/docs/db-priority.html (accessed February 22, 2006)

lasts sixty days, but may be extended in some cases. Within forty-five days of proposal issuance, interested parties can request public hearings be held on the issues involved with listing. Such hearings are also held in cases where public interest is high in the listing outcome.

In February 2006 there were fifteen species proposed for listing under the ESA: twelve species of pomace fly, two fish species—cowhead lake tui chub and coho salmon—and a flowering plant called Graham's beardtongue.

FINAL DECISION. After a listing has been proposed the Agency must take one of three possible actions:

- Withdraw the proposal—the biological information is found not to support listing the species

- Extend the proposal period—there is substantial disagreement within the scientific community regarding the listing. Only one six-month extension is allowed, and then a final decision must be made.

FIGURE 2.2

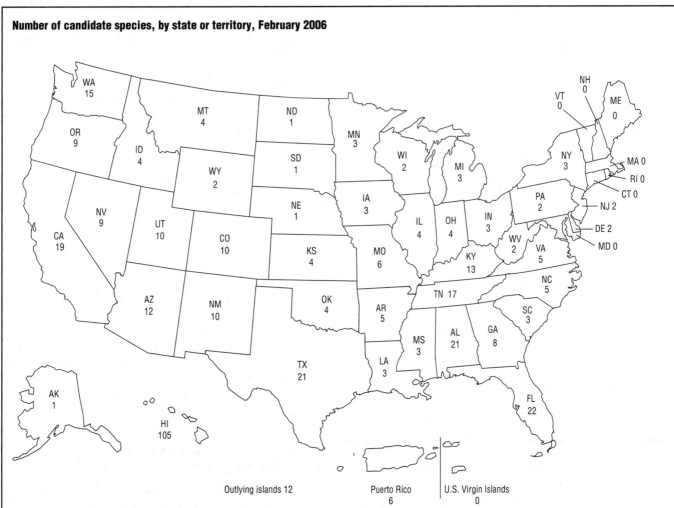

Number of candidate species, by state or territory, February 2006

Note: Distributions reflect known historic range. Total U.S. species is 282. Numbers are not additive, a species often occurs in multiple states.

SOURCE: "Candidate Species Range by State/Territory as of Wed Feb 1 01:00:32 MST 2006," in *Threatened and Endangered Species System*, U.S. Department of the Interior, U.S. Fish and Wildlife Service, February 1, 2006, http://www.fws.gov/endangered/wildlife.html#maps (accessed February 1, 2006)

TABLE 2.4

Delisted U.S. and foreign species, March 2006

Inverted common name	Scientific name	Listing status[a]
Alligator, American	*Alligator mississippiensis*	SAT
Barberry, truckee	*Berberis (=mahonia) sonnei*	DR
Bidens, cuneate	*Bidens cuneata*	DR
Broadbill, Guam	*Myiagra freycineti*	D3A
Butterfly, Bahama swallowtail	*Heraclides andraemon bonhotei*	DA
Cactus, Lloyd's hedgehog	*Echinocereus lloydii*	DR
Cactus, spineless hedgehog	*Echinocereus triglochidiatus var. inermis*	DR
Cinquefoil, Robbins'	*Potentilla robbinsiana*	DM
Cisco, longjaw	*Coregonus alpenae*	D3A
Deer, Columbian white-tailed (Douglas County DPS[b])	*Odocoileus virginianus leucurus*	DM
Dove, Palau ground	*Gallicolumba canifrons*	DM
Duck, Mexican (U.S.A. only)	*Anas "diazi"*	DR
Falcon, American peregrine	*Falco peregrinus anatum*	DM
Falcon, Arctic peregrine	*Falco peregrinus tundrius*	DM
Flycatcher, Palau fantail	*Rhipidura lepida*	DM
Gambusia, Amistad	*Gambusia amistadensis*	D3A
Globeberry, Tumamoc	*Tumamoca macdougalii*	DP
Goose, Aleutian Canada	*Branta canadensis leucopareia*	DM
Hedgehog cactus, purple spined	*Echinocereus engelmannii var. purpureus*	DR
Kangaroo, eastern gray	*Macropus giganteus*	DM
Kangaroo, red	*Macropus rufus*	DM
Kangaroo, western gray	*Macropus fuliginosus*	DM
Mallard, Mariana	*Anas oustaleti*	D3A
Milk-vetch, Rydberg	*Astragalus perianus*	DP
Monarch, Tinian (old world flycatcher)	*Monarcha takatsukasae*	DM
Owl, Palau	*Pyrroglaux podargina*	DM
Pearlymussel, Sampson's	*Epioblasma sampsoni*	D3A
Pelican, brown (U.S. Atlantic coast, Florida, Alabama)	*Pelecanus occidentalis*	DM
Pennyroyal, Mckittrick	*Hedeoma apiculatum*	DP
Pike, blue	*Stizostedion vitreum glaucum*	D3A
Pupfish, Tecopa	*Cyprinodon nevadensis calidae*	D3A
Shrew, Dismal Swamp southeastern	*Sorex longirostris fisheri*	DP
Sparrow, dusky seaside	*Ammodramus maritimus nigrescens*	D3A
Sparrow, Santa Barbara song	*Melospiza melodia graminea*	D3A
Sunflower, Eggert's	*Helianthus eggertii*	DM
Treefrog, pine barrens	*Hyla andersonii*	DP
Trout, coastal cutthroat	*Oncorhynchus clarki clarki*	DR
Turtle, Indian flap-shelled	*Lissemys punctata punctata*	DO
Whale, gray (except where listed)	*Eschrichtius robustus*	DM
Woolly-star, Hoover's	*Eriastrum hooveri*	DP

Note: Entire range unless otherwise noted.

[a]Listing status:

D3A	Delisted taxon, evidently extinct
DA	Delisted taxon, amendment of the act
DM	Delisted taxon, recovered, being monitored first five years
DO	Delisted taxon, original commercial data erroneous
DP	Delisted taxon, discovered previously unknown additional populations and/or habitat
DR	Delisted taxon, taxonomic revision (improved understanding)
SAT	Similarity of appearance to a threatened taxon

[b]Distinct population segment.

SOURCE: "Delisted Species Report as of 3/9/2006," in *Threatened and Endangered Species System (TESS)*, U.S. Department of the Interior, U.S. Fish and Wildlife Service, March 9, 2006, http://ecos.fws.gov/tess_public/SpeciesReport.do?listingType=D (accessed March 9, 2006)

• Publish a final listing rule in the *Federal Register*—the listing becomes effective thirty days after publication, unless otherwise indicated.

After a species is listed, its condition and situation are reviewed at least every five years to decide whether it still requires government protection.

EMERGENCY LISTING. The ESA authorizes the Agencies to issue temporary emergency listings for species when evidence indicates an immediate and significant risk to the well-being of a species; for example, following a natural disaster. Two designations are possible: endangered emergency listing (EmE) and threatened emergency listing (EmT). The listing must be published in the *Federal Register* and is effective only for 240 days. During this time the normal status review procedure proceeds.

Petitioners also have the right under the ESA to ask the Agencies for an emergency listing for a species. In July 2005 a coalition of groups petitioned the Fish and Wildlife Service for an EmE listing for the *rufus* subspecies of the red knot, an imperiled shorebird found in New Jersey. The petitioners argued that the species faces imminent threats and "simply does not have the luxury of time to await the Service's normal status review." The FWS denied the petition claiming that recent population data show the bird's condition is improving and steps are already planned or taking place to protect the bird's status.

As of February 24, 2006, there were no emergency listings in effect for endangered or threatened species listed under the ESA.

DELISTING. Delisting occurs when a species is removed from the candidate list, proposed list, or final list of endangered and threatened species. Delisting takes place for a variety of reasons, as indicated by the "D" codes in Table 2.2. In general, delisting occurs when the agencies find that a species has recovered or become extinct or on various procedural grounds, including discovery of additional habitats or populations.

Listed species that have been delisted are shown in Table 2.4. Of the forty delisted species, fifteen recovered, nine became extinct, and the remainder had procedural issues.

According to the U.S. Fish and Wildlife Service, between September 1997 and February 2006 more than seventy candidate or proposed species were delisted; primarily because new information became available indicating that populations were greater or threats were less serious than originally believed. However, eight species were delisted because of extinction: four flowering plants and four insects.

RECOVERY ACTIONS UNDER THE ENDANGERED SPECIES ACT

Once a species becomes listed as endangered or threatened under the Endangered Species Act it is afforded the following protections:

• Import, export, and interstate or foreign sales are prohibited without a special permit.

- Taking is illegal—Taking is killing, harming, harassing, pursuing, or removing the species from the wild.

- Federal agencies must conduct their activities in such a way as to conserve the species.

- Federal agencies that manage lands and/or waters must consult with the U.S. Fish and Wildlife Service or National Marine Fisheries Service regarding conserving listed species in those habitats. Any activities funded or authorized by those federal agencies or carried out on lands or waters managed by them can not jeopardize the survival of the listed species.

Civil and criminal penalties can be levied for violations of these provisions. However, exemptions are granted for native peoples of Alaska that rely on certain endangered or threatened animals for food or other products needed for subsistence. In addition, section 4(d) of the Endangered Species Act allows the Fish and Wildlife Service to grant other exemptions from the "taking" rule for threatened species. For example, the gray wolf in Minnesota falls under a 4(d) rule that allows certain government agents to kill wolves that prey on domestic animals. The rule was created to prevent private citizens from performing wolf control to protect livestock. A 4(d) rule is commonly referred to as a "special rule" under the ESA.

Endangered species have different needs and require different conservation measures. Some fish are endangered only because of a history of overfishing. Halting or reducing fishing is sufficient for population recovery. In most cases, however, more active forms of intervention are necessary. The single most important conservation measure for many threatened and endangered species is habitat conservation or restoration. For some species, captive breeding followed by reintroduction into the wild may help increase numbers. In all cases, knowledge of the natural history of endangered species is essential to acquiring a better understanding of species' needs, as well as to the development of measures that will aid in conservation.

Critical Habitat

Under the Endangered Species Act the FWS or NMFS must decide whether critical habitat should be designated for a listed species. Critical habitat is specific geographical areas of land, water, and/or air space that contain features essential for the conservation of a listed species and that may require special management and protection. For example, these could be areas used for breeding, resting, and feeding. If the agencies decide that critical habitat should be designated, a proposal notice is published in the *Federal Register* for public comment. If it is decided that critical habitat is needed, then the final boundaries are published in the *Federal Register*.

The role of critical habitat is often misunderstood by the public. Critical habitat designation does not set up a refuge or sanctuary for a species in which no development can take place. It can provide additional protection for a specific geographical area that might not occur without the designation. For example, if the FWS determines that an area not currently occupied by a species is needed for species recovery and designates that area as critical habitat, any federal actions involving that area have to avoid adverse modifications. Critical habitat designation has no regulatory impact on private landowners unless they wish to take actions on their land that involve federal funding or permits.

The original ESA did not provide a time limit for the setting of critical habitat. In 1978 the law was amended to require that critical habitat be designated at the same time a species is listed. However, the designation is only required "when prudent." For example, the Fish and Wildlife Service or National Marine Fisheries Service can refuse to designate critical habitat for a species if doing so would publicize the specific locations of organisms known to be targets for illegal hunting or collection. Historically the agencies have broadly used the "when prudent" clause to justify not setting critical habitat for many listed species. This has been a very contentious issue between the government and conservation groups.

As of February 23, 2006, critical habitat had been designated for 473 species. This represents just over one-third of all U.S. species listed under the ESA. Plants make up more than half of the listed species for which critical habitat has been designated.

Experimental Populations

For a small number of species, primarily mammals, birds, fish, and aquatic invertebrates, recovery efforts include the introduction of individuals into new areas. Typically this is accomplished by moving a small group of imperiled animals from an established area to one or more other locations within their historical range of distribution.

Experimental populations of a species are not subject to the same rigorous protections under the Endangered Species Act as other members of the species. Experimental populations can be considered threatened, even if the rest of the species is listed as endangered. In addition, the FWS can designate an experimental population as essential or nonessential. A nonessential designation indicates that the survival of this population is not believed essential to the survival of the species as a whole. A nonessential experimental population (EXPN or XN) is treated under the law as if it is proposed for listing, not already listed. This results in less protection under the ESA.

As of February 2006 there were thirty-seven experimental populations listed under the ESA for thirty-three

TABLE 2.5

Recovery potential priority ranking system

Priority rank	Degree of threat	Recoverability potential	Taxonomy
1	High	High	Monotypic genus
2	High	High	Species
3	High	High	Subspecies
4	High	Low	Monotypic genus
5	High	Low	Species
6	High	Low	Subspecies
7	Moderate	High	Monotypic genus
8	Moderate	High	Species
9	Moderate	High	Subspecies
10	Moderate	Low	Monotypic genus
11	Moderate	Low	Species
12	Moderate	Low	Subspecies
13	Low	High	Monotypic genus
14	Low	High	Species
15	Low	High	Subspecies
16	Low	Low	Monotypic genus
17	Low	Low	Species
18	Low	Low	Subspecies

Note: A species that is a monotypic genus is the only remaining species representing the entire genus.

SOURCE: "Table 2. Fish and Wildlife Service's Recovery Priority Ranking Schedule," in *Endangered Species: Fish and Wildlife Service Generally Focuses Recovery Funding on High-Priority Species, But Needs to Periodically Assess Its Funding Decisions,* U.S. Government Accountability Office, April 2005, http://www.gao.gov/new.items/d05211.pdf (accessed February 25, 2006)

separate species. Clams and snails comprise more than half the animals represented. Notable experimental populations for mammals include the grizzly bear and gray wolf. Both have been reintroduced into portions of western states.

Recovery Plans

The ESA requires that a recovery plan be developed and implemented for every listed species unless "such a plan will not promote the conservation of the species." The Fish and Wildlife Service and National Marine Fisheries Service are directed to give priority to those species that are most likely to benefit from having a plan in place. The recovery potential of species is ranked from 1 to 18 as shown in Table 2.5. Low rankings indicate a greater likelihood that the species can be recovered. Priority is based on the degree of threat, potential for recovery, and taxonomy (genetic distinctiveness). In addition, rankings can be appended with the letter "c" when species recovery is in conflict with economic activities. Species with a "c" designation have higher priority than other species within the same numerical ranking.

Each recovery plan must include the following three elements:

- Site-specific management actions to achieve the plan's goals

- Objective and measurable criteria for determining when a species is recovered

- Estimates of the amount of time and money that will be required to achieve recovery

Recovery plans include precisely defined milestones for recovery achievement. For example, recovery may be considered accomplished when a certain number of individuals is reached and specifically named threats are eliminated.

Notices regarding proposed new or revised recovery plans must be placed in the *Federal Register* so that public comment can be obtained and considered before a plan is finalized.

Incidental Take Permits and Habitat Conservation Plans

When the original ESA was passed it included exceptions that allowed "taking" of listed species only for scientific research or other conservation activities authorized by the act. In 1982 Congress added a provision in Section 10 of the ESA that allows "incidental take" of listed species of wildlife by nonfederal entities. Incidental take is defined as take that is incidental to, but not the purpose of, an otherwise lawful activity. Incidental taking cannot appreciably reduce the likelihood of the survival and recovery of listed species in the wild. The incidental take provision was added to allow private landowners some freedom to develop their land even if it provides habitat to listed species.

In order to obtain an incidental take permit, an applicant has to prepare a Habitat Conservation Plan (HCP). An HCP describes the impacts likely to result from the taking of the species and the measures the applicant will take to minimize and mitigate the impacts. HCPs are generally partnerships drawn up by people at the local level, working with officials from the Fish and Wildlife Service or the National Marine Fisheries Service. The plans frequently represent compromises between developers and environmentalists.

Included in the agreement is a "no surprise" provision that assures landowners or developers that the overall cost of species protection measures will be limited to what has been agreed to under the Habitat Conservation Plan. In return, landowners make a long-term commitment to conservation as negotiated in the HCP. Many HCPs include the preservation of significant areas of habitat for endangered species.

Although the HCP program was implemented in 1982, it was little used before 1992, with only fourteen permits issued in that time period. As of February 28, 2006, there were 446 HCPs in place covering dozens of species. More than half of the Habitat Conservation Plans were issued in FWS regions for the southwest and southeast states. By far, the animal with the most plans issued is the Houston toad with more than 200 HCPs in place.

Information about HCPs is available in a database at the FWS Web site (http://ecos.fws.gov/conserv_plans/public.jsp). The database includes the locations covered by the plans as well as information on the applicants and the listed and unlisted species involved.

ENDANGERED SPECIES ACT LITIGATION

In a 2004 speech to the American Farm Bureau Federation, Gale Norton, Secretary of the Department of the Interior, described the Endangered Species Act as follows: "it is a powerful law designed for confrontation." Many confrontations over the law have taken place in the courts. The ESA includes provisions for civil lawsuits against government agencies alleged to be in violation of the ESA. Citizens can also sue if they believe the U.S. Fish and Wildlife Service has failed to perform actions required under the ESA or to compel the FWS to apply ESA prohibitions regarding "taking." Only two lawsuits were filed against the agency regarding the ESA between 1974 and 1991. Over the next decade more than three dozen suits were filed.

In *Endangered Species Act: Successes and Challengesin Agency Collaboration and the Use of Scientific Information in the Decision Making Process* (May 19, 2005), the Government Accountability Office (GAO) noted that the FWS had become "overburdened by litigation." Many of the lawsuits were filed by conservationist and animal groups regarding the listing process and designation of critical habitat. In 1992 a coalition of groups sued the Department of Interior charging that the listing process was proceeding too slowly. At that time more than 500 species were awaiting listing. The suit was settled out of court later that year when the FWS agreed to specific time limits for listings of the species at issue.

Designation of critical habitat has also been a contentious issue. In 1997 the Natural Resources Defense Council sued the Department of the Interior (DOI) over the long-standing policy of the U.S. Fish and Wildlife Service to avoid designating critical habitat under the "when prudent" clause. At that time the agency had set critical habitat for only approximately 10% of all listed species. The FWS lost the lawsuit, as well as many subsequent suits in the same vein. In 2000 the agency put a one-year hold on all work related to listing new species so that court-ordered critical habitat work could be tackled.

In 2004 the Fish and Wildlife Service lost a case that focused on the agency's decision to ignore petitions submitted for species that are candidate species. The lawsuit specifically dealt with the Gunnison sage grouse, a large ground-dwelling bird found only in parts of Colorado and Utah. In January 2000 a coalition of conservationist groups submitted a petition to the FWS on behalf of the species. The FWS responded that no action was needed on its part, because it planned to designate the species as a candidate species. This decision was in keeping with the agency's long-standing "Petition Management Guidance." In September 2000 the petitioning groups sued the agency claiming that the Guidance violated the intent of the ESA. In 2004 the U.S. District Court for the District of Columbia ruled against the FWS and ordered the agency to respond to petitions that had been submitted for more than 200 candidate species.

Since the 1990s the Fish and Wildlife Service has repeatedly complained that many of its decisions and activities are driven by court orders, rather than scientific priorities. Conservation and animal groups have taken advantage of ESA provisions that allow citizen involvement in petition submittals and lawsuits. Critics claim that the groups flood the FWS with petitions so that lawsuits can be brought when the agency is unable to respond in a timely manner. Environmentalists counter that the lawsuits are necessary, because the FWS fails to do the job assigned to the agency under the Endangered Species Act to protect imperiled species.

ENDANGERED SPECIES ACT SPENDING

Various federal agencies spend money in support of the ESA. The primary spending agency is the U.S. Fish and Wildlife Service, a division of the Department of the Interior. For accounting purposes the federal government operates on a fiscal year that begins in October and runs through the end of September. Thus, fiscal year 2007 covers the time period of October 1, 2006, through September 30, 2007. Each year by the first Monday in February the President of the United States must present a proposed budget to the U.S. House of Representatives. This is the amount of money that the president estimates will be required to operate the federal government during the next fiscal year.

In February 2006 the president proposed a $10.5 billion budget for the Department of the Interior for fiscal year 2007. This amount is 3% less than the amount funded to the DOI for fiscal year 2006. Just under $1.3 billion was requested for the Fish and Wildlife Service for fiscal year 2007. An additional $808 million is available under permanent appropriations. (This is money allocated to the agency on a continuing basis, not requested each year). According to the FWS, most of the permanent appropriations for fiscal year 2007 will be turned over to the states for restoration and conservation of fish and wildlife resources.

A breakdown by FWS mission goal for the nearly $1.3 billion budget for fiscal year 2007 is shown in Figure 2.3. More than half the money is devoted to sustaining biological communities. Budget appropriations specific to endangered species are shown in Table 2.6 for fiscal years 2005 through 2007. For fiscal year 2007

FIGURE 2.3

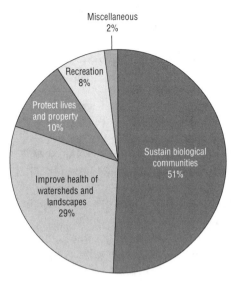

U.S. Fish and Wildlife Service budget request for fiscal year 2007

Miscellaneous 2%

Recreation 8%

Protect lives and property 10%

Improve health of watersheds and landscapes 29%

Sustain biological communities 51%

SOURCE: Adapted from "Appendix B. 2007 Request by Mission Goal," in "Bureau Highlights: Fish and Wildlife Service," *The Department of the Interior Fiscal Year 2007 Interior Budget in Brief,* U.S. Department of the Interior, February 2, 2006, http://www.doi.gov/budget/2007/07Hilites/BH55.pdf (accessed February 10, 2006)

just over $141 million is requested for endangered species programs. Most of the money is allocated to recovery programs ($65.9 million), followed by consultations with other agencies and groups ($49 million), listing activities ($17.8 million), and candidate species conservation ($8.1 million).

The Endangered Species Act requires the Department of the Interior to file an annual report detailing certain expenditures made for the conservation of threatened and endangered species under the act. The most recent report available was published in January 2005 and is titled

Federal and State Endangered and Threatened Species Expenditures: Fiscal Year 2004. The DOI collects spending data from other federal agencies and states receiving certain federal grants. The report indicates that $1.4 billion was spent during fiscal year 2004, broken down as follows:

- Specific individual species—$793 million
- Land acquisition—$60 million
- Other ESA expenses—$559 million

Other ESA expenses include salaries, operational expenses, and maintenance costs that are not assignable to a particular species. Total ESA expenditures for fiscal years 1994 through 2004 are shown in Figure 2.4 along with the number of listed species for each year.

Expenditures by Agency

The Department of the Interior reports that thirty-three federal agencies had ESA expenditures during fiscal year 2004; however, only thirty-one of the agencies were able to provide details on spending, as shown in Table 2.7. The federal agencies with the highest expenditures were the Department of Energy's Bonneville Power Administration ($309 million), FWS ($247 million), and the U.S. Department of Commerce's National Oceanic and Atmospheric Administration or NOAA ($197 million). The National Marine Fisheries Service is an agency of NOAA and handles ESA management of marine mammals, such as whales and seals, and anadromous fish (which migrate between ocean and fresh waters). State spending under the Endangered Species Act during fiscal year 2004 amounted to $205 million.

The Bonneville Power Administration (BPA) operates an extensive electric transmission system throughout the northwest United States that provides electricity generated at federal dams and nonfederal facilities,

TABLE 2.6

U.S. Fish and Wildlife Service budgets for endangered species program, fiscal years 2005–07

[In thousands of dollars]

Appropriation: resource management, by appropriation activity/subactivity	2005 actual	2006 enacted	2007 request	Change from 2006 enacted
Ecological services				
Endangered species				
Candidate conservation	9,142	8,619	8,063	−556
Listing	15,710	17,630	17,759	+129
Consultation	47,281	47,997	49,337	+1,340
Recovery	69,270	73,562	65,879	−7,683
Subtotal, endangered species	141,403	147,808	141,038	−6,770

SOURCE: "Highlights of Budget Changes: Appropriation: Resource Management," in "Bureau Highlights: Fish and Wildlife Service," *The Department of the Interior Fiscal Year 2007 Interior Budget in Brief,* U.S. Department of the Interior, February 2, 2006, http://www.doi.gov/budget/2007/07Hilites/BH55.pdf (accessed February 10, 2006)

FIGURE 2.4

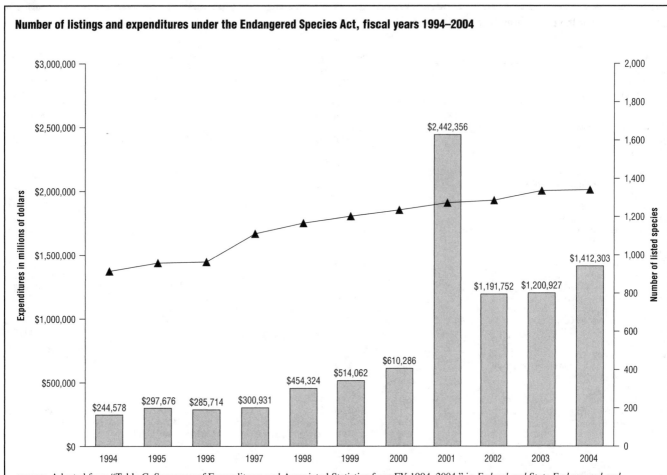

Number of listings and expenditures under the Endangered Species Act, fiscal years 1994–2004

SOURCE: Adapted from "Table C. Summary of Expenditures and Associated Statistics from FY 1994–2004," in *Federal and State Endangered and Threatened Species Expenditures: Fiscal Year 2004*, U.S. Department of the Interior, U.S. Fish and Wildlife Service, January 2005, http://www.fws.gov/endangered/expenditures/reports/FWS%20Endangered%20Species%202004%20Expenditures%20Report.pdf (accessed February 11, 2006)

including one nuclear power plant and a number of hydroelectric and wind energy plants. BPA is headquartered in Portland, Oregon. It is not funded by tax dollars, but by proceeds from the sale of electricity. Most BPA power comes from dams operated in the Columbia River basin. These waterways are also home to many endangered and threatened freshwater and anadromous fish species. BPA, the U.S. Army Corps of Engineers, and the Bureau of Reclamation operate the Federal Columbia River Power System and coordinate competing river uses, such as power generation, irrigation, flood control, navigation, recreation, and aquatic habitat.

Expenditures by Species

Table 2.8 shows the ten species with the highest reported expenditures under the Endangered Species Act in fiscal year 2004. The list is dominated by fish species. More than $161 million was spent on the Chinook salmon, followed by $117 million for the steelhead. Both species are anadromous and found in the waters of the Pacific Northwest. There are two marine

(ocean-based) mammals on the top-ten list: the Steller sea lion and the right whale. The red-cockaded woodpecker is the only nonaquatic species in the top ten.

Table 2.9 shows the ten entities (species, subspecies, distinct population segment or evolutionarily significant unit) with the highest reported expenditures during fiscal year 2004. Eight of the ten entities are anadromous fish. The exceptions are the western population of the Steller sea lion and the bull trout (a freshwater fish) found in the coterminous United States. Anadromous fish are often designated by their season of upriver migration and the primary body of water in which migration takes place. The entity with the highest expenditure ($40.6 million) during fiscal year 2004 was the population of Chinook salmon that migrate up the Snake River from spring through summer.

How best to use the funds allocated to endangered species has been a contentious issue for years. Approximately half of the money allocated to individual species in fiscal year 2004 was spent on only about 1.5% of the

TABLE 2.7

Expenditures under the Endangered Species Act, fiscal year 2004

Agency	Species total	Land total	Total
DHS[a] Coast Guard	$33,090,997	$17,114	$33,108,111
DHS Customs and Border Protection	$334,000	$0	$334,000
DOC[b] National Oceanic and Atmospheric Administration	$197,158,000	$0	$197,158,000
DOD[c] Air Force	$12,293,047	$0	$12,293,047
DOD Army	$26,539,300	$0	$26,539,300
DOD Army Corps of Engineers	$83,107,413	$0	$83,107,413
DOD Defense Logistics Agency	$131,005	$0	$131,005
DOD Marine Corps	$1,943,062	$0	$1,943,062
DOD Navy	$4,988,842	$0	$4,988,842
DOE[d] Bonneville Power Administration	$309,004,814	$50,271	$309,055,085
DOE Southwestern Power Administration	$13,500	$0	$13,500
DOE Western Area Power Administration	$6,492,268	$0	$6,492,268
DOI[e] Bureau of Indian Affairs	$2,327,681	$0	$2,327,681
DOI Bureau of Land Management	$21,153,074	$412,170	$21,565,244
DOI Bureau of Reclamation	$93,786,700	$1,851,000	$95,637,700
DOI Minerals Management Service	$2,707,347	$0	$2,707,347
DOI National Park Service	$10,902,792	$0	$10,902,792
DOI US Geologic Survey	$14,200,585	$0	$14,200,585
DOT[f] Federal Aviation Administration	$202,295	$0	$202,295
DOT Federal Highway Administration	$31,792,297	$6,484,000	$38,276,297
Environmental Protection Agency	$5,262,500	$0	$5,262,500
Federal Communications Commission	$27,500	$0	$27,500
Federal Energy Regulatory Commission	$226,800	$0	$226,800
Nuclear Regulatory Commission	$143,800	$0	$143,800
Smithsonian Institution	$994,200	$0	$994,200
Tennessee Valley Authority	$105,500	$0	$105,500
USDA[g] Animal and Plant Health Inspection Service	$6,580,276	$0	$6,580,276
USDA Farm Service Agency	$64,250	$0	$64,250
USDA Forest Service	$35,652,300	$0	$35,652,300
USDA Natural Resources Conservation Service	$30,016,143	$19,798,572	$49,814,715
US Fish and Wildlife Service	$217,050,166	$30,083,961	$247,134,127
State governments	$127,719,076	$77,594,400	$205,313,476
Total	**$1,276,011,530**	**$136,291,488**	**$1,412,303,018**

[a]DHS is Department of Homeland Security.
[b]DOC is Department of Commerce.
[c]DOD is Department of Defense.
[d]DOE is Department of Energy.
[e]DOI is Department of the Interior.
[f]DOT is Department of Transportation.
[g]USGA is United States Department of Agriculture.

SOURCE: "Table 4A. Species and Land Expenditures, Including Other ESA Expenses and Foreign Species, by Reporting Agency for FY2004," in *Federal and State Endangered and Threatened Species Expenditures: Fiscal Year 2004*, U.S. Department of the Interior, U.S. Fish and Wildlife Service, January 2005, http://www.fws.gov/endangered/expenditures/reports/FWS%20Endangered%20Species%202004%20Expenditures%20Report.pdf (accessed February 11, 2006)

listed species. In general, this disproportionate spending occurs because Congress and some states appropriate money for specific species. The DOI report *Federal and State Endangered and Threatened Species Expenditures: Fiscal Year 2004* notes the following benefits from this practice: "State and Federal natural resource managers use the public interest in these high-profile species to help protect other species in the same habitats or imperiled by the same threats. The species identified by Congress as deserving of specific appropriations are the same species that drive interest and participation in the considerable State and private sector efforts on behalf of all listed species."

The number of species being added to the federal threatened and endangered species list is likely to continue to grow. Although vertebrate species dominated the list during the first years of the act, plants and inverte-brate animals now make up a much greater proportion of listed species. (See Table 1.2 in Chapter 1.) These species are politically more difficult to defend than either mammals or birds, which are more inherently appealing to most Americans because of the "warm and fuzzy" factor. These circumstances raise questions about the continued feasibility of a species-by-species preservation strategy, and the FWS struggles under intense legal and political pressures to decide which species to protect first.

OPPOSITION TO THE ENDANGERED SPECIES ACT

Opponents of the Endangered Species Act believe the law violates private property rights and stifles economic growth by curbing development. They also charge that environmental protection often results in the loss of jobs and business profits.

TABLE 2.8

The ten listed species with the highest expenditures under the Endangered Species Act, fiscal year 2004

2004 rank	Species (50CFR[a]Part17)	Status[b]	Total ($000s)	2003 rank
1	Salmon, chinook[c]	E,T	161,309.5	1
2	Steelhead[c]	E,T	117,380.4	2
3	Sea-lion, steller[c]	E,T	42,557.3	3
4	Salmon, coho[c]	T	36,648.2	4
5	Trout, bull	T	32,570.6	5
6	Salmon, sockeye[c]	E,T	21,827.6	6
7	Woodpecker, red-cockaded	E	14,125.1	10
8	Sturgeon, pallid	E	13,370.2	34
9	Salmon, chum[c]	T	13,257.9	7
10	Whale, right	E	12,369.6	8

[a]Code of Federal Regulations.
[b]E=endangered; T=threatened.
[c]All subspecies, evolutionary significant units (ESUs), or distinct population segments (DPSs) combined.

SOURCE: "Table B. The Ten Species with the Highest Reported Expenditures in FY 2004," in *Federal and State Endangered and Threatened Species Expenditures: Fiscal Year 2004*, U.S. Department of the Interior, U.S. Fish and Wildlife Service, January 2005, http://www.fws.gov/endangered/expenditures/reports/FWS%20Endangered%20Species%202004%20Expenditures%20Report.pdf (accessed February 11, 2006)

TABLE 2.9

The ten listed entities with the highest expenditures under the Endangered Species Act, fiscal year 2004

Rank	Species	Population	Status*	2004 expenses
1	Salmon, chinook	Spring/summer, Snake River	T	$40,578,600
2	Trout, bull	U.S.A., coterminous, lower 48 states	T	$32,570,600
3	Sea-lion, steller	Western population	E	$31,746,200
4	Steelhead	Snake River basin	T	$28,203,300
5	Steelhead	Middle Columbia River	T	$27,959,600
6	Salmon, chinook	Fall, Snake River	T	$27,428,300
7	Salmon, chinook	Puget Sound	T	$24,084,900
8	Salmon, coho	Oregon, California populations	T	$23,405,700
9	Salmon, chinook	Spring, upper Columbia River	E	$20,254,600
10	Salmon, sockeye	U.S.A., Snake River	E	$17,550,200

*E=endangered; T=threatened.
Note: Entity can be a species, subspecies, distinct population segment (DPS), or evolutionary significant unit (ESU).

SOURCE: Adapted from "Table A. The Ten Listed Entities with the Highest Reported Expenditures in FY 2004," in *Federal and State Endangered and Threatened Species Expenditures: Fiscal Year 2004*, U.S. Department of the Interior, U.S. Fish and Wildlife Service, January 2005, http://www.fws.gov/endangered/expenditures/reports/FWS%20Endangered%20Species%202004%20Expenditures%20Report.pdf (accessed February 11, 2006)

One vocal critic of the ESA is Republican Congressman Richard Pombo of California. In 1996 Pombo coauthored the book *This Land Is Our Land: How to End the War on Private Property*, in which he asserted that the ESA and other federal laws infringe upon private property rights. Since taking office in 1993, the Congressman has sponsored several bills calling for sweeping reforms of the ESA. The most recent legislation (H.R. 3824) was introduced in September 2005 and had ninety-five cosponsors. The bill calls for elimination of critical habitat designation, authorizes government payments for landowners prevented from carrying out planned developments, and grants greater decision-making powers to the Secretary of the Interior regarding the scientific data involved in ESA decisions. The bill was passed by the House, and was sent to the U.S. Senate for consideration.

In December 2005 Republican Senator Mike Crapo of Idaho and Democratic Senator Blanche Lincoln of Arkansas introduced Senate bill S. 2110, which also calls for major reforms of the Endangered Species Act. The Senate bill seeks greater collaboration between landowners and local, state, and federal officials in decision-making and offers incentives (such as tax breaks) for landowners to cooperate in recovery activities. In a press release Congressman Pombo expressed his support for the Senate bill noting, "The ESA must be updated to incorporate more than thirty years of lessons learned. It must be modernized to provide flexibility for innovation to achieve results (http://resourcescommittee.house.gov/Press/releases/2005/121505crapolincolnstat.htm). As of May 2006 neither H.R. 3824 or S. 2110 had been passed by the Senate, but remained in committee.

IS THE ENDANGERED SPECIES ACT ENOUGH?

Other critics argue, on the other hand, that the ESA is not enough. In May 2005 a group of ten prominent scientists sent a letter to the U.S. Senate in which they urged strengthening of the Act. The letter was spearheaded by Professors E. O. Wilson of Harvard University and Paul Ehrlich of Stanford University. It warns that Earth is facing an "extinction crisis" and that large numbers of species could be lost over the next few decades. The scientists note the importance of the ESA in U.S. efforts to preserve biological diversity and conclude, "Viewing our looming extinction crisis as a crisis for humans as well as wildlife, the importance of the Endangered Species Act takes on even greater significance. In the face of this crisis, we must strengthen the Act and broaden its protections, not weaken them" (http://www.edcnews.se/Research/Extinction.html).

In March 2006 more than 5,700 U.S. scientists signed a letter to the U.S. Senate regarding concerns of the scientific community about proposed changes to the ESA. The letter highlights the historical successes of the Act as encouraging signs that progress is being made against the loss of imperiled species. It argues that the Act does not need a substantial overhaul, but a greater emphasis on implementation and use of objective scientific information in decision-making. The scientists wrote: "For species conservation to continue, it is imperative both that the scientific principles embodied in the Act are maintained, and that the Act is strengthened, fully implemented, and adequately funded" (http://www.ucsusa.org/scientific_integrity/restoring/science-in-the-endangered.html).

CHAPTER 3
HABITAT AND ECOSYSTEM CONSERVATION

The Endangered Species Act (ESA) is designed to protect plant and animal species in danger of extinction. During the 1990s there was a growing concern that traditional methods of species protection, which take a species-by-species approach, were ineffective. Many alternatives were proposed. One of the most popular was a method variously termed the "habitat," "ecosystem," or "community" approach. The U.S. Fish and Wildlife Service (FWS) defines an ecosystem as a "geographic area including all the living organisms (people, plants, animals, and microorganisms), their physical surroundings (such as soil, water, and air), and the natural cycles that sustain them." Central to the new approaches is a focus on conservation of large intact areas of habitat. It is hoped that by focusing on entire habitats, rather than individual species recovery, numerous species will be protected before they reach critically low population sizes.

THE ECOSYSTEM APPROACH

Ecosystem conservation considers entire communities of species as well as their interactions with the physical environment and aims to develop integrated plans involving wildlife, physical resources, and sustainable use. Such an approach sometimes requires compromise between environmentalists and developers. This is the case for several Habitat Conservation Plans (HCPs) developed by the U.S. Fish and Wildlife Service in recent years. In Southern California developers and environmentalists had long battled over hundreds of thousands of biologically rich acres lying between Los Angeles and Mexico that were home to uncounted species of plants and animals. Developers wanted to build there, while federal regulators wanted to protect the habitat for wildlife. Haggling over small parcels of land had already cost significant time and money and caused frustration on both sides. A compromise resolution permitted developers to develop some large parcels of land while setting aside other large, intact regions as conservation areas.

A similar agreement between developers and environmentalists was reached in the Texas Hill Country in 1996 and is effective for thirty years from that date. The Balcones Canyonlands Conservation Plan set aside 111,428 acres for ecosystem enhancement while allowing uncontested development of many thousands of acres of land in the central Texas corridor.

Endangered U.S. Ecosystems.

In 1995 the first full review of the health of the American landscape was compiled by the National Biological Service and published by the U.S. Geological Survey (Reed F. Noss et al., *Endangered Ecosystems of the United States: A Preliminary Assessment of Loss and Degradation*, 1995). It is still considered the definitive study of U.S. ecosystem health. Although individual species had been studied previously, the health of the larger ecosystems had never before been considered. The study was based on surveys of state databases and the scientific literature. The report concluded that vast stretches of natural habitat, totaling nearly half the area of the forty-eight contiguous states, had declined to the point of endangerment. Ecosystems suffered in two ways. Quantitative losses were measured by a decline in the area of an ecosystem. Qualitative losses involved degradation in the structure, function, or composition of an ecosystem.

Of the ecosystems that had declined by over 70%, 58% were terrestrial, 32% were wetland areas, and 10% were aquatic. Forests, grasslands, barrens, and savannas dominated the list. (See Figure 3.1.) American ecosystems identified by the National Biological Service as suffering the greatest overall decline include grasslands, savannas, and barrens (55%), followed by shrublands (24%) and forests (17%).

The National Biological Service found that thirty-two American ecosystems had declined by more than

FIGURE 3.1

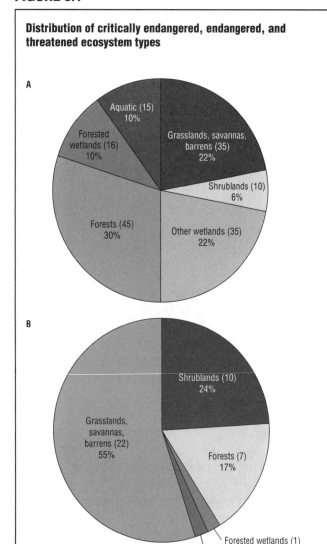

Distribution of critically endangered, endangered, and threatened ecosystem types

A

Aquatic (15) 10%

Forested wetlands (16) 10%

Grasslands, savannas, barrens (35) 22%

Shrublands (10) 6%

Forests (45) 30%

Other wetlands (35) 22%

B

Shrublands (10) 24%

Grasslands, savannas, barrens (22) 55%

Forests (7) 17%

Forested wetlands (1) 2%

Aquatic (1) 2%

(A) Distribution of critically endangered, endangered, and threatened ecosystem types in six general categories. To include general wetland-loss statistics, which are usually organized by state, a number was added in the wetland category for each state with declines of more than 70%. The greatest number of reported declines is among forest and wetland habitats and communities. (B) For ecosystems that have declined by more than 98% (i.e., critically endangered), the greatest losses are among grassland, savanna, and barrens communities.

Note: Number in parentheses indicates the number of ecosystem types.

SOURCE: Reed F. Noss, Edward T. LaRoe III, and J. Michael Scott, "Figure 1," in *Endangered Ecosystems of the United States: A Preliminary Assessment of Loss and Degradations*, U.S. Geological Survey, 1995, http://biology.usgs.gov/pubs/ecosys.htm (accessed April 4, 2006)

98% and were classified as "critically endangered." Fifty-eight had declined by 85% to 98% and were classified as "endangered." Thirty-eight others declined by 70% to 84% and were listed as "threatened."

Endangered ecosystems were found in all major regions of the United States except Alaska. The greatest losses occurred in the Northeast, the South, and the Midwest, as well as in California. Native grasslands,

needlegrass steppes, and alkali sink scrubs are among the communities that have declined most precipitously in California.

FORESTS

Forests perform a wide variety of social and ecological functions. They provide homes and sustenance for forest dwellers, protect and enrich soils, affect local and regional climate through the evaporation and storage of water, and help stabilize the global climate by processing carbon dioxide.

Forests are broadly classified by latitude as either tropical, temperate, or boreal. Tropical forests, or rainforests, are predominantly evergreen and occur close to the equator, in areas with plentiful rain and little temperature variation year-round. There are tropical forests in Central and South America, Africa, South and Southeast Asia, and Australia. Tropical forests are characterized by the greatest diversity of biological species. For example, as many as 100 distinct tree species may inhabit a square kilometer (about 0.38 square miles). Vegetation is often so dense in tropical forests that very little light penetrates to the ground.

Temperate forests are found in areas with distinct warm and cold seasons, including North America, northern Asia, and western and central Europe. Many temperate forests are made up of deciduous trees—species that shed their leaves during winter. Plant diversity is not as great in temperate forests as in rainforests. There are perhaps three or four tree species per square kilometer.

Boreal forests, also known as taiga, are found at high latitudes in extremely cold climates where the growing season is short. Precipitation generally falls as snow rather than rain. Boreal forest flora include evergreen trees and lichen ground cover. Boreal forests are present in Siberia, Scandinavia, Alaska, and Canada.

North American Forests

Many U.S. forests are highly imperiled. One of the greatest threats to forests is deforestation via clear cutting, a method of logging in which all the trees in an area are cut. Serious damage to the old-growth forests of the Pacific Northwest, for example, is visible from National Aeronautics and Space Administration (NASA) satellite photos. Old-growth forests harbor many unique species, including numerous species that are threatened or endangered. An alternative to clear-cutting is selective management, in which only some trees are removed from an area. Even selective management practices, however, frequently deplete forests more quickly than they are able to recover. The lumber industry continues to battle with environmentalists and the U.S. Forest Service over the right to log national forest lands, including the unique redwood forests of the West Coast.

Huge forest fires raged through the western United States in 2000 and 2002. The Forest Service reported that these were two of the worst fire seasons in over fifty years. In 2002 forest fires scorched over seven million acres and caused over $1.7 billion in damages. The fires were partly the result of long decades of fire suppression. In response, President Bush announced the "Healthy Forest Initiative" in 2002. This initiative was immediately attacked by conservationists, who claimed that its only aim was to roll back federal regulations on logging, and that it was intended to benefit logging companies rather than to protect people or wildlife. Conservationists further argued that the Bush Administration was merely using the forest fires as an excuse for forwarding its pro-business/anti-environment agenda.

In addition to logging and fire risk, there are several other major threats to forests. These threats are highlighted by the U.S. Forest Service in *America's Forests: 2003 Health Update* (2003, http://www.fs.fed.us/publications/documents/forest-health-update2003.pdf). These threats include:

- *Invasive insects and pathogens.* Sudden Oak Death, caused by a new, unidentified pathogen, has killed thousands of oak and other species in coastal forests, mixed evergreen forests, and urban-wildland interfaces in California and southern Oregon. White pine blister rust is a nonnative fungus from Asia that has killed white pine trees in the western United States and Canada. The gypsy moth, first introduced from native habitats in Europe and Asia in the 1800s, continues to damage eastern U.S. forests. The hemlock woolly adelgid, native to Asia and introduced in the 1920s, continues to kill hemlock trees in the eastern United States.

- *Invasive plants.* About 1,400 species of nonnative plants are recognized as pest species that threaten forests and grasslands. Table 3.1 lists some of the most common ones. Invasive plant species currently affect over 100 million acres of U.S. forestland. The Forest Service spends about $16 million annually in preventing the spread of invasive plants such as the "mile-a-minute" weed, which infests northeastern forests, and leafy spurge, which affects ecosystems in southern Canada and the northern United States.

- *Outbreaks of native insects.* Certain native insects, including bark beetles, mountain pine beetles, and southern pine beetles, can also lay waste to native forests when they occur in large outbreaks.

TONGASS NATIONAL FOREST. During the first millennium CE, an expanse of ancient forest flourished along the entire western coast of the United States and Canada. Today, a portion of this habitat, a 500-mile expanse along the southeastern coast of Alaska, has been preserved as Tongass National Forest. Tongass National Forest represents an unblemished stretch of trees and other wildlife that has existed as a completely intact ecosystem for over a thousand years. It includes nearly eighteen million acres of virtually pristine woodland. The Tongass preserve comprises about one-fourth of the world's temperate rainforest and is the largest on earth.

In the mid-twentieth century, however, the federal government began to negotiate with logging companies to open small portions of the ancient forest for clear-cutting. This has generated ongoing debate in Congress. In the 1990s loggers appealed to the government to open more access roads to facilitate logging, whereas environmentalists fought to preserve the area from human tampering altogether. In May 2000 the National Forest Service drafted a proposal urging renewed protection of roadless areas. A successful lawsuit brought by the Natural Resources Defense Council in 2003 appeared to protect Tongass and other roadless national forests from logging. However, the Bush Administration exempted Tongass from these protections and has continued attempts to open more acreage of the forest to logging.

In June 2005 an amendment was voted down by the U.S. Senate that would have banned federal subsidies for new roads in Tongass. Proponents of the amendment argued that taxpayers should not have to pay for building roads that allow timber producers better access to old-growth trees in the forest. Critics charged that the roads serve many purposes, including the enhancement of tourism, recreational activities, and access by Forest Service rangers. At that time approximately 4% of the Tongass National Forest was open to logging.

Deforestation

Deforestation refers to the destruction of forests through the removal of trees, most often by clear-cutting or burning. It results in habitat loss for countless species of plants as well as animals. Deforestation is occurring globally, but is proceeding at a particularly alarming rate in the world's tropical rainforests, which comprise the most diverse ecosystems in the world. Deforestation is one of the most pressing environmental issues today.

In addition to destruction of habitat for numerous plant and animal species, the loss of forests has other effects as well. For example, forests play a crucial role in the global cycling of carbon—vegetation stores two trillion tons of carbon worldwide, roughly triple the amount stored in the atmosphere. When forest trees are cleared, the carbon they contain is oxidized and released to the air, adding to the carbon dioxide in the atmosphere. The burning of the Amazon rainforests and other forests thus has a two-fold effect—the release of large amounts of carbon dioxide into the atmosphere and the loss of the trees that help absorb carbon dioxide.

TABLE 3.1

Invasive plants

Species	Common name	Species	Common name
Acer platanoides	Norway maple	*Imperata cylindrica*	Cogon grass
Acroptilon repens	Russian knapweed	*Kochia scoparia*	Summer-cypress
Agropyron cristatum	Crested wheatgrass	*Lepidium latifolium*	Perennial pepperweed
Agropyron desertorum	Desert wheatgrass	*Lespedeza bicolor*	Bicolor lespedeza
Agrostis gigantea	Redtop	*Lespedeza cuneata*	Sericea lespedeza
Ailanthus altissima	Tree-of-heaven	*Lespedeza striata*	Common lespedeza
Alliaria petiolata	Garlic mustard	*Ligustrum amurense*	Amur privet
Amaranthus retroflexus	Rough pigweed	*Ligustrum japonicum*	Japanese privet
Artemisia abrotanum	Oldman wormwood	*Ligustrum sinense*	Chinese privet
Artemisia absinthium	Absinth wormwood	*Ligustrum vulgare*	European privet
Artemisia dracunculus	Tarragon	*Linaria dalmatica*	Dalmatian toadflax
Arundo donax	Giant reed	*Linaria vulgaris*	Yellow toadflax
Bromus hordeaceus	Soft chess	*Lolium perenne*	Perennial ryegrass
Bromus inermis	Smooth brome	*Lolium multiflorum*	Italian ryegrass
Bromus japonicus	Japanese brome	*Lonicera × bella*	Bell's honeysuckle
Bromus madritensis	Foxtail chess, red brome	*Lonicera fragantissima*	Winter honeysuckle
Bromus tectorum	Cheatgrass	*Lonicera japonica*	Japanese honeysuckle
Calluna vulgaris	Heather	*Lonicera maackii*	Amur honeysuckle
Cardaria chalapensis	Lens-podded hoary cress	*Lonicera morrowii*	Morrow's honeysuckle
Cardaria draba	Heart-podded hoary cress	*Lonicera tatarica*	Tatarian honeysuckle
Cardaria pubescens	Globe-podded hoary cress	*Lonicera xylosteum*	European fly honeysuckle
Carduus nutans	Musk thistle	*Lygodium japonicum*	Japanese climbing fern
Casuarina cunninghamiana	River sheoak	*Lygodium microphyllum*	Old World climbing fern
Casuarina equisetifolia	Australian-pine	*Lythrum salicaria*	Purple loosestrife
Casuarina glauca	Gray sheoak	*Medicago sativa*	Alfalfa
Celastrus orbiculatus	Oriental bittersweet	*Melaleuca quinquenervia*	Melaleuca
Centaurea diffusa	Diffuse knapweed	*Melilotus alba*	White sweetclover
Centaurea maculosa	Spotted knapweed	*Melilotus officinalis*	Yellow sweetclover
Centaurea solstitialis	Yellow starthistle	*Microstegium vimineum*	Nepalese browntop
Chondrilla juncea	Rush skeletonweed	*Phalaris arundinacea*	Reed canarygrass
Cirsium arvense	Canada thistle	*Phleum pratense*	Timothy
Cirsium vulgare	Bull thistle	*Poa pratensis*	Kentucky bluegrass
Convolvulus arvensis	Field bindweed	*Potentilla recta*	Sulfur cinquefoil
Cynodon dactylon	Bermuda grass	*Psathyrostachys juncea*	Russian wildrye
Cynoglossum officinale	Houndstongue	*Pueraria montana var. lobata*	Kudzu
Cytisus scoparius	Scotch broom	*Rosa multiflora*	Multiflora rose
Cytisus striatus	Portuguese broom	*Rubus discolor*	Himalayan blackberry
Dactylis glomerata	Orchard grass	*Rubus laciniatus*	Evergreen blackberry
Descurainia sophia	Flixweed tansymustard	*Rumex acetosella*	Sheep sorrel
Echinochloa crus-galli	Barnyard grass	*Salsola kali*	Russian-thistle
Elaeagnus angustifolia	Russian-olive	*Schinus terebinthifolius*	Brazilian peppertree
Elaeagnus umbellata	Autumn-olive	*Sisymbrium altissimum*	Tumblemustard
Elytrigia repens	Quackgrass	*Sonchus arvensis*	Perennial sowthistle
Eragrostis curvula	Weeping lovegrass	*Sorghum halepense*	Johnson grass
Eragrostis lehmanniana	Lehmann lovegrass	*Spartium junceum*	Spanish broom
Eremochloa ophiuroides	Centipede grass	*Taeniatherum caput-medusae*	Medusahead
Erodium cicutarium	Cutleaf filaree	*Tamarix aphylla*	Athel tamarisk
Eucalyptus globulus	Bluegum eucalyptus	*Tamarix chinensis*	Saltcedar
Euphorbia esula	Leafy spurge	*Tamarix gallica*	French tamarisk
Festuca arundinaceum	Tall fescue	*Tamarix parviflora*	Small-flowered tamarisk
Genista monspessulana	French broom	*Tamarix ramosissima*	Saltcedar
Halogeton glomeratus	Halogeton	*Taraxacum officinale*	Dandelion
Hypericum perforatum	St. Johnswort	*Triadica sebifera*	Tallowtree
Imperata brasiliensis	Brazilian satintail	*Xanthium strumarium*	Common cocklebur

SOURCE: Adapted from "Invasive Plants List," in *Fire Effects Information System: Invasive Plants*, U.S. Department of Agriculture, U.S. Forest Service, Rocky Mountain Research Station, Fire Sciences Laboratory, Undated, http://www.fs.fed.us/database/feis/plants/weed/index.html (accessed March 8, 2006)

Furthermore, deforestation also results in forest fragmentation, which is itself detrimental for several reasons. First, forest fragmentation creates more "edge" habitats and destroys habitat for deep-forest creatures. Second, fragmentation isolates plant and animal populations, making them more vulnerable to local extinction. Third, some nonnative species thrive in edge habitats, and are able to invade and displace native species in a fragmented habitat. In North America, for example, songbirds like the wood thrush and the promontory warbler are declining due to increasing numbers of blue jays and parasitic brown-headed cowbirds, both of which flourish at forest edges. Finally, most trees are more susceptible to weather at forest edges.

Rainforests

Tropical forests are found in a band along the equator from Mexico into South America and across the Caribbean, central Africa, and parts of Asia. These forests include both lowland and upland (hill and mountainous) formations and vary in vegetative type. Most tropical forests are either dry or moist and are composed of deciduous vegetation that sheds its leaves at the end of the growing season. Lying closest to the equator are the tropical rainforests. They experience very warm temperatures year round and high amounts of precipitation. The vegetation is thick and lush and characterized by a large number of flowering and fruit-producing trees and vines. The largest concentration of tropical rainforests occurs in northern South America. However, they are also found in west central Africa and scattered across parts of Southeast Asia and northernmost Australia. Tropical rainforests are the world's most biologically rich habitats and are estimated to harbor 50% to 90% of the world's species. Biologists believe that many rainforest species have yet to be discovered and described by humans. In February 2006, the BBC reported that an international team of scientists had found a previously unknown jungle in Indonesia containing new species of butterflies, frogs, birds, and plants (http://newsvote.bbc.co.uk/mpapps/pagetools/print/news.bbc.co.uk/1/hi/sci/tech/4688000.stm).

Throughout the twentieth century tropical forests were depleted by logging and clearing for farms and ranches. The United Nations Food and Agriculture Organization (FAO) published an assessment of the world's tropical forests in *Forest Resources Assessment 1990: Survey of Tropical Forest Cover and Study of Change Processes* (1993). The FAO reported at that time that tropical forests covered 4.34 billion acres at the end of 1990, down from 4.72 billion acres at the end of 1980. The highest rates of deforestation were reported in Africa, Asia, Central America, and Mexico. During the 1980s an average of approximately thirty-eight million acres per year was deforested. The deforestation rate for tropical rainforests was eleven million acres per year. In an update, the FAO estimated that all tropical forests were deforested at an average of 22.7 million acres per year during the 1990s (*Global Forest Resources Assessment 2000*, 2005, http://www.fao.org/documents/show_cdr.asp?url_file=/DOCREP/004/Y1997E/Y1997E00.HTM). The deforestation rate for tropical rainforests was 14.8 million acres per year.

The major underlying causes of tropical deforestation are economic—underdevelopment, unemployment, and poverty among the growing populations of tropical countries. Unrestricted by enforceable regulations, farmers clear forests to create meager cropland that is often useless three years after its conversion—this is because tropical forest soils are poor, because almost all available nutrients are locked up in the trees and other biomatter. Logging and the conversion of forestland to unsustainable, short-term agricultural use have resulted in the destruction of habitats, declining fisheries, erosion, and flooding. Forest loss also disrupts regional weather patterns and contributes to global climate change. Finally, it eliminates plant and animal species that may serve

important medical, industrial, and agricultural purposes. However, arguments for protective measures that might not reap economic benefits for many decades are of little interest to farmers with families to feed. Developing countries frequently voice resentment over what they see as the hypocrisy of industrialized nations, which invariably engaged in similarly destructive practices to build their own economies.

Conservation of tropical forests presents a considerable challenge. The creation of protected areas alone has often proven ineffectual, mostly because the people who exploit forests are given no other options for meeting their economic needs. Many conservationists have started to focus on the promotion of sustainable development within rainforests. Agroforestry describes an agricultural strategy that involves the maintenance of diversity within developed tropical forest areas. This includes planting many different types of crops in patches that are mixed in among grazing lands and intact forest. Agroforestry often focuses on crops that produce goods for an indefinite period of time, including citrus fruits, bananas, cacao, coffee, and rubber.

Agroforestry can help to maintain soil quality as well as tropical biodiversity, allowing for a sustained productivity that makes it unnecessary to clear more and more areas of forest. In addition, rainforest conservationists have promoted the harvest of sustainable rainforest products, rather than unsustainable products such as timber. Sustainable harvests include those of medicines, food, and rubber.

WETLANDS

Wetlands are transitional areas between land and water bodies where water periodically floods the land or saturates the soil. The term wetland includes environments such as marshes, swamps, bogs, and estuaries. Wetlands may be covered in shallow water most of the year or be wet only seasonally. Plants and animals found in wetlands are uniquely adapted to these conditions.

Wetlands in the United States are highly diverse because of regional differences in climate, geology, soils, and vegetation. According to the National Audubon Society there are approximately 100 million acres of wetlands in the country. The majority of this is freshwater wetland. The rest is tidal, or saltwater, wetland and is found along the coasts. Wetlands are found in nearly all states—there are Arctic tundra wetlands in Alaska, peat bogs in the Appalachians, and riparian (riverbank) wetlands in the arid West.

The Audubon Society reported that in 2006 well over half the original North American wetlands had vanished. A few states had lost nearly all their original wetlands. With the recognition of the importance of wetlands and the institution of protective measures, the pace of wetland loss has slowed in recent decades. The U.S. Environmental Protection Agency (EPA) reported that about 58,500 wetland acres were lost each year between 1986 and 1997, with forested wetlands suffering the most damage. Although this represents an 80% drop from the previous decade, wetland loss is still significant. Wetlands provide critical habitats for fish and wildlife. They also purify polluted water and check the destructive power of floods and storms. Finally, wetlands provide recreational opportunities such as fishing, hunting, photography, and wildlife observation. As of December 2004 the EPA estimated that approximately 60,000 acres of wetland habitat continued to be lost each year in the United States (http://www.epa.gov/owow/wetlands/pdf/overview.pdf).

Endangered Bogs

Bogs are nontidal wetland ecosystems that form where poor drainage and low oxygen levels combine with a low mineral content to retard the decay of organic material. Over time, peat (partially decayed organic substances) begins to solidify, forming layers over the surface of ponds. Migrating birds and amphibians, including some salamanders, are among the animals most commonly found in bog habitats. Bog flora include coarse, grass-like plants called sedges and unusual carnivorous plants such as sundew and pitcher plants. Carnivorous plants capture and digest small insects in order to obtain nutrients unavailable in their unique environments, most often minerals such as nitrogen and phosphorus. The leaves of the sundew are covered with hundreds of tiny "tentacles" that are used to trap insects. The sundew traps an average of five insects per month. Pitcher plants maintain a pool of acidic fluid at the bottom of their "pitchers." Hairs on the inside of the pitchers point downward, preventing insects from exiting once they enter. Insects are attracted to the pitchers by the enticing red color inside.

Bog plants are threatened primarily by encroaching urbanization. Boggy wetlands are either drained or filled for use as dumping grounds. In addition, the suppression of naturally occurring fires discourages the formation of bog ecosystems. One bog species, the funnel-shaped green pitcher plant, first appeared on the Endangered Species List in 1979. Found in Alabama, North Carolina, and Georgia, it has declined largely due to collection by humans, who find these insect-eating plants both interesting and exotic. The collection of carnivorous plant species has also disrupted bog ecosystems by allowing mosquitoes and flies to proliferate.

The Florida Everglades

The Everglades covers approximately 5,000 square miles of southern Florida. (See Figure 3.2.) It includes a wide diversity of both temperate and tropical habitat types, including sawgrass prairies, mangrove swamps, pine forests, cypress forests, marshes, and estuaries, and represents one of the wildest and most inaccessible areas in the United States. The area was formed by centuries of water flow from Lake Okeechobee in south-central Florida to Florida Bay, and is often described as a shallow "river of grass." The highest land in the Everglades is a mere seven feet above sea level. Everglades National Park is the largest remaining subtropical wilderness in the United States, and is home to such endangered species as the American crocodile, Florida panther, wood stork, and West Indian manatee. The Everglades became a National Park in 1947, and the region has also been designated an International Biosphere Reserve, a World Heritage Site, and a Wetland of International Importance.

Everglades habitats are now threatened by many factors. First, water control through an extensive system of canals and levees has brought both droughts and floods to Everglades lands. Much of the Everglades' water has traditionally been diverted for irrigation or to supply metropolitan areas. In fact, the portion of the Everglades inundated by water was reduced drastically over the twentieth century, destroying numerous habitat areas. Occasional releases of large amounts of water, on the other hand, flood habitats, harming species such as alligators, whose nests may be washed away. Pollution is a second factor in Everglades deterioration. Harmful pollutants now found in the Everglades include fertilizers and pesticides from agricultural runoff, as well as mercury. Fertilizers encourage the rampant growth of vegetation that chokes wetlands, while pesticides and mercury poison species. One plant species that is affected is Garber's spurge, a beach herb that thrives in sandy peripheral soil. With its decline, parts of the Everglades have been more prone to soil erosion.

Invasive species have also altered Everglades habitats. Alien species such as Brazilian pepper and Australian pine have reduced native plant populations. Finally, fire suppression related to human encroachment has caused habitat alteration. Park officials now adhere to a prescribed burn schedule, setting fires in three- to ten-year intervals as necessary.

Multiple efforts were made in the 1990s and early 2000s to help restore the Everglades. Florida's Everglades Forever Act, passed in 1994, attempted to limit agricultural runoff as well as set water quality standards. The Comprehensive Everglades Restoration Plan, passed by Congress in 2000, is a thirty-eight year project drawn up by the U.S. Army Corps of Engineers. It aims to restore natural water flow patterns in the Everglades and to redirect water to the marshes.

Tidal Wetlands—The Mangroves

Mangrove forests are among the most biodiverse wetland ecosystems on earth. They are found in tropical

FIGURE 3.2

Map of south Florida

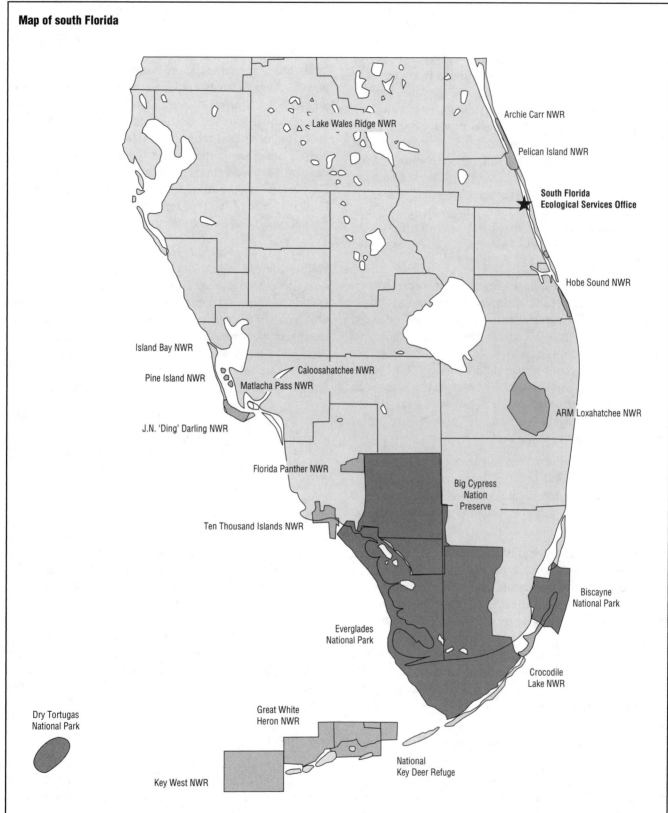

Note: NWR is National Wildlife Refuge.

SOURCE: "The 19-Counties That Comprise the Area of Responsibility for the Vero Beach Office Is Equal to a Combination of the States of Massachusetts and New Hampshire," in *Vero Beach, South Florida Ecological Services Office*, U.S. Department of the Interior, U.S. Fish and Wildlife Service, Undated, http://www.fws.gov/verobeach/ Fact%20Sheets/ES%20Office.pdf (accessed March 2, 2006)

coastal waters, often near river mouths. The tree species found in mangrove forests possess special roots that allow them to survive in brackish water. Mangrove forests harbor numerous unique species worldwide, such as crab-eating monkeys, fishing cats, and diverse species of birds and fish. They also provide food and wood for local communities, stabilize coastlines, and provide barriers from the sea during storms. Mangrove forests once lined three-quarters of the world's tropical coasts. Now, according to the World Resources Institute, an environmental advocacy group, less than half these forests remain ("Scorecard of Ecosystem Conditions and Changing Capacities," http://pubs.wri.org/pubs_content_print.cfm? ContentID=184). Indonesia, a country of more than 13,000 islands, possesses the most mangrove forestland of any country. Brazil and Australia also have extensive mangrove habitats.

Mangroves are disappearing in part because they have traditionally been regarded as sinister, malarial wastelands. In Florida, for example, mangroves were flooded every year to control mosquito populations. Mangrove forests have also been sold to logging companies for paper pulp, pest-proof timber, and chipboard for coastal development. Many mangrove forests have also been replaced with saltwater ponds for commercial shrimp farming. The shrimp industry is perhaps the most immediate threat to mangrove forests today.

During the Vietnam War, herbicides were dumped on an estimated 124,000 hectares (approximately 306,410 acres) of mangrove forests in South Vietnam. These areas remain, for the most part, entirely barren—a true wasteland.

The continued survival of endangered and threatened species is dependent on the presence of suitable habitat for them. Due to agricultural and urban development, much of the land in the United States has been rendered unsuitable for this purpose. However, federal, state, and private efforts to preserve land from harmful development have been successful to some degree. As a result there are conservation areas throughout the country that provide varying levels of refuge for endangered and threatened species.

U.S. LAND CONSERVATION EFFORTS

The early American colonists were impressed by the abundance of natural resources they found in North America and by the vast expanses of land available for settlement. Settlers migrated to the West and South, building towns and developing land for agriculture and industry. New modes of transportation allowed access to areas previously undisturbed by humans. Widespread development and demand for food, water, lumber, and other goods began to stress some natural resources. Massive areas of forest were cleared of trees. Passenger pigeons

and heath hens were driven to extinction. Buffalo, elk, and beaver stocks were nearly destroyed.

In the United States's first century as a nation, the federal government owned about 80% of the nation's land. The government started surveying and selling its land holdings to states, settlers, and railroad companies in about 1785. During the nineteenth century awareness began growing in the United States about the scarcity and value of natural resources. In 1892 John Muir (1838–1914) established the Sierra Club, an organization devoted to recreation, education, and conservation. President Theodore Roosevelt (1858–1919) set aside millions of acres of land under federal government control for national refuges, forests, and parks.

By the end of the nineteenth century, the government had transferred most of its lands to private ownership. It also allowed private use of remaining federal lands. After several decades of rapid development and unrestricted use, much of the nation's land and natural resources were significantly degraded. Responding to mounting concerns, Congress slowly redefined the federal government's role in land management from temporary to permanent retention as well as active stewardship.

During the 1960s, increasing scientific and public concern about the declining condition of the country's natural resources led Congress to enact a number of laws to conserve both federal and nonfederal lands. These laws regulate activities that affect air, water, soil, plants, and animals. With increasing environmental legislation, the land management framework evolved into a complex collection of agencies, land units, and laws. Different agencies have different priorities, which are reflected in how they manage the resources under their care. The effects of these different missions are particularly evident in places where two agencies hold adjacent lands. For example, the National Park Service (Department of the Interior) oversees Yellowstone National Park, where timber harvesting is prohibited, whereas the U.S. Forest Service (Department of Agriculture) allows large areas to be clear-cut in the adjacent Targhee National Forest in Idaho.

The National Park System

In 1849 the U.S. Congress passed a bill creating the U.S. Department of the Interior (DOI). The DOI was responsible for a wide variety of matters, including constructing water systems, exploring wilderness areas in the West, and managing public lands and public parks. In 1872 Yellowstone National Park was created by an act of Congress and was the first national park established in the world. Over the next four decades more than a dozen national parks were established in the United States, along with twenty-one national monuments. In 1916 a

FIGURE 3.3

The National Park System

■ National Park System

SOURCE: "The National Park System (in Red) Represents Ecosystem throughout the United States," in "Endangered Species and the National Park Service," *Endangered Species Bulletin,* vol. XXVII, no. 1, January/February 2002, U.S. Department of the Interior, U.S. Fish and Wildlife Service, http://www.fws.gov/endangered/esb/2002/01-02/04-07.pdf (accessed January 31, 2006)

new agency, the National Park Service (NPS), was created under the DOI to manage these federal lands.

As of 2006 there were 388 units in the National Park System covering nearly eighty million acres. The units include national parks, monuments, preserves, lakeshores, seashores, wild and scenic rivers, trails, historic sites, military parks, battlefields, historical parks, recreation areas, memorials, and parkways. The map in Figure 3.3 shows the location and ranges of National Parks in the United States. In addition to preserving habitats that range from Arctic tundra to tropical rain forest, the system protects many imperiled plant and animal species.

In late 2005 the NPS published a proposed revision of the *National Park Service Management Policies* (2005, http://parkplanning.nps.gov/document.cfm?projectId=13746 &documentID=12825). Section 4.4.2.3 of the document

discusses the management of endangered and threatened species on NPS lands. The agency notes that it engages in the following activities:

- Cooperates with the U.S. Fish and Wildlife Service and National Marine Fisheries Service to ensure that National Park Service actions comply with the Endangered Species Act

- Operates programs to inventory, monitor, restore, and maintain the habitats of listed species

- Works to control invasive nonnative species

- Prevents visitors from damaging vital habitats

- Reestablishes depleted populations to maintain the species

- Manages critical habitat and recovery areas designated under the ESA

TABLE 3.2

Areas located within National Forest Service boundaries, September 30, 2005

Area kind	Number of units	Gross acreage	Non forest service acreage	Other acreage
National totals				
National forests	155	225,316,632	188,009,261	37,307,371
Purchase units	63	2,316,288	370,546	1,945,742
National grasslands	20	4,264,663	3,838,166	426,497
Land utilization projects	6	1,876	1,876	0
Research and experimental areas	20	73,154	64,871	8,283
Other areas	35	361,967	357,910	4,057
National preserves	1	89,716	89,716	0
Totals	**300**	**232,424,296**	**192,732,346**	**39,691,950**
Western regional totals (regions 1 through 6)				
National forests	101	156,025,042	141,226,878	14,798,164
Purchase units	19	164,239	12,244	151,995
National grasslands	18	4,080,564	3,799,984	280,580
Land utilization projects	4	1,834	1,834	0
Research and experimental areas	6	60,598	60,598	0
Other areas	29	171,717	167,660	4,057
National preserves	1	89,716	89,716	0
Totals	**178**	**160,593,710**	**145,358,914**	**15,234,796**
Eastern regional totals (regions 8 and 9)				
National forests	52	44,932,472	24,809,244	20,123,228
Purchase units	44	2,152,049	358,302	1,793,747
National grasslands	2	184,099	38,182	145,917
Land utilization projects	2	42	42	0
Research and experimental areas	14	12,556	4,273	8,283
Other areas	6	190,250	190,250	0
Totals	**120**	**47,471,468**	**25,400,293**	**22,071,175**
Alaska region totals (region 10)				
National forests	2	24,359,118	21,973,139	2,385,979
Totals	**2**	**24,359,118**	**21,973,139**	**2,385,979**

Note: Other acreage refers to areas located within National Forest System boundaries that are not federally owned or administered by the U.S. Forest Service.

SOURCE: "Table 1. National and Regional Areas Summary," in *Land Areas Report as of September 30, 2005*, U.S. Department of the Interior, 2005, http://www.fs.fed.us/land/staff/lar/LAR05/table1.htm (accessed March 8, 2006)

• Cooperates with other agencies involved in setting critical habitat and recovery areas and participates in the recovery planning process

• Works with federal and state agencies and nongovernmental organizations to promote conservation agreements for candidate species

• Conducts activities and allocates funds to address endangered, threatened, proposed, and candidate species.

The National Parks have played a significant role in the return of several species, including red wolves and peregrine falcons. National Parks also contain designated critical habitat for numerous listed species. However, not all of these are publicly disclosed, in order to protect rare species from collectors, vandals, or curiosity seekers.

The National Forests

In 1905 the U.S. Forest Service was established as an agency of the U.S. Department of Agriculture. As of February 2006 the Forest Service managed nearly 193 million acres of public lands in 155 national forests and twenty national grasslands. (See Table 3.2.) A map of the locations of U.S. national forests and grasslands is shown in Figure 3.4. National forest lands also include numerous lakes and ponds. National forest land is, in general, not conserved to the same degree as National Park lands. For example, much logging occurs within these forests.

Within the Forest Service, the Threatened, Endangered, and Sensitive Species Program focuses on wildlife conservation. The Secretary of Agriculture's Policy on Fish and Wildlife directs the Forest Service to "manage habitats for all native and desired nonnative plants, fish and wildlife species to maintain viable populations of each species; identify and recover threatened and endangered plant and animal species" and to avoid actions "which may cause species to become threatened or endangered." In addition, the Forest Service has another designation called "sensitive species" for species considered unique, rare, endemic or meeting other criteria.

FIGURE 3.4

A map of the National Forests

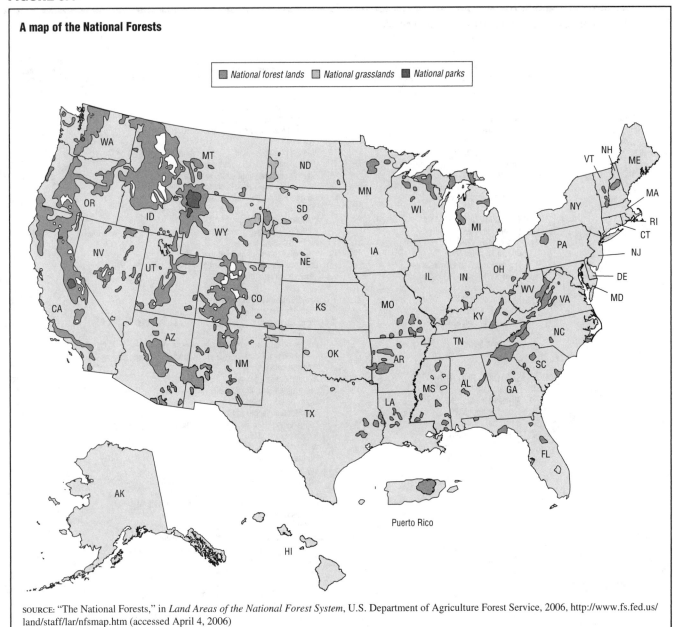

SOURCE: "The National Forests," in *Land Areas of the National Forest System*, U.S. Department of Agriculture Forest Service, 2006, http://www.fs.fed.us/land/staff/lar/nfsmap.htm (accessed April 4, 2006)

Endangered, threatened and sensitive species on national forest lands are subjected to biological evaluations to determine the effects on them of management activities. Conservation measures are also incorporated to preserve these species.

The National Wildlife Refuge System

In 1903 President Theodore Roosevelt established the National Wildlife Refuge System (NWRS) and designated the first refuge at Pelican Island, Florida. The refuge was home to a population of brown pelicans, which were being slaughtered for their popular feathers. Over the next century hundreds of additional refuges were designated throughout the country.

The NWRS is the only network of federal lands and waters managed principally for the protection of fish and wildlife. As of March 2006 it covered ninety-six million acres and included 545 refuges and thousands of small wetlands around the country. Yukon Delta, the largest of the Alaskan refuges, comprises twenty million acres. Approximately one-third of the total refuge acreage is wetland habitat, reflecting the importance of wetlands for wildlife survival.

Fifty-nine of the refuges were established specifically for endangered species, as shown in Table 3.3. These refuges cover more than 360,000 acres and are located in twenty states and the U.S. Virgin Islands. California is home to fourteen of the refuges, followed by Florida with

TABLE 3.3

National Wildlife Refuges established for endangered species

State	Unit name	Species of concern	Unit acreage
Alabama	Sauta Cave NWR	Indiana bat, gray bat	264
	Fern Cave NWR	Indiana bat, gray bat	199
	Key Cave NWR	Alabama cavefish, gray bat	1,060
	Watercress Darter NWR	Watercress darter	7
Arkansas	Logan Cave NWR	Cave crayfish, gray bat, Indiana bat, Ozark cavefish	124
Arizona	Buenos Aires NWR	Masked bobwhite quail	116,585
	Leslie Canyon	Gila topminnow, yaqui chub, peregrine falcon	2,765
	San Bernardino NWR	Gila topminnow, yaqui chub, yaqui catfish, beautiful shiner, Huachuca water umbel	2,369
California	Antioch Dunes NWR	Lange's metalmark butterfly, Antioch Dunes evening-primrose, Contra Costa wallflower	55
	Bitter Creek NWR	California condor	14,054
	Blue Ridge NWR	California condor	897
	Castle Rock NWR	Aleutian Canada goose	14
	Coachella Valley NWR	Coachello Valley fringe-toed lizard	3,592
	Don Edwards San Francisco Bay NWR	California clapper rail, California least tern, salt marsh harvest mouse	21,524
	Ellicott Slough NWR	Santa Cruz long-toed salamander	139
	Hopper Mountain NWR	California condor	2,471
	Sacramento River NWR	Valley elderberry longhorn beetle, bald eagle, Least Bell's vireo	7,884
	San Diego NWR	San Diego fairy shrimp, San Diego mesa mint, Otay Mesa mint, California orcutt grass, San Diego button-celery	1,840
	San Joaquin River NWR	Aleutian Canada goose	1,638
	Seal Beach NWR	Light-footed clapper rail, California least tern	911
	Sweetwater Marsh NWR	Light-footed clapper rail	316
	Tijuana Slough NWR	Light-footed clapper rail	1,023
Florida	Archie Carr NWR	Loggerhead sea turtle, green sea turtle	29
	Crocodile Lake NWR	American crocodile	6,686
	Crystal River NWR	West Indian manatee	80
	Florida Panther NWR	Florida panther	23,379
	Hobe Sound NWR	Loggerhead sea turtle, green sea turtle	980
	Lake Wales Ridge NWR	Florida scrub jay, snakeroot, scrub blazing star, Carter's mustard, papery whitlow-wort, Florida bonamia, scrub lupine highlands scrub hypericum, Garett's mint, scrub mint, pygmy gringe-tree, wireweed, Florida ziziphus, scrub plum, eastern indigo snake, bluetail mole skink, sand skink	659
	National Key Deer Refuge	Key deer	8,542
	St. Johns NWR	Dusky seaside sparrow	6,255
Hawaii	Hakalau Forest NWR	Akepa, akiapolaau, `o`u, Hawaiian hawk, Hawaiian creeper	32,730
	Hanalei NWR	Hawaiian stilt, Hawaiian coot, Hawaiian moorhen, Hawaiian duck	917
	Huleia NWR	Hawaiian stilt, Hawaiian coot, Hawaiian moorhen, Hawaiian duck	241
	James C. Campbell NWR	Hawaiian stilt, Hawaiian coot, Hawaiian moorhen, Hawaiian duck	164
	Kakahaia NWR	Hawaiian stilt, Hawaiian coot	45
	Kealia Pond NWR	Hawaiian stilt, Hawaiian coot	691
	Pearl Harbor NWR	Hawaiian stilt	61
Iowa	Driftless Area NWR	Iowa pleistocene snail	521
Massachusetts	Massasoit NWR	Plymouth red-bellied turtle	184
Michigan	Kirtland's Warbler WMA	Kirtland's warbler	6,535
Mississippi	Sandhill Crane NWR	Mississippi sandhill crane	19,713
Missouri	Ozark Cavefish NWR	Ozark cavefish	42
	Pilot Knob NWR	Indiana bat	90
Nebraska	Karl E. Mundt NWR	Bald eagle	19
Nevada	Ash Meadows NWR	Devil's Hole pupfish, Warm Springs pupfish, Ash Meadows Amargosa pupfish, Ash Meadows speckled dace, Ash Meadows naucorid, Ash Meadows blazing star, Amargosa niterwort, Ash Meadows milk-vetch, Ash Meadows sunray, spring-loving centaury, Ash Meadows gumplant, Ash Meadows invesia	13,268
	Moapa Valley NWR	Moapa dace	32
Oklahoma	Ozark Plateau NWR	Ozark big-eared bat, gray bat	2,208

TABLE 3.3

National Wildlife Refuges established for endangered species [CONTINUED]

State	Unit name	Species of concern	Unit acreage
Oregon	Bear Valley NWR	Bald eagle	4,200
	Julia Butler Hansen Refuge for Columbian White-tail Deer	Columbian white-tailed deer	2,750
	Nestucca Bay NWR	Aleutian Canada goose	457
South Dakota	Karl E. Mundt NWR	Bald eagle	1,044
Texas	Attwater Prairie Chicken NWR	Attwater's greater prairie chicken	8,007
	Balcones Canyonlands NWR	Black-capped vreo, golden-cheeked warbler	14,144
Virgin Islands	Green Cay NWR	St. Croix ground lizard	14
	Sandy Point NWR	Leatherback sea turtle	327
Virginia	James River NWR	Bald eagle	4,147
	Mason Neck NWR	Bald eagle	2,276
Washington	Julia Butler Hansen Refuge for Columbian White-tail Deer	Columbian white-tailed deer	2,777
Wyoming	Mortenson Lake NWR	Wyoming toad	1,776

Note: NWR=National Wildlife Refuge, WMA=Wildlife Management Area.

SOURCE: "National Wildlife Refuges Established for Endangered Species," in *America's National Wildlife Refuge System*, U.S. Department of the Interior, U.S. Fish and Wildlife Service, 2006, http://www.fws.gov/refuges/habitats/endSpRefuges.html (accessed February 28, 2006)

eight refuges and Hawaii with seven refuges. The refuges range in size from the seven-acre Watercress Darter refuge in Alabama to the 116,585-acre Buenos Aires refuge in Arizona. Protected species include a variety of plants and animals.

Table 3.4 shows all federally listed threatened and endangered animal species known to occur on units of the NWRS. The list comprises 185 species in total, including fifty-five species of birds, forty-five species of mammals, and thirty-three species of fish. In addition, ninety-eight threatened and endangered plant species are found in the NWRS system, as shown in Table 3.5.

Many other listed animal species use refuge lands on a temporary basis for breeding or migratory rest stops. Virtually every species of bird in North America has been recorded in the refuge system.

Wilderness Preservation System Areas

In 1964 the U.S. Congress passed the Wilderness Act. Its purpose was to designate certain areas of undeveloped federal land as the National Wilderness Preservation System. The act noted that these areas were to be "where the earth and its community of life are untrammeled by man, where man himself is a visitor who does not remain."

As of 2006 nearly 700 of these so-called wilderness areas have been designated across the country covering more than 105 million acres. (See Figure 3.5.) The lands are owned or administered by the USFWS, the USDA Forest Service, the National Park Service, or the Bureau of Land Management. All of the wilderness areas occur within national wildlife refuges, expect for one—the Mount Massive Wilderness Area located at the Leadville National Fish Hatchery in Colorado. Alaska,

California, and other western states are home to most of the wilderness areas.

Unlike National Parks, which are intended for use by large numbers of visitors, wilderness areas are intended to be pristine, with limited access and no amenities. True wilderness remains, for most humans, a place to visit only rarely. Nonetheless, the number of people using wilderness areas has increased steadily. Many visitors, as well as park managers, have complained about the intrusions of civilization—cell phones, snowmobiles, and aircraft—into wilderness areas.

The Debate over Use of Federally Protected Lands

Since federal conservation lands were first set aside, a national debate has raged over how they should be used. Many of these lands contain natural resources of great value in commercial markets, including timber, oil, gas, and minerals. Political and business interests that wish to harvest these resources are pitted against environmentalists who want to preserve the lands in as pristine condition as possible. During the 1990s such a battle raged over the issue of logging in old-growth forests of the Pacific Northwest—the same forests that provided habitat for endangered northern spotted owls. A similar controversy has been brewing for decades over the drilling of oil and gas in the Arctic National Wildlife Refuge (ANWR).

OIL DRILLING IN THE ARCTIC NATIONAL WILDLIFE REFUGE? The Arctic National Wildlife Refuge is located in northern Alaska as shown in Figure 3.6. Covering nineteen million acres, it is the largest national wildlife refuge in the United States. ANWR was established in 1980 by passage of the *Alaska National Interest Lands Conservation Act* (http://alaska.fws.gov/asm/anilca/toc.html). In Section 1002 of the act, the U.S. Congress

TABLE 3.4

Threatened and endangered animal species known to occur on units of the National Wildlife Refuge system

Amphibians
- Frog, California red-legged
- Salamander, Cheat Mountain
- Salamander, Santa Cruz long-toed
- Toad, Arroyo
- Toad, Wyoming

Birds
- Akepa, Hawaii
- Akiapolaau
- Albatross, short-tailed
- Blackbird, yellow-shouldered
- Bobwhite, masked (quail)
- Broadbill, Guam
- Caracara, Audubon's crested
- Condor, California
- Coot, Hawaiian
- Crane, Mississippi sandhill
- Crane, whooping
- Creeper, Hawaii
- Crow, Mariana
- Curlew, Eskimo
- Duck, Hawaiian
- Duck, Laysan
- Eider, spectacled
- Eider, Stellar's
- Elepaio, Ohau
- Falcon, northern Aplomado
- Finch, Laysan
- Finch, Nihoa
- Flycatcher, southwestern willow
- Gnatcatcher, coastal California
- Goose, Hawaiian (=nene)
- Hawk, Hawaiian
- Jay, Florida scrub
- Kingfisher, Guam Micronesian
- Kite, Everglade snail
- Millerbird, Nihoa
- Moorhen (=gallilnule), Hawaiian common
- Moorhen, Mariana common
- Murrelet, marbled
- `O`u (honeycreeper)
- Owl, northern spotted
- Pelican, brown
- Plover, piping
- Plover, western snowy (Pacific coastal)
- Prairie-chicken, Attwater's greater
- Pygmy-owl, cactus ferruginous
- Rail, California clapper
- Rail, light-footed clapper
- Rail, Yuma clapper
- Stilt, Hawaiian
- Stork, wood
- Swiftlet, Vanikoro
- Tern, California least
- Tern, least (interior)
- Tern, roseate
- Vireo, black-capped
- Vireo, least Bell's
- Warbler, Bachman's
- Warbler, golden-cheeked
- Warbler, Kirtland's
- White-eye, bridled
- Woodpecker, red-cockaded

Clams
- Clubshell
- Fanshell

- Mussel, ring pink (=golf stick pearly)
- Mussel, winged mapleleaf
- Pearlymussel, Higgin's eye
- Pearlymussel, orange-footed pimple back
- Pearlymussel, pink mucket
- Pigtoe, rough
- Pocketbook, fat
- Riffleshell, northern

Crustaceans
- Cambarus aculabrum (crayfish with no common name)
- Fairy shrimp, riverside
- Fairy shrimp, San Diego
- Tadpole shrimp, vernal pool

Fishes
- Catfish, Yaqui
- Cavefish, Alabama
- Cavefish, Ozark
- Chub, bonytail
- Chub, humpback
- Chub, Oregon
- Chub, Yaqui
- Dace, Ash Meadows speckled
- Dace, Moapa
- Darter, watercress
- Gambusia, Pecos
- Goby, Tidewater
- Madtom, Neosho
- Madtom, pygmy
- Minnow, Rio Grande silvery
- Poolfish (=killifish), Pahrump
- Pupfish, Ash Meadows Amargosa
- Pupfish, desert
- Pupfish, Devils Hole
- Pupfish, Warm Springs
- Salmon, Chinook
- Shiner, beautiful
- Shiner, Pecos bluntnose
- Shiner, Topeka
- Squawfish, Colorado
- Sturgeon, Gulf
- Sturgeon, pallid
- Sturgeon, shortnose
- Sturgeon, white, Kootenai River population
- Sucker, Lost River
- Sucker, razorback
- Sucker, short-nose
- Topminnow, gila (includes Yaqui)

Insects
- Beetle, American burying
- Beetle, valley elderberry longhorn
- Butterfly, Karner blue
- Butterfly, Lange's metalmark
- Butterfly, Quino checkerspot
- Butterfly, Schaus swallowtail
- Butterfly, Smith's blue
- Dragonfly, Hine's emerald
- Naucorid, Ash Meadows

Mammals
- Bat, gray
- Bat, Hawaiian goary
- Bat, Indiana
- Bat, lesser (=Sanborn's) long-nosed
- Bat, little Mariana fruit

- Bat, Mariana fruit
- Bat, Ozark big-eared
- Bear, grizzly
- Bear, Louisiana black
- Deer, Columbian white-tailed
- Deer, key
- Ferret, black-footed
- Fox, San Joaquin kit
- Jaguar
- Jaguarundi
- Manatee, West Indian (Florida)
- Mouse, Alabama Beach
- Mouse, Key Largo cotton
- Mouse, salt marsh harvest
- Mouse, Southeastern Beach
- Ocelot
- Panther, Florida
- Pronghorn, Sonoran
- Puma, eastern
- Rabbit, Lower Keys
- Rabbit, riparian brush
- Rat, Morro Bay kangaroo
- Rat, rice (=silver rice)
- Rat,Tipton kangaroo
- Sea-lion, steller (=northern)
- Seal, Hawaiian monk
- Squirrel, Delmarva Peninsula fox
- Squirrel, Virginia northern flying
- Whale, blue
- Whale, bowhead
- Whale, finback
- Whale, gray
- Whale, humpback
- Whale, right
- Whale, sei
- Whale, sperm
- Wolf, gray
- Wolf, Mexican
- Wolf, red
- Wood rat, Key Largo

Reptiles
- Anole, Culebra Island giant
- Crocodile, American
- Lizard, Blunt-nosed leopard
- Lizard, Coachella Valley fringe-toed
- Lizard, St. Croix ground
- Skink, Blue-tailed mole
- Skink, dand
- Snake, Atlantic dalt marsh
- Snake, rastern indigo
- Snake, giant garter
- Snake, northern copperbelly water
- Tortoise, desert
- Tortoise, gopher
- Turtle, green sea
- Turtle, hawksbill sea
- Turtle, Kemp's (=Atlantic) ridley sea
- Turtle, leatherback sea
- Turtle, loggerhead sea
- Turtle, Plymouth redbelly
- Turtle, ringed map (= sawback)

Snails
- Snail, Iowa pleistocence
- Snail, Oahu tree
- Snail, Stock Island tree

SOURCE: "Threatened and Endangered Animal Species Found on the National Wildlife Refuge System," in *America's National Wildlife Refuge System*, U.S. Department of the Interior, U.S. Fish and Wildlife Service, 2006, http://www.fws.gov/refuges/habitats/endSpAnimals.html (accessed March 8, 2006)

deferred a decision on the future management of 1.5 million acres of ANWR, because of conflicting interests between potential oil and gas resources thought to be located there and the area's importance as a wildlife habitat. This disputed area of coastal plain came to be known as the 1002 area. It is shown in detail in Figure 3.7.

TABLE 3.5

Threatened and endangered plant species known to occur on units of the National Wildlife Refuge system

- *Aconitum noveboracense*—northern wild monkshood
- *Aeschynomene virginica*—sensitive Joint-vetch
- *Agalinis acuta*—sandplain gerardia
- *Amaranthus brownii*—Brown's pigweed
- *Amaranthus pumilus*—seabeach Amaranth
- *Apios priceana*—Price's potato-bean
- *Arenaria paludicola*—marsh sandwort
- *Aristida chasae*—no common name
- *Asclepias meadii*—Mead's milkweed
- *Asimina tetramera*—four-petal pawpaw
- *Asplenium scolopendrium* var. *Americana*—American Hart's-tongue fern
- *Astragalus phoenix*—Ash Meadows milk-vetch
- *Boltonia decurrens*—decurrent false aster
- *Bonamia grandiflora*—Florida bonamia
- *Calyptranthes thomasiana*—Thomas' lidflower
- *Centaurium namophilum*—spring-loving centaury
- *Cereus eriophorus* var. *fragrans*—fragrant prickly-apple
- *Cereus robinii*—key tree-cactus
- *Chamaesyce garberi* (= *euphorbia garberi*) Garber's spurge
- *Chamaesyce rockii*—àkoko
- *Chionanthus pygmaeus*—pygmy fringe-tree
- *Chorizante pungens* var *pungens*—monterey spineflower
- *Cirsium pitcheri*—Pitcher's thistle
- *Clermontia pyrularia*—òhawai
- *Clitoria fragrans*—pigeon wings
- *Cordylanthus maritimus* ssp. *maritimus*—salt marsh bird's-beak
- *Cordylanthus palmatus*—palmate-bracted bird's-beak
- *Coryphantha sneedii* var. *robustispina*—pima pineapple cactus
- *Coryphantha sneedii* var. *sneedii*—sneed pincushion cactus
- *Cyanea acuminata*—haha
- *Cyanea humboldtiana*—haha
- *Cyanea koolauensis*—haha
- *Cyanea schipmanii*—haha
- *Cyrtandra subumbellata*—haìwale
- *Cyrtandra viridiflora*—haìwale
- *Dicerandra christmaii*—Garett's mint
- *Echinocereus fendleri* var. *kuenzleri*—Kuenzler hedgehog cactus
- *Enceliopsis nudicaulis* var. *corrugata*—Ash Meadows sunray
- *Eriogonum longifolium* var. *gnaphalifolium*—scrub buckwheat
- *Eryngium aristulatum* var. *parishii*—San Diego button-celery
- *Erysimum capitatum* var. *angustatum*—Contra Costa wallflower
- *Eugenia woodburyana*—no common name
- *Frankenia johnstonii*—Johnston's frankenia
- *Gardenia manii*—nanu, na`u
- *Goetzea elegans*—beautiful goetzea
- *Grindelia fraxino*—*pratensis*—Ash Meadows gumplant
- *Harrisia portorricensis*—Higo chumbo
- *Helianthus pardoxius*—Pecos sunflower
- *Helonias bullata*—swamp pink
- *Hesperomanni arborescens*—no common name
- *Howellia aquatilus*—water howellia
- *Hymenoxys aculis* var. *glabra*—lakeside daisy
- *Iris lacustris*—Dwarf Lake iris
- *Isodendrion laurifolium*—aupaka
- *Ivesia kingii* var. *eremica*—Ash Meadows ivesia
- *Lespedeza leptosyachya*—prairie bush-clover
- *Liatris ohlingerae*—scrub blazingstar
- *Lilaeopsis schaffneriana* var. *recurva*—Huachuca water umbel
- *Lobelia gaudichaudii* spp. *koolauensis*—no common name
- *Lobelia oahuensis*—no common name
- *Lomatium bradshawii*—Bradshaw's desert-parsley
- *Manihot walkerae*—Walker's manioc
- *Mariscus pennatiformis* ssp. *bryanii*—no common name
- *Mentzelia leucophylla*—Ash Meadows blazing-star
- *Nitrophila mohavensis*—Amargosa niterwort
- *Oenothera deltoides*—ssp. *howellii*—Antioch Dunes Evening-primose
- *Orcuttia californica*—California orcutt grass
- *Oxypolis canbyi*—Canby's dropwort
- *Oxytropis campestris* var. *chartacea*—Fassett's locoweed
- *Paronychia chartacea* (= *nyachia pulvinata*)—papery whitlow-wort
- *Penstemon haydenii*—blowout penstemon
- *Peperomia wheeleri*—Wheeler's peperomia
- *Phlegmariurus nutans*—wawae`iole
- *Phyllostegia hirsuta*—no common name
- *Phyllostegia racemosa*—kiponapona
- *Platanthera leucophaea*—Eastern Prairie fringed orchid
- *Platanthera praeclara*—Western Prairie fringed orchid
- *Pogogyne abramsii*—San Diego Mesa mint
- *Pogogyne nudiuscula*—Otay Mesa mint
- *Polygonella basiramia* (= *p. ciliata* var. *b.*)—wireweed
- *Polystichum aleuticum*—Aleutian shield-fern
- *Pritchardia remota*—loulu
- *Prunus geniculata*—scrub plum
- *Pteris lydgatei*—no common name
- *Sanicula purpurea*—no common name
- *Sarracenia oreophila*—green pitcher-plant
- *Schiedea verticillata*—whorled schiedea
- *Schwalbea americana*—American chaffseed
- *Sclerocactus glaucus*—Unita Basin hookless cactus
- *Sedum integrifolium leedyi*—Leedy's roseroot
- *Serianthes nelsonii*—hayun lagu
- *Sesbania tomentosa*—`ohai
- *Sidalcea nelsoniana*—Nelson's checker-mallow
- *Stahlia monosperma*—cobana negra
- *Tetraplasandra gymnocarpa*—no common name
- *Thymophylla tephroleuca*—ashy dogweed
- *Trifolium stoloniferum*—running buffalo clover
- *Viola oahuensis*—no common name

SOURCE: "Threatened and Endangered Plant Species Found on the National Wildlife Refuge System," in *America's National Wildlife Refuge System*, U.S. Department of the Interior, U.S. Fish and Wildlife Service, 2006, http://www.fws.gov/refuges/habitats/endSpPlants.html (accessed March 8, 2006)

There has been interest in tapping the oil deposits in northern Alaska since the early 1900s. The area was first explored for oil and gas resources in the 1940s and 1950s. It was also in the 1950s, however, that people became aware of the ecological value of these lands, and a compromise was reached in which the northeastern part of the state was set aside as a wildlife range (later refuge), while drilling began—and continues—in the northwestern part of the state. Production of oil and gas in the refuge area—the 5% of Alaska's North Slope not already open to drilling—was also prohibited at that time unless specifically authorized by Congress.

In 1987 the Department of the Interior (DOI) submitted a report to Congress on the resources of the 1002 area. At that time only a few oil accumulations had been found near ANWR. Over the next decade, much larger oil fields were discovered as shown by the shaded areas in Figure 3.7. In 1998 the U.S. Geological Survey (USGS) performed a petroleum assessment of the 1002 area and the adjacent state waters. An updated assessment performed in 2001 found that there was a 95% probability of 5.7 billion barrels of oil being recoverable from the assessed area, with most of the oil coming from the undeformed part of the 1002 area. The undeformed area has a geologic structure composed of rock layers that are mostly horizontal. This makes for more successful drilling than in the deformed area where rock layers are folded and faulted.

FIGURE 3.5

National Wilderness Preservation System areas

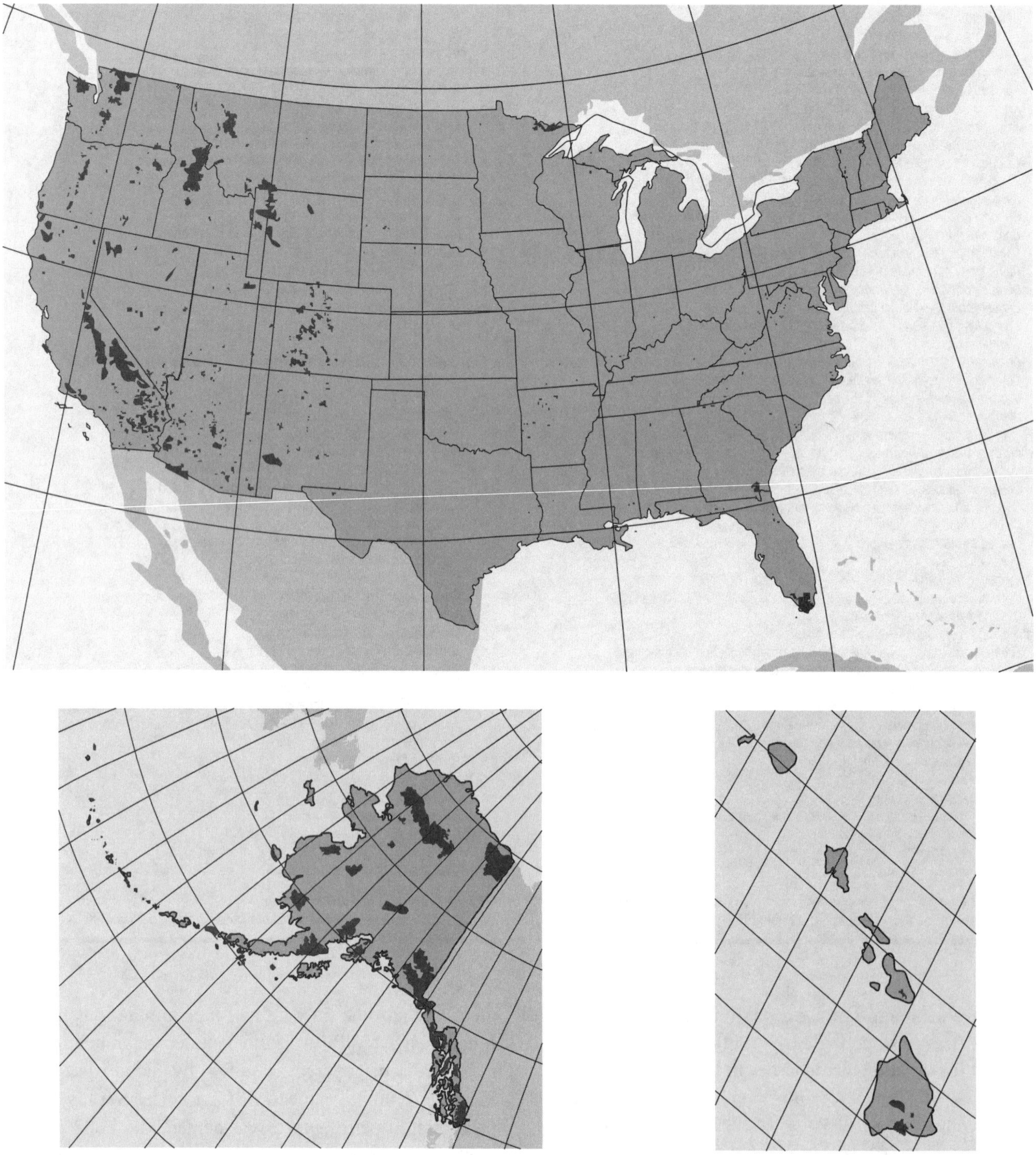

SOURCE: Adapted from "National Wilderness Preservation System Areas," in *National Atlas of the United States* U.S. Department of the Interior, 2006, http://www.nationalatlas.gov (accessed March 10, 2006)

The protected status of ANWR has been challenged by large oil companies and their political supporters. When Republicans took control of Congress in 1995, they passed legislation to allow for drilling in ANWR, but President Clinton vetoed the bill. The succeeding administration under President George W. Bush has been much more supportive of drilling in the refuge.

Environmentalists argue that studies by the Fish and Wildlife Service suggest that oil drilling in the refuge

FIGURE 3.6

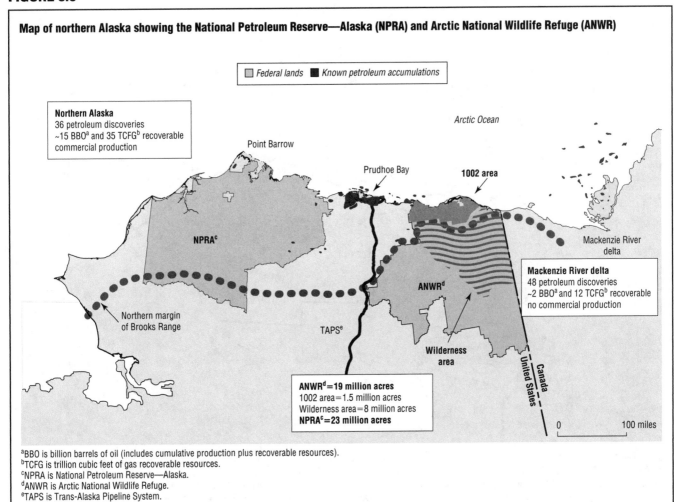

Map of northern Alaska showing the National Petroleum Reserve—Alaska (NPRA) and Arctic National Wildlife Refuge (ANWR)

☐ *Federal lands* ■ *Known petroleum accumulations*

Northern Alaska
36 petroleum discoveries
~15 BBO[a] and 35 TCFG[b] recoverable
commercial production

Arctic Ocean

Point Barrow

Prudhoe Bay

1002 area

NPRA[c]

Mackenzie River delta

Mackenzie River delta
48 petroleum discoveries
~2 BBO[a] and 12 TCFG[b] recoverable
no commercial production

Northern margin
of Brooks Range

ANWR[d]

TAPS[e]

**Wilderness
area**

Canada
United States

ANWR[d]=19 million acres
1002 area=1.5 million acres
Wilderness area=8 million acres
NPRA[c]=23 million acres

0   100 miles

[a]BBO is billion barrels of oil (includes cumulative production plus recoverable resources).
[b]TCFG is trillion cubic feet of gas recoverable resources.
[c]NPRA is National Petroleum Reserve—Alaska.
[d]ANWR is Arctic National Wildlife Refuge.
[e]TAPS is Trans-Alaska Pipeline System.

SOURCE: "Figure 1. Map of Northern Alaska and Nearby Parts of Canada Showing Locations of the Arctic National Wildlife Refuge (ANWR), the 1002 Area, and the National Petroleum Reserve—Alaska (NPRA). Locations of Known Petroleum Accumulations and the Trans-Alaska Pipeline System (TAPS) Are Shown, as Well as Summaries of Known Petroleum Volumes in Northern Alaska and the Mackenzie River Delta of Canada. BBO, Billion Barrels of Oil (Includes Cumulative Production Plus Recoverable Resources), TCFS, Trillion Cubic Feet of Gas Recoverable Resources," in *Arctic National Wildlife Refuge, 1002 Area, Petroleum Assessment, 1998, Including Economic Analysis*, U.S. Department of the Interior, U.S. Geological Survey, April 2001, http://pubs.usgs.gov/fs/fs-0028-01/fs-0028-01.pdf (accessed March 2, 2006)

will harm many Arctic species, by taking over habitat, damaging habitats through pollution, interfering with species activities directly, or increasing opportunities for invasive species. ANWR harbors the greatest number of plant and animal species of any park or refuge in the Arctic, including a multitude of unique species such as caribou, musk oxen, polar bears, arctic foxes, and snow geese. Because of the harsh climate, Arctic habitats are generally characterized by short food chains and extreme vulnerability to habitat disturbance. The majority of Arctic species already live "on the edge." Consequently, the decline of even a single species is likely to have dramatic effects on the entire community.

Some environmentalists consider the 1002 area to be one of the most ecologically diverse and valuable parts of the refuge. Among the species that would be affected if drilling is permitted are polar bears, whose preferred sites for building dens are in the 1002 area (see Figure 3.8) and

caribou, which use this area for calving—giving birth to young (see Figure 3.9.)

In 2001 the House of Representatives again passed a bill allowing for drilling within the refuge. However, the Senate rejected this proposal in 2002. The terrorist attacks of September 11, 2001, and heightened tensions in the Middle East have encouraged some politicians to emphasize the national security aspects of oil development in ANWR. They argue that the United States cannot be truly secure until it reduces its dependence on foreign oil. The Bush administration has continued to press for oil drilling in ANWR. During 2005 ANWR drilling measures were added to bills related to energy, the fiscal year 2006 budget, and defense appropriations. Various versions of these bills were approved by either the Congress or the Senate at one time or another; however, the drilling measures were ultimately dropped from the final bills.

FIGURE 3.7

Map of Arctic National Wildlife Refuge (ANWR)

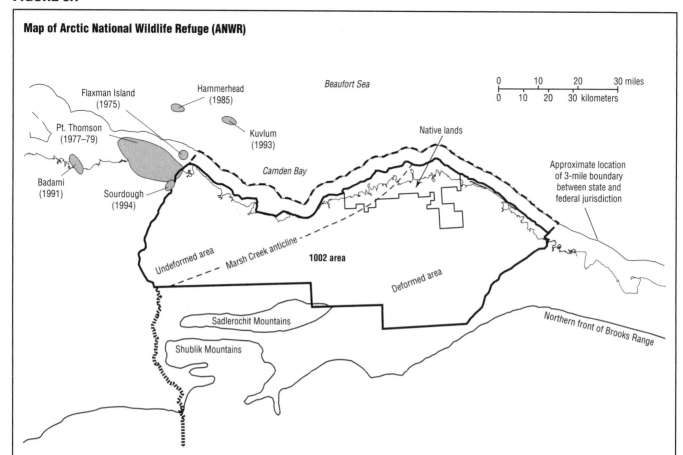

SOURCE: E.D. Attanasi, "Figure 1. Map Showing the Entire Study Area That Included the Federal Part of the 1002 Area of the Arctic National Wildlife Refuge, Native Lands within the 1002 Area, and Lands Underlying Adjacent Alaska State Waters and the Undeformed and Deformed Areas of the 1002 Area. Also Shown Are Oil Accumulations Discovered Near the Entire Study Area during the Past Three Decades," in *Economics of 1998 U.S.Geological Survey's 1002 Area Regional Assessment: An Economic Update*, U.S. Department of the Interior, U.S. Fish and Wildlife Service, 2005, http://pubs.usgs .gov/of/2005/1359/OF2005-1359.pdf (accessed March 1, 2006)

Private Lands Conservation

Federal and state governments are not the only entities involved in land conservation. Increasingly environment-minded private organizations and citizens are purchasing land with the intent of preserving it for wild life. Such national environmental groups as the Nature Conservancy participate in these endeavors. The Nature Conservancy Web site states that the organization helps to protect approximately fifteen million acres in the United States. Other major groups engaged in private land conservation include the Conservation Fund, the Trust for Public Land, the Land Trust Alliance, Society for the Protection of New Hampshire Forests, and the Rocky Mountain Elk Foundation.

Every three years the Land Trust Alliance conducts a census on lands held for private conservation. The latest census was completed in 2003 and found that more than 9.3 million acres of land were held in local and regional land trusts, up from 4.7 million acres in 1998. Land trusts either purchase land outright or develop private, voluntary agreements called conservation easements or restrictions that limit future development of the land. The census estimated that an additional twenty-five million acres in land were protected by national land trusts.

INTERNATIONAL EFFORTS AT CONSERVATION

The United Nations Environment Programme (UNEP) was established to address diverse environmental issues on an international level. Many of its conventions have been extremely valuable in protecting global biodiversity and natural resources. UNEP has also helped to regulate pollution and the use of toxic chemicals.

THE CONVENTION ON INTERNATIONAL TRADE IN ENDANGERED SPECIES (CITES)

The Convention on International Trade in Endangered Species of Wild Fauna and Flora (CITES) is an international agreement administered under UNEP that regulates international trade in wildlife. CITES is perhaps the single most important international agreement relating to endangered species and has contributed critically to the protection of many threatened species.

FIGURE 3.8

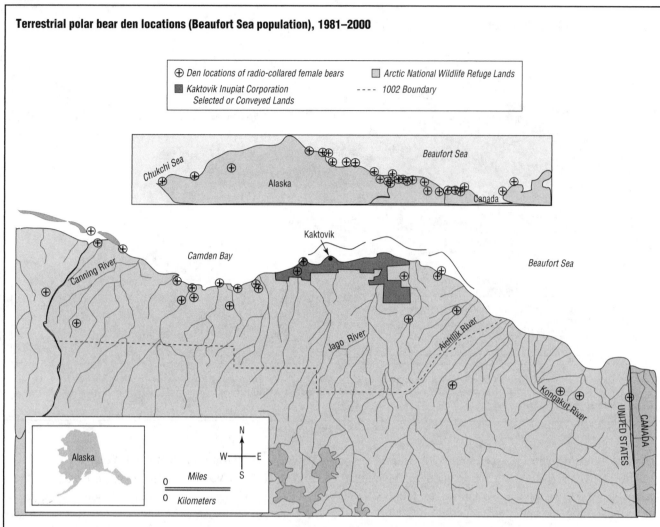

Terrestrial polar bear den locations (Beaufort Sea population), 1981–2000

SOURCE: "Terrestrial Polar Bear Den Locations (Beaufort Sea Population) 1981–2000," in *Potential Impacts of Proposed Oil and Gas Development on the Arctic Refuge's Coastal Plain: Historical Overview and Issues of Concern*, U.S. Fish and Wildlife Service, January 17, 2001, http://library.fws.gov/Pubs7/arctic_oilandgas_impact.pdf (accessed April 4, 2006)

The international wildlife trade is estimated to involve hundreds of millions of specimens annually.

CITES was first drafted in 1963 at a meeting of the International Union for Conservation of Nature and Natural Resources (IUCN; now the World Conservation Union), and went into effect in 1975. Protected plant and animals are listed in three separate CITES appendices depending on degree of endangerment. Appendix I includes species that are in immediate danger of extinction. CITES generally prohibits international trade of these species. Appendix II lists species that are likely to become in danger of extinction without strict protection from international trade. Permits may be obtained for the trade of Appendix II species only if trade will not harm the survival prospects of the species in the wild. Appendix III lists species whose trade is regulated in one or more nations. Any member nation can list a species in Appendix III to request international cooperation in order to prevent unsustainable levels of international trade. Nations agree to abide by CITES rules voluntarily. In 2006 there were more than 150 nations participating in the agreement.

Convention on Biological Diversity

The United Nations Convention on Biological Diversity was set up to conserve biodiversity and to promote the sustainable use of biodiversity. The Convention supports national efforts in the documentation and monitoring of biodiversity, the establishment of refuges and other protected areas, and the restoration of degraded ecosystems. It also supports goals related to the maintenance of traditional knowledge of sustainable resource use, the prevention of invasive species introductions, and the control of invasive species that are already present. Finally, it funds education programs promoting public awareness of the value of natural resources.

FIGURE 3.9

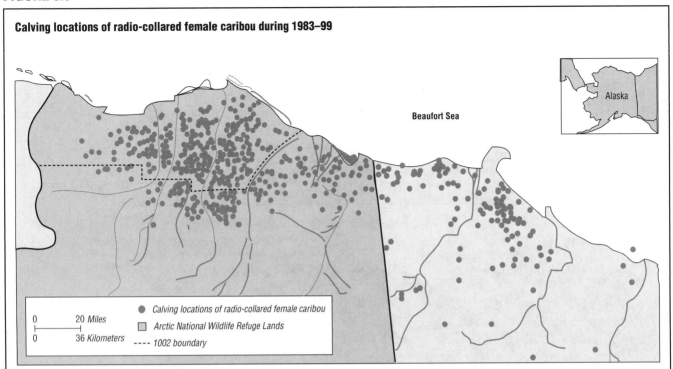

Calving locations of radio-collared female caribou during 1983–99

SOURCE: "Calving Locations of Radio-Collared Female Caribou during 1983–1999," in *Potential Impacts of Proposed Oil and Gas Development on the Arctic Refuge's Coastal Plain: Historical Overview and Issues of Concern*, U.S. Fish and Wildlife Service, January 17, 2001, http://library.fws.gov/Pubs7/arctic_oilandgas_impact.pdf (accessed April 4, 2006)

Convention on Migratory Species of Wild Animals

The Convention on the Conservation of Migratory Species of Wild Animals (also known as the CMS or Bonn Convention) recognizes that certain migratory species cross national boundaries and require protection throughout their range. This convention aims to "conserve terrestrial, marine, and avian migratory species throughout their range." CMS was originally signed in Bonn, Germany, in 1979 and went into force in November 1983. As of February 2006 more than ninety nations in Africa, Central and South America, Asia, Europe, and Oceania were involved in the agreement. The United States and several other nations are not official parties to the agreement but nonetheless abide by its rules.

CMS provides two levels of protection to migratory species. Appendix I species are endangered and strictly protected. Appendix II lists species that are less severely threatened but would nonetheless benefit from international cooperative agreements. Appendix II agreements have been drawn up for groups such as European bats, Mediterranean and Black Sea cetaceans (whales and related species), Baltic and North Sea cetaceans, Wadden Sea seals, African-Eurasian migratory water birds, and marine turtles. In 2004 the Agreement on the Conservation of Albatrosses and Petrels came into effect. Because these sea birds are highly migratory, their conservation requires broad international agreements in addition to efforts by individual nations.

World Commission on Protected Areas

The IUCN's World Commission on Protected Areas (WCPA) is the leading international body dedicated to the selection, establishment, and management of national parks and protected areas. It has helped set up many natural areas around the world for the protection of plant and animal species, and also maintains a database of protected areas. Protected areas often consist of a core zone where wildlife cannot legally be disturbed by human beings, surrounded by "buffer zones," transitional spaces that act as shields for the core zone. On the periphery are areas for managed human living. A protected area is defined as "an area of land and/or sea especially dedicated to the protection and maintenance of biological diversity, and of natural and associated cultural resources, and managed through legal or other effective means."

Conservation biology theory advocates that protected areas should be as large as possible in order to increase biological diversity and to buffer refuges from outside pressures. The world's largest protected areas are Greenland National Park (Greenland), Ar-Rub'al-khali Wildlife Management Area (Saudi Arabia), Great Barrier Reef Marine Park (Australia), Qiang Tang Nature Reserve (China), Cape Churchill Wildlife Management Area (Canada), and the Northern Wildlife Management Zone (Saudi Arabia).

CHAPTER 4
THREATS TO AQUATIC ENVIRONMENTS

According to the U.S. Geological Survey in "How Much Water Is There on (and in) the Earth?" (http://ga.water.usgs.gov/edu/earthhowmuch.html), about 326 million trillion gallons of water make up the total water supply of the planet. This provides an enormous aquatic habitat for a wide variety and number of animal and plant species. The aquatic environment is threatened by many human activities around the world. Humans consume vast amounts of freshwater and exert control over water flows in many rivers and streams. Land development, agricultural practices, industrialization, and commercial fishing have all affected the aquatic environment in some way.

DAMS

Dams have affected rivers, the lands abutting them, the water bodies they join, and aquatic wildlife throughout the United States. Water flow is reduced or stopped altogether downstream of dams, altering aquatic habitats and drying wetlands. Some rivers, including the large Colorado River, no longer reach the sea at all, except in years of unusually high precipitation. Keeping enough water in rivers is especially difficult in the arid West. Of the major rivers in the lower forty-eight states (those more than 600 miles in length), only the Yellowstone River still flows freely. In fact, University of Alabama biologist Arthur Benke, the editor of *Rivers of North America* (Elsevier, 2005), notes that it is difficult to find any river in the United States that has not been dammed or channeled. According to Benke, "All human alterations of rivers, regardless of whether they provide services such as power or drinking water supply, result in degradation. The only exception is when we try to restore them."

Dams have epitomized progress, American ingenuity, and humankind's mastery of nature. In North America, more than two 200 major dams were completed each year between 1962 and 1968. Dams were promoted for

their role in water storage, energy generation, flood control, irrigation, and recreation.

The very success of the dam-building endeavor accounted, in part, for its decline. By 1980 nearly all the nation's best-suited sites—and many dubious ones—had been dammed. Three other factors, however, also contributed to the decline in dam construction: public resistance to the enormous costs, a growing belief that dams were unnecessary "pork-barrel" projects being used by politicians to boost their own popularity, and a developing awareness of the profound environmental degradation caused by dams. In 1986 Congress passed a law requiring the U.S. Bureau of Reclamation to balance issues of power generation and environmental protection when it licenses dams.

The U.S. Army Corps of Engineers maintains the National Inventory of Dams (NID) at the Web site http://crunch.tec.army.mil/nid/webpages/nid.cfm. As of 2006 the inventory included approximately 76,000 dams throughout the country. Dams are listed that are at least six feet tall or hold back at least fifteen acre-feet (nearly five million gallons) of water. Dams are built for a variety of purposes. The most frequent purposes listed in the NID database are recreation, fire protection, stock or small farm pond creation, flood control, and storm water management. As shown in Figure 4.1 these purposes account for 70% of all purposes listed.

Although only a small percentage of dams listed with the NID produce hydroelectric power, these dams tend to be the largest in size and affect large watersheds. Figure 4.2 shows the components of a typical impoundment dam producing hydroelectric power. These structures provide numerous challenges to aquatic species, besides impeding water flow and migration paths. Turbines operate like massive underwater fans. Passage through running turbine blades can result in the death of many small aquatic creatures unable to escape their path. Some modern

FIGURE 4.1

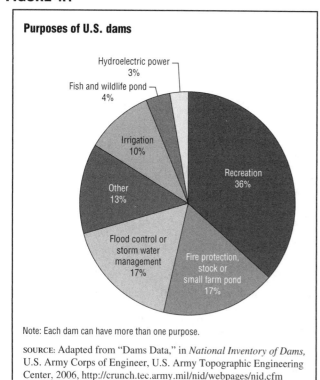

Purposes of U.S. dams

- Hydroelectric power 3%
- Fish and wildlife pond 4%
- Irrigation 10%
- Recreation 36%
- Other 13%
- Flood control or storm water management 17%
- Fire protection, stock or small farm pond 17%

Note: Each dam can have more than one purpose.

SOURCE: Adapted from "Dams Data," in *National Inventory of Dams,* U.S. Army Corps of Engineer, U.S. Army Topographic Engineering Center, 2006, http://crunch.tec.army.mil/nid/webpages/nid.cfm (accessed January 31, 2006)

FIGURE 4.2

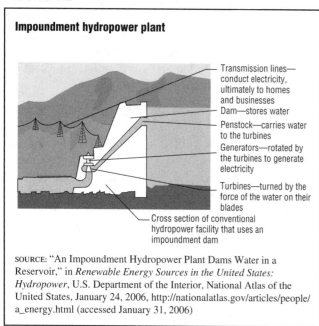

Impoundment hydropower plant

- Transmission lines—conduct electricity, ultimately to homes and businesses
- Dam—stores water
- Penstock—carries water to the turbines
- Generators—rotated by the turbines to generate electricity
- Turbines—turned by the force of the water on their blades
- Cross section of conventional hydropower facility that uses an impoundment dam

SOURCE: "An Impoundment Hydropower Plant Dams Water in a Reservoir," in *Renewable Energy Sources in the United States: Hydropower,* U.S. Department of the Interior, National Atlas of the United States, January 24, 2006, http://nationalatlas.gov/articles/people/a_energy.html (accessed January 31, 2006)

hydroelectric dams include stair-like structures called fish ladders that provide migrating fish a path to climb up and over the dams.

The Snail Darter

The snail darter, a small fish species related to perch, was at the center of a dam-building controversy during the 1970s. The U.S. Fish and Wildlife Service (FWS) listed the snail darter as endangered in 1975. At the time it was believed to exist only in the Little Tennessee River, and this area was designated as critical habitat for the species. That same year, the Tellico Dam was near completion on the Little Tennessee River, and the filling of the Tellico Reservoir would have destroyed the entire habitat of the snail darter. A lawsuit was filed to prevent this from happening. The case went all the way to the Supreme Court, which ruled in 1978 that under the Endangered Species Act (ESA) species protection must take priority over economic and developmental concerns. One month after this court decision, Congress amended the Endangered Species Act to allow for exemptions under certain circumstances.

In late 1979 the Tellico Dam received an exemption and the Tellico Reservoir was filled. The snail darter is now extinct in that habitat. Fortunately, however, snail darter populations were later discovered in other river systems. In addition, the species has been introduced into several other habitats. Due to an increase in numbers, the snail darter was reclassified as threatened in 1984.

The Missouri "Spring Rise" Issue

During the 2000s a heated debate has surrounded the issue of water flow on the Missouri River. The U.S. Fish and Wildlife Service determined in 2000 that existing water flow patterns—managed to create a steady depth for barge traffic—were endangering three listed species: the pallid sturgeon (a fish) and two bird species, the piping plover and least tern. The FWS argued that increased water flow in the spring—a "spring rise"— was necessary for sturgeon spawning. In addition, it called for less water flow in the summer, which is necessary for exposing the sandbars used by the bird species as nesting grounds. The FWS and the Army Corps of Engineers, which manages the flow of water on the Missouri River, implemented a water management plan beginning with the 2003 season. The issue has been extremely controversial in the Midwest, with environmentalists, recreation interests, and upper-basin officials favoring a spring rise, and farmers, barge interests, and Missouri leaders opposed.

Salmon and Dams

Numerous species of salmon are in decline, at least partly due to the effects of dams. Salmon have an unusual life cycle that involves a migration from freshwater habitats to oceans and back. Hatching and the juvenile period occur in rivers, followed by a long downstream migration to the ocean, where individuals mature. Adult salmon eventually make an arduous, upstream return to freshwater habitats, where they spawn (lay their eggs, burying them in gravel nests) and then die. Dams are associated

FIGURE 4.3

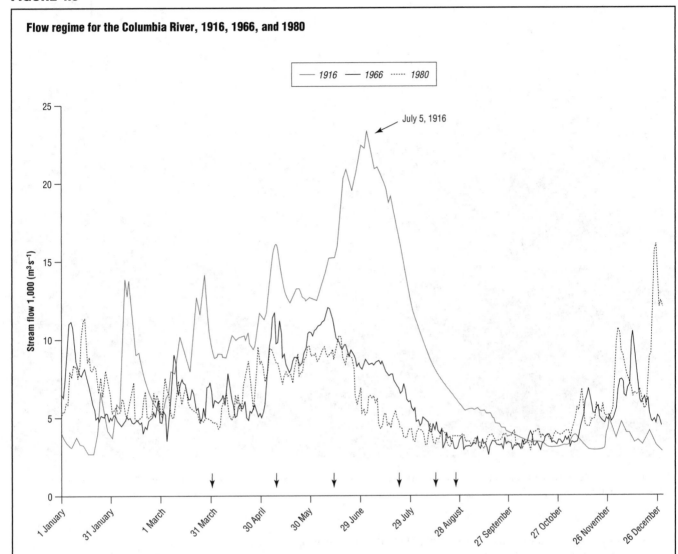

Flow regime for the Columbia River, 1916, 1966, and 1980

— 1916   — 1966   ······ 1980

July 5, 1916

Note: Arrows at base of graph indicate sampling dates during 1920. Flows compiled from The Dalles gauge (United States Geological Survey, 2001) and estimates of Willamette River contribution at Salem, OR.

SOURCE: D.L. Bottom, C.A. Simestad, J. Burke, A.M. Baptista, D.A. Jay, K.K. Jones, E. Casillas, and M.H. Schiewe, "Figure 83. River Flows (Cubic Meters per Second) for 1916, 1966, and 1980," in *Salmon at River's End: The Role of the Estuary in the Decline and Recovery of Columbia River Salmon*, U.S. Department of Commerce, National Oceanic and Atmospheric Administration, National Marine Fisheries Service, Northwest Fisheries Science Center 2005, http://www.nwfsc.noaa.gov/assets/25/6294_09302005_153156_SARETM68Final.pdf (accessed February 13, 2006)

with high salmon mortality during both downstream and upstream migrations.

Scientists are increasingly learning of the importance of estuaries to juvenile salmon in the Pacific Northwest. Estuaries are areas where freshwater meets and mixes with ocean water. Juvenile salmon pass through estuaries on their downstream trip to the sea. Prior to excessive damming of the Columbia River system, spring and summer floods (called freshets) would have spread juvenile salmon throughout the estuaries into various marshes and natural channels. From there the salmon would make their way to the sea. Flow regulation has dramatically changed the river flows in this area and limited the amount of estuary

habitat available to the salmon. Figure 4.3 shows daily river flows recorded in 1916, 1966, and 1980. The flows in 1916 were highly variable on a seasonal basis, reflecting the natural effects of melting snows and heavy spring rains. Damming the river dampened these seasonal changes and virtually eliminated freshets from occurring. This result has been beneficial for residents and farmers living along the river, but detrimental to the habitat of the Pacific salmon.

Tearing Down Dams?

In November 1997, for the first time in U.S. history, the Federal Energy Regulatory Commission ordered a dam removed when the Edwards Dam was ordered

FIGURE 4.4

The Three Gorges Dam, currently under construction on the Yangtze River in China, will be the largest dam in the world when it is completed. (AP/Wide World Photos.)

removed from the Kennebec River in Augusta, Maine, to restore habitats for sea-run fish. The dam's owner, Edwards Manufacturing, appealed the decision, but the federal government prevailed. The 160-year old dam produced 1% of Maine's electricity. Normal river conditions were achieved at the site within days of water release. Environmentalists viewed the removal of the dam as a boon to both aquatic species and the terrestrial species that feed on them.

Conservationists and fisheries have also argued for the removal of four dams on the Snake River in the Pacific Northwest to allow salmon runs to recover. The issue was extremely contentious, with more than 8,700 people attending public hearings on the debate and over 230,000 written comments submitted. The Army Corps of Engineers announced in February 2002 that the dams would not be removed, citing the fact that they produce $324 million in electricity and water with operating costs of only $36.5 million. The Corps did agree, however, to budget $390 million over a ten-year period to improve salmon survival, including trucking juvenile salmon around the dams. This decision represented the culmination of nearly ten years of debate regarding the Snake River dams.

Foreign Dams

As the era of big dams faded in North America, construction increased in Asia, fueled by growing demand for electricity and irrigation water. The Three Gorges Dam on the Yangtze River in China (see Figure 4.4) will be the largest dam in the world when it becomes operational in 2009. It will be 6,600 feet—more than a mile—wide and over 600 feet high. The creation of a water reservoir upstream from the dam will flood thirteen cities and countless villages, and displace more than a million people. In addition, the dam will disrupt water flow and increase water pollution, threatening unique species such as the Yangtze River dolphin, one of only five freshwater dolphin species in the world.

The Yangtze River dolphin was placed on the Endangered Species List in 1989 and is at extreme risk of extinction, with only 150 individuals remaining. Other species likely to be threatened or wiped out altogether include the Chinese sturgeon, the Chinese tiger, the Chinese alligator, the Siberian crane, the giant panda, and countless species of fish, freshwater invertebrates, and plants. Several U.S. agencies provided much technical assistance in planning the Three Gorges Dam. However,

U.S. government involvement ceased due to a challenge under the Endangered Species Act, which prohibits government activity detrimental to listed species. The main part of dam construction has been completed, and filling of the Three Gorges Dam began in June 2003. However, generators have yet to be installed as of 2006.

FRESHWATER DIVERSION AND USE

Freshwater is a vital resource to humans. It is used for a variety of purposes—drinking water, hydroelectric power production, irrigation of crops, watering of livestock, and for commercial and industrial applications. Diversion of water from natural waterways, such as rivers and streams, stresses aquatic animals living in those habitats.

Klamath Basin

The Klamath Basin in southern Oregon and northern California is the site of a heated battle pitting farmers against a coalition of fishermen and environmentalists who wish to protect three listed species: the coho salmon, shortnose sucker fish, and Lost River sucker fish. Opponents are battling over water, which is needed for irrigation purposes by farmers in the area.

The Klamath River once supported the third-largest salmon run in the country. However, in recent years, water diversion has caused river water levels to be too low to maintain healthy stream conditions and temperatures. Over 7,000 fishing jobs have been lost due to salmon declines. Water diversion practices also violate agreements with Native American tribes to avoid harming healthy salmon runs. Over the years many of the wetlands in the Klamath Basin have been drained for agricultural purposes; however, there are still scattered wetlands and lakes throughout the area. This habitat supports the shortnose sucker and the Lost River sucker, which were listed as endangered in their entire ranges in California and Oregon in 1988.

A lawsuit regarding the distribution of Klamath Basin waters was brought against the U.S. Bureau of Reclamation (BOR) by the Pacific Coast Federation of Fishermen's Associations, the Klamath Forest Alliance, the Institute for Fisheries Resources, the Oregon Natural Resources Council, and other groups. The plaintiffs argued that the BOR had met farmers' demands for water but left Klamath River flows much lower than required for survival of the coho salmon, shortnose suckerfish, and Lost River suckerfish. Furthermore, the Bureau was charged with violating the ESA by not consulting with the National Marine Fisheries Service regarding endangered species conservation. Farmers were also accused of wasting water.

In April 2001 the U.S. Bureau of Reclamation was found by a federal district court to have knowingly violated the ESA when it allowed delivery of irrigation water required to maintain habitat of the three listed species. As a result of the court decision, federal agencies cut water to irrigation canals in order to preserve water levels in the Upper Klamath Lake for the two species of suckerfish and to increase water flow in the Klamath River for coho salmon. In April 2002 a lawsuit was filed on behalf of the farmers to remove all three species from the Endangered Species List. Water flow was an issue again in 2002. After a federal judge decided not to force the BOR to provide water to listed species in 2002, there was a massive fish-kill involving approximately 33,000 salmon.

Between 2000 and 2002 the Bureau of Reclamation developed numerous operating plans for water flows in the Klamath Basin; however, these plans were continually challenged in court. In 2002 the agency issued a ten-year plan designed to achieve full protection for the river's salmon by 2012. A lengthy court battle over the plan culminated in March 2006 when a federal judge ruled that the plan had to be implemented immediately. The judge noted that salmon water requirements must outweigh the needs of farmers for irrigation water. Because a wet winter had produced large flows in the Klamath River, no immediate effects of the ruling on irrigation supply were anticipated. However, the issue is expected to continue to be a subject of continued litigation.

WATER POLLUTION POSES A THREAT

Water pollution poses a considerable threat to many aquatic species. Contaminants include chemicals, biological substances (such as manure and sewage), solid waste materials, and dirt and soil eroded from riverbanks or nearby lands. In general, aquatic creatures are not killed outright by water contamination. A major exception is an oil spill, which can kill many creatures through direct contact. The more widespread and common threat is overall degradation of water quality and habitats due to pollutants. Exposure to contaminants can weaken the immune systems of aquatic animals and make them more susceptible to disease and other health and reproductive problems.

Pesticides

Pesticides are chemicals used to kill insects that feed on crops and vegetation. The first documented use of pesticides was by the ancient Greeks. Pliny the Elder (23–79) reported using common compounds such as arsenic, sulfur, caustic soda, and olive oil to protect crops. The Chinese later used similar substances to retard infestation by insects and fungi. In the 1800s Europeans used heavy metal salts such as copper sulfate and iron sulfate as weed killers.

The invention of DDT (dichloro-diphenyl-trichlor-oethane) in 1939 marked a revolution in the war against pests. DDT was effective, relatively cheap, and apparently safe for people—on the face of it, a miracle chemical that promised a world with unprecedented crop yields. Its discoverer, Paul Muller, received a Nobel Prize for discovering the high efficiency of DDT as a contact poison against pests. In the United States, pesticide use in agriculture nearly tripled after 1965, as farmers began to use DDT and other pesticides, herbicides, and fungicides intensively and began to accept these chemicals as essential to agriculture.

For many years, it was thought that if pesticides were properly used, the risk of harm to humans and wildlife was slight. As the boom in pesticide use continued, however, it eventually became apparent that pesticides were not safe after all. The fundamental reason that pesticides are dangerous is that they are poisons purposely designed to kill living organisms. Part of the problem is biomagnification—a predator that eats organisms with pesticides in their bodies ends up concentrating all those pesticides in its own tissues. Eventually, the concentration of pesticides causes serious problems. DDT was eventually shown to have harmed numerous bird species, particularly those high in the food chain, such as bald eagles and peregrine falcons. DDT caused the production of eggs with shells so thin they could not protect the developing chick.

As the dangers of pesticides became more apparent in the 1960s and 1970s, some of the most dangerous, like DDT, were banned in the United States. However, the use of other chemical pesticides increased until the 1980s. Use levels have generally held steady since then. The primary reason that pesticide use has leveled off in recent decades is not concern regarding its safety, but declines in its effectiveness. This is due to the fact that pest species quickly evolve resistance to pesticides. Worldwide the number of resistant pests continues to climb. Unfortunately increased resistance has only created a demand for new and more powerful chemicals.

Nutrient Pollution

Nutrient pollution is primarily composed of nitrogen and phosphorus. These chemicals are commonly used in inorganic fertilizers and are naturally found in biological wastes, such as manure and sewage. In addition, nitrogen compounds are emitted into the air during the combustion of fossil fuels, such as oil and coals. All of these factors combine to produce a heavy load of nutrients that enter waterbodies via land runoff, direct discharges, and atmospheric deposition.

While nutrients are not poisonous by nature, large quantities of them can cause serious health problems in aquatic animals. Nutrients also encourage the growth of

FIGURE 4.5

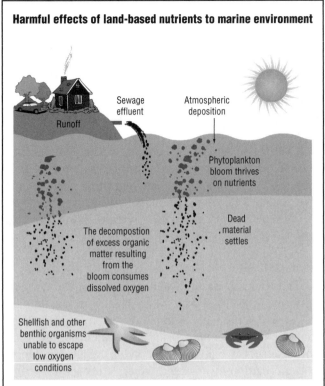

Harmful effects of land-based nutrients to marine environment

SOURCE: "Figure 14.2. Nutrient Pollution in Coastal Waters," in *An Ocean Blueprint for the 21st Century, Final Report*, U.S. Commission on Ocean Policy, 2004, http://www.oceancommission.gov/documents/full_color_rpt/000_ocean_full_report.pdf (accessed February 1, 2006)

aquatic plant life, disrupting food webs and biological communities. Aquatic plants and algae may grow so rapidly that they block sunlight or deplete oxygen essential to other species. (See Figure 4.5.)

Oils

Oil enters waterbodies through a variety of means, including natural and anthropogenic (human-related) sources. Figure 4.6 shows the sources of oil input to the North American marine (oceanic) environment in 2002. Natural seepage accounts for 63% of marine oil exposure. Anthropogenic activities are blamed for the other 37%. Runoff of oil in municipal and industrial waste discharges is the primary source of oil exposure attributed to human activities. Smaller amounts are blamed on atmospheric fallout from additional anthropogenic sources, including air pollution (8%), marine transportation vehicles (3%), recreational marine vehicles (2%), and offshore oil and gas development (2%).

Oil spills are devastating accidents to aquatic life. Oil spilled into the ocean floats on the water surface, cutting off oxygen to the sea life below and killing mammals, birds, fish, and other animals. The dangers presented by oil spills have grown worse over the years. In 1945 the largest tanker held 16,500 tons of oil. Now, supertankers

FIGURE 4.6

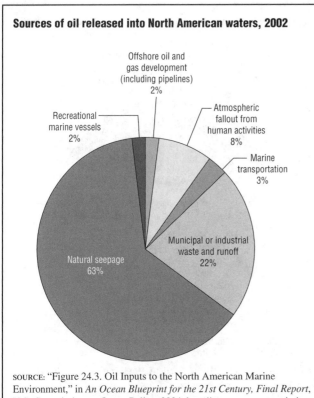

Sources of oil released into North American waters, 2002

Offshore oil and gas development (including pipelines) 2%

Atmospheric fallout from human activities 8%

Recreational marine vessels 2%

Marine transportation 3%

Natural seepage 63%

Municipal or industrial waste and runoff 22%

SOURCE: "Figure 24.3. Oil Inputs to the North American Marine Environment," in *An Ocean Blueprint for the 21st Century, Final Report*, U.S. Commission on Ocean Policy, 2004, http://www.oceancommission.gov/documents/full_color_rpt/000_ocean_full_report.pdf (accessed February 1, 2006)

the length of several football fields regularly carry more than 550,000 tons.

In 1989 the tanker *Exxon Valdez* ran aground on the pristine Alaskan coastline, spilling eleven million gallons of oil into Prince William Sound and killing millions of animals. In 1994 a federal jury assessed $5 billion in punitive damages and $3.5 billion in criminal fines and cleanup costs against Exxon. The *Valdez* spill led to additional safety requirements for tankers, including double hulls. Larger oil spills than the *Valdez* have occurred both before and since, but the incident alerted many people to the damage that can be done to marine habitats. Many species affected by the spill, particularly seabird species, had yet to recover more than a decade later.

In January 2001 the tanker *Jessica* released 150,000 gallons of fuel near the Galapagos Islands, a biologically rich area harboring numerous unique species including Darwin's famous finches, marine iguanas, and a tropical penguin population. There was widespread relief when winds blew the oil slick seaward rather than towards the islands. Sea bird and sea lion deaths numbered in the dozens, and it was believed that a true catastrophe had been avoided. Ongoing studies of the Galapagos' unique marine iguanas, however, revealed in June 2002 that numerous iguanas likely died due to oil-related injuries

after the spill. In particular, 60% of the marine iguanas on Santa Fe Island died in 2001, despite the fact that oil contamination was relatively low, with only about one quart of oil per yard of shoreline. Similar deaths were not found on another island where there was no contamination. Scientists believe that the deaths occurred when oil contamination killed the iguanas' gut bacteria, making them unable to digest seaweed and causing them to starve. Marine iguanas have no natural predators and generally die either of starvation or old age.

The U.S. National Research Council warns that, even without large catastrophic oil spills, many marine habitats are regularly exposed to oil pollution. Harbors and aquatic habitats near developed areas are in particular jeopardy. In 2003 the agency estimated that each year approximately twenty-nine million gallons of petroleum enter North American ocean waters due to human activities. Nearly 85% of this amount is attributed to street runoff, polluted rivers, and losses from airplanes, small boats, and jet skis. As little as one part of oil per million parts of water can be detrimental to the reproduction and growth of fish, crustaceans, and plankton.

Ocean Dumping and Debris

Ocean debris comes from many sources and affects diverse marine species. Waterborne litter entangles wildlife, masquerades as a food source, smothers beach and bottom-dwelling plants, provides a means for small organisms to invade nonnative areas, and contributes to toxic water pollution. Records of interactions between ocean debris and wildlife date back to the first half of the twentieth century. Northern fur seals entangled in debris were spotted as early as the 1930s. In the 1960s various seabirds were found to have plastic in their stomachs. By the early twenty-first century, a total of 255 species were documented to have become entangled in marine debris or to have ingested it.

Some scientists once thought it was safe to dump garbage into the oceans, believing the oceans were large enough to absorb sludge without harmful effects. Other scientists argued dumping would eventually lead to the pollution of the oceans. Metropolitan centers such as New York City once loaded their sludge and debris onto barges, took the vessels out to sea, and dumped the refuse, in a practice called ocean dumping. Problems with ocean dumping were not fully recognized until floating plastic particles were found throughout the Atlantic and Pacific Oceans.

The perils of ocean dumping and debris struck home both literally and figuratively in the summer of 1988, when debris from the ocean, including sewage, garbage, and biohazards from medical waste, washed up on the Atlantic seaboard, forcing an unprecedented 803 beach closures. In some cases authorities were alerted to beach

TABLE 4.1

How long does marine debris stay in the environment?

Cardboard box	2 weeks
Paper towels	2–4 weeks
Newspaper	6 weeks
Cotton glove	1–5 months
Apple core	2 months
Waxed milk carton	3 months
Cotton rope	3–14 months
Photodegradable 6-pack ring	6 months
Biodegradable diaper	1 year
Wool glove	1 year
Plywood	1–3 years
Painted wooden stick	13 years
Foam cup	50 years
Tin can	50 years
Styrofoam buoy	80 years
Aluminum Can	200 years
Plastic 6-pack ring	400 years
Disposable diapers	450 years
Plastic bottles	450 years
Microfilament fishing line	600 years
Glass bottles/jars	Undetermined

SOURCE: Adapted from "Marine Debris Timeline," U.S. Environmental Protection Agency, Gulf of Mexico Program, October 9, 2003, http://www.epa.gov/gmpo/edresources/debris_t.html (accessed April 4, 2006)

FIGURE 4.7

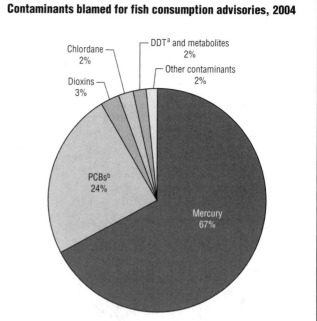

Contaminants blamed for fish consumption advisories, 2004

[a]DDT is dichlorodiphenyltrichloroethane, an insecticide.
[b]PCB is polychlorinated biphenyls.

SOURCE: Adapted from "Bioaccumulative Pollutants," in *Ten Individual Slides Providing National Summaries and Statistics for the 2004 National Listing of Fish Advisories (NLFA) Database*, U.S. Environmental Protection Agency, September 15, 2005, http://epa.gov/waterscience/fish/advisories/2004slides.ppt#3 (accessed February 11, 2006) and "Other Contaminants," in *2004 National Listing of Fish Advisories*, U.S. Environmental Protection Agency, Office of Water, September 2005, http://epa.gov/waterscience/fish/advisories/fs2004.pdf (accessed February 11, 2006)

wash-ups when children turned up hypodermic needles in the sand. Aquatic species also faced serious dangers from these materials, including absorbing or ingesting hazardous waste substances, and ingesting needles, forceps, and other dangerous solid debris. In 1994 hundreds of dead dolphins washed up on Mediterranean beaches, killed by a virus linked to water pollution. Scientists pointed to this event as an indication of what may happen to other marine animals (and humans) if pollution continues.

At the urging of the Environmental Protection Agency (EPA), the dumping of potentially infectious medical waste into ocean waters from public vessels was prohibited in 1988. In 1992 the federal government banned ocean dumping. In 1995 the EPA stepped up efforts to educate people about the dangers of polluting coastal waters through improper disposal of trash on land, sewer overflows to rivers and streams, and dumping by ships and other vessels. The EPA further warned that marine debris poses not only a serious threat to wildlife, but remains in the environment for many years. (See Table 4.1.)

Mercury and Other Toxic Pollutants

Since 1993 the EPA has published an annual listing of all fish advisories issued around the country. These advisories are issued by states to protect residents from the adverse health risk of eating fish contaminated with certain pollutants. The EPA's *2004 National Listing of Fish Advisories* (September 2005, http://www.epa.gov/OST/fish/advisories/fs2004.pdf) showed that 3,221 advisories were issued during 2004 affecting 35% of the

nation's total lake acreage and 24% of its total river miles. Nearly 14.3 million lake acres and just over 839,000 river miles were under advisory during 2004. As shown in Figure 4.7 more than two-thirds of the advisories were issued due to mercury contamination. Polychlorinated biphenyls (PCBs) accounted for another 24% of advisories. Dioxins, pesticides, and other contaminants contributed the other 9% of the total.

MERCURY. Mercury contamination is a problem in many of the nation's waterbodies. Scientists believe that the main source of mercury pollution is rainwater that carries mercury from coal-burning power plants, incinerators that burn garbage, and smelters that make metals. Because mercury becomes concentrated in organic tissues like DDT, even small concentrations of mercury in the water can be harmful to health. (See Figure 4.8.)

Mercury can cause brain damage and other serious health problems in wild species and in humans. During the 1990s scientists began to report widespread mercury contamination in fish, including those inhabiting remote lakes that were assumed pristine. As a result, many states now warn people against eating certain types of fish.

FIGURE 4.8

Biomagnification of mercury in the food chain

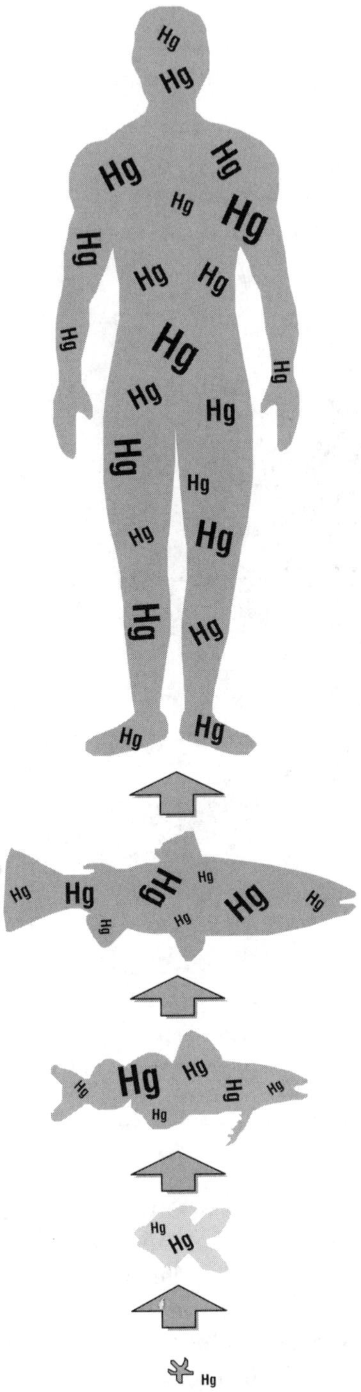

Note: Even at very low input rates to aquatic ecosystems that are remote from point sources, biomagnification effects can result in mercury levels of toxicological concern.

SOURCE: David P. Krabbenhoft and David A. Rickert, "Figure 4. Mercury (Hg) Biomagnifies from the Bottom to the Top of the Food Chain," in *Mercury Contamination of Aquatic Ecosystems*, U.S. Geological Survey, 1995, http://water.usgs.gov/wid/FS_216-95/FS_216-95.pdf (accessed April 4, 2006)

The Environmental Protection Agency's National Fish and Wildlife Contamination Program reported that

in 2004 mercury was the cause of 2,436 fish and wildlife consumption advisories. Figure 4.9 shows the advisories in effect as of December 2004. Most states across the nation's northern border and in the Northeast had state-wide advisories in effect for all their rivers and lakes, as did Florida. All of the Gulf Coast, Hawaiian coast, and much of the eastern seaboard were under advisory for mercury contamination in marine fish.

SEDIMENT—GOOD AND BAD

Erosion of river and stream banks brings dirt into waterbodies. Once in the water, this dirt is known as silt or sediment. Most of these particles settle to the bottom. However, sediment is easily stirred up by the movement of fish and other aquatic creatures, many of which spawn or lay eggs at the bed of their habitats. The dirt that remains in suspension in the water is said to make water turbid. The measure of the dirtiness (lack of clarity) of a waterbody is called its turbidity.

Freshwater aquatic creatures are sensitive to turbidity levels and choose their habitats based in part on their sediment preferences. Some fish prefer waters with large amounts of sediment. It provides cover that prevents predator fish from seeing them. Other species prefer clean waters with low turbidity levels. Excessive sediment may clog their gills or smother their eggs. (See Figure 4.10.)

Sediment levels in a water system can be drastically changed by deforestation of banks and nearby lands through forestry or agricultural practices. Excessive grazing of livestock along riverbanks can strip vegetation and permit large amounts of dirt to enter the water. Likewise, timber harvesting and crop production can expose loosened dirt to wind and rain that carry it into water bodies. Dams and diversion structures trap sediments behind them, interrupting the natural downstream flow of sediments that takes place in moving waters.

AIR POLLUTION AFFECTS WATER QUALITY

Water quality can be affected by pollutants emitted into the air during fossil fuel combustion or industrial, agricultural and forestry activities. Nutrients, oil and dirt particles, and some chemicals (such as mercury) are known to be carried through the air and deposited onto waterbodies. This process is called atmospheric disposition. In addition, aquatic environments can be harmed indirectly, through changes in climate and atmospheric phenomena due to human activities.

Phytoplankton

Phytoplankton (planktonic plant life) are microscopic photosynthesizing species that form the basis of nearly all marine food chains. (See Figure 4.11.) In many parts of the world, phytoplankton seems to be declining. The most severe damage appears to be in the waters off Antarctica,

FIGURE 4.9

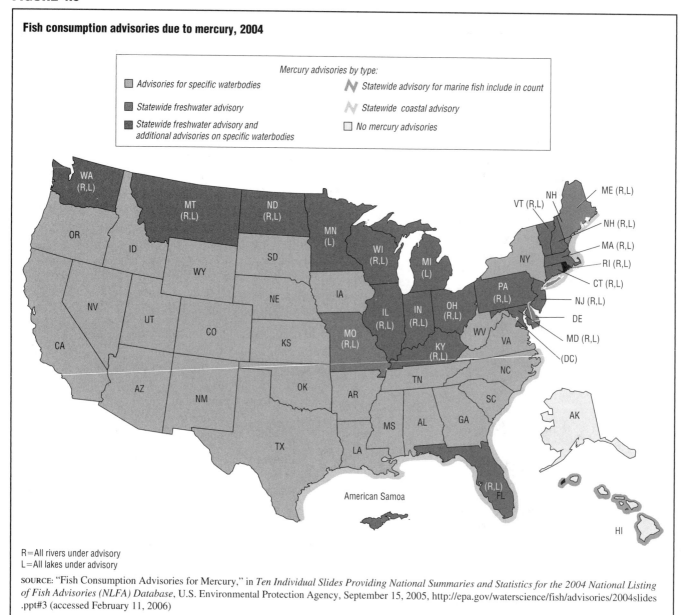

Fish consumption advisories due to mercury, 2004

Mercury advisories by type:

- Advisories for specific waterbodies
- Statewide freshwater advisory
- Statewide freshwater advisory and additional advisories on specific waterbodies
- Statewide advisory for marine fish include in count
- Statewide coastal advisory
- No mercury advisories

R=All rivers under advisory
L=All lakes under advisory

SOURCE: "Fish Consumption Advisories for Mercury," in *Ten Individual Slides Providing National Summaries and Statistics for the 2004 National Listing of Fish Advisories (NLFA) Database*, U.S. Environmental Protection Agency, September 15, 2005, http://epa.gov/waterscience/fish/advisories/2004slides .ppt#3 (accessed February 11, 2006)

where phytoplankton are severely depleted. The depletion of phytoplankton has implications all the way up the food chain, affecting not only the zooplankton that consume them but larger species such as penguins, seals, and whales. Scientists believe that phytoplankton declines are a result of the thinning atmospheric ozone layer (caused by industrial pollutants such as chlorofluorocarbons, or CFCs), which allows increasing amounts of ultraviolet radiation to penetrate the Earth's surface. Ultraviolet radiation decreases the ability of phytoplankton to photosynthesize and also damages their genetic material.

FISHING—FAR-REACHING CONSEQUENCES

Worldwide, the demand for fish and other edible aquatic creatures has risen dramatically in recent decades. The National Marine Fisheries Service in *Fisheries*

of the United States–2004 (November 2005, http:// www.st.nmfs.gov/st1/fus/fus04/index.html) summarizes data collected about commercial and recreational fisheries. The report notes that in 2003 the world's commercial fishery and aquaculture industries harvested 146 million tons of products. In 2004 U.S. commercial fishery and aquaculture industries produced 11.2 billion pounds of fish and shellfish. Per capita annual consumption of fishery products in the United States was 16.6 pounds of meat in 2004. This is up from fifteen pounds per person annual consumption reported in 1990. U.S. consumers spent nearly $62 billion on fishery products in 2004.

Overfishing

Up to a certain point, fishermen are able to catch fish without damaging the ecological balance. This is known

FIGURE 4.10

Effects of siltation on aquatic life

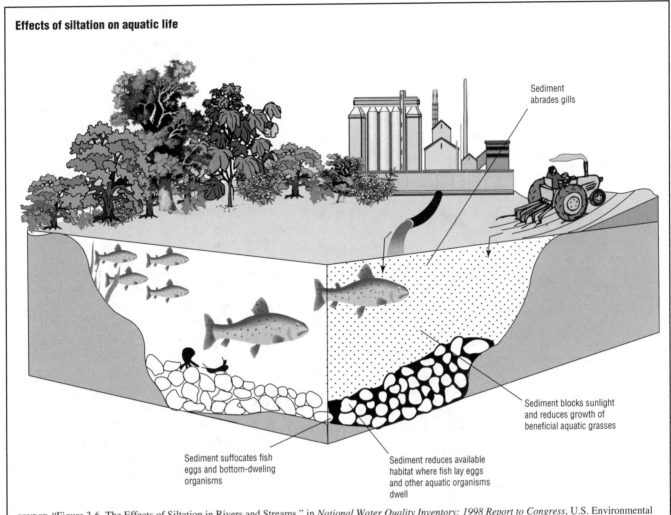

Sediment abrades gills

Sediment blocks sunlight and reduces growth of beneficial aquatic grasses

Sediment suffocates fish eggs and bottom-dwelling organisms

Sediment reduces available habitat where fish lay eggs and other aquatic organisms dwell

SOURCE: "Figure 3-6. The Effects of Siltation in Rivers and Streams," in *National Water Quality Inventory: 1998 Report to Congress*, U.S. Environmental Protection Agency, June 2000, http://www.epa.gov/305b/98report/chap3.pdf (accessed March 9, 2006)

as the maximum sustainable yield. Catches beyond the maximum sustainable yield represent overfishing.

Overfishing removes fish faster than they can reproduce and causes serious population declines. This can have far-reaching consequences on other species that rely on the depleted fish for food. Furthermore, once fishermen deplete all the large fish of a species, they often begin to target smaller, younger individuals. Targeting young fish undermines future breeding populations and guarantees a smaller biological return in future years. Swordfish have been seriously depleted in this way. In the early 1900s the average weight of a swordfish when caught was about 300 pounds. By 1960, according to the NMFS, it was 266 pounds, and at the close of the twentieth century it was ninety pounds.

Technological advances have enabled numerous marine fisheries to be depleted in a short amount of time. The U.S. Commission on Ocean Policy published *An Ocean Blueprint for the 21st Century* (September

2004, http://www.oceancommission.gov/documents/full_color_rpt/welcome.html). Commission members were appointed by President George W. Bush to develop recommendations for a new national ocean policy. The report noted: "Experts estimate that 25 to 30 percent of the world's major fish stocks are overexploited, and many U.S. fisheries are experiencing serious difficulties."

MAGNUSON-STEVENS ACT. The U.S. government attempted to eliminate overfishing in U.S. coastal waters by passing the Magnuson-Stevens Fishery Conservation and Management Act (P.L. 94-265) in 1976. This act established U.S. control over fishery resources within 200 nautical miles of the coast. (See Figure 4.12.) This area was later deemed the Exclusive Economic Zone (EEZ). Under international law the United States has sovereign rights to explore, exploit, conserve, and manage living and nonliving resources within and below ocean waters within the EEZ.

FIGURE 4.11

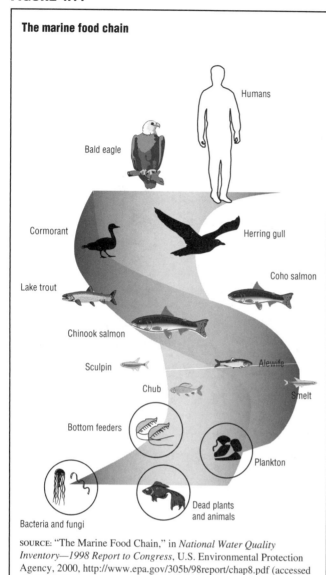

The marine food chain

Humans

Bald eagle

Cormorant

Herring gull

Coho salmon

Lake trout

Chinook salmon

Sculpin

Alewife

Chub

Smelt

Bottom feeders

Plankton

Bacteria and fungi

Dead plants and animals

SOURCE: "The Marine Food Chain," in *National Water Quality Inventory—1998 Report to Congress*, U.S. Environmental Protection Agency, 2000, http://www.epa.gov/305b/98report/chap8.pdf (accessed April 4, 2006)

When the Magnuson-Stevens Act was passed it prevented foreign fishing fleets from exploiting the affected waters. However, with foreign fleets gone, American fishermen built up their own fleets, buying large, well-equipped vessels with low-interest loans from the federal government. For several years U.S. fishermen reported record catches. Then these declined.

The act established eight Regional Fishery Management Councils as follows:

- Caribbean Fishery Management Council
- Gulf of Mexico Fishery Management Council
- Mid-Atlantic Fishery Management Council
- New England Fishery Management Council
- North Pacific Fishery Management Council
- Pacific Fishery Management Council
- South Atlantic Fishery Management Council
- Western Pacific Fishery Management Council

The councils were instructed to prepare Fishery Management Plans (FMPs) covering domestic and foreign fishing efforts within their area of authority. FMPs must be approved by the Secretary of Commerce before being implemented. They are enforced by the National Marine Fisheries Service and the U.S. Coast Guard. The Fishery Management Plans for some species, such as highly migratory fishes that enter and leave the Exclusive Economic Zone, are prepared by the U.S. Department of Commerce. As of February 2006 more than forty FMPs have been finalized for various species. The plans can be accessed at the Web site http://www.nmfs.noaa.gov/sfa/domes_fish/FMPS.htm.

The Fishery Management Councils were intended to eliminate overfishing, while ensuring that the "optimum yield" was obtained from each fishery. Critics say the system has failed to do this. The National Academy of Public Administration in *Courts, Congress, and Constituencies: Managing Fisheries by Default* (July 2002, http://www.napawash.org/Pubs/NMFS_July_2002.pdf? OpenDocument) concluded that fisheries management in the United States was being driven by litigation and political processes, rather than sound science. At that time more than 100 lawsuits were pending against the NMFS; most involved stock assessments and catch limits and were filed by the fishing industry or conservation groups.

The *Ocean Blueprint for the 21st Century* complains: "Social, economic, and political considerations have often led the Councils to downplay the best available scientific information, resulting in overfishing and the slow recovery of overfished stocks." However, the report does acknowledge that overfishing has been relieved in some areas. During the 1990s increases were reported in stocks of Mid-Atlantic flounder, New England groundfish, and Atlantic striped bass.

SHARK OVERFISHING. According to the San Diego Natural History Museum, sharks have been predators of the seas for nearly 400 million years. There are more than 350 species of sharks, ranging in size from the tiny pygmy shark to the giant whale shark.

Shark populations are being decimated because of the growing demand for shark meat and shark fins. Fins and tails sell for as much as $100 a pound. In 2003 the Pew Institute for Ocean Science instituted a project called the Pew Global Shark Assessment. Its purpose is to collect data regarding declines in global shark populations. According to the project's Web site (http://www.pewoceanscience.org/projects/Pew_Global_Shar/intro.php?ID=56) populations of dusky, oceanic whitetip, and silky sharks in the Gulf of Mexico have declined by

FIGURE 4.12

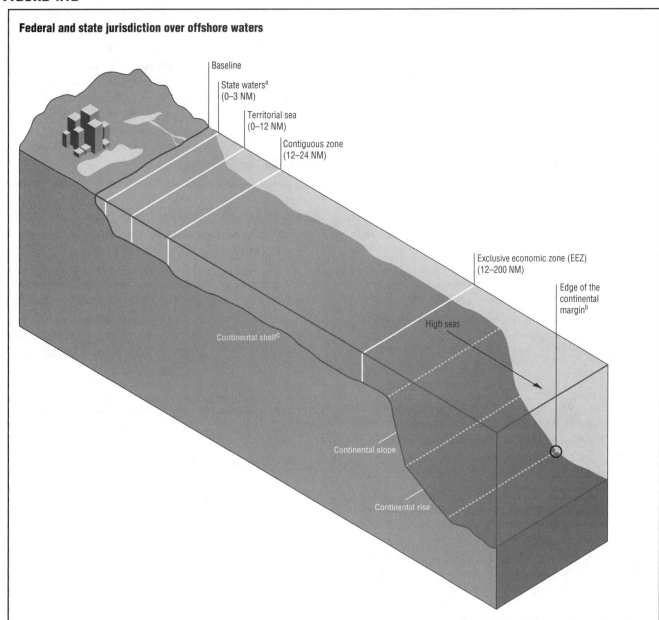

Federal and state jurisdiction over offshore waters

Baseline

State waters[a]
(0–3 NM)

Territorial sea
(0–12 NM)

Contiguous zone
(12–24 NM)

Exclusive economic zone (EEZ)
(12–200 NM)

Edge of the
continental
margin[b]

High seas

Continental shelf[c]

Continental slope

Continental rise

[a]Three nautical miles is the jurisdictional limit for U.S. states and some territories under domestic law, with the exception of Texas, Florida's west coast, and Puerto Rico, whose jurisdictions extend to 9 nautical miles offshore.
[b]The outer edge of the continental margin is a principal basis for determining a coastal nation's jurisdiction over seabed resources beyond 200 nautical miles from the baseline.
[c]The continental shelf is depicted here based on its geological definition. The term is sometimes used differently in international law.

SOURCE: "Figure P.1 Lines of U.S. Authority in Offshore Waters," in *An Ocean Blueprint for the 21st Century, Final Report*, U.S. Commission on Ocean Policy, 2004, http://www.oceancommission.gov/documents/full_color_rpt/000_ocean_full_report.pdf (accessed February 1, 2006)

79% to 97% since the 1950s due to overfishing. Massive declines are also reported over the same time period for blue, mako, oceanic whitetip, silky, and thresher sharks in the tropical Pacific Ocean. Overfishing is particularly harmful to sharks because they reproduce slowly. In 1997 the Fisheries Service cut quotas on commercial harvests of some shark species by half and completely banned harvest of the most vulnerable species—whale sharks, white sharks, basking sharks, sand tiger sharks, and bigeye sand tiger sharks. A few shark species, including whale sharks and basking sharks, were given protection

by the Convention on International Trade in Endangered Species (CITES) for the first time in 2002. This was considered a landmark decision because CITES had never before addressed fisheries.

Biologists Julia Baum and Ransom Myers of Dalhousie University in Canada in "Collapse and Conservation of Shark Populations in the Northwest Atlantic" (*Science*, January 17, 2003), showed that many shark populations in the Gulf of Mexico have plummeted since the 1950s. In particular, whitetip shark populations have declined by 90%. The researchers blamed the decline on overfishing due to demand for sharkfin soup, which is considered a luxury. Myers said, "Researchers in the 1960s suggested that oceanic whitetip sharks were the most common large species on Earth. What we have shown is akin to the herds of buffalo disappearing from the Great Plains and no one noticing." Other species which have been affected include the silk shark, whose populations have dropped by 90%, and the mako shark, which has declined 79%.

FISH DECLINES AND DEEP-SEA HARVESTING. As catches of shallow water fishes decline, trawlers have increasingly been used to scour the deep seas for new varieties of fish, such as the nine-inch long royal red shrimp, rattails, skates, squid, red crabs, orange roughy, oreos, hoki, blue ling, southern blue whiting, and spiny dogfish. Although limited commercial deep-sea fishing has occurred for decades, new technologies are making it considerably more practical and efficient. As stocks of better-known fish shrink and international quotas tighten, experts say deep ocean waters will increasingly be targeted as a source of seafood.

Bycatch

Bycatch is the term used for nontargeted animals captured during fishing. For example, during the 1960s, hundreds of thousands of dolphins per year were caught in the nets of tuna fishing boats and drowned. Although dolphins were not the targets of the fishing operations, they became victims anyway. Public outcry over dolphin deaths led to passage of the Marine Mammal Protection Act and promises by tuna canneries to sell only "dolphin-safe" tuna. Unfortunately bycatch continues to be a problem for many aquatic species, including those that are endangered and threatened.

FROM DRIFT NETS TO LONGLINES. Drift nets are the world's largest fishing nets, reaching lengths of up to thirty miles. Conservationists refer to them as "walls of death" because they indiscriminately catch and kill marine species. Over 100 species—including whales, sea turtles, dolphins, seabirds, sharks, salmon, and numerous other fish species—have been killed in drift nets. Drift nets were eventually banned because of their destructiveness to wildlife.

After the banning of drift nets, many fishermen turned to longlines. Longlines are fishing lines with a single main line attached to many shorter lines that terminate in baited hooks. They are used to catch wide-ranging oceanic species such as tuna, swordfish, and sharks, as well as bottom dwellers such as cod and halibut. A single boat can trail thousands of hooks from lines stretching twenty to eighty miles.

Longline fishing kills fewer marine mammals than drift nets but captures more surface-feeding sea birds,

particularly the rare albatrosses. Longline fishing has in fact resulted in the decline of numerous albatross species, almost all of which are now listed by the World Conservation Union (IUCN) as endangered. Australian scientists estimate that longline fishing kills more than 40,000 albatrosses each year. Longline fishing has also caused rapid declines in some fish species. Longlining is an old practice, but modern technology has vastly increased its efficiency and ecological impact.

Ghost Fishing

"Ghost fishing" is a term used by biologists to refer to the accidental entanglement of aquatic animals in abandoned or lost fishing gear. According to the 2004 report *An Ocean Blueprint for the 21st Century* ghost fishing kills hundreds of thousands of marine mammals worldwide each year. Dolphins, porpoises, and small whales are the primary victims. However, even large whales can be injured by entanglements or become exhausted after towing heavy nets and gear over long distances. Ghost fishing is one of the main causes blamed for the endangered status of the North Atlantic right whale.

Ghost fishing is an international problem. The U.S. Commission on Ocean Policy reports that between 1998 and 2002 more than 150 tons of fishing nets and lines were removed from reefs near the northwestern Hawaiian Islands. Oftentimes the nets were not the type used by local fisheries; instead, they are believed to have drifted from thousands of miles away in the North Pacific Ocean. Possible solutions to the problem of ghost fishing include the assessment of fees or deposits on fishing nets with the money raised used to collect derelict fishing gear, achieving international cooperation in identifying and removing derelict fishing gear, and development of biodegradable fishing gear. The NMFS already requires commercial U.S. fisheries to mark fishing gear with identifying information.

UNWELCOME GUESTS—AQUATIC INVASIVE SPECIES

Invasive species can be domestic or foreign. Some aquatic invasive species have been introduced purposely to U.S. waterbodies, for example, to improve sport and recreational fishing. Others have been introduced unintentionally. The primary source of these aquatic invasive species has traditionally been ship ballast water, which is generally picked up in one location and released in another. According to Leo O'Brien, executive director of Baykeeper (a group trying to protect and improve the water quality of the San Francisco Bay/Delta Estuary), it is estimated that a new invasive species becomes established every fourteen weeks through ballast water in the San Francisco Bay alone. Invasive species are also established through transfer from recreational boating vessels;

dumping of live bait; release of aquarium species; and accidental escapes from research facilities and aquaculture pens.

The Nonindigenous Aquatic Nuisance Prevention and Control Act of 1990 and the National Invasive Species Act of 1996 are intended to help prevent unintentional introductions of aquatic nuisance species.

Invasive aquatic species include the common carp, bluegill, largemouth bass, smallmouth bass, shad, walleye, and brook trout. The common carp was purposely brought to the United States during the 1800s from Europe. It thrived so well that it soon spread across the country. Today the fish is considered a pest. It competes against native species for food and habitat.

In the state of Georgia, invasive Asian eels have increased in number in many habitats. These species were brought over from Southeast Asia or Australia, where they are considered delicacies. The three-foot-long, flesh-eating eel preys on species such as largemouth bass and crawfish in and around the Chattahoochee River. The eels have gills but can also breathe air—this enables them to worm their way across dry ground to get from one body of water to another. Asian eels have few predators in their new habitat, and humans have found no effective way to control them. As of 2006 three populations of Asian eel had been identified in Florida, confirming fears that the eel would spread beyond Georgia. According to a fact sheet prepared by the Florida Integrated Science Center of the U.S. Geological Survey, one colony was living in canals in the northern Miami area, once colony was near Tampa Bay, and one colony was within a mile of the eastern edge of Everglades National Park.

MULTIPLE THREATS COMBINE

Most aquatic lifeforms are not imperiled by a single threat to their survival, but by multiple threats that combine to produce daunting challenges to recovery. The lethal combination of historical overfishing and habitat degradation is blamed for the problems of many endangered and threatened aquatic species. Habitat degradation can be caused by many factors, including dams, water pollution, and invasive species.

Overcrowding of stressed fish populations into smaller and smaller areas has contributed to hybridization—uncharacteristic mating between closely related species resulting in hybrid offspring. According to the U.S. Fish and Wildlife Service environmental degradation appears to inhibit natural reproductive instincts that historically prevented fish from mating outside their species. In addition, shortage of suitable space for spawning has resulted in more mating between species. Cross-mating can be extremely detrimental to imperiled species, because the offspring can be sterile.

Coral Reefs

Coral reefs are the largest living structures on Earth. Biologically, the richness of coral reef ecosystems is comparable to that of tropical rainforests. The reefs themselves are formed from calcium carbonate skeletons secreted by corals. Corals maintain a close relationship with certain species of photosynthetic algae, providing shelter to them and receiving nutrients in exchange. Most people are familiar with the colorful coral reefs found in coastal, tropical waters. (See Figure 4.13.) These reefs are located in relatively shallow waters, making them more susceptible to human activities. Only 1% to 2% of warm-water corals are found in U.S. waters. Most warm-water corals are located in the waters of the South Pacific and around Indonesia. In addition there are numerous cold-water reefs around the world that scientists are just beginning to learn about. These reefs are found in cold deep waters from depths of 100 feet to more than three miles.

According to *An Ocean Blueprint for the 21st Century*, one-third of coral reefs around the world are severely damaged and all U.S. warm-water reefs have been damaged to some degree. Coral reefs are imperiled by diseases and coastal development that spurs the growth of unfriendly algae. Coastal development also increases the danger of the reefs being trampled by divers and boat anchors. Other serious threats to reef ecosystems include marine pollution, blast fishing, and cyanide fishing. Collection of tropical reef specimens for the aquarium trade has also damaged a number of species. Perhaps the greatest immediate threat to coral reefs is rising water temperature due to global climate change. This has caused extensive coral bleaching in recent years. (See Figure 4.14.)

FIGURE 4.13

Locations of tropical coral reefs

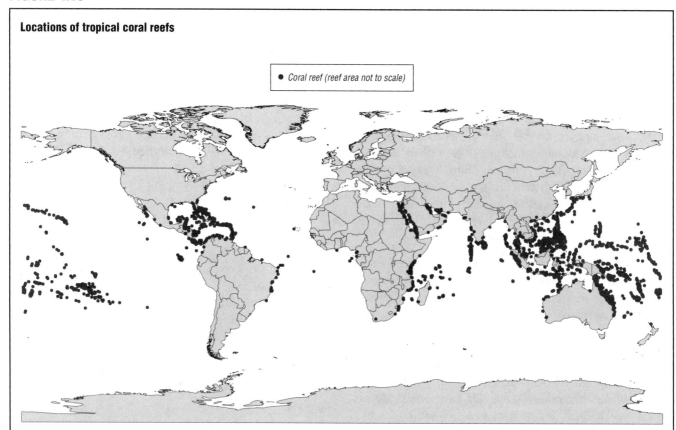

SOURCE: "Figure 21.1. Tropical Waters Are Home to the Majority of Known Reefs," in *An Ocean Blueprint for the 21st Century, Final Report*, U.S. Commission on Ocean Policy, 2004, http://www.oceancommission.gov/documents/full_color_rpt/000_ocean_full_report.pdf (accessed February 1, 2006)

FIGURE 4.14

Coral reefs are among the most diverse ecosystems in the world. They are also immediately threatened by global warming, which has caused unprecedented episodes of coral bleaching in recent years. (AP/Wide World Photos.)

CHAPTER 5

MARINE MAMMALS

around the ocean. They
...e hair at some point in
...(as opposed to laying
...by secreting milk.
...valruses, polar bears,
...latives) fall into this

...e garnered a high
...ection. During the
...rtained American
...elligent and love-
...t a family. Such
...a and SeaWorld
...dolphins and
...g environmen-
...est in marine
...otect animals
...ly smart and
social

At ....ng was widely practiced by com......... ..shers in the eastern tropical Pacific Ocean. This fishing method involved the use of enormous nets, often hundreds of miles long that were circled around schools of tuna. Many dolphins were inadvertently captured because they tend to mingle with fleets of tuna in this part of the ocean. Nontargeted animals captured during commercial fishing activities are called "bycatch." Dolphin bycatch became a major public issue. Hauling in the enormous tuna-filled nets was a lengthy process. As a result, the air-breathing dolphins were trapped for long periods under water, and often drowned. It is estimated that more than 400,000 dolphins and porpoises died per year in this manner during the late 1960s. Public outcry over these killings and general concern for the welfare of marine mammals led the U.S. Congress to pass the Marine Mammal Protection Act of 1972.

THE MARINE MAMMAL PROTECTION ACT

The Marine Mammal Protection Act (MMPA) was passed in 1972 and substantially amended in 1994. The original act noted that "certain species and population stocks of marine mammals are, or may be, in danger of extinction or depletion as a result of man's activities." However, it was acknowledged that "inadequate" information was available concerning the population dynamics of the animals being protected.

The Marine Mammal Protection Act prohibits the taking (hunting, killing, capturing, and harassing) of marine mammals. The act also bars importation of most marine mammals or their products. Exceptions are occasionally granted for scientific research, public display in aquariums, traditional subsistence hunting by Alaska Natives, and some incidental capture during commercial fishing operations. The goal of the MMPA is to maintain marine populations at or above "optimum sustainable" levels.

Whales, dolphins, seals, and sea lions were put under the jurisdiction of the National Marine Fisheries Service (NMFS), an agency of the National Oceanic and Atmospheric Administration (NOAA) in the U.S. Department of Commerce. Polar bears, walruses, sea otters, manatees, and dugongs were put under the jurisdiction of the U.S. Fish and Wildlife Service (FWS), an agency of the U.S. Department of Interior.

The Marine Mammal Protection Act requires the NMFS and FWS to conduct periodic surveys to estimate populations and predict population trends for marine mammals in three regions of U.S. waters: Pacific Ocean coast (excluding Alaska), Atlantic Ocean coast (including the Gulf of Mexico), and the Alaskan coast. The survey results are published in annual Stock Assessment Reports. Reports dating back to 1995 are available online at http://www.nmfs.noaa.gov/pr/sars/.

The Marine Mammal Protection Act was passed a year before the Endangered Species Act. The MMPA was driven largely by public affection for marine mammals, rather than specific knowledge about impending species extinction. According to Eugene H. Buck in *Fishery, Aquaculture, and Marine Mammal Legislation in the 109th Congress* (Congressional Research Service, September 9, 2005), "some critics assert that the MMPA is scientifically irrational because it identifies one group of organisms for special protection unrelated to their abundance or ecological role." However, the MMPA is credited with promoting research about marine mammals and drawing attention to issues associated with bycatch mortality.

THE ENDANGERED SPECIES ACT

As shown in Table 2.1 in Chapter 2, there were only three marine mammal species on the first list of native endangered species issued in 1967. Over the following decades additional marine mammals were added as information became available on their population status. As of February 2006 there were fourteen species of marine mammals listed as endangered or threatened in the United States. (See Table 5.1.) Another fourteen foreign species were also listed.

Table 5.2 shows that $71.2 million was spent by federal and state agencies during fiscal year 2004 on specific marine mammal species listed under the Endangered Species Act (ESA).

In February 2006 the U.S. Fish and Wildlife Service announced its intention to conduct a status review to determine if polar bears should be proposed for listing under the ESA as a threatened species. The decision was driven by what the agency called "substantial scientific

TABLE 5.1

Endangered and threatened aquatic mammals, February 2006

U.S. species

Status*	Type	Common name	Scientific name	Note
E	Whale	Blue whale	*Balaenoptera musculus*	Baleen plate
E	Whale	Bowhead whale	*Balaena mysticetus*	Baleen plate
E	Whale	Finback whale	*Balaenoptera physalus*	Baleen plate
E	Whale	Humpback whale	*Megaptera novaeangliae*	Baleen plate
E	Whale	Right whale (northern & southern)	*Balaena glacialis incl. australis*	Baleen plate
E	Whale	Sei whale	*Balaenoptera borealis*	Baleen plate
E	Whale	Sperm whale	*Physeter catodon= macrocephalus*	Toothed
E	Sea-lion	Steller sea-lion	*Eumetopias jubatus*	Eared
E	Seal	Caribbean monk seal	*Monachus tropicalis*	Earless, presumed extinct
T	Seal	Guadalupe fur seal	*Arctocephalus townsendi*	Eared
E	Seal	Hawaiian monk seal	*Monachus schauinslandi*	Earless
T	Otter	Northern sea otter	*Enhydra lutris kenyoni*	Southwest Alaska stock
T (XN at San Nicolas Island)	Otter	Southern sea otter	*Enhydra lutris nereis*	California stock
E	Manatee	West Indian manatee	*Trichechus manatus*	Florida stock
Foreign species				
E	Whale	Gray whale	*Eschrichtius robustus*	Western north Pacific Ocean
E	Dolphin	Chinese River dolphin	*Lipotes vexillifer*	China
E	Dolphin	Indus River dolphin	*Platanista minor*	Pakistan
E	Porpoise	Cochito (or vaquita)	*Phocoena sinus*	Mexico (Gulf of California)
E	Seal	Mediterranean monk seal	*Monachus monachus*	Mediterranean, northwest African coast and Black Sea
E	Seal	Saimaa seal	*Phoca hispida saimensis*	Finland
E	Otter	Cameroon clawless otter	*Aonyx congicus=congica microdon*	Nigeria
E	Otter	Giant otter	*Pteronura brasiliensis*	South America
E	Otter	Long-tailed otter	*Lontra= lutra longicaudis*	South America
E	Otter	Marine otter	*Lontra lutra felina*	Peru south to Straits of Magellan
E	Otter	Southern river otter	*Lontra=lutra provocax*	Argentina, Chile
E	Manatee	Amazonian manatee	*Trichechus inunguis*	South America
T	Manatee	West African manatee	*Trichechus senegalensis*	West coast of Africa
E	Dugong	Dugong	*Dugong dugon*	Palau (western Pacific Ocean)

*E=endangered; T=threatened; XN=nonessential experimental population

SOURCE: Adapted from "Listed U.S. Species by Taxonomic Group," in *Threatened and Endangered Species System (TESS)*, U.S. Department of the Interior, U.S. Fish and Wildlife Service, February 10, 2006, http://ecos.fws.gov/tess_public/SpeciesReport.do?kingdom=V&listingType=L (accessed February 10, 2006)

TABLE 5.2

**The ten listed marine mammal entities with the highest
expenditures under the Endangered Species Act, fiscal year 2004**

Common name	Species total
Steller sea-lion (western & eastern)	$42,557,321
Right whale (northern & southern)	$12,369,623
West Indian manatee	$9,861,677
Hawaiian monk seal	$2,321,146
Sperm whale	$2,270,475
Southern sea otter	$734,386
Humpback whale	$666,282
Bowhead whale	$190,117
Finback whale	$72,160
Blue whale	$66,594
Sei whale	$66,129
Guadalupe fur seal	$1,000
Total	**$71,176,910**

SOURCE: Adapted from "Table 1. Reported FY2004 Expenditures for
Endangered and Threatened Species, Not Including Land Acquisition Costs,"
in *Federal and State Endangered and Threatened Species Expenditures:
Fiscal Year 2004*, U.S. Department of the Interior, U.S. Fish and Wildlife
Service, January 2005, http://www.fws.gov/endangered/expenditures/
reports/FWS%20Endangered%20Species%202004%20Expenditures%20
Report.pdf (accessed February 11, 2006)

and commercial information" indicating that polar bear
populations may be imperiled.

As of February 2006 ESA-listed endangered and
threatened marine mammals fell into five main categories: whales, dolphins and porpoises, seals and sea
lions, sea otters, and manatees and dugongs.

WHALES

Whales are cetaceans, or marine mammals that live
in the water all the time and have torpedo-shaped, nearly
hairless bodies. (See Figure 5.1.) There are approximately seventy known whale species. The so-called
"great" whales are the largest animals on Earth. In general, the great whale species range in size from thirty to
100 feet in length. There are thirteen whale species nor-
mally considered to be "great" whales. The blue whale is
the largest of these species.

Whales are found throughout the world's oceans;
however, many species are concentrated in cold northern

FIGURE 5.1

A humpback whale, seen off the coast of Massachusetts. (AP/Wide World Photos.)

FIGURE 5.2

Baleen plates

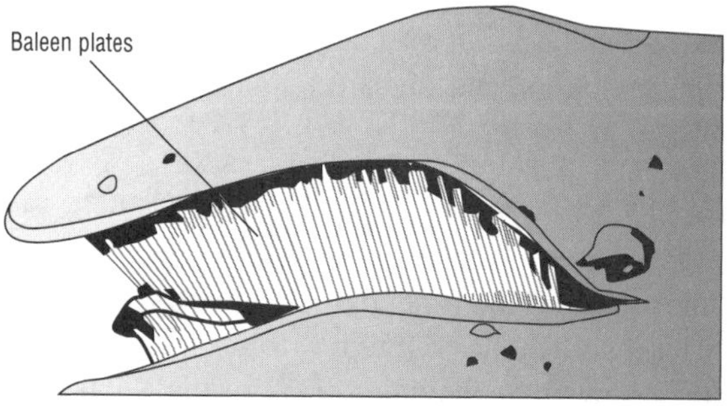

Baleen plates

SOURCE: "What Are Baleen Whales Like?" in *Groups of Cetaceans*, U.S. Department of Commerce, National Oceanic and Atmospheric Administration, National Marine Mammal Laboratory, March 3, 2004, http://nmml.afsc.noaa.gov/education/cetaceans/groupsofcetaceans.htm (accessed January 18, 2006)

waters. Although they are warm-blooded and do not have fur, whales can survive in very cold waters because they have a thick layer of dense fat and tissue known as blubber lying just beneath the skin. This blubber layer can be up to a foot thick in larger species.

Most whales have teeth. A handful of species filter their food through strong flexible plates called baleen. (See Figure 5.2.) Baleen is informally known as "whalebone." It is composed of a substance similar to human fingernails. Baleen whales strain large amounts of water to obtain their food, mostly zooplankton and tiny fish and crustaceans. Nearly all of the "great" whales are baleen whales.

Many marine mammals can vocalize (make sound). Whales, in particular, use sound to communicate with each other and for navigational purposes. Some whale vocalizations are audible to human ears. These sounds are known as "whalesong."

Whales are believed to be highly intelligent. Scientists use a measure called the Encephalization Quotient (EQ) to compare the relative intelligence of different species. EQ is a number based on the ratio of brain mass to body mass. For example, the average human brain is much larger than needed just to operate an organism the size of a human. This extra capacity indicates higher intelligence. Likewise, the brains of cetaceans, such as whales, are larger than expected, indicating that they probably are very intelligent animals.

Imperiled Whale Populations

As of February 2006 seven whale species had been listed for protection under the ESA in U.S. waters: humpback whales, sperm whales, bowhead whales, northern right whales, sei whales, fin whales, and blue whales. In addition, the ESA covers southern right whales in the southern hemisphere and gray whales, a species that inhabits the northwest Pacific Ocean. All of these whales are considered "great" whales. All but the sperm whale have baleen plates.

The National Marine Fisheries Service publishes annual Stock Assessment Reports (http://www.nmfs.noaa.gov/pr/sars/) that provide population estimates for endangered whale species in U.S. waters. Surveys of all species are not conducted every year. As of February 2006 final reports were available for the Pacific Coast (2004), Atlantic and Gulf Coasts (2003), and Alaskan Coast (2003). Summing survey results from each report provides a rough estimate of the minimum population of each species:

- Blue whale—1,692
- Bowhead whale—8,886
- Fin whale—5,004
- Humpback whale—5,655
- Northern right whale—291
- Sei whale—72 (based on incomplete data)
- Sperm whale—10,956

The NMFS notes that sei whale populations are extremely difficult to estimate. The whales prefer the open sea and rarely enter U.S. waters. Also, they tend to travel alone or in small groups, making them difficult to count.

The northern right whale is also known as the North Atlantic right whale because it is primarily found along the eastern coast of the United States. Although a few sightings have been confirmed in the North Pacific Ocean, there is no official estimate of that population. The National Marine Fisheries Service considers both populations to be of the same species. However, this opinion is disputed by some scientists. As of 2006 the World Wildlife Fund estimated that there were only 350 northern right whales in existence worldwide (http://www.worldwildlife.org/cetaceans/pubs/whales_current_status.pdf).

The northern right whale is the most endangered of the great whales. It was once the "right" whale to hunt because it swims slowly, prefers shallow coastal waters, and floats upon death. The species was nearly driven to extinction by whaling, which was banned in 1937 when the population had been reduced to an estimated 100. Despite decades of protection, the northern right whale population has not recovered, and as of 2006 the WWF estimated no population increase at all since the 1980s. Some scientists believe the animal is in grave danger of becoming extinct within only a few decades.

Threats to Whales

Whale populations are imperiled due to a long history of hunting by humans. As early as the eighth century, humans hunted whales for meat and whalebone (baleen). Whales were relatively easy for fishermen to catch because the animals spend a great deal of time at the surface of the water and provide a large target for harpoons. Advances in shipbuilding and the invention of the steam engine allowed fishermen greater access to whale populations, even those in Arctic areas that had previously been out of reach. By the nineteenth century, large numbers of whales were being killed for blubber and baleen. Blubber was rendered to extract whale oil, which was used to light lamps. Baleen was valued for making fans, corsets, and other consumer goods.

On December 2, 1946, the representatives of fourteen nations signed the *International Convention for the Regulation of Whaling* to form the International Whaling Commission (IWC). The signatory nations were Argentina, Australia, Brazil, Canada, Chile, Denmark, France, the Netherlands, New Zealand, Peru, South Africa, United Kingdom, United States, and the Union of Soviet Socialist Republics. The IWC was formed as a means to regulate the industry and limit the number and type of whales that could be killed. The Marine Mammal Protection Act of 1972 banned commercial whaling in U.S. waters. As of February 2006 there were sixty-six member nations in the IWC.

Centuries of whaling severely depleted whale populations. Low birth rates and high mortality rates due to a variety of factors have prevented many species from recovering. Like other marine animals, whales are endangered by water pollution and loss or degradation of habitat. However, the biggest threats to the northern right whale are believed to be entanglement in fishing gear and ship strikes.

ENTANGLEMENT IN FISHING GEAR. Entanglement of whales in fishing gear is a major problem, as noted by the National Marine Fisheries Service in "What Kinds of Fishing Gear Most Often Entangle Right Whales?" (*Right Whale News*, November 2005). The article describes recently published research related to whale entanglement. According to studies conducted in 2003 by the New England Aquarium, 71.9% of all known northern right whales have been entangled at least once in fishing gear. In 2005 researchers from Duke University investigated thirty-one cases of right whale entanglements and tried to identify the type of fishing gear involved in each case. They found that nearly a third of the whales had become entangled in lobster pot gear, mostly buoy lines. It was concluded that any type of fishing line that rises vertically in the water column poses a "significant entanglement risk" to northern right whales.

SHIP STRIKES. As shown in Figure 5.3 the National Marine Fisheries Service documented nearly 300 ship strikes on large whales off the U.S. East Coast between 1975 and 2002. Strikes on northern right whales are particularly troublesome because so few of the animals remain in existence. According to the NMFS fourteen northern right whales were confirmed killed by ship strikes between 1991 and 2002.

Figure 5.4 shows the locations of ship strikes on northern right whales that occurred between 1990 and 2000 along the North American coastline. Most strikes in U.S. waters occurred along the Massachusetts coast near Cape Cod and along the Georgia and northern Florida coastline. These areas are near or within critical habitats designated by the National Marine Fisheries Service for the whales. The southern critical habitat is the only known calving area of the northern right whale and is used from mid-November to mid-April. During calving season the NMFS performs aerial surveys and alerts ships about whales in their vicinity. In addition, federal law requires that ships remain 500 yards from right whales. Any sightings of dead, injured, or entangled whales must be reported to authorities.

In January 2006 the NMFS announced that a dead right whale calf had been reported by a fishing crew near the Florida shore. The animal was towed to shore and found to have large propeller marks and other wounds on its body, indicating it had been struck by a ship. The whale was male and only one month old.

In 2004 the National Marine Fisheries Service announced plans to propose rules requiring routing changes and speed limits for large vessels traveling in U.S. coastal waters frequented by northern right whales. The agency was still developing the rules in May 2005 when several environmental and animal groups petitioned the NMFS requesting that a temporary emergency regulation be imposed until the permanent rules could be issued. The petitioners asked for a speed limit of 12 knots (13.8 miles per hour) for all ships entering and leaving major East Coast ports during time periods of high use by right whales. In September 2005 the NMFS formally denied the petition. Two months later, three of the petitioners—the Defenders of Wildlife, the Humane Society of the United States, and the Ocean Conservancy—filed a lawsuit against the NMFS accusing the agency of "failing to protect" northern right whales as required by law. The lawsuit had not been resolved as of early 2006, when the petitioners filed papers that added the U.S. Coast Guard as defendants in the suit for their failure to adequately protect the whales in U.S. waters.

Whale Recovery Plans

Table 5.3 is a table published by the National Marine Fisheries Service in 2004 showing the status of recovery

FIGURE 5.3

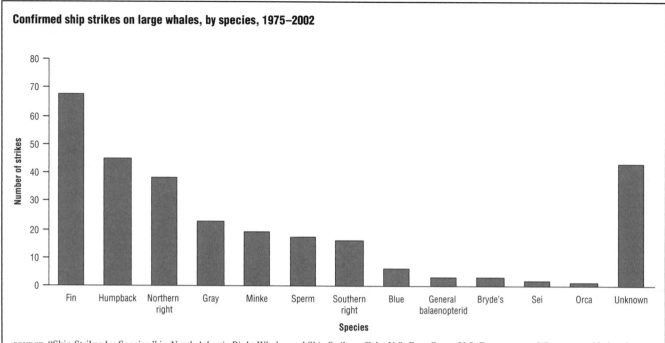

Confirmed ship strikes on large whales, by species, 1975–2002

SOURCE: "Ship Strikes by Species," in *North Atlantic Right Whales and Ship Strikes off the U.S. East Coast*, U.S. Department of Commerce, National Oceanic and Atmospheric Administration, National Marine Fisheries Service, Northeast Fisheries Science Center, June 2, 2004, http://nefsc.noaa.gov/press_release/2004/advisory04.02.pdf (accessed February 11, 2006)

FIGURE 5.4

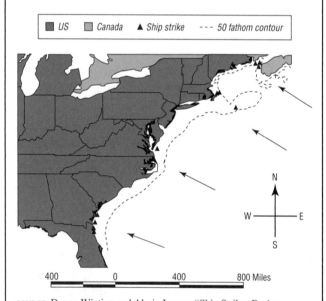

Locations of confirmed ship strikes on North Atlantic right whales, 1990–2000

SOURCE: Donna Wieting and Aleria Jensen, "Ship Strikes During 1990–2000: North Atlantic Right Whales," in *NOAA Fisheries' Proposed Strategy to Reduce Ship Strikes of North Atlantic Right Whales*, U.S. Department of Commerce, National Oceanic and Atmospheric Administration, National Marine Fisheries Service, Office of Protected Resources, 2004, http://www.nmfs.noaa.gov/pr/pdfs/shipstrike/ss_meetings.pdf (accessed March 28, 2006)

plans for endangered whale species. As of February 2006 no recovery plans had been developed for bowhead or sperm whales. A draft recovery plan was published in 1998 for fin and sei whales and is undergoing revision. A recovery plan for the Pacific population of the northern right whale is under development. Final plans have been published for the blue whale (1998), humpback whale (1991), and the Atlantic population of the northern right whale (2005).

Table 5.3 also shows the recovery priority numbers assigned by the NMFS to each endangered whale species. Priority numbers can range from a value of 1 (highest priority) to 12 (lowest priority). The northern right whale has a priority level of 1, indicating strong concern about its abundance and chances for survival as a species.

The recovery plan for the North Atlantic right whale lists five goals for recovering the species. In order of importance, the goals are:

- Significantly reduce sources of human-caused death, injury and disturbance

- Develop recovery criteria based on demographic criteria

- Identify, characterize, protect, and monitor important habitats

TABLE 5.3

Endangered and threatened whale species in the United States, 2004

Species/ESU/DPS[a]	Date listed reclassified	Endangered Species Act status	Population/ ESU[a] trend	Recovery priority number[b]	Status of recovery plan
Whales					
Blue whale	6/2/1970	Endangered	Increasing	7	Completed 07/1998
Bowhead whale	6/2/1970	Endangered	Increasing	9	None
Fin whale	6/2/1970	Endangered	Unknown	7	Draft completed 07/1998—under revision
Humpback whale	6/2/1970	Endangered	Increasing	3	Completed 11/1991
Northern right whale[c]	6/2/1970	Endangered	Unknown	1	Completed 12/1991 *(Atlantic)*, draft revision completed 2004; under development *(Pacific)*
Sei whale	6/2/1970	Endangered	Unknown	3	Draft completed 07/1998—under revision
Sperm whale	6/2/1970	Endangered	Unknown	7	None

[a]ESU=evolutionarily significant unit; DPS=distinct population segment.
[b]Recovery priority numbers are designated according to guidelines published by the National Marine Fisheries Service (NMFS) on June 15, 1990 (55 FR 24296). Priorities are designated from 1 (high) to 12 (low) based on the following factors: degree of threat, recovery potential, and conflict with development projects or other economic activity.
[c]During the timeframe for this report (2002–2004), two separate endangered species of right whale in the Northern Hemisphere were listed: the North Atlantic right whale (Eubalaena glacialis) and the North Pacific right whale (Eubalaena japonica). In January 2005, NMFS published a final rule to remove this distinction, thereby reverting to the previously used taxonomy of one endangered species—the northern right whale (Eubalaena glacialis)—for both North Pacific and North Atlantic populations. This report, therefore, uses the taxonomy at time of publication (northern right whale), noting that the taxonomic split may be reinstated in the future pending an upcoming status review and following ESA listing procedures.

SOURCE: Adapted from "Table 1. ESA-Listed Species under NMFS' Jurisdiction Including Listing Status, Trends, Priority Numbers, and Recovery Plan Status," in *Biennial Report to Congress on the Recovery Program for Threatened and Endangered Species (October 1, 2002–September 30, 2004)*, U.S. Department of Commerce, National Oceanic and Atmospheric Administration, National Marine Fisheries Service, Office of Protected Resources, 2004, http://www.nmfs.noaa.gov/pr/readingrm/ESABiennial/bien04.pdf (accessed February 14, 2006)

- Monitor the status and trends of abundance and distribution of the whale population

- Coordinate federal, state, local, international and private efforts to implement the recovery plan

DOLPHINS AND PORPOISES

Dolphins and porpoises are toothed cetaceans. They are similar in shape; however, dolphins are generally larger than porpoises and prefer shallower, warmer waters. Dolphins tend to have long bottlenoses and cone-shaped teeth, as opposed to the flatter noses and teeth found in porpoises. Porpoises are members of the Phocoenidae family, which includes only six existing species. Dolphins are members of the Delphinidae family, a large family containing at least thirty known species. Most dolphin and porpoise populations around the world are hardy and not in danger of extinction. However, there are several species that are in trouble due to limited geographical distribution.

There are no U.S. species of dolphin or porpoises listed under the ESA. There are three foreign species listed as endangered as shown in Table 5.1: the Chinese River dolphin, the Indus River dolphin, and the cochito. The Chinese River and Indus River dolphins live in freshwater rivers in China and Pakistan, respectively. Their numbers are considered to be extremely small. In both cases extensive river damming, water drawdown due to human consumption, fishing, and pollution are blamed for the declines.

The cochito (or vaquita) is a kind of porpoise found only in the Gulf of California, a narrow body of water that separates the western Mexican mainland from the Baja California peninsula. This stretch of water is known in the United States as the Sea of Cortez and contains a great diversity of sea life. Cochitos are among the rarest of all marine mammals. According to the NMFS the cochito species has been nearly eliminated because so many of the animals have become entangled in fishing lines and drowned.

Protection of Prevalent Dolphins

Although they are not considered endangered or threatened, dolphins receive special consideration under U.S. law because of public concern about them. Dolphins are believed to be highly intelligent. They have a high encephalization quotient, perhaps the highest of any animal, besides humans. In addition, many people have been exposed to dolphins through marine entertainment parks, movies, television shows, and even personal encounters and sightings at tourist beaches. As a result, there is widespread public fondness for the animals.

Dolphins are protected by the Marine Mammal Protection Act and laws designed to limit their capture during tuna fishing. In 1990 large U.S. tuna canning companies announced they would no longer purchase tuna caught in a manner that endangered dolphins. The companies began labeling their products "Dolphin Safe" if their practices met specific standards established by the U.S. government. The International Dolphin

Conservation Program Act, passed in 1992, reduced the number of legally permitted dolphin deaths. This act also made the United States a dolphin-safe zone in 1994, when it became illegal to sell, buy, or ship tuna products obtained using methods that kill dolphins.

SEALS AND SEA LIONS

Seals, sea lions, and walruses are considered pinnipeds. This designation comes from the Latin word *pinnipedia*, which means "feather or fin foot." Pinnipeds have fin-like flippers. Although they spend most of their time in the ocean, pinnipeds come on shore to rest, breed, give birth, and nurse their young. Areas preferred for breeding, birthing, and nursing are called rookeries. Pinnipeds not yet of reproductive age congregate at shore areas known as "haul-outs."

Seals and sea lions were hunted extensively during the 1800s and early 1900s for their blubber, fur, and meat. They continue to be imperiled by human encroachment of haul-out beaches, entanglement in marine debris and fishing nets, incidental catches, disease, and lack of food due to competition from humans for prey species.

Imperiled Seal and Sea Lion Populations

As of February 2006 there were four U.S. species and two foreign species of seals and sea lions listed under the ESA as shown in Table 5.1. The species are Caribbean monk seal, Guadalupe fur seal, Hawaiian monk seal, Mediterranean monk seal, Saimaa seal, and Steller sea lion. However, the Caribbean monk seal has not been sighted since 1952 and is presumed by the NMFS to be extinct.

GUADALUPE FUR SEALS. The Guadalupe fur seal breeds along the eastern coast of Isla de Guadalupe, Mexico. The island is approximately 400 miles west of Baja California. Although populations once included as many as 20,000 to 100,000 individuals, decline and endangerment resulted from extensive fur hunting in the 1700s and 1800s. The species was believed extinct in the early twentieth century, but a small population was discovered in 1954. NMFS scientists believe that the population is now on the increase.

HAWAIIAN MONK SEALS. Hawaiian monk seals are the only pinnipeds found on Hawaii and are endemic to those islands—that is, they occur nowhere else on Earth. Hunting was the primary cause of population decline. Hawaiian monk seals are also extremely sensitive to human activity and disturbance and now breed exclusively on the remote northwestern Hawaiian Islands, which are not inhabited by humans. Most females give birth to a single pup every two years, a reproductive rate lower than other pinniped species. The seals also fall prey to shark attacks and mobbing, violent mating acts perpetuated by adult male seals on females and pups of both sexes. Mobbing can result in fatal wounds or drowning. Scientists monitoring seal populations have relocated males guilty of repeated mobbing. The National Marine Fisheries Service Web site (http://www.nmfs.noaa.gov/) estimates the species population at around 1,400 animals.

MEDITERRANEAN MONK SEALS. Mediterranean monk seals inhabit remote areas around the Mediterranean Sea and northwest African coast. Most are found off the coasts of Mauritania/Western Sahara, Greece, and Turkey. According to the Seal Conservation Society there are only about 300 of the seals believed to be in existence. Mediterranean monk seals are very sensitive to disturbance. As humans have encroached on beaches and coastal areas, the seals have retreated to isolated caves.

In 1997 there was a massive die-off in a colony of the seals near Mauritania. The exact cause is not known; however, a virus or "red tide" event is generally blamed. This was a severe blow to the seal population. The animals are also purposely killed by fishermen, who consider them a nuisance and competition for limited fish stocks. Scientists fear that Mediterranean monk seals could become extinct with a few decades.

SAIMAA SEALS. Saimaa seals are found only in the cold waters of the Saimaa Lake system in eastern Finland. Their numbers were decimated by hunting over the centuries to the point of extinction. However, protection measures and fishing restrictions allowed some measure of recovery. In 2005 the World Wildlife Fund estimated that there were approximately 250 Saimaa seals remaining, making them one of the most endangered species in the world. Although the number of seals has been slowly increasing, they are still imperiled by entanglement in fishing nets when they leave protected areas of the lake.

STELLER SEA LIONS. Steller sea lions are large animals, with males reaching a length of about eleven feet and weight of 2,500 pounds. Females are significantly smaller. Steller sea lions are found in Pacific waters from Japan to central California, but most populations breed near Alaska and the Aleutian Islands. The breeding season is from May through July. The species was named after George Wilhelm Steller, a German scientist who studied the animals when he accompanied Russian explorer Vitus Bering on an expedition to Alaska in 1741.

The Steller sea lion population is divided into two stocks as shown in Figure 5.5. The eastern stock inhabits the area east of Cape Suckling, Alaska, and extends down the west coast of Canada and the U.S. mainland. The western stock is found west of Cape Suckling and extends across the Aleutian Islands to Russia and Japan.

According to the National Marine Fisheries Service, the western stock declined by 75% between 1976 and 1990. In April 1990 the Steller sea lion was listed under

FIGURE 5.5

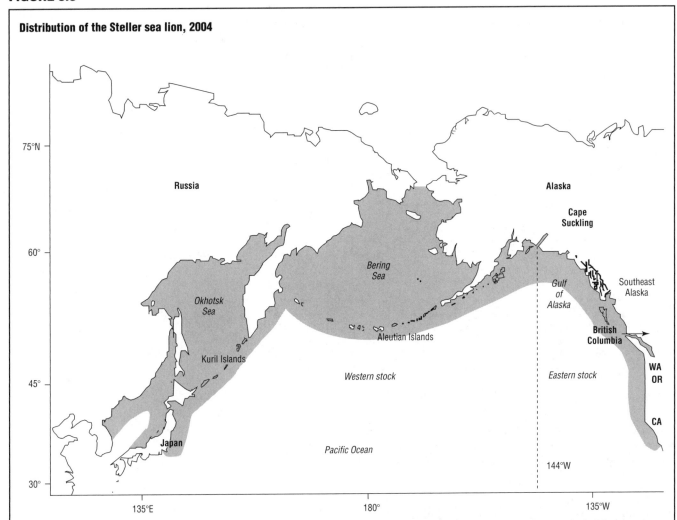

Distribution of the Steller sea lion, 2004

SOURCE: "Steller Sea Lion Distribution," in *Steller Sea Lion Research*, U.S. Department of Commerce, National Oceanic and Atmospheric Administration, National Marine Mammal Laboratory, March 8, 2004, http://nmml.afsc.noaa.gov/AlaskaEcosystems/sslhome/distrib.htm (accessed February 9, 2006)

the ESA as threatened. Over the following decade the western stock continued to decline. This stock was declared endangered in 1997. The eastern stock increased at a rate of approximately 3% per year from the 1980s to the 1990s as shown in Figure 5.6. This stock remains classified as threatened.

Steller sea lion populations have declined for a variety of reasons including bycatch, illegal and legal hunting, predation, and disease. In addition, scientists believe that the animal has experienced reduced productivity due to the indirect effects of climate change and competition from humans for prey species (food fish).

In February 2004 the North Pacific Universities Marine Mammal Consortium reported that population declines may be explained by the fact that Steller sea lions had switched from eating fatty fish to fish with low fat content. In particular, their diet now consists primarily of pollock and flatfish, rather than herring. The low fat content of the new diet prevents Steller sea lions from

building up enough blubber to survive and reproduce in their cold aquatic habitat.

The NMFS has conducted surveys of Steller sea lion populations since 1985. These surveys are primarily aerial. The most popular rookeries and haul-outs are photographed from the air, and the animals are counted from examination of detailed photographs. During the summer of 2005 the first Alaska-wide aerial pup count was conducted. The results are shown in Figure 5.7 for target rookeries in the Gulf of Alaska and the Aleutian Islands. Pup populations have declined dramatically since the 1980s. However, the numbers appeared to level off during the early 2000s.

As shown in Table 5.2 species-specific expenditures under the ESA for Steller sea lions totaled $42.6 million in fiscal year 2004, accounting for 60% of expenditures on all marine mammals. The Steller sea lion ranked third in spending among all species covered by the ESA. (See Table 2.8 in Chapter 2.)

FIGURE 5.6

FIGURE 5.7

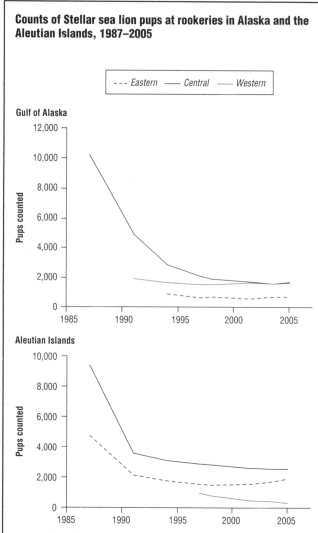

Trends in Steller sea lion populations, through 2005

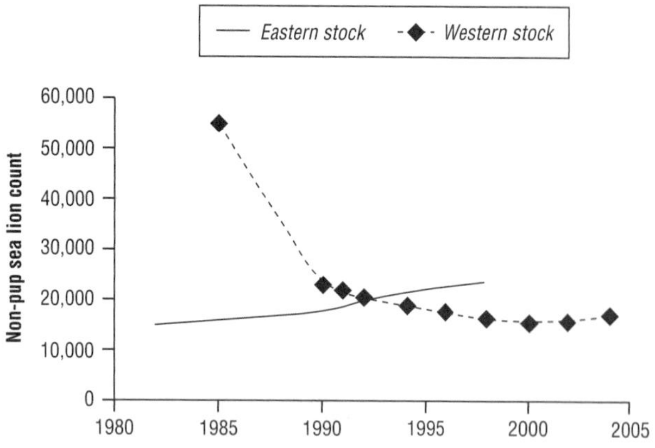

— Eastern stock - ♦ - Western stock

SOURCE: "Steller Sea Lion Decline," in *Steller Sea Lion Research*, U.S. Department of Commerce, National Oceanic and Atmospheric Administration, National Marine Mammal Laboratory, August 1, 2005, http://nmml.afsc.noaa.gov/AlaskaEcosystems/sslhome/DECLINE.htm (accessed February 9, 2006)

Counts of Stellar sea lion pups at rookeries in Alaska and the Aleutian Islands, 1987–2005

- - - Eastern — Central — Western

Gulf of Alaska

Aleutian Islands

SOURCE: Lowell Fritz, Tom Gelatt, Charles Stinchcomb, and Wayne Perryman, "Figure 3. Steller Sea Lion Pup Counts at Trend Rookeries in the Range of the Western Stock in Alaska by Region from the Late 1980s to 2005 in the Gulf of Alaska (A) and Aleutian Islands (B)," in *Memorandum: Steller Sea Lion Pup Counts, June–July 2005*, U.S. Department of Commerce, National Oceanic and Atmospheric Administration, National Marine Fisheries Service, Northeast Fisheries Science Center, October 20, 2005, http://nmml.afsc.noaa.gov/ AlaskaEcosystems/sslhome/sslpdf/SSLPupCount2005Memo.pdf (accessed February 11, 2006)

Recovery Plans for Seals and Sea Lions

Table 5.4 shows the status of recovery plans for endangered seal and sea lion species as of February 2006. No plans have been developed for Caribbean monk seals (which are believed to be extinct) or Guadalupe fur seals. A recovery plan published in 1983 for the Hawaiian monk seal is currently being revised. Likewise, a plan published in 1992 for the eastern and western stocks of the Steller sea lion is also being revised.

Table 5.4 also shows the recovery priority numbers assigned by the NMFS to each endangered seal and sea lion species. Priority numbers can range from a value of 1 (highest priority) to 12 (lowest priority). The Hawaiian monk seal has a priority level of 1, indicating strong concern about its abundance and chances for survival as a species.

SEA OTTERS

Sea otters are the smallest marine mammals in North America. They are furry creatures that grow to be about four feet in length and weigh up to sixty-five pounds. Otters are related to weasels and mink and are members of the *Mustelidae* family. Sea otters are almost entirely aquatic and inhabit relativly shallow waters along rocky coasts of the North Pacific Ocean. They eat a wide variety of marine invertebrate. Sea otters are the only animals, besides primates, known to use tools. They use rocks and other objects to smash open the hard shells of clams and crabs to get the meat inside.

Although they inhabit cold waters, sea otters do not have a blubber layer to keep them warm. Instead, they have extremely dense fur coats and high metabolism rates. Their fur coats are waterproof, but only if kept clean. This makes sea otters very susceptible to water contaminants, such as oil.

Imperiled Otter Populations

At one time sea otters were very populous along the entire U.S. West Coast from Southern California to Alaska. Their thick and lustrous fur made them a target of intesive hunting for many centuries. By the dawn of the twentieth century sea otters were on the brink of

TABLE 5.4

Endangered and threatened seal and sea lion species in the United States, February 2006

Species/ESU/DPS[a]	Date listed reclassified	Endangered Species Act status	Population/ ESU[a] trend	Recovery priority number[b]	Status of recovery plan
Seals and sea lions					
Caribbean monk seal	3/11/1967	Endangered	Presumed extinct	12	None
Guadalupe fur seal	12/16/1985	Threatened	Increasing	10	None
Hawaiian monk seal	11/23/1976	Endangered	Declining	1	Completed 03/1983; under revision
Stellar sea lion —eastern distinct population segment (DPS)	4/10/1990; 11/26/1990; 5/5/97[c]	Threatened	Increasing	10	Completed 12/1992; under revision
Stellar sea lion —western distinct population segment (DPS)	4/10/1990; 11/26/1990; 5/5/97[c]	Endangered	Declining	7	Completed 12/1992; under revision

[a]ESU=evolutionarily significant unit; DPS=distinct population segment.
[b]Recovery priority numbers are designated according to guidelines published by the National Marine Fisheries Service (NMFS) on June 15, 1990 (55 FR 24296). Priorities are designated from 1 (high) to 12 (low) based on the following factors: degree of threat, recovery potential, and conflict with development projects or other economic activity.
[c]This species was first listed as threatened via a 240-day emergency rule on 4/10/1990, then officially listed as threatened in a final rule on 11/26/1990. NMFS separated the species into western and eastern DPSs via a final rule on 5/5/1997, which maintained the eastern DPS as threatened and reclassified the western DPS as endangered.

SOURCE: Adapted from "Table 1. ESA-Listed Species under NMFS' Jurisdiction Including Listing Status, Trends, Priority Numbers, and Recovery Plan Status," in *Biennial Report to Congress on the Recovery Program for Threatened and Endangered Species (October 1, 2002–September 30, 2004)*, U.S. Department of Commerce, National Oceanic and Atmospheric Administration, National Marine Fisheries Service, Office of Protected Resources, 2004, http://www.nmfs.noaa .gov/pr/readingrm/ESABiennial/bien04.pdf (accessed February 14, 2006)

extinction. In 1911 they became protected under the International Fur Seal Treaty and their numbers began to increase. By the mid-1980s there were approximately 110,000 to 148,000 sea otters around the world. Nearly half lived in the Aleutian Islands off the coast of Alaska. A much smaller population survived off the California coast.

Figure 5.8 shows the distribution of sea otters in 1995. Biologists recognize two distinct populations. The northern sea otter extends from Russia across the Aleutian Islands and the coast of Alaska south to the state of Washington. The southern sea otter is found only off the California coast.

Beginning in the 1960s the U.S. Fish and Wildlife Service began translocating (moving) limited numbers of sea otters from established locations to new locations within their traditional range of distribution. Attempted translocations to Oregon failed; however, translocated colonies were established at four locations: southeast Alaska, Washington, and San Nicolas Island, California, in the United States, and Vancouver, British Columbia, in Canada. (See Figure 5.8.)

SOUTHERN SEA OTTERS. Southern (or California) sea otters were designated a threatened species in 1977. At that time the animals inhabited a small stretch of coastline in central California. Scientists feared that this isolated population was in grave danger of being wiped out by a single catastrophe, such as an oil spill. In 1987 the U.S. Fish and Wildlife Service decided to establish an

FIGURE 5.8

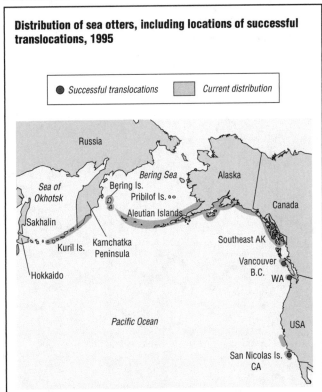

Distribution of sea otters, including locations of successful translocations, 1995

SOURCE: James L. Bodkin, Ronald J. Jameson, and James A. Estes, "Fig.1b. Current Distribution of Sea Otters Including Locations of Successful Translocations," in "Alaska," *Our Living Resources: A Report to the Nation on the Distribution, Abundance, and Health of U.S. Plants, Animals, and Ecosystems*, U.S. Department of the Interior, U.S. Geological Survey, National Biological Service, 1995, http:// biology.usgs.gov/s+t/pdf/Alaska.pdf (accessed March 1, 2006) "experimental population" of sea otters at another location. Over the next few years 140 sea otters were moved, a few at a time, to San Nicolas Island. It was hoped that these translocated animals would thrive and develop an independent growing colony. Unfortunately, the venture achieved only limited success. Many of the otters swam back to their original habitat; others died, apparently from the stress of moving. During the early 1990s the transport effort was abandoned. The FWS spent $3.8 million on the program between 1987 and 1995.

In October 2005 the U.S. Fish and Wildlife Service proposed officially ending the translocation program and removing the designation of "experimental population" for the thirty or so sea otters remaining at San Nicolas Island. These animals would be considered threatened under the ESA, just like their fellow southern sea otters. The FWS collected comments on this proposal and expected to make a final decision in 2006.

Figure 5.9 shows annual survey results for southern sea otter populations from 1983 through 2005. These surveys were conducted during the springtime and count both independent otters and pups. As indicated in Figure 5.9 the populations have been gradually increasing. In spring 2005 just over 2,700 otters were counted (2,417 independent otters and 318 pups).

In 2005 the U.S. Geological Survey (USGS) reported that the California otter population declined during the late 1990s for a surprising reason. The USGS National Wildlife Health Center found that more than 40% of otter deaths occurring between 1992 and 2002 were the result of parasitic, fungal, or bacterial infections. (See Figure 5.10.) Toxicological analyses indicated that the immune systems of the animals had been damaged by water pollutants, particularly butyltins and organochlorine compounds, such as polychlorinated biphenyls (PCBs). Butyltins are tin compounds widely used as wood preservatives and as a component of ship paints.

A revised recovery plan was issued for threatened southern sea otters in 2003. The primary recovery objective is management of human acitivities that could damage or destroy habitat (for example, oil spills). The plan notes that southern sea otters can be considered for delisting under the ESA when the average population level over a three-year period exceeds 3,090 animals. As shown in Figure 5.9 population trends through 2005 are encouraging. Absent of any catastrophic events, the

FIGURE 5.9

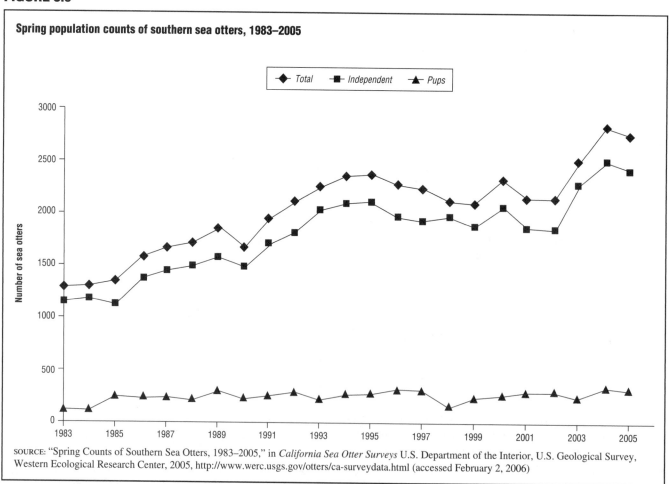

SOURCE: "Spring Counts of Southern Sea Otters, 1983–2005," in *California Sea Otter Surveys* U.S. Department of the Interior, U.S. Geological Survey, Western Ecological Research Center, 2005, http://www.werc.usgs.gov/otters/ca-surveydata.html (accessed February 2, 2006)

FIGURE 5.10

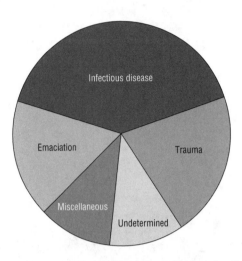

Causes of mortality in southern sea otters, 1992–2002

Sample size=312

SOURCE: Nancy Thomas, "Causes of Mortality in Southern Sea Otters," in *Sea Otter Mortality*, U.S. Department of the Interior, U.S. Geological Survey, National Wildlife Health Center, May 2005, http://www.nwhc .usgs.gov/publications/fact_sheets/pdfs/SeaOtter2005.pdf (accessed March 9, 2006)

TABLE 5.5

Survey results for sea otter populations in southwest Alaska, 1986–2001

Location	Year	Count or estimate	Decline
Aleutian Islands	1992	8,044	
	2000	2,442	70%
North Alaska peninsula	1986	9,061–13,091	
	2000	5,756	36–56%
South Alaska peninsula	1986	15,346–17,835	
	2001	1,344	91–92%
Kodiak Archipelago	1989	13,526	
	1994	9,817	
	2001	5,893	56%

SOURCE: "Table 1. Southwest Alaska Sea Otter Survey Results, 1986–2001," in *Sea Otter Declines in Southwest Alaska: A Growing Concern*, U.S. Department of the Interior, U.S. Fish and Wildlife Service, October 2001, http://alaska.fws.gov/media/sotter/declineotter.pdf (accessed February 13, 2006)

southern sea otter could achieve delisting within the next decade.

SOUTHWEST ALASKA DISTINCT POPULATION SEGMENT (DPS). Translocations of northern sea otters to southeast Alaska, British Columbia, and Washington established thriving colonies in those areas. Likewise, populations in south central Alaska are believed to be stable or increasing. However, the stock of sea otters in southwest Alaska has experienced severe decline. In August 2005 the U.S. Fish and Wildlife Service listed the southwest Alaska distinct population segment (DPS) of the northern sea otter as "threatened" under the ESA.

The southwest Alaska DPS extends from the tip of the Aleutian Islands to a point roughly beneath the letter "A" in the word "Alaska" in Figure 5.8. Populations in this area have decreased dramatically since the mid-1980s, when more than 70,000 sea otters inhabited southwest Alaska. Table 5.5 shows the decline in sea otter populations across the region since the 1980s and early 1990s. According to Douglas Burn in "Alaska Sea Otters: The Southwest Decline Continues" (February 2004, http://alaska.fws.gov/media/seaotter2004/fact-sheet.pdf), surveys conducted in 2003 in the Aleutian Islands found that sea otter counts were down by 63% from the year 2000. Scientists are not sure of the reasons for the decline; however, there is suspicion that orca whales are preying on the otters.

Foreign Species of Sea Otters

As shown in Table 5.1 there were five foreign otter species listed as endangered under the ESA as of February 2006. They populate areas of Africa and South America. All species are imperiled by illegal hunting for meat and fur. Loss of habitat and water pollution are also threats to their survival. The southern river otter of South America is in dire danger of extinction. According to the International Union for Conservation of Nature and Natural Resources' *IUCN Red List of Threatened Species*, the species is found in only a handful of isolated areas, all of which are threatened by massive deforestation and expanding fishing operations.

MANATEES AND DUGONGS

Manatees are large stout mammals that inhabit fresh waters and coastal waterways. They are from the Sirenian order, along with dugongs. There are only five Sirenian species, and all are endangered or extinct. Scientists believe that Steller's sea cow, the only species of cold-water manatee, was hunted to extinction during the 1700s.

The West Indian manatee, also known as the Florida manatee, primarily swims in the rivers, bays, and estuaries of Florida and surrounding states. (See Figure 5.11.) As shown in Table 5.1 this species is listed as endangered under the ESA.

Manatees are often called "sea cows" and can reach weights of up to 2,000 pounds. They swim just below the surface of the water and feed on vegetation. West Indian manatees migrate north in the summer, though generally no farther than the North Carolina coast. In 1995 a manatee nicknamed "Chessie" made headlines by swimming all the way to Chesapeake Bay. Eventually biologists, concerned about his health in cooler waters, had him airlifted back to Florida. During the winter many manatees huddle around warm water discharges from

FIGURE 5.11

A Florida manatee nurses its calves. (© Douglas Faulkner/Corbis. Reproduced by permission.)

power plants and other industrial facilities. Although this can keep them warm, scientists worry that overcrowding in small areas makes the animals more susceptible to sickness.

Imperiled Manatee Populations

Each year during cold weather biologists conduct surveys to determine the number of Florida manatees remaining in the wild. The numbers are estimates based on surveys conducted at known wintering habitats. The latest survey was performed in January 2005 and found 3,143 manatees living along the Florida coast. This number is up from 1,267 reported in 1991. Many manatees have scars on their backs from motorboat propellers—these allow individual manatees to be recognized. In a press release entitled "FWC Biologists Release Preliminary 2005 Manatee Mortality Data" (January 6, 2006, http://www.floridamarine.org/news/view_article.asp?id=26330), the Florida Fish and Wildlife Conservation Commission noted that "the manatee population appears to be doing fairly well" throughout much of the state. Populations in the northern and central parts of Florida are increasing or remaining stable. However, manatees in southwest Florida face extra threats due to their exposure to red tide incidents (proliferation of harmful algae in the water). Scientists warn that these populations "could decline significantly."

Threats to Manatees

Manatees are imperiled for a variety of reasons. Although they can live for fifty or sixty years, their birth rate is low. Mature females bear a single offspring only every three to five years. Many baby manatees die in the womb or soon after birth for unknown reasons. These are called perinatal fatalities. Disease, natural pathogens, and cold water temperatures are also deadly. However, motorboat strikes are the major documented cause of manatee mortalities. Manatees are large and swim slowly at the surface of the water. They often cannot move away from boats quickly enough to avoid being hit. Environmentalists have tried to protect manatees from boat collisions, and have successfully had several Florida waterways declared boat-free zones. There are also areas where boaters are required to lower their speeds.

During 1995 and 1996 a pneumonia-like virus killed more than 100 manatees in southern Florida. The disease, according to marine microbiologist John H. Paul and his colleagues, was caused by a red tide that occurred when toxin-producing aquatic organisms called *dinoflagellates* bloomed in large quantities ("A Filterable Lytic Agent Obtained from a Red Tide Bloom That Caused Lysis of *Karenia Brevis* [*Gymnodinum breve*] Cultures," *Aquatic Microbial Ecology*, 2002). The Florida Marine Research Institute reported in 2006 that human-related activity accounted for 30% of all manatee deaths between April 1974 and June 2005, most from watercraft collisions. (See Figure 5.12.) The cause of death could not be determined in 28% of the cases. Nonhuman causes were blamed for 42% of the deaths.

A lawsuit by the Save the Manatee Club and other environmental and conservation organizations in 2000 successfully required the state to implement new low-speed zones for boats and establish safe-haven areas for manatees. The rules were immediately challenged by individual boaters and boating organizations; however, the restrictions were upheld by Florida courts in 2002.

Foreign Manatee and Dugong Species

There are two surviving foreign species of manatees found in western Africa and in and around the Amazon River in South America. Both species are designated under the ESA as endangered and are in grave danger of extinction due to illegal hunting, deforestation, habitat destruction, and water pollution. The only remaining dugongs live in the coastal waters of the Indian Ocean and Pacific Ocean. Their populations are also considered imperiled. Dugongs around the tiny island of Palau in the western Pacific Ocean are considered endangered under the ESA.

FIGURE 5.12

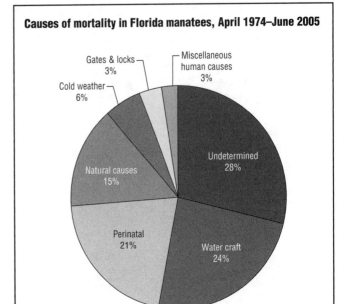

Causes of mortality in Florida manatees, April 1974–June 2005

Gates & locks 3%
Miscellaneous human causes 3%
Cold weather 6%
Undetermined 28%
Natural causes 15%
Perinatal 21%
Water craft 24%

Note: Total mortalities: 5,560 manatees.

SOURCE: Adapted from "Summary Report by County, Month, Year and Probable Cause of Death," in *Manatee Mortality Database*, Florida Fish and Wildlife Conservation Commission, Fish and Wildlife Research Institute, 2005, http://research.myfwc.com/manatees/ (accessed January 20, 2006)

CHAPTER 6
FISH, CLAMS, SNAILS, AND CRUSTACEANS

Fish, clams, snails, and crustaceans are aquatic creatures. Fish are vertebrates, meaning they have an internal skeleton made of bone or cartilage. Clams, snails, and crustaceans are invertebrates.

FISH

Fish are cold-blooded vertebrates with fins. They occur in nearly all permanent water environments, from deep oceans to remote alpine lakes and desert springs. Marine fish inhabit the salty waters of oceans and seas. Freshwater fish inhabit inland rivers, lakes, and ponds. Anadromous fish are born in freshwater, migrate to the ocean to spend their adulthood, and then return to freshwater to spawn.

Fish are the most diverse vertebrate group on the planet and include thousands of different species. The largest known fish are the whale sharks, which can grow to be in excess of fifty feet long and weigh several tons. At the other end of the spectrum is *Paedocypris progenetica*, a tiny fish discovered in Sumatra, Indonesia, that is less than one-third of an inch in length.

FishBase (http://filaman.ifm-geomar.de/home.htm) is a comprehensive online database of scientific information about fish. It was developed by the WorldFish Center of Malaysia in collaboration with the Food and Agriculture Organization of the United Nations and is supported by many government and research institutions. As of February 2006 FishBase contains information on 29,300 fish species around the world, a number it calls "practically all fish species known to science." Scientists report that only a small fraction of these species have been assessed for their conservation status.

The U.S. Fish and Wildlife Service (FWS) listed a total of eighty-five endangered and forty-three threatened fish species in the United States as of February 2006. Nearly $475 million was spent under the Endangered Species Act (ESA) during fiscal year 2004 on imperiled fish.

General Threats to Fish

Fish species have become endangered and threatened in the United States for a variety of reasons, both natural and anthropogenic (caused by humans). Some scientists believe that natural threats, such as disease, have been aggravated by human actions that stress fish populations. Dams and other structures used for power generation, flood control, irrigation, and navigation have dramatically changed water flow patterns in many rivers. These impediments disrupt migration patterns and affect water temperature and quality. Likewise, dredging of river and stream beds to produce channels and filling of wetlands and swamps have changed water habitats.

Large nonnative fish species introduced to water bodies to improve recreational fishing prey on small imperiled fish and compete with large imperiled fish for food and space. Crowding also leads to uncharacteristic mating between fish species. This phenomenon results in hybrid offspring, some of which are sterile (cannot reproduce).

Many river and stream banks and adjacent lands have been stripped of vegetation by timber harvesting, crop growing, and excessive grazing of livestock. This eliminates habitat for insects and other tiny creatures that serve as foodstuff for fish. It also aggravates erosion problems and allows large amounts of dirt and silt to enter the water, effectively smothering the fish. In agricultural areas there is runoff of manure, fertilizers, and pesticides. Discharges of sewage and storm water contain high levels of biological contaminants. Industrial pollution introduces metal and organic chemicals to water bodies. Although not typically lethal, chemical and biological pollutants stress the immune systems of fish, placing them at greater risk of disease.

Imperiled Freshwater Fish

Freshwater fish listed under the Endangered Species Act are under the jurisdiction of the U.S. Fish and Wildlife Service. They include a wide variety of species and are found all over the country. The U.S. Geological Survey (USGS) estimates that the United States contains approximately 800 native freshwater species. Although most of these species are found in the eastern part of the country, the highest percentages of imperiled fish species are in the western states. According to the USGS this is because aquatic ecosystems in the western United States, particularly in the Southwest, have very high rates of endemism (that is, species found there are particular to that location).

Table 6.1 provides information about the freshwater fish species listed as endangered or threatened under the ESA as of February 2006. Most of the species have recovery plans in place. In general, imperiled freshwater fish are small in size and associated with flowing (lotic) waters, such as rivers and streams, rather than still (lentic) waters, such as lakes and ponds. Nearly half of the listed freshwater fish fall into four species groups: darters, chubs, daces, and shiners.

Table 6.2 shows the ten freshwater species with the highest expenditures under the ESA during fiscal year 2004. More than $45 million was spent on only two of the fish, the bull trout ($32.6 million) and the pallid sturgeon ($13.4 million).

BULL TROUT. Bull trout are relatively large fish that live in streams, lakes, and rivers. They can grow to weigh more than twenty pounds; however, those that inhabit small streams seldom exceed four pounds in weight. Bull trout are members of the char subgroup of the salmon family (Salmonidae). (See Figure 6.1.) Their backs are dark in color (green to brown) with small light-colored spots (crimson to yellow), while their undersides are pale. The fish prefer very cold and clean inland waters in the Northwest.

Historically bull trout were found throughout much of the northwestern United States and as far north as Alaska. Large populations have disappeared from major rivers, leaving mostly isolated pockets of smaller-sized fish in headwater streams. A variety of factors have contributed to the decline of the bull trout. The species is very sensitive to changes in water temperature and purity. Its survival is threatened by water pollution, degraded habitat, and dams and other diversion structures. In addition, introduction of a nonnative game fish called brook trout has been devastating. The two species are able to mate, but produce mostly sterile offspring—a genetic dead-end for the imperiled bull trout.

The legal history of the bull trout is extensive. In 1992 three environmental groups petitioned the U.S. Fish and Wildlife Service to list the fish as an endangered species under the ESA. In 1993 the agency concluded that listing for the species was warranted, but low in priority compared to other work of the FWS. This set off a long series of court battles that culminated in 1999 when all bull trout in the coterminous United States were listed as threatened under the ESA. In 2001 two of the original petitioners (Alliance for the Wild Rockies, Inc. and Friends of the Wild Swan, Inc.) filed a lawsuit against the FWS for failing to designate critical habitat for the bull trout. A settlement was reached in 2002. In September 2005 the FWS designated critical habitat for the bull trout as follows:

- Idaho—294 stream miles and 50,627 acres of lakes or reservoirs

- Montana—1,058 stream miles and 31,916 acres of lakes or reservoirs

- Oregon—939 stream miles and 27,322 acres of lakes or reservoirs

- Oregon/Idaho—17 stream miles

- Washington—1,519 stream miles, 33,353 acres of lakes or reservoirs, and 985 miles of marine shoreline

The shaded river basins in Figure 6.2 were designated as critical habitat. The unshaded river basins were considered, but excluded from the final ruling.

PALLID STURGEON. The pallid sturgeon is a unique and rare freshwater fish. The Fish and Wildlife Service calls it "the swimming dinosaur." It is descended from fishes that were common more than fifty million years ago. The pallid sturgeon has a long flat snout and a slender body that ends with a pronounced tail fin. (See Figure 6.3.) Adults range in size from three to five feet and typically weigh twenty-five to fifty pounds. The fish is a bottom-feeder and prefers large rivers of relatively warm free-flowing water with high turbidity (high mud content).

Historically the pallid sturgeon was found throughout the Mississippi and Missouri River systems from Montana and North Dakota south to the Gulf of Mexico. In the early 1900s specimens as large as eighty-five pounds and six feet long were reported. Over the next century the fish virtually disappeared. In 1990 it was listed under the ESA as endangered. Three years later a recovery plan was published by the FWS. The recovery plan blames human destruction and modification of habitat as the primary cause for the pallid sturgeon's decline.

Figure 6.4 shows the consequences of human alteration on the main stem of the Missouri River, one of the last known habitats of the fish. Forty percent of the river has been channelized (reconfigured to flow in a restricted path). Another 36% has been removed from contention due to construction of earthen dams during the early decades of the 1900s. The last 24% of river habitat has

TABLE 6.1

Endangered and threatened freshwater fish species in the United States, February 2006

Common name	Scientific name	Listing status[a]	Recovery plan date	Recovery plan stage[b]
Alabama cavefish	Speoplatyrhinus poulsoni	E	10/25/1990	RF(2)
Alabama sturgeon	Scaphirhynchus suttkusi	E	None	—
Amber darter	Percina antesella	E	6/20/1986	F
Apache trout	Oncorhynchus apache	T	9/22/1983	RF(1)
Arkansas River shiner	Notropis girardi	T	None	—
Ash Meadows amargosa pupfish	Cyprinodon nevadensis mionectes	E	9/28/1990	F
Ash Meadows speckled dace	Rhinichthys osculus nevadensis	E	9/28/1990	F
Bayou darter	Etheostoma rubrum	T	7/10/1990	RF(1)
Beautiful shiner	Cyprinella formosa	T	3/29/1995	F
Big Bend gambusia	Gambusia gaigei	E	9/19/1984	F
Big Spring spinedace	Lepidomeda mollispinis pratensis	T	1/20/1994	F
Blackside dace	Phoxinus cumberlandensis	T	8/17/1988	F
Blue shiner	Cyprinella caerulea	T	8/30/1995	F
Bluemask (=jewel) darter	Etheostoma species	E	7/25/1997	F
Bonytail chub	Gila elegans	E	8/28/2002	RF(2)
Borax Lake chub	Gila boraxobius	E	2/4/1987	F
Boulder darter	Etheostoma wapiti	E, EXPN	7/27/1989	F
Bull trout	Salvelinus confluentus	T	None	—
Cahaba shiner	Notropis cahabae	E	4/23/1992	F
Cape Fear shiner	Notropis mekistocholas	E	10/7/1988	F
Cherokee darter	Etheostoma scotti	T	11/17/2000	F
Chihuahua chub	Gila nigrescens	T	4/14/1986	F
Clear Creek gambusia	Gambusia heterochir	E	1/14/1982	F
Clover Valley speckled dace	Rhinichthys osculus oligoporus	E	5/12/1998	F
Colorado pikeminnow (=squawfish)	Ptychocheilus lucius	E, EXPN	None	—
Comanche Springs pupfish	Cyprinodon elegans	E	9/2/1981	F
Conasauga logperch	Percina jenkinsi	E	6/20/1986	F
Cui-ui	Chasmistes cujus	E	5/15/1992	RF(2)
Delta smelt	Hypomesus transpacificus	T	11/26/1996	F
Desert dace	Eremichthys acros	T	5/27/1997	F
Desert pupfish	Cyprinodon macularius	E	12/8/1993	F
Devils Hole pupfish	Cyprinodon diabolis	E	9/28/1990	F
Devils River minnow	Dionda diaboli	T	9/13/2005	
Duskytail darter	Etheostoma percnurum	E, EXPN	None	—
Etowah darter	Etheostoma etowahae	E	11/17/2000	F
Foskett speckled dace	Rhinichthys osculus ssp.	T	None	—
Fountain darter	Etheostoma fonticola	E	2/14/1996	RF(1)
Gila chub	Gila intermedia	E	None	—
Gila topminnow (including yaqui)	Poeciliopsis occidentalis	E	None	—
Gila trout	Oncorhynchus gilae	E	9/10/2003	RF(3)
Goldline darter	Percina aurolineata	T	11/17/2000	F
Greenback cutthroat trout	Oncorhynchus clarki stomias	T	3/1/1998	RF(2)
Hiko White River springfish	Crenichthys baileyi grandis	E	5/26/1998	F
Humpback chub	Gila cypha	E	8/28/2002	RF(3)
Hutton tui chub	Gila bicolor ssp.	T	None	—
Independence Valley speckled dace	Rhinichthys osculus lethoporus	E	5/12/1998	F
June sucker	Chasmistes liorus	E	6/25/1999	F
Kendall Warm Springs dace	Rhinichthys osculus thermalis	E	7/12/1982	F
Lahontan cutthroat trout	Oncorhynchus clarki henshawi	T	1/30/1995	F
Leon Springs pupfish	Cyprinodon bovinus	E	8/14/1985	F
Leopard darter	Percina pantherina	T	5/3/1993	RD(1)
Little Colorado spinedace	Lepidomeda vittata	T	1/9/1998	F
Little Kern golden trout	Oncorhynchus aguabonita whitei	T	Exempt	—
Loach minnow	Tiaroga cobitis	T	9/30/1991	F
Lost River sucker	Deltistes luxatus	E	3/17/1993	F
Maryland darter	Etheostoma sellare	E	2/2/1982	F
Moapa dace	Moapa coriacea	E	5/16/1996	RF(1)
Modoc sucker	Catostomus microps	E	Exempt	—
Mohave tui chub	Gila bicolor mohavensis	E	9/12/1984	F
Neosho madtom	Noturus placidus	T	9/30/1991	F
Niangua darter	Etheostoma nianguae	T	7/17/1989	F
Okaloosa darter	Etheostoma okaloosae	E	10/26/1998	RF(1)
Oregon chub	Oregonichthys crameri	E	9/3/1998	F
Owens pupfish	Cyprinodon radiosus	E	9/30/1998	F
Owens tui chub	Gila bicolor snyderi	E	9/30/1998	F
Ozark cavefish	Amblyopsis rosae	T	12/17/1986	F
Pahranagat roundtail chub	Gila robusta jordani	E	5/26/1998	F
Pahrump poolfish	Empetrichthys latos	E	3/17/1980	F
Paiute cutthroat trout	Oncorhynchus clarki seleniris	T	9/10/2004	RF(1)
Palezone shiner	Notropis albizonatus	E	7/7/1997	F
Pallid sturgeon	Scaphirhynchus albus	E	11/7/1993	F

TABLE 6.1

Endangered and threatened freshwater fish species in the United States, February 2006 [CONTINUED]

Common name	Scientific name	Listing status[a]	Recovery plan date	Recovery plan stage[b]
Pecos bluntnose shiner	*Notropis simus pecosensis*	T	9/30/1992	F
Pecos gambusia	*Gambusia nobilis*	E	5/9/1985	F
Pygmy madtom	*Noturus stanauli*	E	9/27/1994	F
Pygmy sculpin	*Cottus paulus (=pygmaeus)*	T	8/6/1991	F
Railroad Valley springfish	*Crenichthys nevadae*	T	3/15/1997	F
Razorback sucker	*Xyrauchen texanus*	E	8/28/2002	RF(1)
Relict darter	*Etheostoma chienense*	E	7/31/1994	D
Rio Grande silvery minnow	*Hybognathus amarus*	E	7/8/1999	F
Roanoke logperch	*Percina rex*	E	3/20/1992	F
San Marcos gambusia	*Gambusia georgei*	E	2/14/1996	RF(1)
Santa Ana sucker	*Catostomus santaanae*	T	None	—
Scioto madtom	*Noturus trautmani*	E	Exempt	—
Shortnose sucker	*Chasmistes brevirostris*	E	3/17/1993	F
Slackwater darter	*Etheostoma boschungi*	T	3/8/1984	F
Slender chub	*Erimystax cahni*	T	7/29/1983	F
Smoky madtom	*Noturus baileyi*	E, EXPN	None	—
Snail darter	*Percina tanasi*	T	5/5/1983	F
Sonora chub	*Gila ditaenia*	T	9/30/1992	F
Spikedace	*Meda fulgida*	T	9/30/1991	F
Spotfin chub	*Erimonax monachus*	EXPN, T	None	—
Tidewater goby	*Eucyclogobius newberryi*	E	None	—
Topeka shiner	*Notropis topeka (=tristis)*	E	None	—
Unarmored threespine stickleback	*Gasterosteus aculeatus williamsoni*	E	12/26/1985	RF(1)
Vermilion darter	*Etheostoma chermocki*	E	7/21/2005	D
Virgin River chub	*Gila seminuda (=robusta)*	E	4/19/1995	RF(2)
Waccamaw silverside	*Menidia extensa*	T	8/11/1993	F
Warm Springs pupfish	*Cyprinodon nevadensis pectoralis*	E	9/28/1990	F
Warner sucker	*Catostomus warnerensis*	T	4/27/1998	F
Watercress darter	*Etheostoma nuchale*	E	3/29/1993	RF(2)
White River spinedace	*Lepidomeda albivallis*	E	3/28/1994	F
White River springfish	*Crenichthys baileyi baileyi*	E	5/26/1998	F
White sturgeon	*Acipenser transmontanus*	E	None	—
Woundfin	*Plagopterus argentissimus*	E, EXPN	None	—
Yaqui catfish	*Ictalurus pricei*	T	3/29/1995	F
Yaqui chub	*Gila purpurea*	E	3/29/1995	F
Yellowfin madtom	*Noturus flavipinnis*	EXPN, T	None	—

[a]E=endangered, T=threatened, EXPN=experimental population, non-essential.
[b]Recovery plan stages: F=final, D=draft, RD=draft under revision, RF=final revision, O=other.

SOURCE: Adapted from "Listed FWS/Joint FWS and NMFS Species and Populations with Recovery Plans (Sorted by Listed Entity)" and "Listed U.S. Species by Taxonomic Group," in *Threatened and Endangered Species System (TESS)*, U.S. Department of the Interior, U.S. Fish and Wildlife Service, February 17, 2006, http://ecos.fws.gov/tess_public/SpeciesRecovery.do?sort=1 and http://ecos.fws.gov/tess_public/SpeciesReport.do?kingdom=V&listingType=L (accessed February 17, 2006)

experienced changes in water flows due to dam operations. The middle portion of the Mississippi River has also been extensively channelized and diked to prevent flooding and improve barge navigation.

Pallid sturgeons are believed to be very sensitive to changes in the velocity and volume of river flows. They are nearly blind and forage along muddy river bottoms feeding on tiny fish and other creatures that prefer turbid waters. Dams and channelization have reduced erosion of riverbank soil into the Missouri and Mississippi Rivers. This has given other fish species with better eyesight an advantage over the pallid sturgeon at finding small prey. In addition, mating between the pallid sturgeon and the shovelnose sturgeon in the lower Mississippi River has produced a population of hybrid sturgeon that is thriving compared to their imperiled parents.

All of these factors combine to provide a bleak outlook for the future of the pallid sturgeon. The Fish and Wildlife Service recovery plan notes that "it is unlikely that successfully reproducing populations of pallid sturgeon can be recovered without restoring the habitat elements (morphology, hydrology, temperature regime, cover, and sediment/organic matter transport) of the Missouri and Mississippi Rivers necessary for the species continued survival."

Herb Bollig and George Jordan reported in "U.S. Fish and Wildlife Service Stocks Endangered Pallid Sturgeons in Missouri River" (September 2005, http://mountain-prairie.fws.gov/PRESSREL/05-62.htm) that since 1994 more than 100,000 pallid sturgeons have been bred in captivity and placed in river waters in the states of Montana, North Dakota, Nebraska, Iowa, Kansa, Missouri, and Louisiana. The fish are spawned and reared at the agency's Gavins Point National Fish Hatchery near Yankton, South Dakota. This is the only hatchery in the nation engaged in breeding the pallid sturgeon. During 2004 the facility underwent a major construction program

TABLE 6.2

The ten listed freshwater fish entities with the highest expenditures under the Endangered Species Act, fiscal year 2004

Rank	Entity	Status*	2004 expenses
1	Trout, bull	T	$32,570,600
2	Sturgeon, pallid	E	$13,370,173
3	Minnow, Rio Grande silvery	E	$8,073,562
4	Sucker, razorback	E	$7,548,642
5	Chub, humpback	E	$6,670,006
6	Sturgeon, white	E	$5,689,173
7	Pikeminnow (=squawfish), Colorado except Salt and Verde River drainages, Arizona	E	$5,316,746
8	Chub, bonytail	E	$4,864,566
9	Sucker, shortnose	E	$4,453,465
10	Sucker, Lost River	E	$4,253,222

*T=threatened; E=endangered.

SOURCE: Adapted from "Table 1. Reported FY2004 Expenditures for Endangered and Threatened Species, Not Including Land Acquisition Costs," *Federal and State Endangered and Threatened Species Expenditures: Fiscal Year 2004*, U.S. Department of the Interior, U.S. Fish and Wildlife Service, January 2005, http://www.fws.gov/endangered/expenditures/reports/FWS%20Endangered%20Species%202004%20Expenditures%20Report.pdf (accessed February 11, 2006)

FIGURE 6.1

Bull trout

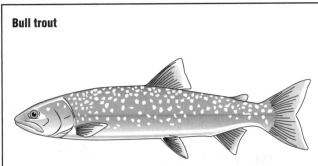

SOURCE: "Bull Trout," in *Bull Trout (Salvelinus confluentus)*, U.S. Department of the Interior, U.S. Fish and Wildlife Service, January 2003, http://training.fws.gov/library/Pubs/bulltrt03.pdf (accessed February 13, 2006)

that included the addition of new specially designed tanks for the endangered fish. Despite the success of the breeding operation, the FWS notes that "this stocking effort alone will not recover the species." Habitat improvement is the only step that biologists believe will save the pallid sturgeon from extinction.

In July 2005 the FWS initiated a five-year status review for the pallid sturgeon. The agency will collect scientific and commercial data that have become available since the species was listed as endangered in 1990. This information will be used to determine if the listing is still appropriate.

RECOVERY PLANS FOR FRESHWATER FISH. As shown in Table 6.1 there were recovery plans for nearly ninety populations or species of freshwater fish as of February 2006. Most of the plans have been finalized. Copies of the plans can be accessed from the Web site of the Threatened and Endangered Species System (TESS) of the U.S. Fish and Wildlife Service (http://ecos.fws.gov/tess_public/TESSWebpageRecovery?sort=1).

Imperiled Marine and Anadromous Fish

Marine and anadromous fish primarily inhabit salty waters. There were only nine such species listed under the Endangered Species Act as of February 2006. They are under the jurisdiction of the National Marine Fisheries Service. Listed species found in the Pacific Northwest and their current status (E—Endangered and T—Threatened) are as follows:

- Chinook salmon—E,T
- Chum salmon—T
- Coho salmon—E,T
- Sockeye salmon—E,T
- Steelhead—E,T

In addition there is an endangered species of Atlantic salmon found in the gulf of Maine. Imperiled non-salmonid species are gulf sturgeon (threatened), shortnose sturgeon (endangered), and smalltooth sawfish (endangered).

More than $79 million was spent under the ESA on marine and anadromous fish in 2004. Expenditures are broken down by species in Table 6.3.

PACIFIC SALMONIDS. Pacific salmonids are found in waters of the northwestern United States and belong to the genus *Oncorhynchus*. There are five species of Pacific salmon: chinook, chum, coho, pink, and sockeye. All but the pink salmon are listed under the ESA as endangered and/or threatened. As shown in Table 2.8 in Chapter 2, four of the ten species with the highest expenditures under the ESA in fiscal year 2004 were Pacific salmonids.

Pacific salmon pose unique protection challenges because they are anadromous. Salmon eggs (or roe) are laid in the bottom gravel of cold freshwater streams where they incubate for five to ten weeks. Each egg ranges in size from one-quarter to one-half inch in size, depending on species. The eggs hatch to release baby fish (or alevin) that are called fry as they mature. Once a fry reaches about three inches in length it is called a fingerling. This typically takes less than a year.

At some point during their first two years the young salmon (now called smolts) migrate downstream to the ocean. There they spend several months or years of their adulthood. When they reach sexual maturity males and females journey back to the streams where they were born to mate and deposit eggs. This is called spawning. Pacific salmon make the round-trip only once. They expend all their energy swimming back upstream and

FIGURE 6.2

Critical habitat designated for bull trout, September 2005

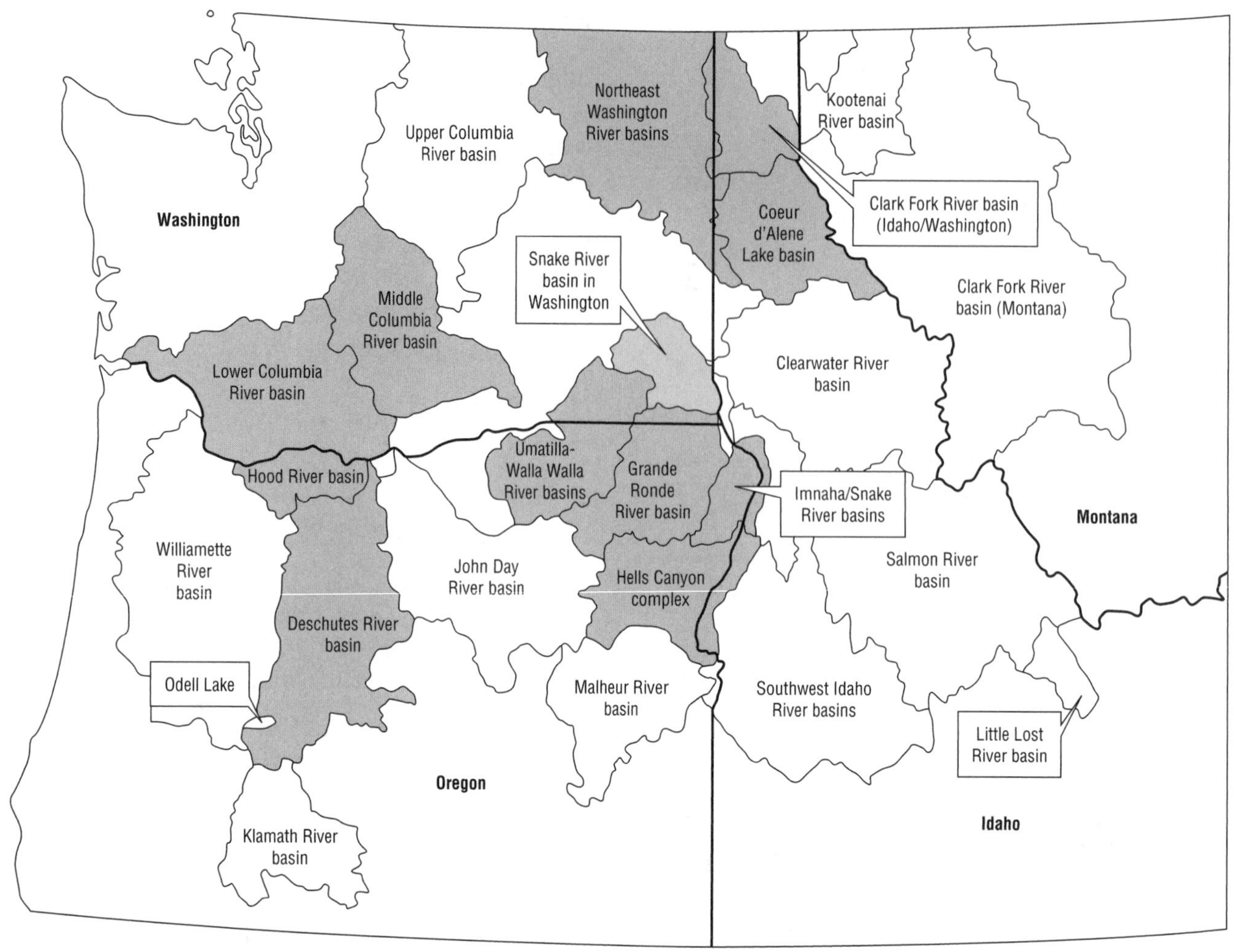

Upper Columbia River basin

Northeast Washington River basins

Kootenai River basin

Washington

Coeur d'Alene Lake basin

Clark Fork River basin (Idaho/Washington)

Clark Fork River basin (Montana)

Snake River basin in Washington

Middle Columbia River basin

Lower Columbia River basin

Clearwater River basin

Hood River basin

Umatilla-Walla Walla River basins

Grande Ronde River basin

Imnaha/Snake River basins

Montana

Williamette River basin

John Day River basin

Hells Canyon complex

Salmon River basin

Deschutes River basin

Odell Lake

Malheur River basin

Southwest Idaho River basins

Little Lost River basin

Oregon

Idaho

Klamath River basin

Note: Shaded river basins are part of final designation.

SOURCE: "Final Critical Habitat," in *Bull Trout, Columbia/Klamath Population*, U.S. Department of the Interior, U.S. Fish and Wildlife Service, Pacific Region, 2006, http://www.fws.gov/pacific/bulltrout/final_colkla/map.html (accessed February 10, 2006)

FIGURE 6.3

Pallid sturgeon

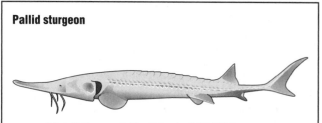

SOURCE: Mark P. Dryer and Alan J. Sandvol, "Pallid Sturgeon (Scaphirhynchus albus)," in *Recovery Plan for the Pallid Sturgeon (Scaphirhynchus albus)*, U.S. Department of the Interior, U.S. Fish and Wildlife Service, November 7, 1993, http://ecos.fws.gov/docs/recovery_plans/1993/931107.pdf (accessed February 13, 2006)

die soon after the eggs are laid and fertilized. Their upstream habitats can be hundreds and even thousands of miles away from their ocean habitats. It is a long and dangerous journey both ways.

Predator fish and birds eat salmon fry, fingerlings, and smolts as they make their way to the ocean. Bears, birds, marine mammals, and humans prey on the adult fish as they migrate upstream. Waterfalls, rapids, dams and other water diversions pose tremendous obstacles to Pacific salmon as they try to travel across long distances.

Salmon heading to the same general location travel upstream in groups called stocks or runs. Stocks migrate at different times of the year depending on geographical and genetic factors. Figure 6.5 illustrates the life cycle of a stock that migrates upstream from late summer through

FIGURE 6.4

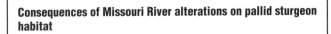

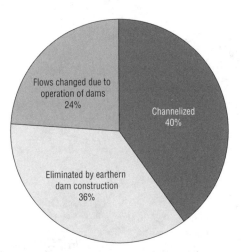

Consequences of Missouri River alterations on pallid sturgeon habitat

- Flows changed due to operation of dams 24%
- Eliminated by earthern dam construction 36%
- Channelized 40%

SOURCE: Adapted from Mark P. Dryer and Alan J. Sandvol, "Habitat Loss," in *Recovery Plan for the Pallid Sturgeon (Scaphirhynchus albus)*, U.S. Department of the Interior, U.S. Fish and Wildlife Service, November 7, 1993, http://ecos.fws.gov/docs/recovery_plans/1993/931107.pdf (accessed February 13, 2006)

TABLE 6.3

The ten listed marine/anadromous fish entities with the highest expenditures under the Endangered Species Act, fiscal year 2004

Species	2004 expenses
Chinook salmon	$32,570,600
Steelhead	$13,370,173
Coho salmon	$8,073,562
Sockeye salmon	$7,548,642
Atlantic salmon	$7,496,334
Chum salmon	$6,670,006
Shortnose sturgeon	$2,311,905
Gulf sturgeon	$933,374
Smalltooth sawfish	$75,900
Total	**$79,050,496**

SOURCE: Adapted from "Table 1. Reported FY 2004 Expenditures for Endangered and Threatened Species, Not Including Land Acquisition Costs," in *Federal and State Endangered and Threatened Species Expenditures: Fiscal Year 2004*, U.S. Department of the Interior, U.S. Fish and Wildlife Service, January 2005, http://www.fws.gov/endangered/expenditures/reports/FWS%20Endangered%20Species%202004%20Expenditures%20Report.pdf (accessed February 11, 2006)

---

early fall. During its lifetime a Pacific salmon is exposed to three different water environments: freshwater streams and rivers, estuaries (areas where freshwater and saltwater meet), and the ocean.

Chinook salmon are the largest of the Pacific salmonids, averaging about twenty-five pounds in adulthood. (See Figure 6.6.) They spend two to seven years in the ocean and travel up to 2,500 miles from their home streams. Coho, sockeye, and chum salmon adults average approximately ten to twelve pounds.

The National Marine Fisheries Service estimates that as many as sixteen million salmon per year migrated upstream in waters of the northwestern United States prior to the arrival of European settlers. Extensive fishing and canning operations quickly decimated the salmon population. As early as 1893 federal officials warned that the future of salmon fisheries had a "disastrous outlook." During the 1890s hatcheries began operating and stocking rivers and streams with "farm-raised" salmon. Over the next century salmon populations were further stressed as natural river flows were dramatically altered with dams, navigational structures, and irrigation systems. Figure 6.7 shows the distribution of salmon hatcheries and dams in the Columbia River basin of the Pacific Northwest. As of 2003 there were twenty-three major dams on mainstem rivers in the basin, more than 300 smaller dams on tributaries, and more than eighty hatcheries.

Endangered and threatened salmon are identified by their water of origin and, in most cases, by their upstream migration season. In 1990 the winter-run stock of Chinook salmon from the Sacramento River was designated as threatened under the ESA, the first Pacific salmon to be listed. It was reclassified to endangered four years later. During the 1990s and early 2000s the NMFS identified thirty-five Evolutionarily Significant Units (ESUs) of Pacific salmonids and listed sixteen of them as endangered or threatened. (See Table 6.4 for the status of these fish as of January 2006.) Two ESUs are "Species of Concern" meaning that the agency has some concerns regarding threats to these species, but lacks sufficient information indicating the need to list them under the ESA.

Biologists blame four main threats, called "the four H's" for the imperiled state of Pacific salmonids:

- Habitat degradation—channelization, dredging, water withdrawals for irrigation, wetland losses, and diking have changed river, stream, and estuary environments.

- Harvesting levels—Over fishing for more than a century has decimated salmon populations.

- Hydropower—Impassable dams have rendered some historical habitat unreachable by salmon. Most modern dams have fish ladders, stepping-stone waterfalls that allow salmon a path up and over the dams. However, all dams affect water temperature, flows, and quality.

- Hatcheries—Biologists fear that hatchery releases overburden estuaries with too many competing fish at the same time.

In addition to these threats, scientists believe that climate changes and the presence of nonnative aquatic species are detrimental to salmon populations.

FIGURE 6.5

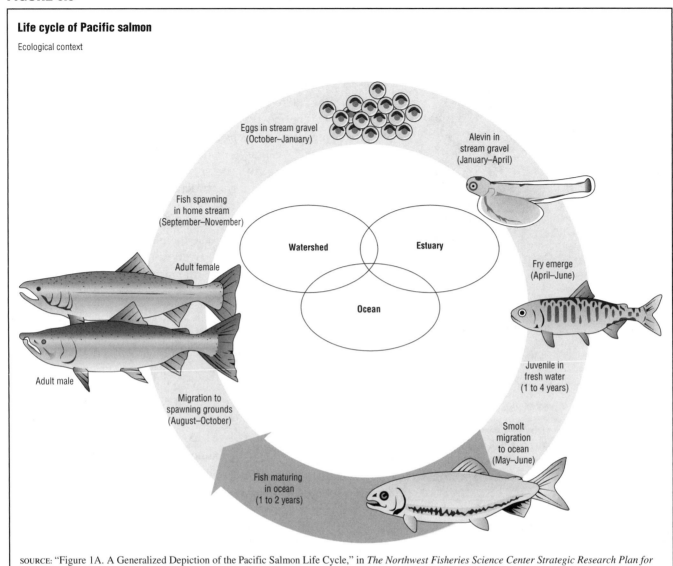

Life cycle of Pacific salmon

Ecological context

SOURCE: "Figure 1A. A Generalized Depiction of the Pacific Salmon Life Cycle," in *The Northwest Fisheries Science Center Strategic Research Plan for Salmon, Final Draft*, U.S. Department of Commerce, National Oceanic and Atmospheric Administration, National Marine Fisheries Service, June 17, 2004, http://www.nwfsc.noaa.gov/publications/researchplans/salmon_research_plan6.17.04%20.pdf (accessed February 13, 2006)

STEELHEAD. Steelhead are members of the *Oncorhynchus* genus and have the scientific name *Oncorhynchus mykiss*. Freshwater steelhead are called rainbow trout. Anadromous steelhead are also trout, but they are associated with salmon due to similarities in habitat and behavior. Steelhead are found in the Pacific Northwest and are anadromous like salmon with two major differences: steelhead migrate individually, rather than in groups, and can spawn numerous times, not just once.

As of January 2006 the National Marine Fisheries Service had identified fifteen distinct population segments (DPSs) of steelhead as shown in Table 6.5. Ten of these DPSs are listed under the ESA as endangered or threatened. In addition, there is one DPS classified as a "Species of Concern," and a DPS in Washington's Puget Sound is undergoing status review. Table 6.3 indicates

that $13.4 million was spent on steelhead under the ESA during fiscal year 2004.

Steelhead face the same threats as Pacific salmon—habitat loss and alteration, over-harvesting, dams and other water obstacles, and competition with hatchery fish.

RECOVERY PLANS FOR MARINE AND ANADROMOUS FISH. Final recovery plans have been published by the NMFS for the shortnose sturgeon (1998), gulf sturgeon (2005), and Atlantic salmon (2005). Copies of the recovery plans are available at the Web site of the NMFS Office of Protected Resources (http://www.nmfs.noaa.gov/pr/recovery/).

In July 2005 the National Marine Fisheries Service announced its intention to develop recovery plans for sixteen populations of Pacific salmon and steelhead

FIGURE 6.6

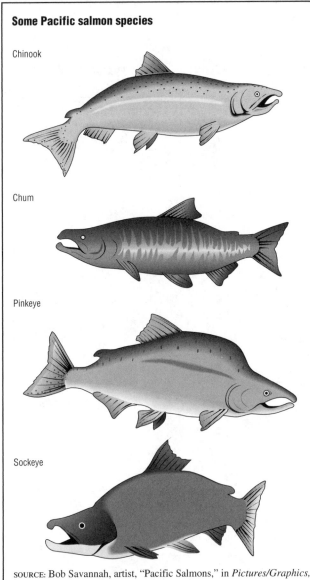

Some Pacific salmon species

Chinook

Chum

Pinkeye

Sockeye

SOURCE: Bob Savannah, artist, "Pacific Salmons," in *Pictures/Graphics, Wildlife Sketches*, U.S. Department of the Interior, U.S. Fish and Wildlife Service, Undated, http://www.fws.gov/pictures/lineart/bobsavannah/pacificsalmons.html (accessed February 15, 2006)

found in Washington, Oregon, and Idaho that are listed as endangered or threatened under the Endangered Species Act. The agency will collect data and information from state, tribal, and local entities regarding the status and threats associated with these fish. The first proposed recovery plan was released by the NMFS for public comment in late December 2005. It covered the Puget Sound area. Plans for populations in other areas were under development in 2006.

Imperiled Fish around the World

The International Union for the Conservation of Nature and Natural Resources (IUCN; now known as the World Conservation Union) listed 800 species of fish as threatened in its *2004 Red List of Threatened Species*, nearly half of the 1,721 species evaluated. However, the IUCN notes that there are in excess of 28,000 known fish species. It is expected that many more fish species will be listed in the future as more evaluations are completed.

As of January 2006 the United States listed eleven foreign species of fish as endangered. The endangered fish and their primary habitat areas are as follows:

- Ala balik (trout)—Turkey
- Ayumodoki (loach)—Japan
- Mexican blindcat (catfish)—Mexico
- Asian bonytongue—Indonesia, Malaysia, Thailand
- Thailand catfish—Thailand
- Thailand giant catfish—Thailand
- Cicek (minnow)—Turkey
- Nekogigi (catfish)—Japan
- Miyako Tango (Tokyo bitterling)—Japan
- Ikan Temoleh (minnow)—Cambodia, Laos, Malaysia, Thailand, and Vietnam
- Totoaba (seatrout or weakfish)—Mexico (Gulf of California)

In addition, there is one foreign fish listed under the ESA as threatened—the beluga sturgeon, which is found in the Caspian and Black Seas and the rivers that drain to them.

Beluga Sturgeon

The beluga sturgeon (Huso huso) is in danger because it is the source of beluga caviar, one of the most coveted luxury foods in the world. Caviar is the processed and salted eggs of large fish. These eggs are called roe while they are still enclosed in the ovarian membrane of the female fish. The sturgeon must be killed to extract its roe. Felicity Barringer and Florence Fabricant reported in the *New York Times* that beluga caviar sold for $200 an ounce in the United States, and the nation consumed 60% of the world's supply of the delicacy ("In Conservation Effort, U.S. Bans Caspian Beluga Caviar," September 30, 2005).

In 2000 a coalition of U.S. environmental groups petitioned the U.S. Fish and Wildlife Service to list the beluga sturgeon as endangered under the ESA. The coalition, named Caviar Emptor (http://www.caviaremptor.org), claimed that the population of the species had declined by 90% between 1980 and 2000 due to overfishing. In 2002 the Natural Resources Defense Council sued the FWS, because the agency had not responded to the petition. Two years later the beluga sturgeon was listed as threatened, rather than endangered, under

FIGURE 6.7

Distribution of salmon hatcheries and dams in the Columbia River basin, 2003

● *Hatchery facilities*   ▲ *Major dam*   ■ *Secondary dam*   ～ *Principal rivers*   *Columbia River basin*   *States and provinces*

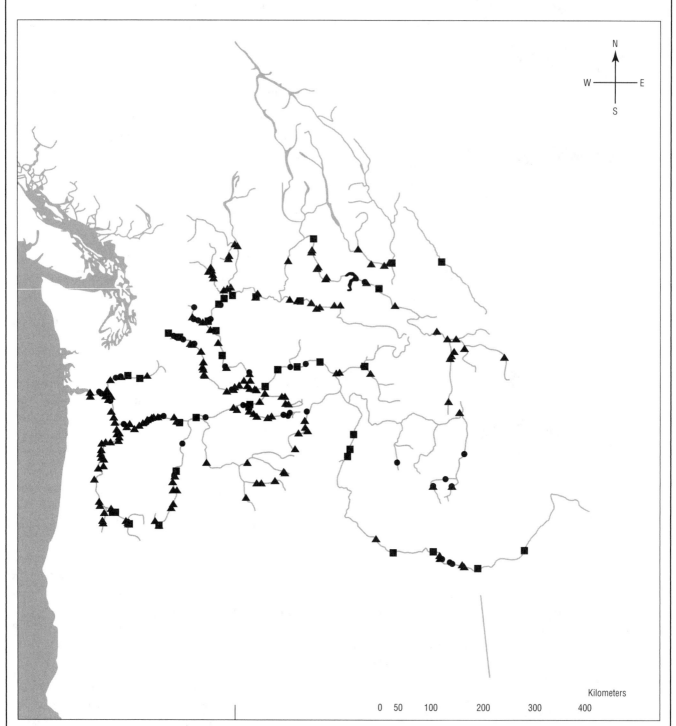

SOURCE: D.L. Bottom, C.A. Simestad, J. Burke, A.M. Baptista, D.A. Jay, K.K. Jones, E. Casillas, and M.H. Schiewe, "Figure 6. Present Distribution of Salmon Hatcheries and Mainstem and Secondary Dams (StreamNet 2003) Along Rivers and Streams of the Columbia River Basin," in *Salmon at River's End: The Role of the Estuary in the Decline and Recovery of Columbia River Salmon*, U.S. Department of Commerce, National Oceanic and Atmospheric Administration, National Marine Fisheries Service, Northwest Fisheries Science Center, 2005, http://www.nwfsc.noaa.gov/assets/25/6294_09302005_153156_SARETM68Final.pdf (accessed February 13, 2006)

TABLE 6.4

Listing status of West Coast salmon populations, January 2006

Species[a]			Current Endangered Species Act listing status[b]
Sockeye salmon (*Oncorhynchus nerka*)	1	Snake River	Endangered
	2	Ozette Lake	Threatened
	3	Baker River	Not warranted
	4	Okanogan River	Not warranted
	5	Lake Wenatchee	Not warranted
	6	Quinalt Lake	Not warranted
	7	Lake Pleasant	Not warranted
Chinook salmon (*O. tshawytscha*)	8	Sacramento River winter-run	Endangered
	9	Upper Columbia River spring-run	Endangered
	10	Snake River spring/summer-run	Threatened
	11	Snake River fall-run	Threatened
	12	Puget Sound	Threatened
	13	Lower Columbia River	Threatened
	14	Upper Willamette River	Threatened
	15	Central Valley spring-run	Threatened
	16	California coastal	Threatened
	17	Central Valley fall and late fall-run	Species of concern
	18	Upper Klamath-Trinity Rivers	Not warranted
	19	Oregon coast	Not warranted
	20	Washington coast	Not warranted
	21	Middle Columbia River spring-run	Not warranted
	22	Upper Columbia River summer/fall-run	Not warranted
	23	Southern Oregon and Northern California Coast	Not warranted
	24	Deschutes River summer/fall-run	Not warranted
Coho salmon (*O. kisutch*)	25	Central California coast	Endangered
	26	Southern Oregon/northern California	Threatened
	27	Oregon coast	Not warranted
	28	Lower Columbia River	Threatened
	29	Southwest Washington	Not warranted
	30	Puget Sound/Strait of Georgia	Species of concern
	31	Olympic peninsula	Not warranted
Chum salmon (*O. keta*)	32	Hood Canal summer-run	Threatened
	33	Columbia River	Threatened
	34	Puget Sound/Strait of Georgia	Not warranted
	35	Pacific Coast	Not warranted

[a]The Endangered Species Act (ESA) defines a "species" to include any distinct population segment of any species of vertebrate fish or wildlife. For Pacific salmon, National Oceanic & Atmospheric Administration (NOAA) fisheries considers an evolutionarily significant unit, or "ESU," a "species" under the ESA. For Pacific steelhead, NOAA fisheries has delineated distinct population segments (DPSs) for consideration as "species" under the ESA.
[b]Updated final listing determinations for 16 salmon species were issued on June 28, 2005 (70 FR 37160). Updated final listing determinations for 10 West Coast steelhead species were issued on January 5, 2006 (71 FR 834). The final "not warranted" listing determination for Oregon Coast coho salmon was announced on January 19, 2006 (71 FR 3033). On September 2, 2005, we issued final critical habitat designations for 19 West coast salmon and steelhead species (70 FR 52488 and 52630).

SOURCE: "Endangered Species Act Status of West Coast Salmon & Steelhead," in *Salmon Populations: Snapshot of ESU Status*, U.S. Department of Commerce, National Oceanic and Atmospheric Administration, National Marine Fisheries Service, January 19, 2006, http://www.nwr.noaa.gov/ESA-Salmon-Listings/Salmon-Populations/upload/1pgr.pdf (accessed February 13, 2006)

the ESA. Environmentalists were highly critical of the decision.

In March 2005 the FWS imposed conditions that limited imports and domestic trade in sturgeon products. The agency gave importing nations six months to provide information regarding their conservation measures to prevent overfishing of the species. In September 2005 the FWS announced that it had not received the required information from five countries around the Caspian Sea. A ban was imposed on imports of beluga sturgeon products from Azerbaijan, Iran, Kazakhstan, the Russian Federation, and Turkmenistan. The ban can be lifted in the future if the proper information is submitted to the FWS. Conservation information was submitted by Black Sea countries and was being reviewed by the agency in 2006.

CLAMS, SNAILS, AND CRUSTACEANS

Clams, snails, and crustaceans are invertebrates. Clams and snails are in the phylum Mollusca. Mollusks have soft bodies usually enclosed in a thin hard shell made of calcium. The U.S. Fish and Wildlife Service uses the generic term "clam" to refer to clams and mussels, but there are physical and reproductive differences between the two creatures. In general, mussels are larger than clams and have an oblong lopsided shell, as opposed to the round symmetrical shell of the clam.

Crustaceans are a large class of creatures with a hard exoskeleton, appendages, and antennae. This class includes lobsters, shrimps, and crabs.

As shown in Table 1.2 in Chapter 1, there were 131 species of clams (including mussels), snails, and

TABLE 6.5

Listing status of West Coast steelhead populations, January 2006

		Species[a]	Current Endangered Species Act listing status[b]	ESA listing actions under review
Steelhead *(O. mykiss)*	36	Southern California	Endangered	
	37	Upper Columbia River	Threatened	
	38	Central California Coast	Threatened	
	39	South central California Coast	Threatened	
	40	Snake River basin	Threatened	
	41	Lower Columbia River	Threatened	
	42	California Central Valley	Threatened	
	43	Upper Willamette River	Threatened	
	44	Middle Columbia River	Threatened	
	45	Northern California	Threatened	
	46	Oregon Coast	Species of concern	
	47	Southwest Washington	Not warranted	
	48	Olympic peninsula	Not warranted	
	49	Puget Sound	Under review	• ESA listing status[c]
	50	Klamath Mountains province	Not warranted	

[a]The Endangered Species Act (ESA) defines a "species" to include any distinct population segment of any species of vertebrate fish or wildlife. For Pacific salmon, National Oceanic & Atmospheric Administration (NOAA) fisheries considers an evolutionarily significant unit, or "ESU," a "species" under the ESA. For Pacific steelhead, NOAA fisheries has delineated distinct population segments (DPSs) for consideration as "species" under the ESA.
[b]Updated final listing determinations for 16 salmon species were issued on June 28, 2005 (70 FR 37160). Updated final listing determinations for 10 West Coast steelhead species were issued on January 5, 2006 (71FR 834). The final "not warranted" listing determination for Oregon Coast coho salmon was announced on January 19, 2006 (71 FR 3033). On September 2, 2005, we issued final critical habitat designations for 19 West Coast salmon and steelhead species (70 FR 52488 and 52630).
[c]A petition to list Puget Sound steelhead was received on September 13, 2004. The species is currently under review.

SOURCE: "Endangered Species Act Status of West Coast Salmon & Steelhead," in *Salmon Populations: Snapshot of ESU Status*, U.S. Department of Commerce, National Oceanic and Atmospheric Administration, National Marine Fisheries Service, January 19, 2006, http://www.nwrnoaa.gov/ESA-Salmon-Listings/Salmon-Populations/ (accessed February 13, 2006)

TABLE 6.6

The ten listed clam, snail, and crustacean entities with the highest expenditures under the Endangered Species Act, fiscal year 2004

Ranking	Entity	Category	Listing*	Expenditure
1	Higgins eye pearlymussel	Clam	E	$1,302,660
2	Vernal pool fairy shrimp	Crustacean	T	$1,018,842
3	Carolina heelsplitter	Clam	E	$991,892
4	Vernal pool tadpole shrimp	Crustacean	E	$665,972
5	Oahu tree snail	Snail	E	$613,532
6	Riverside fairy shrimp	Crustacean	E	$542,464
7	Utah valvata snail	Snail	E	$481,764
8	Clubshell (except where listed as experimental populations)	Clam	E	$475,560
9	Pink mucket peralymussel	Clam	E	$366,725
10	San Diego fairy shrimp	Crustacean	E	$311,484

*E=endangered, T=threatened.

SOURCE: Adapted from "Table 1. Reported FY 2004 Expenditures for Endangered and Threatened Species, Not Including Land Acquisition Costs," in *Federal and State Endangered and Threatened Species Expenditures: Fiscal Year 2004*, U.S. Department of the Interior, U.S. Fish and Wildlife Service, January 2005, http://www.fws.gov/endangered/expenditures/reports/FWS%20Endangered%20Species%202004%20Expenditures%20Report.pdf (accessed February 11, 2006)

---

crustaceans listed under the ESA as endangered or threatened as of February 2006. Most imperiled are clams/mussels (seventy U.S. species and two foreign species). There were thirty-six U.S. species of snails and one foreign species listed under the ESA. Listed crustaceans include twenty-two U.S. species. Table 6.6 shows the ten clam, snail, and crustacean entities with the highest expenditures under the ESA during fiscal year 2004.

The vast majority of imperiled clams/mussels, snails, and crustaceans in the United States are freshwater species that inhabit inland rivers, primarily in the Southeast.

Freshwater Mussels in the United States

Mussels are bivalved (two-shelled) creatures encased in hard hinged shells made of calcium. The freshwater species can grow to be up to six inches in length. The United States, with nearly 300 species, has the greatest diversity of freshwater mussels in the world. According to the U.S. Geological Survey (USGS) (March 2006, http://cars.er.usgs.gov/Southeastern_Aquatic_Fauna/Freshwater_Mussels/freshwater_mussels.html), approximately 90% of these creatures live in southeastern states. Most of them are found burrowed into the sand and gravel beds of rivers and streams making up the Mississippi River system. Mussels have a foot-like appendage that acts like an anchor to hold them in place. They can use this appendage to move themselves very slowly over small distances. Mussels tend to congregate in large groups called colonies.

Mussels are filter-feeders. They have a siphoning system that sucks in food and oxygen from the water. Their gills can filter impurities out of the water. Thus, mussels are tiny natural water purifiers.

Most mussel species have a unique way of spreading their offspring. A female mussel can produce several thousand eggs in a year. After the eggs are fertilized they develop into larva and are released. The larva latch on to the fins or gills of passing fish and they stay there until they have grown into baby clams. At that point they turn loose of the fish and drop to the river bottom. The larvae are called glochidia. It is believed that glochidia are harmless to the fish upon which they hitchhike. This parasitic relationship allows mussels to spread and distribute beyond their usual range.

MUSSEL DECLINES. Unfortunately, many freshwater mussel populations are in danger of extinction. Information about the seventy U.S. species of endangered and threatened clams and mussels as of February 2006 is shown in Table 6.7. Nearly $7.3 million was spent under the ESA during fiscal year 2004 to protect clams and mussels. Just over $1.3 million of this money was devoted to the Higgins' eye mussel, a species found in the Midwest.

The decline of freshwater mussels began in the 1800s. Many of the creatures have an interior shell surface with a pearl-like sheen. These pearlymussels were in great demand as a source of buttons for clothing until the invention of plastic. Collectors also killed many mussels by prying them open looking for pearls. Until the 1990s mussel shells were ground up and used in the oyster pearl industry. Another cause for decline has been habitat disturbance, especially water pollution and the modification of aquatic habitats by dams. The invasive zebra mussel has also harmed native freshwater mussel species by competing with them for food and other resources.

ZEBRA MUSSELS—AN INFESTATION. In 1988 an unwelcome visitor was discovered in the waters of Lake St. Clair, Michigan—a zebra mussel. The zebra mussel is native to eastern Europe. It is smaller than the freshwater mussels found in the United States and has a different method for spreading its young. The larva of zebra mussels do not require a fish host to develop into babies. They can attach to any hard surface under the water. This allows zebra mussels to spread much easier and quicker than their American counterparts.

It is believed that the first zebra mussels migrated to the United States in the ballast water of ships. This is water held in large tanks below deck to improve the stability and control of ships. Ballast water is pumped in and out as needed during a journey. Zebra mussels have also been found clinging to the hulls of small fishing and recreation boats. These boats are hauled overland on trailers, and this allows the creatures to travel great distances between inland water bodies.

Figure 6.8 shows a USGS map of zebra mussel distribution around the country as of June 2005. Since 1988 this invasive species has spread dramatically from the Great Lakes south to the Gulf of Mexico and east to New England. Zebra mussels have been found on boat hulls as far west as California. Throughout waterways in the Midwest, colonies of zebra mussels have clogged pipes and other structures used for municipal and industrial water supply. In addition, the pests have significantly degraded native mussel colonies by competing for available food, space, and resources.

HIGGINS' EYE PEARLYMUSSEL. Figure 6.9 illustrates Higgins' eye, a species of freshwater pearlymussel native to the United States. These mussels are found in the waters of Iowa, Illinois, Minnesota, Missouri, Nebraska, and Wisconsin. The species was named after its discoverer, Frank Higgins, who found some of the mussels in the Mississippi River near Muscatine, Iowa, during the mid-1800s. Over the next few decades Muscatine developed a thriving pearl-button industry that lasted into the 1940s. Higgins' eye was also harvested for the commercial pearl industry.

In 1976 the Higgins' eye pearlymussel was listed as an endangered species under the ESA. More than a century of scavenging by humans had severely depleted the species. Dams, navigational structures, and water quality problems in the upper Mississippi river system were contributing factors to its decline. In 1983 the FWS published its first recovery plan for the Higgins' eye. The plan identified areas deemed essential habitat for the species and called for limits on construction and harvesting in these areas. Since 2000 scientists have collected and relocated hundreds of Higgins' eye mussels. Fish raised in hatcheries have been artificially infested with glochidia and released into rivers to enhance the spread of the mussel.

In 2004 a revised recovery plan was issued for the Higgins' eye pearlymussel. The new plan examines more recent threats to species survival, primarily the pervasive spread of zebra mussels. It acknowledges that there is no currently feasible way to eliminate zebra mussels to the extent needed to benefit the Higgins' eye. Instead, the plan focuses on development of methods to prevent new zebra mussel infestations and working to lessen the impacts of already infested populations.

CLAM/MUSSEL RECOVERY PLANS. All seventy species of clams and mussels listed under the Endangered Species Act as of February 2006 have recovery plans in draft or final form, as shown in Table 6.7. Conservation efforts for freshwater mussels include the captive breeding and reintroduction of some species, as well as measures to restore damaged habitats.

Snails

Snails belong to the class Gastropoda of mollusks. Snails typically have an external spiral-shaped shell and a distinct head that includes sensory organs. Snails inhabit terrestrial (land), marine, and freshwater

TABLE 6.7

Endangered and threatened clams, U.S. species, February 2006

Population	Scientific name	Listing[b]	Recovery plan date	Recovery plan stage[c]
Alabama (=inflated) heelsplitter	Potamilus inflatus	T	4/13/1993	F
Alabama lampmussel[a]	Lampsilis virescens	E	7/2/1985	F
Alabama moccasinshell	Medionidus acutissimus	T	11/17/2000	F
Appalachian elktoe	Alasmidonta raveneliana	E	8/26/1996	F
Appalachian monkeyface (pearlymussel)	Quadrula sparsa	E	7/9/1984	F
Arkansas fatmucket	Lampsilis powelli	T	2/10/1992	F
Birdwing pearlymussel[a]	Conradilla caelata	E	7/9/1984	F
Black clubshell	Pleurobema curtum	E	11/14/1989	F
Carolina heelsplitter	Lasmigona decorata	E	1/17/1997	F
Catspaw (=purple cat's paw pearlymussel)[a]	Epioblasma obliquata obliquata	E	3/10/1992	F
Chipola slabshell	Elliptio chipolaensis	T	9/30/2003	F
Clubshell[a]	Pleurobema clava	E	9/21/1994	F
Coosa moccasinshell	Medionidus parvulus	E	11/17/2000	F
Cracking pearlymussel[a]	Hemistena lata	E	7/11/1991	F
Cumberland bean (pearlymussel)[a]	Villosa trabalis	E	8/22/1984	F
Cumberland elktoe	Alasmidonta atropurpurea	E	5/24/2004	F
Cumberland monkeyface (pearlymussel)[a]	Quadrula intermedia	E	7/9/1984	F
Cumberland pigtoe	Pleurobema gibberum	E	8/13/1992	F
Cumberlandian combshell[a]	Epioblasma brevidens	E	5/24/2004	F
Curtis pearlymussel	Epioblasma florentina curtisii	E	2/4/1986	F
Dark pigtoe	Pleurobema furvum	E	11/17/2000	F
Dromedary pearlymussel[a]	Dromus dromas	E	7/9/1984	F
Dwarf wedgemussel	Alasmidonta heterodon	E	2/8/1993	F
Fanshell	Cyprogenia stegaria	E	7/9/1991	F
Fat pocketbook	Potamilus capax	E	11/14/1989	RF
Fat three-ridge (mussel)	Amblema neislerii	E	9/30/2003	F
Finelined pocketbook	Lampsilis altilis	T	11/17/2000	F
Finerayed pigtoe[a]	Fusconaia cuneolus	E	9/19/1984	F
Flat pigtoe	Pleurobema marshalli	E	11/14/1989	F
Green blossom (pearlymussel)	Epioblasma torulosa gubernaculum	E	7/9/1984	F
Gulf moccasinshell	Medionidus penicillatus	E	9/30/2003	F
Heavy pigtoe	Pleurobema taitianum	E	11/14/1989	F
Higgins eye (pearlymussel)	Lampsilis higginsii	E	7/14/2004	RF
James spinymussel	Pleurobema collina	E	9/24/1990	F
Littlewing pearlymussel	Pegias fabula	E	9/22/1989	F
Louisiana pearlshell	Margaritifera hembeli	T	12/3/1990	F
Northern riffleshell	Epioblasma torulosa rangiana	E	9/21/1994	F
Ochlockonee moccasinshell	Medionidus simpsonianus	E	9/30/2003	F
Orangefoot pimpleback (pearlymussel)	Plethobasus cooperianus	E	9/30/1984	F
Orangenacre mucket	Lampsilis perovalis	T	11/17/2000	F
Ouachita Rock pocketbook	Arkansia wheeleri	E	9/27/2002	F
Oval pigtoe	Pleurobema pyriforme	E	9/30/2003	F
Ovate clubshell	Pleurobema perovatum	E	11/17/2000	F
Oyster mussel[a]	Epioblasma capsaeformis	E	5/24/2004	F
Pale lilliput (pearlymussel)	Toxolasma cylindrellus	E	8/22/1984	F
Pink mucket (pearlymussel)	Lampsilis abrupta	E	1/24/1985	F
Purple bankclimber (mussel)	Elliptoideus sloatianus	T	9/30/2003	F
Purple bean	Villosa perpurpurea	E	5/24/2004	F
Ring pink (mussel)	Obovaria retusa	E	3/25/1991	F
Rough pigtoe	Pleurobema plenum	E	8/6/1984	F
Rough rabbitsfoot	Quadrula cylindrica strigillata	E	5/24/2004	F
Scaleshell mussel	Leptodea leptodon	E	8/6/2004	D
Shiny pigtoe[a]	Fusconaia cor	E	7/9/1984	F
Shinyrayed pocketbook	Lampsilis subangulata	E	9/30/2003	F
Southern acornshell	Epioblasma othcaloogensis	E	11/17/2000	F
Southern clubshell	Pleurobema decisum	E	11/17/2000	F
Southern combshell	Epioblasma penita	E	11/14/1989	F
Southern pigtoe	Pleurobema georgianum	E	11/17/2000	F
Speckled pocketbook	Lampsilis streckeri	E	1/2/1992	F
Stirrupshell	Quadrula stapes	E	11/14/1989	F
Tan riffleshell	Epioblasma florentina walkeri (=E. walkeri)	E	10/22/1984	F
Tar River spinymussel	Elliptio steinstansana	E	5/5/1992	RF
Triangular kidneyshell	Ptychobranchus greenii	E	11/17/2000	F
Tubercled blossom (pearlymussel)[a]	Epioblasma torulosa torulosa	E	1/25/1985	F
Turgid blossom (pearlymussel)[a]	Epioblasma turgidula	E	1/25/1985	F
Upland combshell	Epioblasma metastriata	E	11/17/2000	F

TABLE 6.7

Endangered and threatened clams, U.S. species, February 2006 [CONTINUED]

Population	Scientific name	Listing[b]	Recovery plan date	Recovery plan stage[c]
White catspaw (pearlymussel)	*Epioblasma obliquata perobliqua*	E	1/25/1990	F
White wartyback (pearlymussel)	*Plethobasus cicatricosus*	E	9/19/1984	F
Winged mapleleaf[a]	*Quadrula fragosa*	E	6/25/1997	F
Yellow blossom (pearlymussel)[a]	*Epioblasma florentina florentina*	E	1/25/1985	F

[a]Entire range, except where listed as experimental populations.
[b]E=endangered; T=threatened.
[c]Recovery plan stages: F=final, D=draft, RF=final revision.

SOURCE: Adapted from "Listed FWS/Joint FWS and NMFS Species and Populations with Recovery Plans (Sorted by Listed Entity)" and "Listed U.S. Species by Taxonomic Group," in *Threatened and Endangered Species System (TESS)*, U.S. Department of the Interior, U.S. Fish and Wildlife Service, February 10, 2006, http://ecos.fws.gov/tess_public/SpeciesRecovery.do?sort=1 and http://ecos.fws.gov/tess_public/SpeciesReport.do?kingdom=V&listingType=L (accessed February 17, 2006)

FIGURE 6.8

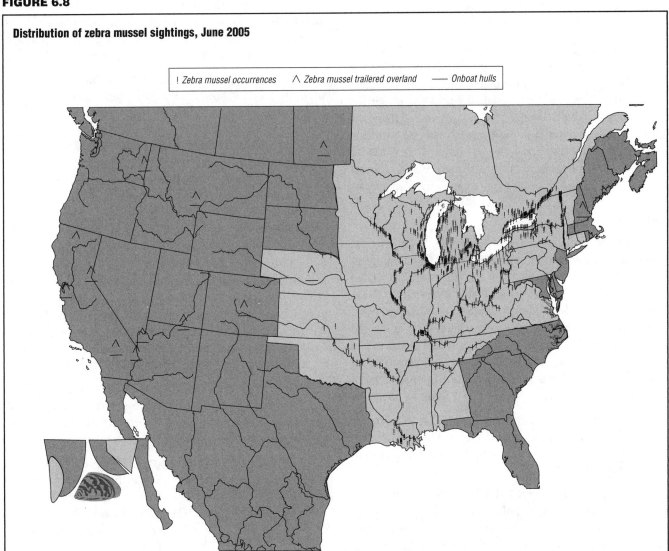

Distribution of zebra mussel sightings, June 2005

! *Zebra mussel occurrences*   ∧ *Zebra mussel trailered overland*   —— *Onboat hulls*

SOURCE: "Zebra Mussel Sightings Distribution," in *Zebra Mussel—U.S. Distribution Information*, U.S. Department of the Interior, U.S. Geological Survey, June 13, 2005, http://nas.er.usgs.gov/taxgroup/mollusks/zebramussel/ (accessed February 18, 2006)

FIGURE 6.9

Higgins' eye, a species of pearlymussel. While the United States harbors the greatest diversity of freshwater mussel species in the world, many of them are now in danger of extinction. (U.S. Fish and Wildlife Service.)

environments. Most land snails prefer moist, heavily vegetated locations.

As of February 2006 there were thirty-six U.S. species of snails and one foreign species listed under the ESA. (See Table 6.8 for a list of the U.S. species). Snails are found throughout the United States. Most imperiled species are located in western states (including Hawaii) and the Southeast (primarily Alabama). Nearly $2.4 million was spent under the ESA during fiscal year 2004 to conserve snail populations in the United States. Almost half of this money was devoted to only two species—Oahu tree snails ($613,532) and Utah valvata snails ($481,764).

OAHU TREE SNAILS. Oahu tree snails belong to the genus *Achatinella* and are endemic to the Oahu island of Hawaii. All forty-one species in the genus are imperiled and are collectively known as Oahu tree snails. These snails were listed as endangered under the ESA in 1981. The snails live in mountainous forests and shrublands and feed on fungi growing on the leaves of native plants. The spread of nonnative vegetation and invasive carnivorous (meat-eating) snails has seriously depleted populations of Oahu tree snails. They are also preyed upon by rats.

In 1992 the FWS released a final recovery plan for the surviving species of *Achatinella* in Oahu. The plan designated areas of essential habitat and called for captive propagation of the snails.

UTAH VALVATA SNAILS. Utah valvata snails were listed as endangered under the ESA in 1992. They are one of five species known as the Snake River snails that inhabit the middle portion of the Snake River in southern Idaho. All five species require cold, clean flowing water with high oxygen levels and low turbidity (suspended sediment) content. Unfortunately their habitat has been

changed considerably over the past few decades by the construction of dams on the river for production of hydroelectric power. These dams have altered the flow and temperature of the river waters. Surviving Utah valvata snails are found in the mainstem of the Snake River and in tributaries fed by cold-water springs.

A recovery plan for the endangered snail has been in effect since 1995. The plan notes that the Utah valvata snail has a high degree of threat and a low degree of recovery potential. Restoration of habitat and water quality is indicated as the only means for saving the snail from extinction.

In late 2003 Utah valvata snails were discovered on a bridge being demolished near Firth, Idaho. Prior to that that time the species had not been found that far south in the Snake River. The Idaho Transportation Department suspended the demolition project so that biologists could conduct a survey of the snails. In 2004 the FWS announced that bridge removal could continue because it did not pose a threat to the survival of the species at that location. However, the discovery of the snails is expected to affect other construction projects planned for that part of the river.

RECOVERY PLANS FOR SNAILS. Table 6.8 lists the snail species for which recovery plans have been published as of February 2006. Two of the species that do not have plans—Pecos assiminea snails and Roswell springsnails—were listed under the ESA during 2005. The white abalone snail is under the jurisdiction of the National Marine Fisheries Service. It is a marine snail that inhabits deep waters off the coast of Southern California.

Crustaceans

Crustaceans are a large class of mandibulate (jawed) creatures in the phylum Arthropoda. They are mostly aquatic and inhabit marine and fresh waters. As of February 2006 there were twenty-two U.S. species listed as endangered or threatened under the Endangered Species Act as shown in Table 6.9. They are found throughout the United States. However, California is home to more imperiled crustacean species than any other state.

More than $2.8 million was spent under the ESA during fiscal year 2004 on endangered and threatened crustaceans. Just over $1 million of these expenditures was devoted to the vernal pool fairy shrimp.

VERNAL POOL FAIRY SHRIMP. The vernal pool fairy shrimp was listed under the ESA as threatened in 1994. It is found in California and Oregon. Vernal is from the Latin word for "spring." This species inhabits temporary small ponds and pools of water that appear in the springtime and dry up after a time. The shrimp lay their eggs in these pools when they contain water. The eggs can go dormant in the dirt when the pools become dry. Baby shrimp hatch only when exposed to water at less than

TABLE 6.8

Endangered and threatened snail species in the United States, February 2006

Population	Scientific name	Listing[b]	Recovery plan date	Recovery plan stage[c]
Alamosa springsnail	*Tryonia alamosae*	E	8/31/1994	F
Anthony's riversnail[a]	*Athearnia anthonyi*	E	8/13/1997	F
Armored snail	*Pyrgulopsis (=marstonia) pachyta*	E	7/1/1994	D
Banbury Springs limpet	*Lanx sp.*	E	11/26/1995	F
Bliss Rapids snail	*Taylorconcha serpenticola*	T	11/26/1995	F
Bruneau hot springsnail	*Pyrgulopsis bruneauensis*	E	9/30/2002	F
Chittenango ovate amber snail	*Succinea chittenangoensis*	T	12/5/2003	RD(1)
Cylindrical lioplax (snail)	*Lioplax cyclostomaformis*	E	12/2/2005	F
Flat pebblesnail	*Lepyrium showalteri*	E	12/2/2005	F
Flat-spired three-toothed snail	*Triodopsis platysayoides*	T	5/9/1983	F
Idaho springsnail	*Fontelicella idahoensis*	E	11/26/1995	F
Iowa pleistocene snail	*Discus macclintocki*	E	3/22/1984	F
Kanab ambersnail	*Oxyloma haydeni kanabensis*	E	10/12/1995	F
Lacy elimia (snail)	*Elimia crenatella*	T	12/2/2005	F
Magazine Mountain shagreen	*Mesodon magazinensis*	T	2/1/1994	F
Morro shoulderband (=banded dune) snail	*Helminthoglypta walkeriana*	E	9/28/1998	F
Newcomb's snail	*Erinna newcombi*	T	3/24/2004	D
Noonday snail	*Mesodon clarki nantahala*	T	9/7/1984	F
Oahu tree snails	*Achatinella spp.*	E	6/30/1992	F
Painted rocksnail	*Leptoxis taeniata*	T	12/2/2005	F
Painted snake coiled forest snail	*Anguispira picta*	T	10/14/1982	F
Pecos assiminea snail	*Assiminea pecos*	E	None	—
Plicate rocksnail	*Leptoxis plicata*	E	12/2/2005	F
Round rocksnail	*Leptoxis ampla*	T	12/2/2005	F
Roswell springsnail	*Pyrgulopsis roswellensis*	E	None	—
Royal marstonia (snail)	*Pyrgulopsis ogmorhaphe*	E	8/11/1995	F
Slender campeloma snail	*Campeloma decampi*	E	None	—
Snake River physa snail	*Physa natricina*	E	11/26/1995	F
Socorro springsnail	*Pyrgulopsis neomexicana*	E	8/31/1994	F
Stock Island tree snail	*Orthalicus reses* (not including *nesodryas*)	T	5/18/1999	F
Stock Island tree snail	*Orthalicus reses* (not including *nesodryas*)	T	4/2/2004	o
Tulotoma snail	*Tulotoma magnifica*	E	11/17/2000	F
Tumbling Creek cavesnail	*Antrobia culveri*	E	9/22/2003	F
Utah valvata snail	*Valvata utahensis*	E	11/26/1995	F
Virginia fringed mountain snail	*Polygyriscus virginianus*	E	5/9/1983	F
White abalone snail	*Haliotis sorenseni*	T	None	—

[a]Entire range, except where listed as experimental populations.
[b]E=endangered, T=threatened.
[c]Recovery plan stages: F=final, D=draft, RD=draft under revision, O=other, —=not applicable.

SOURCE: Adapted from "Listed FWS/Joint FWS and NMFS Species and Populations with Recovery Plans (Sorted by Listed Entity)" and "Listed U.S. Species by Taxonomic Group," in *Threatened and Endangered Species System (TESS)*, U.S. Department of the Interior, U.S. Fish and Wildlife Service, February 17, 2006 http://ecos.fws.gov/tess_public/SpeciesRecovery.do?sort=1 and http://ecos.fws.gov/tess_public/SpeciesReport.do?kingdom=I&listingType=L (accessed February 17, 2006)

approximately 50° Fahrenheit. Adults typically reach 0.4 to 1 inch in length. The shrimp have a lifetime of two to five months.

In 2003 critical habitat was designated for the vernal pool fairy shrimp along with several other species of vernal pool shrimp. During 2004 a draft recovery plan was issued by the U.S. Fish and Wildlife Service for dozens of imperiled plant and animal species that inhabit vernal pool ecosystems in California and southern Oregon. The plan notes that vernal pool life forms are threatened by urban and agricultural development and invasion of nonnative species. The recovery of vernal pool species will require an ecosystem-wide approach. The FWS proposes establishing conservation areas and reserves to protect primary vernal pool habitat.

CRUSTACEAN RECOVERY PLANS. As shown in Table 6.9 nearly all endangered and threatened species of crus-

taceans found in the United States had recovery plans as of February 2006. Most plans were in final form. Two listed species (Hay's spring amphipod and squirrel chimney cave shrimp) are exempt from the requirement for a recovery plan.

Imperiled Mollusks and Crustaceans around the World

The IUCN listed 974 species of mollusks and 429 species of crustaceans as threatened in its *2004 IUCN Red List of Threatened Species* (2004, http://www.redlist.org/). For mollusks, this number comprises 45% of the 2,163 species evaluated. The IUCN reports that approximately 70,000 mollusk species are known. Only 498 crustacean species were evaluated for the 2004 report. Threatened species comprise 86% of this total. However, the IUCN notes that there are approximately 40,000 known species of crustaceans.

TABLE 6.9

Endangered and threatened crustacean species in the United States, February 2006

Population	Scientific name	Listing[a]	Recovery plan date	Recovery plan stage[b]
Alabama cave shrimp	*Palaemonias alabamae*	E	9/4/1997	F
California freshwater shrimp	*Syncaris pacifica*	E	7/31/1998	F
Cave crayfish	*Cambarus aculabrum*	E	10/30/1996	F
Cave crayfish	*Cambarus zophonastes*	E	9/26/1988	F
Conservancy fairy shrimp	*Branchinecta conservatio*	E	11/18/2004	D
Hay's Spring amphipod	*Stygobromus hayi*	E	Exempt	—
Illinois cave amphipod	*Gammarus acherondytes*	E	9/20/2002	F
Kauai cave amphipod	*Spelaeorchestia koloana*	E	2/9/2005	D
Kentucky cave shrimp	*Palaemonias ganteri*	E	10/7/1988	F
Lee County cave isopod	*Lirceus usdagalun*	E	9/30/1997	F
Longhorn fairy shrimp	*Branchinecta longiantenna*	E	11/18/2004	D
Madison cave isopod	*Antrolana lira*	T	9/30/1996	F
Nashville crayfish	*Orconectes shoupi*	E	2/8/1989	RF(1)
Noel's cave amphipod	*Gammarus desperatus*	E	None	—
Peck's cave amphipod	*Stygobromus (=stygonectes) pecki*	E	None	—
Riverside fairy shrimp	*Streptocephalus woottoni*	E	9/3/1998	F
San Diego fairy shrimp	*Branchinecta sandiegonensis*	E	9/3/1998	F
Shasta crayfish	*Pacifastacus fortis*	E	8/28/1998	F
Socorro isopod	*Thermosphaeroma thermophilus*	E	2/16/1982	F
Squirrel chimney cave shrimp	*Palaemonetes cummingi*	T	Exempt	E
Vernal pool fairy shrimp	*Branchinecta lynchi*	T	11/18/2004	D
Vernal pool tadpole shrimp	*Lepidurus packardi*	E	11/18/2004	D

[a]E=endangered, T=threatened.
[b]Recovery plan stages: F=final, D=draft, RD=draft under revision, RF=final revision, O=other.

SOURCE: Adapted from "Listed FWS/Joint FWS and NMFS Species and Populations with Recovery Plans (Sorted by Listed Entity)" and "Listed U.S. Species by Taxonomic Group," in *Threatened and Endangered Species System (TESS)*, U.S. Department of the Interior, U.S. Fish and Wildlife Service, February 17, 2006, http://ecos.fws.gov/tess_public/SpeciesRecovery.do?sort51 and http://ecos.fws.gov/tess_public/SpeciesReport.do?kingdom5I&listingType5L (accessed February 17, 2006)

CHAPTER 7
IMPERILED AMPHIBIANS AND REPTILES

Amphibians and reptiles are collectively known by biologists as herpetofauna. At present, there are over 5,000 described amphibian species and over 6,000 reptiles. New species in both these groups are being discovered every day, particularly in remote tropical regions that are only now being explored.

Most of the herpetofauna native to the United States are found in wetlands and riparian habitat (the banks and immediate areas around waterbodies, such as streams). Biologists say that amphibians and reptiles play a crucial role in these ecosystems by controlling insects, processing dead organic matter into a form that is edible by smaller creatures, and providing an important link in the food chain.

Many herpetofauna species are under threat, primarily due to declines and degradation in their habitats in recent decades.

AMPHIBIANS

Amphibians are vertebrate animals in the taxonomic class Amphibia. They represent the most ancient group of terrestrial vertebrates. The earliest amphibians are known from fossils and date from the early Devonian era, some 400 million years ago. The three groups of amphibians that have survived to the present day are salamanders, frogs (and toads), and caecilians.

Salamanders belong to the orders Caudata or Urodela. They have moist smooth skin, slender bodies, four short legs, and long tails. This category includes the amphibians commonly known as newts (land-dwelling salamanders) and sirens (salamanders with lungs in addition to gills). The majority of salamanders are fairly small in size, most often six inches long or less. The Chinese and Japanese giant salamanders, which grow to be as large as five feet in length, are the largest of all amphibians.

There are approximately 500 salamander species worldwide, and about 150 species in the United States.

Frogs and toads are in the order Anura. These amphibians do not have tails as adults. They have small bodies with two short front legs and two long hind legs. Their feet are webbed, and they are good jumpers and hoppers. True frogs belong to the family Ranidae, while true toads belong to the family Bufonidae. There are many other families in this order whose members are commonly described as tree frogs, tailed frogs, spadefoot toads, horned toads, clawed frogs, Surinam toads, narrow-mouth frogs, or poison dart toads. Many of the species go through a swimming tadpole stage before metamorphosing into an adult. However, in some species, eggs hatch directly as juvenile froglets, which are miniature versions of the adults. Tadpoles are most often herbivorous, although there are some carnivorous tadpoles, including cannibalistic species. Adults are carnivorous and catch prey with their sticky tongues. There are at least 5,000 known frog and toad species, but only about 100 of these species are found in the United States.

Caecilians belong to the orders Gymnophiona or Apoda and share a common ancestor with the other amphibians, but look much different. They are often mistaken for worms or snakes. They have long slender bodies with no limbs and are found primarily in the tropics. There are approximately 160 species of Caecilians worldwide, but none are native to the United States.

"Amphi-" means "both," and amphibians get their name from the fact that many species occupy both aquatic and terrestrial habitats. In particular, a large number of amphibian species undergo a dramatic change called metamorphosis, in which individuals move from an aquatic larval stage to a terrestrial adult stage. In many frog species, for example, aquatic, swimming tadpoles metamorphose into terrestrial jumping frogs. In the process, they lose their muscular swimming tails and acquire

TABLE 7.1

Endangered and threatened amphibian species in the United States, March 2006

Common name	Scientific name	Status[a]	Recovery plan date	Recovery plan status[b]
Coqui, golden	*Eleutherodactylus jasperi*	T	4/19/84	F
Frog, California red-legged (subspecies range clarified)	*Rana aurora draytonii*	T	5/28/02	F
Frog, Chiricahua leopard	*Rana chiricahuensis*	T	None	—
Frog, Mississippi gopher	*Rana capito sevosa*	E	None	—
Frog, mountain yellow-legged	*Rana muscosa*	E	None	—
Guajon	*Eleutherodactylus cooki*	T	9/24/04	F
Salamander, Barton Springs	*Eurycea sosorum*	E	9/21/05	F
Salamander, California tiger	*Ambystoma californiense*	E, T	None	—
Salamander, Cheat Mountain	*Plethodon nettingi*	T	7/25/91	F
Salamander, desert slender	*Batrachoseps aridus*	E	8/12/82	F
Salamander, flatwoods	*Ambystoma cingulatum*	T	None	—
Salamander, Red Hills	*Phaeognathus hubrichti*	T	11/23/83	F
Salamander, San Marcos	*Eurycea nana*	T	2/14/96	RF(1)
Salamander, Santa Cruz long-toed	*Ambystoma macrodactylum croceum*	E	7/2/99	RD(2)
Salamander, Shenandoah	*Plethodon shenandoah*	E	9/29/94	F
Salamander, Sonora tiger	*Ambystoma tigrinum stebbinsi*	E	9/24/02	F
Salamander, Texas blind	*Typhlomolge rathbuni*	E	2/14/96	RF(1)
Toad, Arroyo (=arroyo southwestern)	*Bufo californicus (=microscaphus)*	E	7/24/99	F
Toad, Houston	*Bufo houstonensis*	E	9/17/84	F
Toad, Puerto Rican crested	*Peltophryne lemur*	T	8/7/92	F
Toad, Wyoming	*Bufo baxteri (=hemiophrys)*	E	9/11/91	F

[a]E=endangered, T=threatened.
[b]Recovery plan stages: F=final, RD=draft under revision, RF=final revision.

SOURCE: Adapted from "Listed FWS/Joint FWS and NMFS Species and Populations with Recovery Plans (Sorted by Listed Entity)" and "Listed U.S. Species by Taxonomic Group," in *Threatened and Endangered Species System (TESS)*, U.S. Department of the Interior, U.S. Fish and Wildlife Service, March 6, 2006, http://ecos.fws.gov/tess_public/SpeciesRecovery.do?sort=1 and http://ecos.fws.gov/tess_public/SpeciesReport.do?kingdom=I&listingType=L (accessed March 6, 2006)

forelimbs and hind limbs. Many amphibian species occupy terrestrial habitats through most of the year, but migrate to ponds to breed. However, there are also species that are either entirely aquatic or entirely terrestrial. Whatever their habitat, amphibians generally require some moisture to survive. This is because amphibians pass some oxygen and other chemicals in and out of their body directly through their living skin, using processes that require water to function.

A large number of amphibian species are in serious decline due to factors such as habitat loss, pollution, and climate change. Amphibians are particularly vulnerable to pollution because their skin readily absorbs water and other substances from the environment. For this reason, amphibians are frequently considered biological indicator species, meaning that their presence, condition, and numbers are monitored as a gauge of the overall well-being of their habitat.

THREATENED AND ENDANGERED SPECIES OF AMPHIBIANS

As of March 2006 there were twenty-one U.S. amphibian species listed as threatened or endangered under the Endangered Species Act (ESA). (See Table 7.1.) The list contains eleven species of salamander and ten species of frogs and toads (including the golden coqui and the guajón, which are Puerto Rican frogs). Most of the listed species are endangered and nearly all have

recovery plans in place. Geographically the list is dominated by western states, where thirteen of the imperiled species are found, primarily in California or Texas.

The U.S. Fish and Wildlife Service (FWS) reports that $8.4 million was spent under the ESA during fiscal year 2004 on amphibian species. The ten species with the highest expenditures are shown in Table 7.2.

Imperiled Salamanders in the United States

Of the eleven salamanders listed in Table 7.1, only four species are found outside the western states. The primary ranges of all species are as follows:

- Texas—Barton Springs, San Marcos, and Texas blind salamanders (See Figure 7.1.)

- California—California tiger, Desert slender, and Santa Cruz long-toed salamanders

- Arizona—Sonora tiger salamander

- Alabama—Red Hills salamander

- Virginia—Shenandoah salamander

- West Virginia—Cheat Mountain salamander

The Flatwoods salamander is found in the coastal plain areas of Florida, Georgia, and South Carolina.

Some endangered salamanders, including many cave species, have highly restricted habitats. The Barton Springs salamander is only found in and around spring-fed pools

TABLE 7.2

The ten listed amphibian entities with the highest expenditures under the Endangered Species Act, fiscal year 2004

Ranking	Common name	Listing*	Expenditure
1	Barton Springs salamander	E	$1,884,500
2	California red-legged frog	T	$1,576,949
3	California tiger salamander	T	$1,261,128
4	Arroyo (=arroyo southwestern) toad	E	$1,062,719
5	Mississippi gopher frog (wherever found west of Mobile and Tombigbee Rivers in AL, MS, and LA)	E	$ 589,700
6	Chiricahua leopard frog	T	$ 519,850
7	Flatwoods salamander	T	$ 461,610
8	Wyoming toad	E	$ 241,267
9	Mountain yellow-legged frog	E	$ 220,977
10	Houston toad	E	$ 187,040

*E=endangered, T=threatened.

SOURCE: Adapted from "Table 1. Reported FY 2004 Expenditures for Endangered and Threatened Species, Not Including Land Acquisition Costs," in *Federal and State Endangered and Threatened Species Expenditures: Fiscal Year 2004*, U.S. Department of the Interior, U.S. Fish and Wildlife Service, January 2005, http://www.fws.gov/endangered/expenditures/reports/FWS%20Endangered%20Species%202004%20Expenditures%20Report.pdf (accessed February 11, 2006)

FIGURE 7.1

The Texas blind salamander lives in underground caves and has only vestigial eyes, found below the skin. (U.S. Fish and Wildlife Service.)

in Zilker Park in Austin, Texas. The species was first listed as endangered in 1997. Urban development has contributed to degradation of the local groundwater that feeds the spring. In addition, flows from the spring have decreased due to increasing human use of groundwater from the aquifer. Finally, the Barton Springs salamander has been the subject of contentious debate between conservationists and those who wish to expand development around the area of the pools.

In 2005 the U.S. Fish and Wildlife Service published a final recovery plan for the Barton Springs salamander and began a five-year review of its listing status.

Imperiled Frogs and Toads in the United States

The ten species of imperiled frogs and toads found in the United States are geographically diverse. Their habitats are located in the West, Southeast, and Puerto Rico. California is home to the California red-legged frog, the arroyo toad, and the mountain yellow-legged frog (which also lives in Nevada). Arizona and New Mexico provide habitat for the Chiricahua leopard frog. The Houston toad and Wyoming toad are found in Texas and Wyoming, respectively.

The Mississippi gopher frog is native to the southeastern United States. Three imperiled amphibians are found in Puerto Rico—the golden coquí, guajón, and Puerto Rican crested toad.

CALIFORNIA RED-LEGGED FROG. The California red-legged frog is the largest native frog in the western United States. The frog was made famous by Mark

Twain's short story "The Celebrated Jumping Frog of Calaveras County," which was published in 1865. The species experienced a significant decline during the mid-twentieth century. According to Environmental Defense (http://www.environmentaldefense.org/documents/3733_Species_CA%20Frog.pdf), by 1960 California red-legged frogs had disappeared altogether from the state's Central Valley, probably due to the loss of most of their habitat. In 1996 the species was listed as threatened under the Endangered Species Act.

California red-legged frogs require riverside habitats covered by vegetation and close to deep-water pools. They are extremely sensitive to habitat disturbance and water pollution—tadpoles are particularly sensitive to varying oxygen levels and siltation (mud and other natural impurities) during metamorphosis. The frogs require three to four years to reach maturity and have a normal life span of eight to ten years.

Water reservoir construction and agricultural or residential development are the primary factors in the decline of this species. Biologists have shown that California red-legged frogs generally disappear from habitats within five years of a reservoir or water diversion project. The removal of vegetation associated with flood control, combined with the use of herbicides and restructuring of landscapes, further degrade remaining habitat. Finally, nonnative species have also attacked red-legged frog populations. These include alien fish predators as well as such competing species as bullfrogs.

A recovery plan for the California red-legged frog was published by the U.S. Fish and Wildlife Service in *Recovery Plan for the California Red-legged Frog (Rana aurora draytonii)* (2002, http://ecos.fws.gov/docs/recovery_plans/2002/020528.pdf). It calls for eliminating threats in current habitats, restoring damaged habitats, and reintroducing populations into the historic range of the species. The U.S. National Park Service helped to preserve one current frog habitat by altering water flow in the Piru Creek connection between Lake Piru and Pyramid Lake, located in the Los Angeles and Los Padres National Forests about sixty miles northwest of Los Angeles. This also benefited another threatened species, the arroyo southwestern toad.

The FWS has taken measures to preserve habitat in the foothills of the Sierra Nevada, in the central coastal mountains near San Francisco, along the Pacific coast near Los Angeles, and in the Tehachapi Mountains. Protected frog habitats have also been established in Marin and Sonoma counties.

GUAJÓN. The guajón is a cave-dwelling species endemic to Puerto Rico. It grows to be about three inches long and is primarily brown, but sometimes has yellow markings. The frog has very large protruding eyes that are rimmed in white, giving it an unusual appearance that some observers consider spooky. Because of its appearance, it has been nicknamed the "demon of Puerto Rico."

Its decline has resulted largely from introductions of alien species such as mongooses, rats, and cats, all of which eat unhatched guajón eggs. In addition the species has experienced habitat loss from garbage dumping in caves and deforestation for agriculture, roads, and dams. Deforestation also creates the potential for future environmental disasters such as flash floods, which drown adult frogs and destroy nests. Encroaching agriculture causes pollution from fertilizer runoff. Finally, the guajón, is frequently killed by superstitious local residents who believe the mere sight of the animal can bring disaster.

Foreign Amphibians in Danger

As of March 2006 there were nine foreign amphibian species listed as threatened or endangered under the Endangered Species Act. (See Table 7.3.) This includes seven frog and toad species and two salamander species.

The World Conservation Union (IUCN) reported in its *2004 Red List of Threatened Species* that 1,770 amphibian species are threatened. This represents nearly one-third of all described amphibian species, the highest percentage for any group of animals.

GIANT SALAMANDERS. There are two species of giant salamanders, the Chinese giant salamander and the Japanese giant salamander. These are by far the largest living amphibian species, reaching lengths of up to five feet. Both are listed under the ESA and are highly endangered. Giant salamanders are aquatic, and have folded and wrinkled skin that allows them to absorb oxygen from their watery habitats. The Chinese giant salamander is found in fast mountain streams in western China. Despite

TABLE 7.3

Foreign endangered and threatened amphibian species, March 2006

Status*	Species name
T	Frog, Goliath (*Conraua goliath*)
E	Frog, Israel painted (*Discoglossus nigriventer*)
E	Frog, Panamanian golden (*Atelopus varius zeteki*)
E	Frog, Stephen Island (*Leiopelma hamiltoni*)
E	Salamander, Chinese giant (*Andrias davidianus (=davidianus d.)*)
E	Salamander, Japanese giant (*Andrias japonicus (=davidianus j.)*)
E	Toad, Cameroon (*Bufo superciliaris*)
E	Toad, Monte Verde golden (*Bufo periglenes*)
E	Toads, African viviparous (*Nectophrynoides spp.*)

*E=endangered, T=threatened.

SOURCE: Adapted from "Foreign Listed Species Report as of 03/06/2006," in *Threatened and Endangered Species System (TESS)*, U.S. Department of the Interior, U.S. Fish and Wildlife Service, March 6, 2006, http://ecos.fws.gov/tess_public/servlet/gov.doi.tess_public.servlets.ForeignListing?listings=0#A (accessed March 6, 2006)

official protection, the species is endangered partly because of hunting for food or medicine. The Chinese giant salamander is also harmed by loss of habitat and aquatic pollution. Its close relative, the Japanese giant salamander, is also endangered and protected. This species inhabits cold, fast mountain streams in northern Kyushu Island and western Honshu in Japan. Japanese giant salamanders have been successfully bred in captivity.

GASTRIC-BROODING FROGS. There are two species of gastric-brooding frogs, both found in Australia. Gastric-brooding frogs are described as timid and are often found hiding under rocks in water. These species were only discovered in the 1970s, and, unfortunately, became extinct only a decade after their discovery. Gastric-brooding frogs get their name from their unusual reproductive strategy—females brood their young in their stomachs. During brooding, the mother does not eat and does not produce stomach acids. The gestation period lasts about eight weeks, and as many as thirty tadpoles may be in the brood. Juveniles eventually emerge as miniature froglets from the mother's mouth. Although it is not certain what led to the extinction of gastric-brooding frogs, one hypothesis is that populations were killed off by the chytrid fungus, which is also responsible for the decline of other frog species.

CAECILIANS. Very little is known about most species of caecilians. Some species are aquatic, but most of these elusive animals are underground burrowers that are difficult to locate and to study. Caecilians generally have very poor eyesight because of their underground habitat—some have no eyes at all or are nearly blind. Because so little is known about this group, it is difficult for environmentalists to assess the level of endangerment of these animals. The loss of tropical habitats worldwide suggests that many caecilians are likely imperiled.

WORLDWIDE THREATS TO AMPHIBIANS

At the end of the twentieth century, biologists uncovered growing evidence of a global decline in amphibian populations. AmphibiaWeb (http://amphibiaweb.org), a conservation organization that monitors amphibian species worldwide, reported in 2006 that more than 160 species have become extinct in recent decades and at least 2,400 other species are declining in population. Amphibian declines have been documented worldwide, though the degree of decline varies across regions. Areas that have been hardest hit include Central America and Australia. In the United States, amphibian declines have been concentrated in California, the Rocky Mountains, the Southwest, and Puerto Rico. Particularly disturbing is the loss of numerous populations within protected and relatively pristine wildlife refuges.

Scientists are concerned because a large number of amphibian species—particularly frogs—has become extinct over a very short period of time. Other species are either declining or showing high levels of gross deformities, such as extra limbs.

The golden toad, named for its unusual and striking orange color, is a prime example of the global amphibian decline. Over a three-year period, golden toads disappeared inexplicably from their only known habitat in the Monteverde Cloud Forest Reserve in Costa Rica. In 1987 herpetologists observed an apparently healthy golden toad population estimated at 1,500 adults along with a new generation of tadpoles. The following year, in 1988, there were only eleven toads. In 1989 only a single surviving toad was found. It was the last individual on record for the species (Britton Windeler, "The Extinction of the Golden Toad [*Bufo periglenes*]—Symptom of a Worldwide Crisis," 2005, http://jrscience.wcp.muohio.edu/fieldcourses05/PapersCostaRicaArticles/TheExtinctionoftheGoldenT.html).

Habitat Destruction

Recent amphibian declines appear to result from a combination of causes. Loss of habitat is a major factor in the decline of numerous amphibian species, as it is for many endangered species. The destruction of tropical forests and wetlands—ecosystems that are rich with amphibians—has done particular damage to populations. In the United States, deforestation is blamed for the loss or decline of salamander species in the Pacific Northwest and Appalachian hardwood forests. In addition, some amphibians have lost appropriate aquatic breeding habitats, particularly small bodies of water such as ponds. These aquatic habitats are often developed or filled in by humans, because they appear to be less biologically valuable than larger aquatic habitats.

Finally, habitat fragmentation may be particularly harmful to amphibian species that migrate during the breeding season. These species require not only that both breeding and nonbreeding habitats remain undisturbed, but also that there be intact habitat along migration routes.

Pollution

Pollution is a second major factor in global amphibian declines. Because amphibians absorb water directly through skin and into their bodies, they are particularly vulnerable to water pollution from pesticides or fertilizer runoff.

Furthermore, air pollution by substances such as chlorofluorocarbons (CFCs) has reduced the amount of protective ozone in the Earth's atmosphere. This has resulted in increased levels of ultraviolet (UV) radiation striking the Earth's surface. UV radiation has wavelengths of 290 to 400 nanometers (nm). Wavelengths between 290 and 315 nm are called UV-B radiation and are the most dangerous, because they can damage deoxyribonucleic acid (DNA) by producing chemicals called cyclobutane pyrimidine dimers. (See Figure 7.2.) Exposure to UV-B radiation causes genetic mutations that can prevent normal development or kill eggs. Increased UV-B levels particularly affect the many frog species whose eggs lack shells and float on the exposed surfaces of ponds. Tadpoles and adults are also at risk, because of their thin delicate skins.

Invasive Species

Many amphibian species have also been affected by the introduction of nonnative species that either compete with them or prey on them. These include fish, crayfish, and other amphibians. The bullfrog, the cane toad (a very large frog species), and the African clawed frog (a species often used in biological research) are some of the invasive species believed to have affected amphibian populations. In addition, introduced trout are blamed for the extinction of several species of harlequin frogs in Costa Rica. It is hypothesized that trout consume tadpoles. Similarly, introduced salmon have affected native frog populations in California.

Disease

Amphibian diseases caused variously by bacteria, viruses, and fungi have devastated certain populations. Of particular importance in recent years is the chytrid fungus. This fungus attacks skin, and was first identified in 1998 in diseased amphibians. There are often no symptoms initially, but eventually affected individuals begin to shed skin and die. The precise cause of death is not known, though damage to the skin can interfere with respiration. The chytrid fungus is believed to be responsible for the demise of numerous species in Australia and Panama. In 2000 it was also documented in populations of the Chiricahua leopard frog in Arizona

FIGURE 7.2

The effects of ultraviolet-B radiation on a living cell

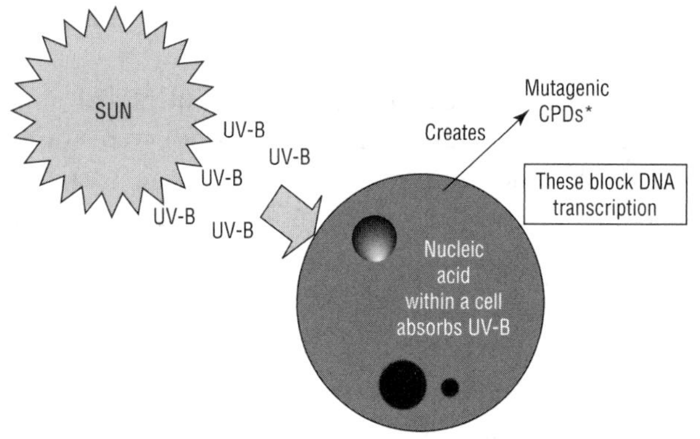

SUN

UV-B
UV-B
UV-B
UV-B
UV-B

Nucleic acid within a cell absorbs UV-B

Creates

Mutagenic CPDs*

These block DNA transcription

*Cyclobutane pyrimidine dimer.

SOURCE: Erin Muths and Steve Corn, "Why Is UV-B 'BAD'?" in *Amphibian Decline: Still an Unexplained Phenomenon—From the Rain Forest to Rocky Mountain National Park*, U.S. Department of the Interior, U.S. Geological Survey, Fort Collins Science Center, Undated, http://www.fort.usgs.gov/products/presentations/amphibian/sld035.html (accessed March 6, 2006)

FIGURE 7.3

A frog showing deformed and extra limbs. The high incidence of amphibian deformities in the United States is cause for concern. (JLM Visuals.)

and the boreal toad in the Rocky Mountains. Officials at the Klondike Gold Rush National Historic Park in Skagway, Alaska, reported in May 2006 that five of nine western toads evaluated there during the summer of 2005 had tested positive for the fungus. The disease was being aggressively investigated as a cause of a decline in toad population in southern Alaska during recent years (http://www.nps.gov/applications/digest/printheadline.cfm?type=Announcements&id=4457).

Global Warming

Global warming is blamed for destroying unique habitats such as cloud forests (forests containing large amounts of water mists) in tropical regions, resulting in the loss of some amphibian species.

Quirin Schiermeier in "The Costs of Global Warming" (*Nature*, January 26, 2006) reported that global warming was also aggravating infectious diseases in the frog populations of Central and South America. The scientists found that warmer temperatures were associated with increased cloud cover over tropical mountain areas. These conditions were conducive to increased growth of the deadly chytrid fungus.

Human Collection

Many amphibian species are vigorously hunted for food, the pet trade, or as medical research specimens.

Amphibian Deformities

Amphibian deformities (see Figure 7.3) first hit the spotlight in 1995, when middle-school students discovered large numbers of deformed frogs in a pond in Minnesota. By 2000 scientists had documented malformed frogs in forty-four states and fifty-seven species. According to FrogWeb, an online service of the National Biological Information Infrastructure (http://frogweb.nbii.gov/index.html), rates of deformity as high as 60% have been documented in some local populations.

The high incidence of amphibian deformities in U.S. species appears to have multiple causes, as no single hypothesis accounts for all the different types of deformities seen. The most common deformities include missing hind limbs and toes, missing feet, misshapen feet, missing eyes, deformed front legs, and extra legs. Some of these malformations are believed to be related to a parasitic trematode, or flatworm, which in experiments causes the development of additional limbs. Aquatic trematodes have increased in number due to human activity, via a complicated chain of events. First, fertilizer runoff increases nutrient levels in ponds, allowing more algae to grow. An increase in algae results in a larger population of algae-eating snails, and snails host juvenile parasitic trematodes. Trematodes move on to frogs when they mature, forming cysts in the vicinity of developing frog legs. Chemical pollution and UV radiation may account for some of the other observed deformities.

The U.S. Geological Survey (USGS) set up a system whereby members of the public can report observations of deformed amphibians. The North American Reporting Center for Amphibian Malformations (NARCAM) is managed by the USGS National Biological Information Infrastructure and the University of Georgia's Savannah River Ecology Lab. Reports can be submitted online at the Web site http://frogweb.nbii.gov/narcam/.

REPTILES

Reptiles belong to the class Reptilia. Although they may appear similar, reptiles differ from amphibians in that their skin is cornified—that is, made of dead cells. All reptiles obtain oxygen from the air using lungs. Most reptiles lay shelled eggs, although some species, particularly lizards and snakes, give birth to live young. Approximately 8,000 species of reptiles have been described. These include turtles, snakes, lizards, and crocodilians. Birds are also technically reptiles (birds and crocodiles are actually close relatives), but have historically been treated separately.

There are four taxonomic orders of reptiles:

- Squamata—More than 7,500 species of lizards, anoles, iguanas, gila monsters, monitors, skinks, geckos, chameleons, snakes (including asps, boas, pythons, and vipers), racerunners, whiptails, and amphisbaenians (worm lizards)

- Testudines—Approximately 300 species of turtles, terrapins, and tortoises

- Crocodilia—Around twenty-four species, including alligators, caimans, crocodiles, and gavials (gharials)

- Rhynchocephalia—Two species of tuataras found only in New Zealand

There are approximately 2,400 species of snakes and 3,800 species of lizards. Together, they represent the largest group of reptiles. Most lizards are carnivorous, although there are some herbivorous species as well, including the iguanas. Snakes are elongate reptiles that have lost their limbs during the course of evolution. All species are carnivorous. Most snakes are adapted to eating relatively large prey items, and have highly mobile jaws that allow them to swallow large prey. In some species, the jaw can be unhinged to accommodate prey. Several groups of snakes are also characterized by a poisonous venom which they use to kill prey.

Many reptiles are in serious decline. Numerous species are endangered due to habitat loss or degradation. In addition, humans hunt reptile species for their skins, shells, or meat. Global climate change has affected some reptile species, particularly turtles, in ominous ways— this is because in some reptiles, ambient temperatures determine whether males or females are produced. Even a small increase in temperature can result in few or no males being born. Natural disasters, such as hurricanes, can also affect reptiles by killing the animals or damaging their habitats. In July 2005 an estimated 84,000 eggs laid by green and loggerhead sea turtles in Mexico's Yucatan peninsula were washed away during Hurricane Emily. According to a report by Eloise Quintanilla in *Christian Science Monitor*, only one nest survived the storm at Akumal beach, representing about 700 eggs, of which 80% were expected to hatch ("Hurricane Emily Takes Toll on Sea Turtles," July 22, 2005).

THREATENED AND ENDANGERED REPTILES

As of March 2006 there were thirty-seven U.S. reptiles listed as threatened or endangered under the ESA, as shown in Table 7.4. Most of the species (twenty-two) are threatened, while fourteen species are endangered. One species, the green sea turtle, has dual status, because it has two separate populations in the United States.

With the exception of the sea turtles, many of the other imperiled reptiles are geographically clustered as follows: California (six species), Puerto Rico (six species), and Florida (four species). Sea turtles spend most of their lives at sea, only coming onto land to nest and lay young. Because there are many potential nesting sites along the U.S. coasts, the sea turtles are listed in numerous states.

Here is a breakdown of imperiled U.S. reptiles by taxonomic order:

- Squamata—twenty-one species

- Testudines—fourteen species (six sea turtles, two tortoises [land-dwelling turtles], and six other turtle species)

- Crocodilia—two species

According to the U.S. Fish and Wildlife Service, nearly $41.6 million was spent under the Endangered Species Act during fiscal year 2004 on threatened and endangered reptiles. Sea turtle species accounted for the vast majority of the expenditures. The ten entities with the highest expenditures are shown in Table 7.5.

Imperiled Sea Turtles in the United States

Sea (or marine) turtles are excellent swimmers and spend nearly their entire lives in water. They feed on a wide array of food items, including mollusks, vegetation, and crustaceans. Some sea turtles are migratory, swimming thousands of miles between feeding and nesting areas. Individuals are exposed to a variety of both natural and human threats. As a result, only an estimated one in 10,000 sea turtles survives to adulthood.

There are seven species of sea turtles that exist worldwide. One species, the flatback turtle, occurs near Australia. The other six species spend part or all of their lives in U.S. territorial waters. The green sea turtle, hawksbill sea turtle, leatherback sea turtle, and loggerhead sea turtle also nest on U.S. lands. (See Figure 7.4.) The Kemp's ridley sea turtle and olive ridley sea turtle nest in other countries.

Imperiled sea turtles fall under the jurisdiction of the U.S. Fish and Wildlife Service while they are on U.S.

TABLE 7.4

Endangered and threatened reptile species in the United States, March 2006

Common name	Scientific name	Listing[a]	Recovery plan date	Recovery plan stage[b]
Alligator, American	*Alligator mississippiensis*	T (S/A)	None	—
Anole, Culebra Island giant	*Anolis roosevelti*	E	01/28/1983	F
Boa, Mona	*Epicrates monensis monensis*	T	04/19/1984	F
Boa, Puerto Rican	*Epicrates inornatus*	E	03/27/1986	F
Boa, Virgin Islands tree	*Epicrates monensis granti*	E	03/27/1986	F
Crocodile, American	*Crocodylus acutus*	E	05/18/1999	F
Gecko, Monito	*Sphaerodactylus micropithecus*	E	03/27/1986	F
Iguana, Mona ground	*Cyclura cornuta stejnegeri*	T	04/19/1984	F
Lizard, blunt-nosed leopard	*Gambelia silus*	E	09/30/1998	F
Lizard, Coachella Valley fringe-toed	*Uma inornata*	T	09/11/1985	F
Lizard, island night	*Xantusia riversiana*	T	01/26/1984	F
Lizard, St. Croix ground	*Ameiva polops*	E	03/29/1984	F
Sea turtle, green (FL, Mexico nesting populations)	*Chelonia mydas*	E	10/29/1991	RF(1)
Sea turtle, green (U.S. East Pacific populations on the west coasts of the U.S., Central America and Mexico and U.S. Pacific populations in Hawaii, Guam, Northern Mariana Islands, American Samoa and other unincorporated U.S. Pacific islands/atolls)	*Chelonia mydas*	T	01/12/1998	RF(1)
Sea turtle, hawksbill (Atlantic populations)	*Eretmochelys imbricata*	E	12/15/1993	RF(1)
Sea turtle, hawksbill (U.S. Pacific populations)	*Eretmochelys imbricata*	E	01/12/1998	RF(1)
Sea turtle, Kemp's ridley	*Lepidochelys kempii*	E	08/21/1992	RF(1)
Sea turtle, leatherback	*Dermochelys coriacea*	E	04/06/1992	RF(1)
Sea turtle, leatherback (U.S. Pacific populations)	*Dermochelys coriacea*	E	01/12/1998	RF(1)
Sea turtle, loggerhead	*Caretta caretta*	T	12/26/1991	RF(1)
Sea turtle, loggerhead (U.S. Pacific populations)	*Caretta caretta*	T	01/12/1998	RF(1)
Sea turtle, olive ridley (U.S. Pacific populations)	*Lepidochelys olivacea*	E	01/12/1998	RF(1)
Skink, bluetail mole	*Eumeces egregius lividus*	T	05/18/1999	F
Skink, sand	*Neoseps reynoldsi*	T	05/18/1999	F
Snake, Alameda whip (=striped racer)	*Masticophis lateralis euryxanthus*	T	04/07/2003	D
Snake, Atlantic salt marsh	*Nerodia clarkii taeniata*	T	12/15/1993	F
Snake, concho water	*Nerodia paucimaculata*	T	09/27/1993	F
Snake, copperbelly water	*Nerodia erythrogaster neglecta*	T	None	—
Snake, eastern indigo	*Drymarchon corais couperi*	T	04/22/1982	F
Snake, giant garter	*Thamnophis gigas*	T	07/02/1999	D
Snake, Lake Erie water (subspecies range clarified)	*Nerodia sipedon insularum*	T	09/25/2003	F
Snake, New Mexican ridge-nosed rattle	*Crotalus willardi obscurus*	T	03/22/1985	F
Snake, San Francisco garter	*Thamnophis sirtalis tetrataenia*	E	09/11/1985	F
Tortoise, desert (U.S.A., except in Sonoran Desert)	*Gopherus agassizii*	T	06/28/1994	F
Tortoise, gopher (west of Mobile/Tombigbee Rivers)	*Gopherus polyphemus*	T	12/26/1990	F
Turtle, Alabama red-belly	*Pseudemys alabamensis*	E	01/08/1990	F
Turtle, bog (=Muhlenberg) (northern)	*Clemmys muhlenbergii*	T	05/15/2001	F
Turtle, flattened musk (species range clarified)	*Sternotherus depressus*	T	02/26/1990	F
Turtle, northern red bellied (= Plymouth) cooter	*Pseudemys rubriventris bangsi*	E	05/06/1994	RF(2)
Turtle, ringed map	*Graptemys oculifera*	T	04/08/1988	F
Turtle, yellow-blotched map	*Graptemys flavimaculata*	T	03/15/1993	F

[a]E=endangered, T=threatened, T (S/A)=similarity of appearance to a threatened taxon.
[b]Recovery plan stages are F=final, D=draft, and RF=final revision.

SOURCE: Adapted from "Listed FWS/Joint FWS and NMFS Species and Populations with Recovery Plans (Sorted by Listed Entity)" and "Listed U.S. Species by Taxonomic Group," in *Threatened and Endangered Species System (TESS)*, U.S. Department of the Interior, U.S. Fish and Wildlife Service, March 6, 2006, http://ecos.fws.gov/tess_public/SpeciesRecovery.do?sort=1 and http://ecos.fws.gov/tess_public/SpeciesReport.do?kingdom=I&listingType=L (accessed March 6, 2006)

land, and under the jurisdiction of the National Marine Fisheries Service while they are at sea.

Information on the distribution of each imperiled sea turtle species is provided below:

- Green sea turtles—found in U.S. waters around Hawaii, U.S. Virgin Islands, Puerto Rico, along the mainland coast from Texas to Massachusetts and from Southern California to Alaska. Key feeding grounds are in Florida coastal waters. Primary nesting sites are the Florida east coast, U.S. Virgin Islands, Puerto Rico, and a remote atoll in Hawaii.

- Hawksbill sea turtles—found in U.S. waters primarily around Hawaii, U.S. Virgin Islands, Puerto Rico, and along the Gulf and southeast Florida coasts. Key nesting sites are in Puerto Rico, the U.S. Virgin Islands, Hawaii, and the southeast coast and keys of Florida.

- Kemp's ridley sea turtles—found in U.S. waters along the Gulf Coast and New England coast. Primary nesting sites are in Mexico and Texas along the Gulf coast.

- Leatherback sea turtles—found in U.S. waters around Hawaii, U.S. Virgin Islands, Puerto Rico,

TABLE 7.5

The ten listed reptile entities with the highest expenditures under the Endangered Species Act, fiscal year 2004

Ranking	Common name	Listing*	Expenditure
1	Loggerhead sea turtle	T	$7,474,119
2	Leatherback sea turtle	E	$7,223,215
3	Desert tortoise (USA, except in Sonoran Desert)	T	$5,413,663
4	Kemps-ridley sea turtle	E	$4,295,166
5	Hawksbill sea turtle	E	$2,949,634
6	Green sea turtle	E	$2,502,218
7	Olive ridley sea turtle (except where endangered)	T	$2,214,790
8	Green sea turtle (Florida, Mexico nesting populations)	E	$2,211,504
9	Gopher tortoise (West of Mobile/ Tombigbee Rivers)	T	$2,102,100
10	Giant garter snake	T	$1,514,823

*E=endangered; T=threatened.

SOURCE: Adapted from "Table 1. Reported FY 2004 Expenditures for Endangered and Threatened Species, Not Including Land Acquisition Costs," in *Federal and State Endangered and Threatened Species Expenditures: Fiscal Year 2004*, U.S. Department of the Interior, U.S. Fish and Wildlife Service, January 2005, http://www.fws.gov/endangered/expenditures/reports/FWS%20Endangered%20Species%202004%20Expenditures%20Report.pdf (accessed February 11, 2006)

FIGURE 7.4

Sea turtles that nest on U.S. coasts

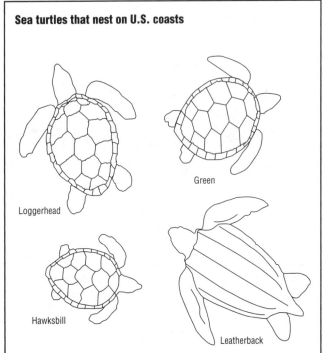

SOURCE: Adapted from "Diagrams," in *You Can Help Protect Sea Turtles*, U.S. Department of the Interior, U.S. Fish and Wildlife Service, North Florida Field Office, Undated, http://www.fws.gov/northflorida/SeaTurtles/SeaTurtleBrochure.pdf (accessed March 10, 2006)

and along the entire Atlantic Coast. Major nesting locations are in the U.S. Virgin Islands and Georgia.

- Loggerhead sea turtles—found in U.S. waters along the entire Atlantic and Pacific coasts. Primary nesting sites occur on the Gulf and east coast of Florida and in Georgia, South Carolina, and North Carolina.

- Olive ridley sea turtles—found occasionally in southwestern U.S. waters. Major nesting sites are in Mexico along the Pacific coast and in other tropical locations.

THREATS TO NESTING TURTLES. Sea turtles bury their eggs in nests on sandy beaches. The building of beachfront resorts and homes has destroyed a large proportion of nesting habitat. Artificial lighting associated with coastal development also poses a problem—lights discourage females from nesting and also cause hatchlings to become disoriented and wander inland instead of out to sea. Finally, beach nourishment—the human practice of rebuilding eroded beach soil—creates unusually compacted sand on which turtles are unable to nest.

SHRIMP-NET CASUALTIES. Shrimp trawling is recognized as one of the most deadly human activities for sea turtles in the Gulf of Mexico and the Caribbean. During the late 1970s the National Marine Fisheries Service began developing turtle excluder devices (TEDs), which allow sea turtles to escape from shrimp nets. By the early 1980s the agency had developed a TED (see Figure 7.5) estimated to exclude 97% of turtles from shrimp nets, while allowing no shrimp to escape. At that time the

NMFS estimated that shrimp trawling killed more than 12,000 sea turtles annually. Despite the proven effectiveness of TEDs and their relatively low cost, use of the devices was bitterly opposed by most shrimpers and the southeastern states in which they were based. The regulatory and legal history of TED usage is described in a chronology compiled by the South Carolina Department of Natural Resources at http://www.dnr.sc.gov/seaturtle/teds.htm.

The chronology reports that during the early 1980s the NMFS asked for voluntary use of the devices by the shrimping industry, but this request was widely ignored. By 1986 less than 2% of the U.S. shrimp fleet was using TEDs. In 1987 federal regulations were published requiring TED usage in certain fisheries during specified seasons. The regulations were challenged in court by the states of North Carolina and Louisiana and by shrimp industry groups. Numerous lawsuits and administrative problems delayed federal enforcement of TED usage until July 20, 1989. Enforcement implementation set off a two-day revolt among Gulf Coast shrimpers. They reportedly "blockaded harbors, impeded navigation, and engaged in other forms of violence to protest against the TED regulations." On July 24, 1989, the federal government backed down, issuing a forty-five-day reprieve in TED enforcement while other options for turtle

FIGURE 7.5

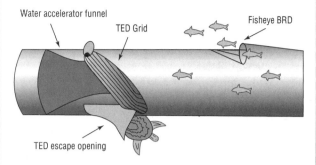

A bycatch reduction device designed to protect sea turtles

Notes: TED is turtle excluder device; BRD is bycatch reduction device.

SOURCE: Richard K. Wallace and Kristen M. Fletcher, "Figure 9," in *Understanding Fisheries Management: A Manual for Understanding the Federal Fisheries Management Process, Including Analysis of the 1996 Sustainable Fisheries Act, Second Edition*, U.S. Department of Commerce, National Oceanic and Atmospheric Administration, National Sea Grant Office, Mississippi Alabama Sea Grant Consortium, 2000, http://nsgl.gso.uri.edu/masgc/masgch00001.pdf (accessed February 28, 2006)

protection were considered. The next day a coalition of environmental groups sued the federal government for failing to enforce the TED regulations and eventually won their case. By 1991 year-round TED use was required for U.S. shrimpers.

On November 21, 1989, Public Law 101-162, Section 609 was enacted in the United States banning the import of shrimp from countries that use harvesting methods deemed harmful to sea turtles. The law was challenged by India, Malaysia, Pakistan, and Thailand as violating commerce agreements under the World Trade Organization (WTO). In 1998 a WTO commission found that the United States was not implementing the law consistently with all countries. In return the United States agreed to change its implementation procedures and offer technical assistance to those countries that requested it.

Each year by May 1 the U.S. Department of State issues a list of nations certified to import shrimp into the United States. Certification is based, in part, on the results of inspections conducted by the Department of State and the National Marine Fisheries Service. On April 28, 2006, the Department of State released a list of thirty-eight nations and one economy (Hong Kong) certified for shrimp imports under Section 609. Certification means that the shrimp were obtained using TEDs, from cold-water regions not populated by sea turtles, from aquaculture (shrimp farming), or by specialized techniques that do not endanger sea turtles. Shrimp imports are allowed from non-certified countries on a shipment-by-shipment basis if the respective governments can show

that the shrimp were harvested in a manner not harmful to sea turtles (http://georgetown.usembassy.gov/guyana/pr_shrimp_08may2006.html).

KEMP'S RIDLEY TURTLE. Kemp's ridley turtle is the smallest sea turtle, with individuals measuring about three feet in length and weighing less than 100 pounds. Kemp's ridley is also the most endangered of the sea turtle species. It has two major nesting sites—Rancho Nuevo, Mexico (the primary nesting location) and the Texas Gulf Coast.

The decline of the Kemp's ridley sea turtle is due primarily to human activities such as egg collecting, fishing for juveniles and adults, and killing of adults for meat or other products. In addition, the turtles have historically been subject to high levels of incidental take by shrimp trawlers. They are also affected by pollution from oil wells, and by floating debris in the Gulf of Mexico, which can choke or entangle turtles. Now under strict protection, the population appears to be in the earliest stages of recovery. In 2001 the Texas Parks and Wildlife Department (TPWD) enacted restrictions on shrimp trawling within Gulf waters near nesting sea turtle populations. In May 2006 the TPWD reported that more than two dozen Kemp's ridley nests had been found along the Texas coast, most at Padre Island National Seashore. Further, the TPWD indicated that nesting activity in Texas is increasing each year and characterized the outlook for the turtles as "mostly good" (http://www.tpwd.state.tx.us/newsmedia/releases/?req=20060508e).

The Desert Tortoise

The desert tortoise (see Figure 7.6) was listed in 1990 as threatened in most of its range in the Mojave and Sonoran Deserts in California, Arizona, Nevada, and Utah. Decline of this species has resulted from collection by humans, predation of young turtles by ravens, off-road vehicles, invasive plant species, and habitat destruction due to development for agriculture, mining, and livestock grazing. Livestock grazing is particularly harmful to tortoises because it results in competition for food, as well as the trampling of young tortoises, eggs, or tortoise burrows. Invasive plant species have caused declines in the native plants that serve as food for tortoises. Off-road vehicles destroy vegetation and sometimes hit tortoises.

Desert tortoise populations are constrained by the fact that females do not reproduce until they are fifteen to twenty years of age (individuals can live eighty to 100 years), and by small clutch sizes, with only three to fourteen eggs per clutch. Juvenile mortality is also extremely high, with only 2% to 3% surviving to adulthood. About half this mortality is due to predation by ravens, whose populations in the desert tortoise's habitat have increased with increasing urbanization of desert

FIGURE 7.6

The desert tortoise is threatened due to habitat destruction, livestock grazing, invasion of nonnative plant species, collection, and predation by ravens. (U.S. Fish and Wildlife Service.)

areas—human garbage provides food for ravens and power lines provide perches.

Protected habitat for the desert tortoise includes areas within Joshua Tree National Park and Lake Mead National Recreation Area in Nevada and Arizona. There is also a desert tortoise research natural area on a Bureau of Land Management habitat in California. A habitat conservation plan for the area around Las Vegas requires developers to pay fees for tortoise conservation.

Snakes and Lizards

SAN FRANCISCO GARTER SNAKE. The San Francisco garter snake is one of the most endangered reptiles in the United States. It was one of the first species to be listed under the Endangered Species Act. The decline of this species can be attributed primarily to habitat loss resulting from urbanization. Most of the snake's habitat was lost when the Skyline Ponds, located along Skyline Boulevard south of San Francisco County along the San Andreas Fault, were drained in 1966 for development. In addition, the building of the San Francisco International Airport and the Bay Area Rapid Transit regional commuter network destroyed additional snake habitat. Pollution and illegal collection have also contributed to the species' decline. Most San Francisco garter snakes today inhabit areas in San Mateo County, south of San Francisco. The species lives close to streams or ponds and feeds mainly on frogs, including Pacific tree frogs, small bullfrogs, and California red-legged frogs, which are also endangered.

LAKE ERIE WATERSNAKE. The Lake Erie watersnake inhabits portions of the Ohio mainland, as well as several small islands in Lake Erie. Its population has declined due primarily to habitat loss and human persecution, among other factors. The Lake Erie watersnake is now extinct on three islands that it previously inhabited. The

species was listed as threatened in 1999, and a recovery plan was completed by the U.S. Fish and Wildlife Service in September 2003.

MONITO GECKO. The endangered Monito gecko is a small lizard less than two inches long. This species exists only on the thirty-eight-acre Monito Island off the Puerto Rican coast. Endangerment of the Monito gecko has resulted from human activity and habitat destruction. After World War II the U.S. military used Monito Island as a site for bombing exercises, causing large-scale habitat destruction. The military also introduced predatory rats, which eat gecko eggs. In 1982 the FWS observed only twenty-four Monito geckos on Monito Island. In 1985 Monito Island was designated critical habitat for the species. The Commonwealth of Puerto Rico is now managing the island for the gecko and as a refuge for seabirds; unauthorized human visitation is prohibited.

HORNED LIZARDS (HORNY TOADS). Horned lizards are native to the deserts of North America. There are fourteen species of horned lizards. All species have flat, broad torsos and spiny scales and feed largely on ants. Although all horned lizards are reptiles, they are often referred to as horny toads because they bear some resemblance to toads in size and shape.

The Texas horned lizard was once abundant in the state of Texas and was designated the official state reptile in 1992. It has declined largely as a result of pesticide pollution, the spread of invasive fire ants across the state, and habitat loss. It is protected by state law in Texas.

In addition to habitat loss, California coastal horned lizards have been negatively affected by the proliferation of tiny black and dark brown Argentine ants, which have displaced the larger native ants on which the horned lizards depend for much of their food. Because the smaller, faster Argentine ants are more difficult to catch, coastal horned lizards from the Mexican border up to Los Angeles have experienced a sharp decline, according to a 2002 study by researchers at the University of California, San Diego (http://ucsdnews.ucsd.edu/newsrel/science/mclizard.htm).

CROCODILIANS. Crocodilians play a crucial role in their habitats. They control fish populations and also dig water holes, which are important to many species in times of drought. The disappearance of alligators and crocodiles has a profound effect on the biological communities these animals occupy. There are two imperiled crocodilian species in the United States—the American alligator and the American crocodile. They are very similar in appearance with only slight differences. The crocodile has a narrower, more pointed snout and an indentation in its upper jaw that allows a tooth to be seen when its mouth is closed.

The American alligator has a unique history under the Endangered Species Act. It was on the first list of endangered species published in 1967. During the 1970s and 1980s populations of the species in many states rebounded in abundance and could have been delisted. Instead they were reclassified as threatened. This measure was taken, in part, because federal officials acknowledged a certain amount of "public hostility" toward the creatures and feared that delisting would open the populations to excessive hunting. Also, it was feared that the American alligator was so similar in appearance to the highly endangered American crocodile that delisting the alligator might lead to accidental "taking" of the crocodile species. By 1987 the alligator was considered fully recovered in the United States. As of March 2006 the alligator is listed as threatened due to similarity of appearance to other crocodilians throughout its entire range.

The American crocodile is another success story of the Endangered Species Act. When the species was originally listed as endangered in 1975, less than 300 individuals existed. Over the next three decades the species thrived and expanded its nesting range to new locations on the east and west coasts of Florida. In March 2005 the U.S. Fish and Wildlife Service proposed downlisting the species in Florida to threatened. At that time the agency estimated there were 500 to 1,000 American crocodiles in the state and that the population was increasing. The FWS also announced plans to conduct a five-year status review of the American crocodile.

TABLE 7.6

Foreign endangered and threatened reptile species, March 2006

Status*	Species name	Status*	Species name
E	Alligator, Chinese (Alligator sinensis)	T	Iguana, Turks and Caicos (Cyclura carinata carinata)
E	Boa, Jamaican (Epicrates subflavus)	E	Iguana, Watling Island ground (Cyclura rileyi rileyi)
E	Boa, Round Island bolyeria (Bolyeria multocarinata)	T	Iguana, White Cay ground (Cyclura rileyi cristata)
E	Boa, Round Island casarea (Casarea dussumieri)	E	Lizard, Hierro giant (Gallotia simonyi simonyi)
E	Caiman, Apaporis River (Caiman crocodilus apaporiensis)	T	Lizard, Ibiza wall (Podarcis pityusensis)
E	Caiman, black (Melanosuchus niger)	E	Lizard, Maria Island ground (Cnemidophorus vanzoi)
E	Caiman, broad-snouted (Caiman latirostris)	E	Monitor, desert (Varanus griseus)
T(S/A)	Caiman, brown (Caiman crocodilus fuscus (includes Caiman crocodilus chiapasius))	E	Monitor, Indian (=Bengal) (Varanus bengalensis)
		E	Monitor, Komodo Island (Varanus komodoensis)
T(S/A)	Caiman, common (Caiman crocodilus crocodilus)	E	Monitor, yellow (Varanus flavescens)
T	Caiman, Yacare (Caiman yacare)	E	Python, Indian (Python molurus molurus)
E	Chuckwalla, San Esteban Island (Sauromalus varius)	T	Rattlesnake, Aruba Island (Crotalus unicolor)
E	Crocodile, African dwarf (Osteolaemus tetraspis tetraspis)	E	Sea turtle, olive ridley Mexican nesting population (Lepidochelys olivacea)
E	Crocodile, African slender-snouted (Crocodylus cataphractus)		
E	Crocodile, Ceylon mugger (Crocodylus palustris kimbula)	T	Skink, Round Island (Leiolopisma telfairi)
E	Crocodile, Congo dwarf (Osteolaemus tetraspis osborni)	E	Snake, Maria Island (Liophus ornatus)
E	Crocodile, Cuban (Crocodylus rhombifer)	E	Tartaruga (Podocnemis expansa)
E	Crocodile, Morelet's (Crocodylus moreletii)	E	Terrapin, river (Batagur baska)
E	Crocodile, mugger (Crocodylus palustris palustris)	E	Tomistoma (Tomistoma schlegelii)
T	Crocodile, Nile (Crocodylus niloticus)	E	Tortoise, angulated (Geochelone yniphora)
E	Crocodile, Orinoco (Crocodylus intermedius)	E	Tortoise, Bolson (Gopherus flavomarginatus)
E	Crocodile, Philippine (Crocodylus novaeguineae mindorensis)	E	Tortoise, Galapagos (Geochelone nigra (=elephantopus))
E	Crocodile, saltwater except Australia & Papua New Guinea (Crocodylus porosus)	E	Tortoise, Madagascar radiated (Geochelone radiata)
		E	Tracaja (Podocnemis unifilis)
T	Crocodile, saltwater Australia (Crocodylus porosus)	E	Tuatara (Sphenodon punctatus)
E	Crocodile, Siamese (Crocodylus siamensis)	E	Tuatara, Brother's Island (Sphenodon guntheri)
E	Gavial (Gavialis gangeticus)	E	Turtle, aquatic box (Terrapene coahuila)
E	Gecko, day (Phelsuma edwardnewtoni)	E	Turtle, black softshell (Trionyx nigricans)
E	Gecko, Round Island day (Phelsuma guentheri)	E	Turtle, Brazilian sideneck (Phrynops hogei)
T	Gecko, Serpent Island (Cyrtodactylus serpensinsula)	E	Turtle, Burmese peacock (Morenia ocellata)
T	Iguana, Acklins ground (Cyclura rileyi nuchalis)	E	Turtle, Cat Island (Trachemys terrapen)
T	Iguana, Allen's Cay (Cyclura cychlura inornata)	E	Turtle, Central American river (Dermatemys mawii)
T	Iguana, Andros Island ground (Cyclura cychlura cychlura)	E	Turtle, Cuatro Cienegas softshell (Trionyx ater)
E	Iguana, Anegada ground (Cyclura pinguis)	E	Turtle, geometric (Psammobates geometricus)
E	Iguana, Barrington land (Conolophus pallidus)	E	Turtle, Inagua Island (Trachemys stejnegeri malonei)
T	Iguana, Cayman Brac ground (Cyclura nubila caymanensis)	E	Turtle, Indian sawback (Kachuga tecta tecta)
T	Iguana, Cuban ground (Cyclura nubila nubila)	E	Turtle, Indian softshell (Trionyx gangeticus)
T	Iguana, Exuma Island (Cyclura cychlura figginsi)	E	Turtle, peacock softshell (Trionyx hurum)
E	Iguana, Fiji banded (Brachylophus fasciatus)	E	Turtle, short-necked or western swamp (Pseudemydura umbrina)
E	Iguana, Fiji crested (Brachylophus vitiensis)	E	Turtle, South American red-lined (Trachemys scripta callirostris)
E	Iguana, Grand Cayman ground (Cyclura nubila lewisi)	E	Turtle, spotted pond (Geoclemys hamiltonii)
E	Iguana, Jamaican (Cyclura collei)	E	Turtle, three-keeled Asian (Melanochelys tricarinata)
T	Iguana, Mayaguana (Cyclura carinata bartschi)	E	Viper, Lar Valley (Vipera latifii)

*E=endangered; T=threatened; T (S/A)=similarity of appearance to a threatened taxon.

SOURCE: Adapted from "Foreign Listed Species Report as of 03/06/2006," in *Threatened and Endangered Species System (TESS)*, U.S. Department of the Interior, U.S. Fish and Wildlife Service, March 6, 2006, http://ecos.fws.gov/tess_public/servlet/gov.doi.tess_public.servlets.ForeignListing?listings=0#A (accessed March 6, 2006)

Threatened and Endangered Foreign Reptile Species

As of March 2006 there were eighty-three foreign reptile species listed under the ESA. (See Table 7.6.) The list is dominated by squamata (lizard and snake species) with thirty-six species, followed by the turtles (twenty-three species), crocodilians (twenty-two species), and tuataras (two species).

The Word Conservation Union's *2004 Red List of Threatened Species* (2004, http://www.redlist.org/) reports that 304 reptile species are threatened. This represents nearly two-thirds of the 499 reptile species evaluated, but only 4% of all described species (8,163).

LIZARDS AND TURTLES. Monitor lizards are among the largest lizard species in existence. The Komodo dragon, native to only a few islands in Indonesia, is the world's largest lizard. It reaches lengths of as much as ten feet and weighs as much as 300 pounds. Despite the fact that the Komodo dragon is protected under Appendix I of the Convention on International Trade in Endangered Species (CITES) treaty, one of the greatest threats to this species is illegal trade. The price on delivery is approximately $30,000 for one Komodo dragon specimen.

Gray's monitor lizard, a species found in forested low mountain habitats of the Philippine Islands, is also prized in illegal trade. Gray's monitor is also protected under CITES Appendix I. Many turtles are highly imperiled, particularly in Asia, where they are hunted for both food and medicine.

CROCODILIANS. Illegal trade poses one of the greatest threats to crocodilians, despite CITES restrictions. Conservation efforts include enforcement of trade restrictions and habitat restoration. Captive breeding programs are also underway for several species.

The Chinese alligator is one of many species listed in CITES Appendix I. Unfortunately, this species is among those most prized by collectors, commanding a black market price of as much as $15,000. The false gavial, a crocodilian that grows to thirteen feet in length and is native to Indonesia, sells for an estimated $5,000 per specimen. Like the Chinese alligator, the false gavial is protected under CITES Appendix I.

TUATARAS. The two-foot long, lizard-like tuatara is sometimes called a living fossil, being the sole existing representative of a once diverse group, the Sphenodontia, which coexisted with dinosaurs. Tuataras are native to New Zealand and the Cook Strait. Like many other reptiles, tuataras are valued by collectors. They are protected by CITES under Appendix I.

CHAPTER 8
TERRESTRIAL MAMMALS

Terrestrial animals are animals that inhabit the land. Mammals are warm-blooded, breathe air, have hair at some point in their lives, give birth to live young (as opposed to laying eggs), and nourish their young by secreting milk.

The biggest cause of terrestrial mammalian decline and extinction in the twentieth-first century is habitat loss and degradation. As humans convert forests, grasslands, rivers, and wetlands for various uses, they relegate many species to precarious existences in small, fragmented habitat patches. In addition, some terrestrial mammals have been purposely eliminated by humans. For example, bison (buffalo), elk, and beaver stocks were severely depleted in the United States following colonization by European settlers. All three species were nearly hunted to extinction by the end of the 1800s. The disappearance of native large game had consequences on other species. Wolves and other predators began preying on livestock and became the subject of massive kill-offs by humans.

Some terrestrial mammal species have been imperiled, in part, because they are considered dangerous to human life. This has been the case for many bears, wolves, and mountain lions. Changing attitudes have led to interest in preserving all species, and conservation measures have allowed several terrestrial mammals to recover.

ENDANGERED AND THREATENED U.S. SPECIES

As of March 2006 there were sixty-seven species of terrestrial mammals in the United States listed under the Endangered Species Act (ESA) as endangered or threatened. (See Table 8.1.) Nearly all have an endangered listing, meaning that they are at risk of extinction. Most have recovery plans in place.

The imperiled species fall into nine broad categories:

- Bats
- Bears
- Canines—foxes and wolves
- Deer, caribou, pronghorns, and bighorn sheep
- Felines—jaguars, jaguarundis, lynx, ocelots, panthers, and pumas
- Ferrets
- Rabbits
- Rodents—beavers, mice, prairie dogs, rats, squirrels, and voles
- Shrews

Approximately $51 million was spent under the ESA during fiscal year 2004 to conserve imperiled terrestrial mammal species. Table 8.2 shows the ten species with the highest expenditures. The grizzly bear was the most expensive ($7.2 million), followed by the Indiana bat ($4.9 million), and the Louisiana black bear ($3.8 million).

Bats

Bats belong to the taxonomic order Chiroptera, which means "hand-wing." They are the only true flying mammals. There are more than 900 species of bats worldwide; however, most are found in warm tropical regions. Only about four dozen species inhabit the United States. They typically weigh less than two ounces and have wingspans of less than twenty inches. Most are insectivores, meaning that insects are their primary food source. Bats prefer to sleep during the day and feed after dusk. Biologists believe that bats are vastly underappreciated for their role in controlling nighttime insect populations.

As of February 2006 there were nine bat species in the United States listed by the U.S. Fish and Wildlife

TABLE 8.1

Endangered and threatened terrestrial mammal species in the United States, March 2006

Inverted common name	Scientific name	Listing status [a]	Recovery plan date	Recovery plan stage [b]
Bat, gray	*Myotis grisescens*	E	7/8/1982	F
Bat, Hawaiian hoary	*Lasiurus cinereus semotus*	E	5/11/1998	F
Bat, Indiana	*Myotis sodalis*	E	10/14/1983	F
Bat, lesser long-nosed	*Leptonycteris curasoae yerbabuenae*	E	3/4/1997	F
Bat, little Mariana fruit	*Pteropus tokudae*	E	11/2/1990	F
Bat, Mariana fruit (=Mariana flying fox)	*Pteropus mariannus mariannus*	T	None	—
Bat, Mexican long-nosed	*Leptonycteris nivalis*	E	9/8/1994	F
Bat, Ozark big-eared	*Corynorhinus (=plecotus) townsendii ingens*	E	3/28/1995	RF(1)
Bat, Virginia big-eared	*Corynorhinus (=plecotus) townsendii virginianus*	E	5/8/1984	F
Bear, American black	*Ursus americanus*	T (S/A)	None	—
Bear, grizzly	*Ursus arctos horribilis*	EXPN, T	9/10/1993	RF(1)
Bear, Louisiana black	*Ursus americanus luteolus*	T	9/27/1995	F
Caribou, woodland	*Rangifer tarandus caribou*	E	3/4/1994	RF(2)
Deer, Columbian white-tailed	*Odocoileus virginianus leucurus*	DM, E	6/14/1983	RF(1)
Deer, key	*Odocoileus virginianus clavium*	E	5/18/1999	F
Ferret, black-footed	*Mustela nigripes*	E, EXPN	8/8/1988	RF(1)
Fox, San Joaquin kit	*Vulpes macrotis mutica*	E	9/30/1998	F
Fox, San Miguel Island	*Urocyon littoralis littoralis*	E	None	—
Fox, Santa Catalina Island	*Urocyon littoralis catalinae*	E	None	—
Fox, Santa Cruz Island	*Urocyon littoralis santacruzae*	E	None	—
Fox, Santa Rosa Island	*Urocyon littoralis santarosae*	E	None	—
Jaguar	*Panthera onca*	E	8/22/1990	F
Jaguarundi, Gulf Coast	*Herpailurus (=felis) yagouaroundi cacomitli*	E	8/22/1990	F
Jaguarundi, Sinaloan	*Herpailurus (=Felis) yagouaroundi tolteca*	E	Exempt	—
Kangaroo rat, Fresno	*Dipodomys nitratoides exilis*	E	9/30/1998	F
Kangaroo rat, giant	*Dipodomys ingens*	E	9/30/1998	F
Kangaroo rat, Morro Bay	*Dipodomys heermanni morroensis*	E	1/25/2000	RD(1)
Kangaroo rat, San Bernardino Merriam's	*Dipodomys merriami parvus*	E	None	—
Kangaroo rat, Stephens'	*Dipodomys stephensi (including d. cascus)*	E	6/23/1997	D
Kangaroo rat, Tipton	*Dipodomys nitratoides nitratoides*	E	9/30/1998	F
Lynx, Canada	*Lynx canadensis*	T	None	—
Mountain beaver, Point Arena	*Aplodontia rufa nigra*	E	6/2/1998	F
Mouse, Alabama beach	*Peromyscus polionotus ammobates*	E	8/12/1987	F
Mouse, Anastasia Island beach	*Peromyscus polionotus phasma*	E	9/23/1993	F
Mouse, Choctawhatchee beach	*Peromyscus polionotus allophrys*	E	8/12/1987	F
Mouse, Key Largo cotton	*Peromyscus gossypinus allapaticola*	E	5/18/1999	F
Mouse, Pacific pocket	*Perognathus longimembris pacificus*	E	9/28/1998	F
Mouse, Perdido Key beach	*Peromyscus polionotus trissyllepsis*	E	8/12/1987	F
Mouse, Preble's meadow jumping	*Zapus hudsonius preblei*	T	None	—
Mouse, salt marsh harvest	*Reithrodontomys raviventris*	E	11/16/1984	F
Mouse, southeastern beach	*Peromyscus polionotus niveiventris*	T	9/23/1993	F
Mouse, St. Andrew beach	*Peromyscus polionotus peninsularis*	E	None	—
Ocelot	*Leopardus (=felis) pardalis*	E	8/22/1990	F
Panther, Florida	*Puma (=felis) concolor coryi*	E	1/31/2006	RD(3)
Prairie dog, Utah	*Cynomys parvidens*	T	9/30/1991	F
Pronghorn, sonoran	*Antilocapra americana sonoriensis*	E	12/3/1998	RF(1)
Puma (=cougar), eastern	*Puma (=felis) concolor couguar*	E	8/2/1982	F
Puma (=mountain lion)	*Puma (=felis) concolor (all subspecies except coryi)*	T (S/A)	None	—
Rabbit, lower keys marsh	*Sylvilagus palustris hefneri*	E	5/18/1999	F
Rabbit, pygmy	*Brachylagus idahoensis*	E	None	—
Rabbit, riparian brush	*Sylvilagus bachmani riparius*	E	9/30/1998	F
Rat, rice	*Oryzomys palustris natator*	E	5/18/1999	F
Sheep, bighorn	*Ovis canadensis*	E	10/25/2000	F
Sheep, bighorn	*Ovis canadensis californiana*	E	7/30/2003	D
Shrew, Buena Vista Lake ornate	*Sorex ornatus relictus*	E	9/30/1998	F
Squirrel, Carolina northern flying	*Glaucomys sabrinus coloratus*	E	9/24/1990	F
Squirrel, Delmarva peninsula fox	*Sciurus niger cinereus*	E, EXPN	6/8/1993	RF(2)
Squirrel, Mount Graham red	*Tamiasciurus hudsonicus grahamensis*	E	5/3/1993	F
Squirrel, northern Idaho ground	*Spermophilus brunneus brunneus*	T	9/16/2003	F
Vole, Amargosa	*Microtus californicus scirpensis*	E	9/15/1997	F
Vole, Florida salt marsh	*Microtus pennsylvanicus dukecampbelli*	E	9/30/1997	F
Vole, Hualapai Mexican	*Microtus mexicanus hualpaiensis*	E	8/19/1991	F
West Virginia northern flying squirrel	*Glaucomys sabrinus fuscus*	E	9/24/1990	F

Service (FWS) as endangered or threatened: gray bat, Hawaiian hoary bat, Indiana bat, lesser long-nosed bat, little Mariana fruit bat, Mariana fruit bat, Mexican long-nosed bat, Ozark big-eared bat, and Virginia big-eared bat.

Bats are imperiled for a variety of reasons, including habitat degradation, disturbance of hibernating and maternity colonies, direct extermination by humans, and the indirect effects of pesticide use on insects. More than $8 million was spent under the ESA on imperiled bat

TABLE 8.1

Endangered and threatened terrestrial mammal species in the United States, March 2006 [CONTINUED]

Inverted common name	Scientific name	Listing status[a]	Recovery plan date	Recovery plan stage[b]
Wolf, gray	*Canis lupus*	E, EXPN,T	8/3/1987	RF(1)
Wolf, red	*Canis rufus*	E, EXPN	10/26/1990	RF(2)
Woodrat, Key Largo	*Neotoma floridana smalli*	E	5/18/1999	F
Woodrat, riparian (=San Joaquin Valley)	*Neotoma fuscipes riparia*	E	9/30/1998	F

[a]E=endangered, T=threatened, DM=delisted taxon, recovered, being monitored first five years, EXPN=experimental population, non-essential, T(S/A)=similarity of appearance to a threatened taxon.
[b]Recovery plan stages: F=final, D=draft, RD=draft under revision, RF=final revision.

SOURCE: Adapted from "Listed FWS/Joint FWS and NMFS Species and Populations with Recovery Plans (Sorted by Listed Entity)" and "Listed U.S. Species by Taxonomic Group," in *Threatened and Endangered Species System (TESS)*, U.S. Department of the Interior, U.S. Fish and Wildlife Service, March 1, 2006, http://ecos.fws.gov/tess_public/SpeciesRecovery.do?sort=1 and http://ecos.fws.gov/tess_public/SpeciesReport.do?kingdom=V&listingType=L (accessed March 1, 2006)

TABLE 8.2

The ten listed terrestrial mammal entities with the highest expenditures under the Endangered Species Act, fiscal year 2004

Rank	Entity	Listing[a]	Expenditures
1	Grizzly bear (lower 48 states, except EXPN[a])	T	$7,240,402
2	Indiana bat	E	$4,920,682
3	Louisiana black bear	T	$3,811,626
4	Canada lynx	T	$3,012,982
5	San Joaquin kit fox	E	$2,641,027
6	Florida panther	E	$2,489,720
7	Gray wolf (eastern DPS[b])	T	$2,280,463
8	Grey wolf (western DPS[b])	T	$2,272,904
9	Key deer	E	$2,116,000
10	Black-footed ferret (in specific portions of Arizona Colorado, Montana, South Dakota, Utah, and Wyoming)	EXPN	$2,019,576

[a]E=endangered, T=threatened, EXPN=experimental population, non-essential.
[b]DPS is distinct population segment.

SOURCE: Adapted from "Table 1. Reported FY2004 Expenditures for Endangered and Threatened Species, Not Including Land Acquisition Costs," in *Federal and State Endangered and Threatened Species Expenditures: Fiscal Year 2004*, U.S. Department of the Interior, U.S. Fish and Wildlife Service, January 2005, http://www.fws.gov/endangered/expenditures/reports/FWS%20Endangered%20Species%202004%20Expenditures%20Report.pdf (accessed February 11, 2006)

---

species during fiscal year 2004. More than half of the money ($4.9 million) was devoted to the Indiana bat.

INDIANA BAT. The Indiana bat is a medium-sized, brown-colored bat found throughout a region encompassing the mid-Atlantic states and into the Midwest. (See Figure 8.1.) There are nine caves considered prime hibernation spots (or hibernacula) for the species during the winter. The bats are very sensitive to any disturbances during hibernation. If they are awakened, they become agitated and waste precious energy flying around frantically. This can leave them too weak and malnourished to survive the remainder of the winter. In the springtime, adult females move to wooded areas near agricultural crops and form maternity colonies. Loss of suitable habi-

tat due to deforestation has disrupted this natural process. In addition, the bats have a low reproductive rate, producing only one baby per year. This makes it difficult for their populations to grow.

During the 1800s some hibernacula became popular winter visiting spots for tourists, cave explorers, bat fanciers, and well-meaning researchers. These disturbances, along with removal of suitable maternity habitat, led to decreased numbers of Indiana bats. The U.S. Fish and Wildlife Service estimates that the species numbered close to one million individuals in 1967 when it was listed under the Endangered Species Act. As of 2003 that number had dropped to around 380,000. In 2002 winter tours were discontinued at the Wyandotte Cave in Indiana, a prime hibernacula for the bats. Biologists report that this measure has resulted in increased bat numbers in the cave.

Bears

Bears belong to the family Ursidae. Their furry bodies are large and heavy, with powerful arms and legs and short tails. For the most part they feed on fruits and insects, but they also eat meat.

As of February 2006 there were three bear species listed as endangered or threatened in the United States: the American black bear, the Louisiana black bear, and the grizzly bear. Many bears are endangered due to habitat loss. According to the U.S. Fish and Wildlife Service, bears have been eliminated from about 50% to 75% of their natural ranges. Some bears have been hunted because they are considered predatory or threatening, while others are hunted for sport.

More than $11 million was spent under the ESA on imperiled bear species during fiscal year 2004. More than half of this money was devoted to the grizzly bear.

GRIZZLY BEARS. Grizzly bears are large animals, standing four feet high at the shoulder when on four paws, and as tall as seven feet when upright. Males weigh

FIGURE 8.1

Range and prime hibernacula for Indiana bats, 1995

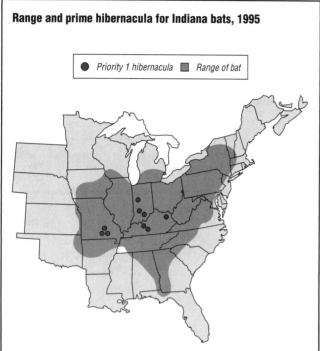

SOURCE: Ronald D. Drobney and Richard L. Clawson, "Figure 1. Range of the Indiana Bat and Locations of Priority 1 Hibernacula," in "Indiana Bats," in "Mammals" *Our Living Resources: A Report to the Nation on the Distribution, Abundance, and Health of U.S. Plants, Animals, and Ecosystems*, U.S. Department of the Interior, U.S. Geological Survey, National Biological Service, 1995, http://biology.usgs.gov/s+t/pdf/Mammals.pdf (accessed March 1, 2006)

FIGURE 8.2

Distribution of grizzly bear ecosystems in the lower 48 states, 1990

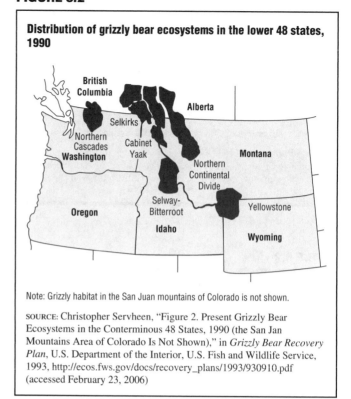

Note: Grizzly habitat in the San Juan mountains of Colorado is not shown.

SOURCE: Christopher Servheen, "Figure 2. Present Grizzly Bear Ecosystems in the Conterminous 48 States, 1990 (the San Jan Mountains Area of Colorado Is Not Shown)," in *Grizzly Bear Recovery Plan*, U.S. Department of the Interior, U.S. Fish and Wildlife Service, 1993, http://ecos.fws.gov/docs/recovery_plans/1993/930910.pdf (accessed February 23, 2006)

500 pounds on average but are sometimes as large as 900 pounds. Females weigh 350 pounds on average. Grizzlies have a distinctive shoulder hump, which actually represents a massive digging muscle. Their claws are two to four inches long.

The grizzly bear was originally found throughout the continental United States, but has now been eliminated from all but a handful of western habitats. The first recovery plan for grizzly bears was published by the Fish and Wildlife Service in 1982. A revised recovery plan was published in 1993. At that time the species was found in a few ecosystems as shown in Figure 8.2; however, the populations were considered distinct from one another. The grizzly bear has declined due primarily to aggressive hunting and habitat loss. It is listed as threatened under the Endangered Species Act, except in nonessential experimental populations in parts of Idaho and Montana.

The federal government has established recovery zones for the grizzly bear in Yellowstone National Park, the North Continental Divide, the Selkirk and Bitterroot Mountains in Idaho, the North Cascades, the San Juan Mountains in Colorado, and the Cabinet/Yaak area on the Canadian border. Recovery plans for this species are coordinated under the Interagency Grizzly Bear Committee, which was created in 1983 (http://www.fs.fed.us/r1/wildlife/igbc/).

In November 2005 the FWS proposed removing the Yellowstone National Park population from the list of endangered and threatened species. Biologists reported that the population had grown from only 200 to 300 individuals in the 1970s to more than 600 bears.

Canines

Canine is the common term used to describe a member of the Canidae family of carnivorous animals. This family includes wolves, foxes, coyotes, jackals, and domestic dogs.

As of February 2006 there were five fox species and two wolf species listed under the Endangered Species Act in the United States. More than $4 million was spent under the ESA during fiscal year 2004 on endangered wolves. Just over $3 million was appropriated for the preservation of endangered fox species.

WOLVES. Wolves were once among the most widely distributed mammals on Earth. Prior to European settlement, wolves ranged over most of North America, from central Mexico to the Arctic Ocean. Their decline has largely resulted from hunting. In 1914 Congress authorized funding for the removal of all large predators, including wolves, from federal lands. By the 1940s wolves had been eliminated from most of the contiguous

United States. In 1973 the wolf, which had all but disappeared, became the first animal listed as endangered under the ESA. Two species of wolves exist in North America today, the gray wolf and the red wolf. Both are imperiled.

In 1991 Congress instructed the U.S. Fish and Wildlife Service to prepare an environmental impact report on the possibility of reintroducing wolves to habitats in the United States. Reintroductions began in 1995. Over a two-year period, sixty-six gray wolves from southwestern Canada were introduced to Yellowstone National Park and central Idaho.

Wolf reintroductions were not greeted with universal enthusiasm. Ranchers, in particular, were concerned that wolves would attack livestock. They were also worried that their land would be open to government restrictions as a result of the wolves' presence. Some ranchers said openly that they would shoot wolves they found on their property. Several measures were adopted to address the concerns of the ranchers. The most significant was that ranchers would be reimbursed for livestock losses from a compensation fund maintained by the Defenders of Wildlife, a private conservation group based in Washington, D.C. Defenders of Wildlife in *The Bailey Wildlife Foundation Wolf Compensation Trust* (http://www.defenders. org/wildlife/wolf/wolfcomp.pdf) state that between 1987 and 2005 the fund had paid out $543,905 to 431 ranchers, covering the losses of 1,378 sheep, 565 cattle, and sixty-one other animals killed by wolves.

Wolf introductions were legally challenged in 1997, when the American Farm Bureau Federation initiated a lawsuit calling for the removal of wolves from Yellowstone. The farm coalition scored an initial victory, but in January 2000 the Tenth Circuit Court of Appeals in Denver overturned the decision upon appeal by the U.S. Department of the Interior, the World Wildlife Fund, and other conservation groups.

Despite the concern of ranchers and livestock owners, a recovered wolf population in the Yellowstone Park area has only slightly reduced populations of cattle, sheep, elk, moose, bison, and deer. In fact, wolves weed out sick and weak animals, thus improving the overall health of prey populations. Wolf predation on herbivorous species also takes pressure off vegetation and produces carrion for an array of scavengers including eagles, ravens, cougars, and foxes. Finally, wolves have increased visitor attendance to Yellowstone National Park, generating an estimated $7–$10 million in additional net income each year.

The U.S. Fish and Wildlife Service issues an annual report on the status of gray wolf populations in the Northern Rocky Mountain states (Idaho, Montana, and Wyoming). The latest report covers calendar year 2005

(http://westerngraywolf.fws.gov/annualrpt05/2005_WOLF_ REPORT_TOTAL.pdf). It places the population of gray wolves at 1,020 individuals, including seventy-one breeding pairs (an adult male and female raising two or more pups). A map of the entire wolf recovery area is shown in Figure 8.3. An historical breakdown of populations by area is shown in Figure 8.4. Gray wolves in central Idaho and the greater Yellowstone Park area have been quite successful. Recovery has been more challenging in the northwest Montana recovery area. In 2003 the Northwest Montana population of the gray wolf was reclassified from endangered to threatened. However, the decision was reversed in 2005 following a court challenge.

As of February 2006 the gray wolf is listed under the Endangered Species Act as endangered throughout the lower forty-eight states, except in Minnesota and where it is an experimental population. Gray wolves in the greater Yellowstone Park area, central Idaho, and portions of Arizona, New Mexico, and Texas are classified as nonessential experimental populations. Gray wolves in Minnesota are designated as threatened.

The red wolf (see Figure 8.5) was once found throughout the eastern United States, but declined as a result of habitat loss and aggressive hunting by humans. The species was first listed as endangered in 1967. The red wolf is a smaller species than its relative, the gray wolf, and, despite its name, may have any of several coat colors including black, brown, gray, and yellow. In 1975, to prevent the immediate extinction of this species, the U.S. Fish and Wildlife Service captured the twenty-some remaining individuals and began a captive breeding program. The red wolf reintroduction program began in 1987, marking the first reintroduction of a species extinct in the wild.

Red wolves now inhabit an area covering about one million acres in North Carolina and Tennessee, including three national wildlife refuges, a Department of Defense bombing range, some state-owned lands, and private property (with the permission and cooperation of landowners). These wolves are classified as nonessential experimental populations. Throughout the remainder of the lower forty-eight states, the red wolf is still considered endangered.

Deer, Caribou, Pronghorn, and Bighorn Sheep

Deer and caribou are members of the Cervidae family, along with elk and moose. Pronghorn are the last surviving members of the Antilocapridae family and are often confused with antelopes. Bighorn sheep belong to the large Bovidae family, which also contains antelopes, bison, gazelles, and domesticated sheep, cattle, and goats. Although these species are diverse in taxonomy, the wild populations share a common threat—they are popular big-game animals for hunters.

FIGURE 8.3

Recovery areas for the gray wolf

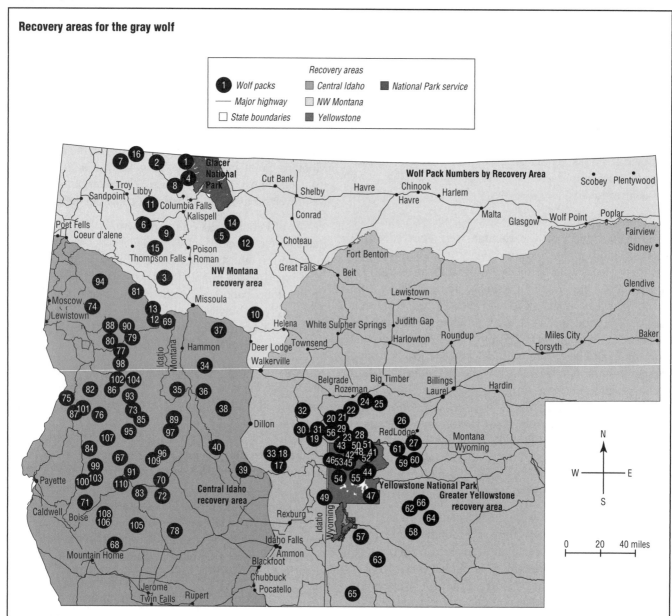

SOURCE: D. Boyd, ed., "Figure 1. Central Idaho, Northwest Montana and Greater Yellowstone Wolf Recovery Areas," in *Rocky Mountain Wolf Recovery 2004 Annual Report*, U.S. Department of the Interior, U.S. Fish and Wildlife Service, 2005, http://westerngraywolf.fws.gov/annualrpt04/index.htm (accessed March 2, 2006)

As of February 2006 there were five species of big game listed under the Endangered Species Act, as follows:

- Woodland caribou
- Columbian white-tailed deer
- Key deer
- Sonoran pronghorn
- Bighorn sheep

According to the U.S. Fish and Wildlife Service, approximately $3.8 million was spent under the ESA during fiscal year 2004 to preserve imperiled big-game species. More than half of the funds ($2 million) were devoted to the Key deer, found only in the Florida Keys.

KEY DEER. The Key deer is a small deer weighing only sixty to eighty pounds when fully grown and standing about two feet tall. It is the smallest subspecies of the North American white-tailed deer. Overhunting during the early 1900s drove the Key deer to the brink of extinction. Only two dozen individuals remained by the early 1950s when a federal refuge was established for them. In 1967 the Key deer was classified as endangered under the ESA. By 1990 the population reached 250–300 individuals and continued to grow, reaching nearly 700

FIGURE 8.4

Population trends for gray wolves in the Rocky Mountains, 1979–2004

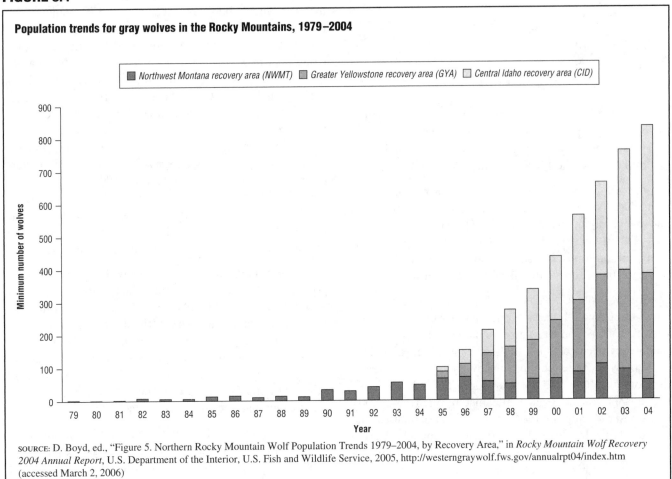

Legend: ■ Northwest Montana recovery area (NWMT) ■ Greater Yellowstone recovery area (GYA) □ Central Idaho recovery area (CID)

y-axis: Minimum number of wolves

x-axis: Year — 79 80 81 82 83 84 85 86 87 88 89 90 91 92 93 94 95 96 97 98 99 00 01 02 03 04

SOURCE: D. Boyd, ed., "Figure 5. Northern Rocky Mountain Wolf Population Trends 1979–2004, by Recovery Area," in *Rocky Mountain Wolf Recovery 2004 Annual Report*, U.S. Department of the Interior, U.S. Fish and Wildlife Service, 2005, http://westerngraywolf.fws.gov/annualrpt04/index.htm (accessed March 2, 2006)

FIGURE 8.5

The red wolf is found in the eastern United States. (U.S. Fish and Wildlife Service.)

by the end of the decade. This number is close to what biologists believe to be the historical population of the animal. However, the future of the Key deer is considered insecure due to continuing threats of loss of habitat, a low reproductive rate, and high mortality caused by vehicle strikes. Biologists fear the entire population could be wiped out by a catastrophic event, such as a hurricane.

Recovery criteria for the Key deer (and dozens of other imperiled species) were laid out in a 1999 document, the *South Florida Multi-Species Recovery Plan*. In 2004 a comprehensive implementation schedule was published for the plan that prioritizes the recovery tasks and identifies the entities, time frames, and costs associated with accomplishing the tasks.

Felines

Feline is the common term used for a member of the Felidae family. This diverse family includes bobcats, cheetahs, cougars, jaguars, jaguarundis, leopards, lions, lynx, panthers, pumas, tigers, and domesticated cats. All of the wild species are under threat as development has left them with less and less natural habitat in which to live.

As of February 2006 there were seven wild feline species listed as endangered or threatened under the ESA in the United States:

- Jaguar

- Gulf Coast jaguarundi

- Sinaloan jaguarundi
- Canada lynx
- Ocelot
- Florida panther
- Puma

Nearly $6 million was spent under the Endangered Species Act to preserve these species during fiscal year 2004. Most of the money was devoted to the Canada lynx ($3 million) and the Florida panther ($2.5 million).

CANADA LYNX. The Canada lynx is a medium-sized feline; adults average thirty to thirty-five inches in length and weigh about twenty pounds. The animal has tufted ears, a short tail, long legs, and large flat paws that allow it to walk on top of the snow. Canada lynx inhabit cold, moist northern forests dominated by coniferous trees.

In 1982 the U.S. Fish and Wildlife Service designated the Canada lynx as a candidate species for listing. However, no action was taken on listing until 1994, when the agency decided to list the species as threatened. This decision was challenged in court by a group of conservation organizations led by Defenders of Wildlife. This began a protracted legal battle that resulted in a 2004 court order forcing the FWS to set critical habitat for the Canada lynx. In November 2005 approximately 18,000 square miles of critical habitat was proposed for the animal by the FWS as follows:

- Maine—approximately 10,633 square miles in portions of Aroostook, Franklin, Penobscot, Piscataquis, and Somerset counties

- Minnesota—approximately 3,546 square miles in portions of Cook, Koochiching, Lake, and St. Louis counties

- Montana and Idaho—approximately 3,549 square miles in portions of Boundary County, Idaho; and Flathead, Glacier, Granite, Lake, Lewis and Clark, Lincoln, Missoula, Pondera, Powell, and Teton counties in Montana

- Washington—approximately 303 square miles in portions of Chelan and Okanogan counties

Also in 2005 the agency developed a preliminary outline for a recovery plan for the Canada lynx including a map of possible recovery areas. (See Figure 8.6.) As of February 2006 the Canada lynx is designated as threatened in fourteen northern states (Colorado, Idaho, Maine, Michigan, Minnesota, Montana, New Hampshire, New York, Oregon, Utah, Vermont, Washington, Wisconsin, and Wyoming).

The Fish and Wildlife Service must make a final determination on critical habitat areas before the end of 2006.

MOUNTAIN LIONS. Mountain lions are large felines that can weigh between seventy and 170 pounds. The twenty-seven subspecies of mountain lion were once found from southern Argentina to northern British Columbia, making them one of the most widely distributed terrestrial species in the Americas. Mountain lions are regionally known as panthers, pumas, or cougars. They prey on large game animals, particularly deer, and wild hogs, rabbits, and rodents. They require large home ranges for securing food—a single individual may have a home range spanning eighty-five square kilometers (about thirty-three square miles). By 1900 mountain lions were nearly extinct due to habitat loss and hunting. Until the 1960s many states offered monetary rewards for the killing of mountain lions. Mountain lions are now found primarily in mountainous, unpopulated areas.

Conservation efforts have met with success in some portions of the country. In fact, there are now so many encounters between humans and mountain lions in California that hikers and park officials are taught how to react to these large cats. Scientists attribute the increased encounter rate to more wilderness ventures by humans as well as a larger mountain lion population—an estimated 6,000 individuals. Because of these events, some people are demanding that hunting be reinstituted.

In California, following a ban on mountain lion hunting, reports of mountain lions rose through the 1990s. In January 2004 a mountain lion killed one bicyclist and severely injured a second in Southern California. The mountain lion was later found and shot. Since 1890 California has reported a total of fourteen mountain lion attacks, of which six were fatal; however, twelve of the attacks occurred between 1986 and 2004.

In most of the eastern United States, however, mountain lions have long been presumed extinct. If they are present, they are still extremely rare. In 1997 several sightings were reported in the Appalachian Mountains, but these have not been confirmed.

The Florida panther is a subspecies of mountain lion that has been considered endangered since 1967. The species has declined due to loss of habitat to urbanization and development, water contamination, and highway traffic. Its population became so small that many individuals began suffering from genetic disorders due to inbreeding. In 1994 and 1995 scientists and wildlife managers introduced Texas cougars, the Florida panthers' closest relatives, into habitats in Florida. Eight female Texas cougars were released. Biologists hoped that interbreeding would strengthen and diversify the Florida panther gene pool. In fact, Florida panthers and Texas cougars once formed a single, interbreeding population that ranged freely throughout the southeastern United States. They were eventually isolated from each other by human encroachment a little more than a hundred years ago.

FIGURE 8.6

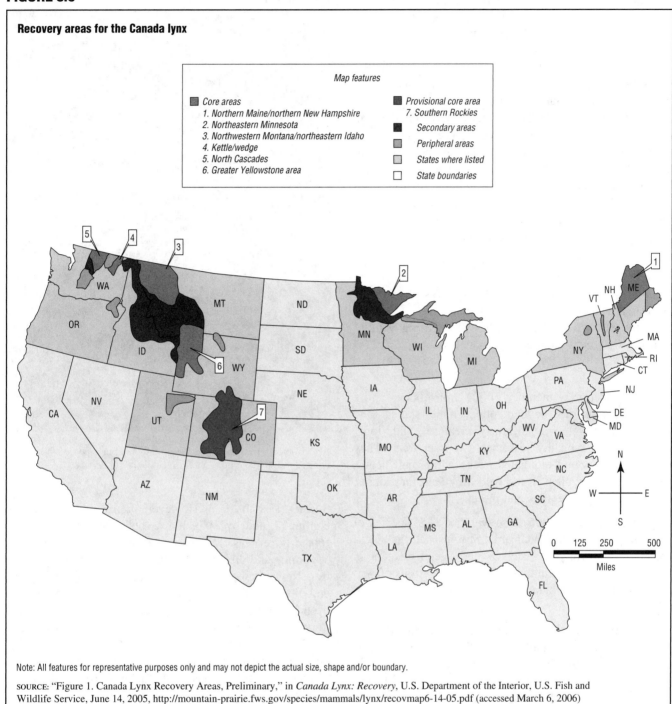

Recovery areas for the Canada lynx

Map features

- Core areas
  1. Northern Maine/northern New Hampshire
  2. Northeastern Minnesota
  3. Northwestern Montana/northeastern Idaho
  4. Kettle/wedge
  5. North Cascades
  6. Greater Yellowstone area

- Provisional core area
  7. Southern Rockies
- Secondary areas
- Peripheral areas
- States where listed
- State boundaries

Note: All features for representative purposes only and may not depict the actual size, shape and/or boundary.

SOURCE: "Figure 1. Canada Lynx Recovery Areas, Preliminary," in *Canada Lynx: Recovery*, U.S. Department of the Interior, U.S. Fish and Wildlife Service, June 14, 2005, http://mountain-prairie.fws.gov/species/mammals/lynx/recovmap6-14-05.pdf (accessed March 6, 2006)

In December 2005 the Florida Fish and Wildlife Conservation Commission (FFWCC) released *Florida Panther Annual Report: 2004–2005* with details on species protection measures (http://www.panther.state.fl.us/news/pdf/FWC2004-2005PantherAnnualReport.pdf). According to the report, there were only thirty to fifty adult Florida panthers in existence as of the late 1980s. The small population size and geographic range combined to limit genetic exchange, resulting in declining health among the species. Five of the Texas cougars released into Florida during the mid-1990s produced at least twenty offspring that began interbreeding with Florida panthers. FFWCC biologists have been tracking subsequent generations of Texas-Florida crossbreeds as part of a genetic restoration project. The scientists hope to develop a long-term management plan that will ensure the survival of the Florida panther as a species. The report estimates that approximately ninety adult individuals make up the Florida panther population.

Other efforts are also underway to help maintain the existing Florida panther gene pool. A captive breeding program was initiated in 1991 with ten panther cubs that had been removed from the wild. It is hoped that captive breeding will allow for the establishment of additional populations in the wild. Scientists are also hopeful that the habitat destruction that threatens the Florida panther has slowed. The primary issue in panther conservation today is providing large enough expanses of protected habitat for the species. This is particularly challenging not simply because the carnivores need large home ranges to feed, but because male panthers are territorial and will not tolerate the presence of other males. About half the area occupied by Florida panthers is private land, including farms, ranches, and citrus groves adjacent to protected reserves. Efforts are being made to secure the cooperation of landowners in conservation efforts.

As a result of the Florida panther's plight and public affection for the animal, in 1982 Florida declared the panther its state animal. Florida businessman Wayne Huizenga named his National Hockey League (NHL) team the Florida Panthers and has pledged many thousands of dollars to panther recovery efforts.

Ferrets

The ferret is a member of the Mustelidae family along with muskrats, badgers, otters, mink, skunks, and weasels. Ferrets are small, furry creatures with long, skinny bodies typically less than two feet long. They have short legs and elongated necks with small heads. Ferrets are carnivores; in the wild they feed on rodents, rabbits, and some reptiles and insects.

As of February 2006 there was one U.S. species of ferret listed under the Endangered Species Act: the black-footed ferret, which is listed as endangered, except in nonessential experimental populations in portions of Arizona, Colorado, Montana, South Dakota, Utah, and Wyoming.

THE BLACK-FOOTED FERRET. The black-footed ferret (see Figure 8.7) is a small, furrow-digging mammal. It is a nocturnal creature and helps to control populations of snakes and rodents, including its primary prey, black-tailed prairie dogs. Black-footed ferrets once ranged over eleven Rocky Mountain states as well as parts of Canada. They have declined drastically because of the large-scale conversion of prairie habitats to farmland, and because their main prey, prairie dogs, have been nearly exterminated by humans. Prairie dogs are considered pests because they dig holes and tunnels just beneath the ground surface. These can cause serious injury to horses or other large animals that step into them. (Some municipalities also poison prairie dogs in city parks, where burrow holes can trip and injure humans.) Poisons used to kill prairie dogs may also kill some ferrets.

Black-footed ferret populations had declined so greatly that the species was put on the Endangered

FIGURE 8.7

Black-footed ferrets are being successfully bred in captivity and reintroduced to the wild. (U.S. Fish and Wildlife Service.)

Species List in 1973. However, prairie dog poisonings continued, and by 1979 it was believed that the black-footed ferret was extinct. In 1981 a ferret was sighted in Wyoming and discovered to be part of a remnant population. Rewards were offered for more sightings, and by the end of the year a few black-footed ferret populations had been located. These typically existed in close proximity to prairie dog populations in areas characterized by heavy sagebrush. In 1985 ferret populations were struck by disease, and by 1987, only eighteen black-footed ferrets were in existence. These individuals were captured and entered into a captive breeding program.

The captive breeding of ferrets has been reasonably successful. There are now core populations of several hundred breeding-age individuals in zoos in the United States and Canada and in one facility operated by the U.S. Fish and Wildlife Service. The agency has also tried to reintroduce black-footed ferrets in several states. Studies suggest that each population requires approximately 10,000 acres of black-tailed prairie dog habitat to survive. Unfortunately, prairie dogs are also in decline due to habitat loss and episodes of sylvatic plague, which have decimated many populations. Although some reintroductions have failed, two are doing well—one in national forest habitat in Conata Basin/Badlands, South Dakota, and another in the Charles M. Russell National Wildlife Refuge in Montana. By 2000 there were already many more wild-born than captive-born ferrets at those sites.

The recovery plan for black-footed ferrets was published in 1988. At that time it was hoped the species could be moved from endangered to threatened status by 2010. This would require that 1,500 breeding adults exist in the wild in a minimum of ten separate locations, with a minimum of thirty breeding adults included in each population. Captive breeding and reintroductions of black-footed ferrets were organized by the Black-Footed Ferret Recovery Implementation Team, and involved twenty-six separate state and federal organizations, conservation groups, and Native American tribes.

Rabbits

Rabbits are members of the Leporidae family, along with hares. Rabbits are generally smaller than hares and have somewhat shorter ears. Both species have tall, slender ears and short bodies with long limbs and thick, soft fur. Domesticated rabbits are all descended from European species.

As of February 2006 there were three rabbit species listed as endangered under the ESA in the United States. The species and their primary locations are as follows:

- Lower Keys marsh rabbit—Florida
- Pygmy rabbit—Western states
- Riparian brush rabbit—California

Approximately $1 million was spent under the Endangered Species Act to preserve imperiled rabbit species during fiscal year 2004. Just over half of the money was devoted to the pygmy rabbit, specifically, a distinct population segment (DPS) inhabiting the Columbia River Basin in the state of Washington.

PYGMY RABBIT. The pygmy rabbit is the smallest species in the Leporidae family. Adults weigh up to one pound and can be up to a foot in length. The animals have relatively short rounded ears and small tails. Their only habitat is underneath sagebrush, a rough scrubby bush found in dry alkaline soils in the western United States. Sagebrush provides shelter and the majority of their food source, particularly during the winter. Pygmy rabbits are burrowers and prefer deep loose soils.

Historically the pygmy rabbit was found throughout the semiarid regions of California, Idaho, Montana, Nevada, Utah, Washington, and Wyoming. There is a distinct population segment (DPS) located in the Columbia River basin, an area extending from northern Oregon through eastern Washington. This DPS is considered to be distinct from other populations within the historic range. The pygmy rabbits in the DPS became a candidate species in 1991. A decade later the U.S. Fish and Wildlife Service was forced to issue an emergency endangered listing for the DPS to settle litigation filed by a number of conservation groups. In 2003 a final listing of endangered was made for the Columbia Basin DPS of the pygmy rabbit. At that time the FWS reported that fewer than thirty individuals made up the DPS.

Since 2001 the Washington Department of Fish and Wildlife and the Oregon Zoo have operated a captive propagation project for the endangered pygmy rabbits. It is hoped that the captive animals can be returned to their native habitat at some point in the future.

Rodents

Rodents are members of the order Rodentia, the single largest group of mammals. This order includes mice, rats, beavers, chipmunks, squirrels, prairie dogs, voles, and many other species. There are approximately 1,500 rodent species. Rodents are characterized by their distinctive teeth, particularly a pair of chisel-shaped incisors in each jaw. Although most rodents are plant-eaters, some species include insects in their diets.

As of February 2006 there were twenty-eight rodent species listed under the ESA as endangered or threatened. They are broken down by animal as follows:

- Kangaroo rat—six species
- Mountain beaver—one species
- Mouse—ten species
- Prairie dog—one species
- Rat—three species
- Squirrel—four species
- Vole—three species

Just over $5.4 million was spent under the ESA to conserve imperiled rodents in the United States during fiscal year 2004. The highest expenditures were for the Utah prairie dog ($1 million) and the Alabama beach mouse and Preble's meadow jumping mouse ($0.6 million each).

UTAH PRAIRIE DOG. Prairie dogs are members of the Scieuridae family, along with chipmunks and squirrels. (See Figure 8.8.) They are endemic to the United States and inhabit mostly arid grasslands. They are found from Montana and North Dakota south to Texas. The nineteenth-century explorers Meriwether Lewis and William Clark allegedly named the animals prairie dogs because of their bark-like calls.

Before settlers moved into the West, it is believed that millions of prairie dogs inhabited the area. Prairie dogs are burrowing creatures and live in colonies. They produce holes, tunnels, and dirt mounds that can be very damaging to land used for agriculture. The holes also

FIGURE 8.8

The prairie dog

SOURCE: Bob Savannah, artist, "Prairie Dogs," in *Pictures/Graphics, Wildlife Sketches*, U.S. Department of the Interior, U.S. Fish and Wildlife Service, Undated, http://www.fws.gov/pictures/lineart/bobsavannah/prairiedogs.html (accessed February 15, 2006)

pose a tripping hazard to horses. As a result, ranchers of the late 1800s and early 1900s tried to eradicate the prairie dog using poison on a large scale. They were assisted in their efforts by the federal government.

The Utah prairie dog is a small furry creature that reaches twelve to fourteen inches in length when full grown. They are reddish brown in color and have short, white-tipped tails. Prior to the control programs of the 1920s, approximately 100,000 of the animals lived in Utah. By 1972 the population had been reduced to about 3,000 individuals. Massive poisoning by humans, disease (a form of plague), and loss of suitable habitat are blamed for the population decline. In 1973 the FWS listed the Utah prairie dog as endangered under the ESA. Over the next decade, conservation efforts began to pay off. More than 3,500 of the animals were counted during a 1982 census. However, angry farmers began reporting massive crop damage caused by the creatures, particularly to summer alfalfa crops, a favorite food source for the prairie dogs. The state of Utah petitioned the U.S. Fish and Wildlife Service to downlist the species from endangered to threatened; this reclassification took place in 1984.

The FWS recognized that Utah farmers were not going to tolerate continuing threats to their crops from the prairie dogs. In a unique action the agency established a special regulation allowing the Utah Division of Wildlife Resources to issue permits to private landowners that wished to kill Utah prairie dogs on their property. A maximum of 5,000 of the "nuisance" animals could be "taken" annually in specific portions of the state. In 1991 the maximum allowable take was raised to 6,000 animals per year, and the area of allowed take was expanded to include all private lands within the species' range. In addition, the FWS began relocating Utah prairie dogs from private lands to lands under control of the federal government. In 2004 the Utah Division of Wildlife Resources estimated the species population at around 8,000 individuals. They are found only in limited areas of the state as shown in Figure 8.9.

In November 2005 the U.S. Fish and Wildlife Service assessed a $10,000 civil penalty against a Utah developer accused of killing Utah prairie dogs without a permit during construction of a residential development in Enoch, Utah, in 1995 (http://mountain-prairie.fws.gov/PRESSREL/05-84.htm). A $15,000 penalty had been originally assessed against the developer, but this amount was reduced to $10,000 following a lengthy court battle.

Shrews

Shrews are members of the order Insectivora, along with moles and hedgehogs. Shrews are small furry creatures with long, pointed snouts.

As of February 2006 there was one shrew species listed as endangered under the ESA—the ornate Buena Vista Lake shrew, which is endemic to California. Less than $200,000 was spent under the ESA on this animal during fiscal year 2004.

The Buena Vista Lake shrew is one of nine subspecies of the ornate shrew. Adult animals reach only about four inches in length and weigh around a quarter of an ounce. Historically the subspecies was found throughout freshwater wetlands near Buena Vista Lake in south-central California. Much of this area has been converted to agricultural purposes, and many of the wetlands have been drained or filled. As a result, populations of the subspecies are believed to be severely depleted.

In 1996 the Buena Vista Lake shrew was designated a candidate species by the U.S. Fish and Wildlife Service. In 2002 the agency was forced under court order to make a listing determination for the animal; it was listed as endangered. Following additional litigation the FWS was ordered to make a final critical habitat determination by 2005. In January 2005 the agency designated eighty-four acres in Kern County, California, as critical habitat for the Buena Vista Lake shrew.

FIGURE 8.9

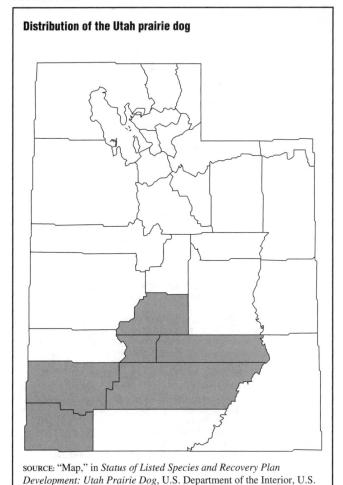

Distribution of the Utah prairie dog

SOURCE: "Map," in *Status of Listed Species and Recovery Plan Development: Utah Prairie Dog*, U.S. Department of the Interior, U.S. Geological Survey, Northern Prairie Wildlife Research Center, Undated, http://www.npwrc.usgs.gov/resource/distr/others/recoprog/states/species/cynoparv.htm (accessed March 3, 2006)

IMPERILED TERRESTRIAL MAMMALS AROUND THE WORLD

As of March 2006 the FWS listed 257 foreign species of terrestrial mammals as endangered or threatened under the Endangered Species Act. (See Table 8.3.) Many of the species are from groups also imperiled in the United States, such as bats, bears, big game, canines, felines, rabbits, and rodents. In addition, there are exotic animals not native to this country, particularly elephants, pandas, primates, and rhinoceroses.

The *2004 IUCN Red List of Threatened Species* of the World Conservation Union listed 1,101 mammals as critically endangered, endangered, or vulnerable. Approximately 960 of these mammals could be considered terrestrial mammals. Orders with large numbers of listed animals are as follows:

- Rodentia (rodents)—315 species
- Chiroptera (bats)—247 species
- Insectivora (moles, shrews & hedgehogs)—124 species
- Primates—114 species
- Artiodactyla (big game, camels, hippos, etc.)—72 species
- Carnivora (bears, big cats, etc.)—56 species

Together, these orders comprise nearly 90% of the terrestrial mammals on the *2004 IUCN Red List.* Among the remaining listed species are some animals that garner high levels of public interest—elephants, koalas, and rhinoceroses.

The habitat types occupied by the largest numbers of threatened mammal species are lowland and tropical rainforests, both of which are being rapidly degraded.

Bears

Bear species are imperiled worldwide. They are killed in large numbers by poachers, who sell bear organs and body parts in the illegal wildlife trade. These organs usually end up in Asia, where they are valued as ingredients in treatments for ailments or illnesses, or to delay the effects of aging—although there is no evidence that such treatments are effective. In North America bears are threatened by loss of habitat and are eliminated for posing a danger to humans and livestock. In 2000 biathlete Mary Beth Miller was mauled to death by a black bear as she ran along a wooded path during her training routine in Quebec, Canada. The tragedy ignited controversy over attempts by Canadian officials to protect the species, including the cancellation of an annual bear hunt.

Big Cats

Wild tigers are found exclusively in Asia, from India to Siberia. Although the world tiger population surpassed 100,000 in the nineteenth century, experts fear that fewer than 10,000 remained in the early 2000s. In addition to habitat loss, countless tigers fall victim to the illegal wildlife trade every year. Many tiger body parts are used as ingredients in traditional Chinese medicine, and the big cats are also prized in the exotic pet industry.

In 1999 the Wildlife Conservation Society reported a rebound in the world tiger population, in part because of a worldwide moratorium on tiger hunting imposed by listing in the Convention on International Trade in Endangered Species (CITES) treaty. However, ecologists warn that tigers, which hunt deer, wild pigs, cattle, antelope, and other large mammals, are threatened seriously by loss of prey, much of which consists of nonprotected species being eliminated by hunters.

THE SIBERIAN TIGER. The Siberian tiger (see Figure 8.10) is the largest cat in the world and one of the world's most endangered species, with only 500 individuals estimated to exist in the wild. There are also several hundred Siberian tigers in captivity. The Siberian tiger, also known as the Amur tiger, once occupied

TABLE 8.3

Foreign endangered and threatened terrestrial mammal species, March 2006

Status*	Species name	Status*	Species name
E	Addax (Addax nasomaculatus)	E	Deer, Ryukyu sika (Cervus nippon keramae)
E	Anoa, lowland (Bubalus depressicornis)	E	Deer, Shansi sika (Cervus nippon grassianus)
E	Anoa, mountain (Bubalus quarlesi)	E	Deer, South China sika (Cervus nippon kopschi)
E	Antelope, giant sable (Hippotragus niger variani)	E	Deer, swamp (Cervus duvauceli)
E, T	Argali (Ovis ammon)	E	Deer, Visayan (Cervus alfredi)
E	Armadillo, giant (Priodontes maximus)	E	Deer, Yarkand (Cervus elaphus yarkandensis)
E	Armadillo, pink fairy (Chlamyphorus truncatus)	E	Dhole (Cuon alpinus)
E	Ass, African wild (Equus asinus)	E	Dibbler (Antechinus apicalis)
E	Ass, Asian wild (Equus hemionus)	E	Dog, African wild (Lycaon pictus)
E	Avahi (Avahi laniger (entire genus))	E	Dolphin, Chinese River (Lipotes vexillifer)
E	Aye-aye (Daubentonia madagascariensis)	E	Dolphin, Indus River (Platanista minor)
E	Babirusa (Babyrousa babyrussa)	E	Drill (Mandrillus (=papio) leucophaeus)
T	Baboon, gelada (Theropithecus gelada)	E	Dugong (Dugong dugon)
E	Bandicoot, barred (Perameles bougainville)	E	Duiker, Jentink's (Cephalophus jentinki)
E	Bandicoot, desert (Perameles eremiana)	E	Eland, western giant (Taurotragus derbianus derbianus)
E	Bandicoot, lesser rabbit (Macrotis leucura)	T	Elephant, African (Loxodonta africana)
E	Bandicoot, pig-footed (Chaeropus ecaudatus)	E	Elephant, Asian (Elephas maximus)
E	Bandicoot, rabbit (Macrotis lagotis)	E	Fox, northern swift (Vulpes velox hebes)
E	Banteng (Bos javanicus)	E	Fox, Simien (Canis simensis)
E	Bat, Bulmer's fruit (=flying fox) (Aproteles bulmerae)	E	Gazelle, Arabian (Gazella gazella)
E	Bat, bumblebee (Craseonycteris thonglongyai)	E	Gazelle, Clark's (Ammodorcas clarkei)
E	Bat, Rodrigues fruit (=flying fox) (Pteropus rodricensis)	E	Gazelle, dama (Gazella dama)
E	Bat, Singapore roundleaf horseshoe (Hipposideros ridleyi)	E	Gazelle, Mhorr (Gazella dama mhorr)
E	Bear, Baluchistan (Ursus thibetanus gedrosianus)	E	Gazelle, Moroccan (Gazella dorcas massaesyla)
E	Bear, brown (Ursus arctos arctos)	E	Gazelle, mountain (=Cuvier's) (Gazella cuvieri)
E	Bear, brown (Ursus arctos pruinosus)	E	Gazelle, Pelzeln's (Gazella dorcas pelzelni)
E	Bear, Mexican grizzly (Ursus arctos)	E	Gazelle, Rio de Oro Dama (Gazella dama lozanoi)
E	Beaver (Castor fiber birulai)	E	Gazelle, sand (Gazella subgutturosa marica)
E	Bison, wood (Bison bison athabascae)	E	Gazelle, Saudi Arabian (Gazella dorcas saudiya)
E	Bobcat, Mexican (Lynx (=felis) rufus escuinapae)	E	Gazelle, slender-horned (Gazella leptoceros)
E	Bontebok (Damaliscus pygarus (=dorcas) dorcas)	E	Gibbons (Hylobates spp. (including nomascus))
E	Camel, Bactrian (Camelus bactrianus)	E	Goral (Naemorhedus goral)
E	Cat, Andean (Felis jacobita)	E	Gorilla (Gorilla gorilla)
E	Cat, Asian golden (=Temmnick's) (Catopuma (=felis) temminckii)	E	Hare, hispid (Caprolagus hispidus)
E	Cat, black-footed (Felis nigripes)	E	Hartebeest, Swayne's (Alcelaphus buselaphus swaynei)
E	Cat, flat-headed (Prionailurus (=felis) planiceps)	E	Hartebeest, Tora (Alcelaphus buselaphus tora)
E	Cat, Iriomote (Prionailurus (=felis) bengalensis iriomotensis)	E	Hog, pygmy (Sus salvanius)
E	Cat, leopard (Prionailurus (=felis) bengalensis bengalensis)	E	Horse, Przewalski's (Equus przewalskii)
E	Cat, marbled (Pardofelis (=felis) marmorata)	E	Huemul, North Andean (Hippocamelus antisensis)
E	Cat, Pakistan sand (felis margarita scheffeli)	E	Huemul, South Andean (Hippocamelus bisulcus)
E	Cat, tiger (Leopardus (=felis) tigrinus)	E	Hutia, Cabrera's (Capromys angelcabrerai)
E	Chamois, Apennine (Rupicapra rupicapra ornata)	E	Hutia, dwarf (Capromys nana)
E	Cheetah (Acinonyx jubatus)	E	Hutia, large-eared (Capromys auritus)
E, T	Chimpanzee (Pan troglodytes)	E	Hutia, little earth (Capromys sanfelipensis)
E	Chimpanzee, pygmy (Pan paniscus)	E	Hyena, Barbary (Hyaena hyaena barbara)
E	Chinchilla (Chinchilla brevicaudata boliviana)	E	Hyena, brown (Parahyaena (=hyaena) brunnea)
E	Civet, Malabar large-spotted (Viverra civettina (=megaspila c.))	E	Ibex, Pyrenean (Capra pyrenaica pyrenaica)
E	Cochito (Phocoena sinus)	E	Ibex, Walia (Capra walie)
E	Deer, Bactrian (Cervus elaphus bactrianus)	E	Impala, black-faced (Aepyceros melampus petersi)
E	Deer, Barbary (Cervus elaphus barbarus)	E	Indri (Indri indri (entire genus))
E	Deer, Calamianes (=Philippine) (Axis porcinus calamianensis)	E	Jaguarundi, Guatemalan (Herpailurus (=felis) yagouaroundi fossata)
E	Deer, Cedros Island mule (Odocoileus hemionus cerrosensis)		
E	Deer, Corsican red (Cervus elaphus corsicanus)	E	Jaguarundi, Panamanian (Herpailurus (=felis) ya gouaroundi panamensis)
E	Deer, Eld's brow-antlered (Cervus eldi)		
E	Deer, Formosan sika (Cervus nippon taiouanus)	E	Kangaroo, Tasmanian forester (Macropus giganteus tasmaniensis)
E	Deer, Indochina hog (Axis porcinus annamiticus)	T	Koala (Phascolarctos cinereus)
E	Deer, Kuhl's (=Bawean) (Axis porcinus kuhli)	E	Kouprey (Bos sauveli)
E	Deer, marsh (Blastocerus dichotomus)	E	Langur, capped (Trachypithecus (=presbytis) pileatus)
E	Deer, McNeill's (Cervus elaphus macneili)	E	Langur, Douc (Pygathrix nemaeus)
E	Deer, musk (Moschus spp. (all species))	E	Langur, Francois' (Trachypithecus (=presbytis) francoisi)
E	Deer, North China sika (Cervus nippon mandarinus)	E	Langur, golden (Trachypithecus (=presbytis) geei)
E	Deer, pampas (Ozotoceros bezoarticus)	E	Langur, gray (=entellus) (Semnopithecus (=presbytis) entellus)
E	Deer, Persian fallow (Dama mesopotamica (=dama m.))	T	Langur, long-tailed (Presbytis potenziani)
		E	Langur, Pagi Island (Nasalis concolor)

mixed deciduous and coniferous forest habitats in the Amur-Ussuri area in Siberia, as well as in northern China and Korea. It is now believed to be extinct, or nearly extinct, in China and Korea. Individuals reach lengths of eight to ten feet and weigh up to 800 pounds. They eat wild boars, Sika deer, and elk. Siberian tigers are territorial and require large home ranges of some 500 to 600 square miles.

Populations have suffered greatly from habitat loss caused by logging and deforestation, as well as illegal trade. The Siberian tiger is sought for its skin, bones,

TABLE 8.3

Foreign endangered and threatened terrestrial mammal species, March 2006 [CONTINUED]

Status*	Species name	Status*	Species name
T	Langur, purple-faced (Presbytis senex)	E	Mouse, Shark Bay (Pseudomys praeconis)
T	Lechwe, red (Kobus leche)	E	Mouse, Shortridge's (Pseudomys shortridgei)
E	Lemurs (Lemuridae (including genera lemur, phaner, hapalemur,	E	Mouse, smoky (Pseudomys fumeus)
	lepilemur, microcebus, allocebus, cheirog aleus, varecia))	E	Mouse, western (Pseudomys occidentalis)
E, T	Leopard (Panthera pardus)	E	Muntjac, Fea's (Muntiacus feae)
E	Leopard, clouded (Neofelis nebulosa)	E	Native-cat, eastern (Dasyurus viverrinus)
E	Leopard, snow (Uncia (=panthera) uncia)	E	Numbat (Myrmecobius fasciatus)
E	Linsang, spotted (Prionodon pardicolor)	E	Orangutan (Pongo pygmaeus)
E	Lion, Asiatic (Panthera leo persica)	E	Oryx, Arabian (Oryx leucoryx)
T	Loris, lesser slow (Nycticebus pygmaeus)	E	Oryx, scimitar-horned (Oryx dammah)
E	Lynx, Spanish (Felis pardina)	E	Otter, Cameroon clawless (Aonyx congicus (=congica) microdon)
T	Macaque, Formosan rock (Macaca cyclopis)	E	Otter, giant (Pteronura brasiliensis)
T	Macaque, Japanese (Macaca fuscata)	E	Otter, long-tailed (Lontra (=lutra) longicaudis (including platensis))
E	Macaque, lion-tailed (Macaca silenus)	E	Otter, marine (Lontra (=lutra) felina)
T	Macaque, stump-tailed (Macaca arctoides)	E	Otter, Southern River (Lontra (=lutra) provocax)
T	Macaque, Toque (Macaca sinica)	E	Panda, giant (Ailuropoda melanoleuca)
E	Manatee, Amazonian (Trichechus inunguis)	E	Pangolin, Temnick's ground (Manis temminckii)
T	Manatee, West African (Trichechus senegalensis)	E	Planigale, little (Planigale ingrami subtilissima)
E	Mandrill (Mandrillus (=papio) sphinx)	E	Planigale, southern (Planigale tenuirostris)
E	Mangabey, Tana River (Cercocebus galeritus galeritus)	E	Porcupine, thin-spined (Chaetomys subspinosus)
E	Mangabey, white-collared (Cercocebus torquatus)	E	Possum, Leadbeater's (Gymnobelideus leadbeateri)
E	Margay (Leopardus (=felis) wiedii)	E	Possum, mountain pygmy (Burramys parvus)
E	Markhor, chiltan (=wild goat) (Capra falconeri (=aegragrus)	E	Possum, scaly-tailed (Wyulda squamicaudata)
	chiltanensis)	E	Prairie dog, Mexican (Cynomys mexicanus)
E	Markhor, Kabul (Capra falconeri megaceros)	E	Pronghorn, peninsular (Antilocapra americana peninsularis)
E	Markhor, straight-horned (Capra falconeri jerdoni)	E	Pudu (Pudu pudu)
E	Marmoset, buff-headed (Callithrix flaviceps)	E	Puma, Costa Rican (Puma (=felis) concolor costaricensis)
E	Marmoset, cotton-top (Saguinus oedipus)	E	Quokka (Setonix brachyurus)
E	Marmoset, Goeldi's (Callimico goeldi)	E	Rabbit, Ryukyu (Pentalagus furnessi)
E	Marmoset, white-eared (=buffy tufted-ear) (Callithrix aurita	E	Rabbit, volcano (Romerolagus diazi)
	(=jacchus a.))	E	Rat, false water (Xeromys myoides)
E	Marmot, Vancouver Island (Marmota vancouverensis)	E	Rat, stick-nest (Leporillus conditor)
E	Marsupial, eastern Jerboa (Antechinomys laniger)	E	Rat-kangaroo, brush-tailed (Bettongia penicillata)
E	Marsupial-mouse, large desert (Sminthopsis psammophila)	E	Rat-kangaroo, desert (=plain) (Caloprymnus campestris)
E	Marsupial-mouse, long-tailed (Sminthopsis longicaudata)	E	Rat-kangaroo, Gaimard's (Bettongia gaimardi)
E	Marten, Formosan yellow-throated (Martes flavigula chrysospila)	E	Rat-kangaroo, Lesuer's (Bettongia lesueur)
E	Monkey, black colobus (Colobus satanas)	E	Rat-kangaroo, Queensland (Bettongia tropica)
T	Monkey, black howler (Alouatta pigra)	E	Rhinoceros, black (Diceros bicornis)
E	Monkey, Diana (Cercopithecus diana)	E	Rhinoceros, great Indian (Rhinoceros unicornis)
E	Monkey, Guizhou snub-nosed (Rhinopithecus brelichi)	E	Rhinoceros, Javan (Rhinoceros sondaicus)
E	Monkey, L'hoest's (Cercopithecus lhoesti)	E	Rhinoceros, northern white (Ceratotherium simum cottoni)
E	Monkey, mantled howler (Alouatta palliata)	E	Rhinoceros, Sumatran (Dicerorhinus sumatrensis)
E	Monkey, Preuss' red colobus (Procolobus (=colobus) preussi	E	Saiga, Mongolian (antelope) (Saiga tatarica mongolica)
	(=badius p.))	E	Saki, southern bearded (Chiropotes satanas satanas)
E	Monkey, proboscis (Nasalis larvatus)	E	Saki, white-nosed (Chiropotes albinasus)
E	Monkey, red-backed squirrel (Saimiri oerstedii)	E	Seal, Mediterranean monk (Monachus monachus)
E	Monkey, red-bellied (Cercopithecus erythrogaster)	E	Seal, Saimaa (Phoca hispida saimensis)
E	Monkey, red-eared nose-spotted (Cercopithecus erythrotis)	E	Seledang (Bos gaurus)
E	Monkey, Sichuan snub-nosed (Rhinopithecus roxellana)	E	Serow (Naemorhedus (=Capricornis) sumatraensis)
E	Monkey, spider (Ateles geoffroyi frontatus)	E	Serval, Barbary (Leptailurus (=Felis) serval constantina)
E	Monkey, spider (Ateles geoffroyl panamensis)	E	Shapo (Ovis vignei vignei)
E	Monkey, Tana River red colobus (Procolobus (=colobus)	E	Shou (Cervus elaphus wallichi)
	rufomitratus (=badius r.))	E	Siamang (Symphalangus syndactylus)
E	Monkey, Tonkin snub-nosed (Rhinopithecus avunculus)	E	Sifakas (Propithecus spp.)
E	Monkey, woolly spider (Brachyteles arachnoides)	E	Sloth, Brazilian three-toed (Bradypus torquatus)
E	Monkey, yellow-tailed woolly (Lagothrix flavicauda)	E	Solenodon, Cuban (Solenodon cubanus)
E	Monkey, Yunnan snub-nosed (Rhinopithecus bieti)	E	Solenodon, Haitian (Solenodon paradoxus)
E	Monkey, Zanzibar red colobus (Procolobus (=colobus)	E	Stag, Barbary (Cervus elaphus barbarus)
	pennantii (=kirki) kirki)	E	Stag, Kashmir (Cervus elaphus hanglu)
E	Mouse, Australian native (Notomys aquilo)	E	Suni, Zanzibar (Neotragus moschatus moschatus)
E	Mouse, Australian native (Zyzomys pedunculatus)	E	Tahr, Arabian (Hemitragus jayakari)
E	Mouse, Field's (Pseudomys fieldi)	E	Tamaraw (Bubalus mindorensis)
E	Mouse, Gould's (Pseudomys gouldi)	E	Tamarin, golden-rumped (Leontopithecus spp.)
E	Mouse, New Holland (Pseudomys novaehollandiae)	E	Tamarin, pied (Saguinus bicolor)

eyes, whiskers, teeth, internal organs, and genitals. These are used for everything from skin cures to tooth medicine. In Russia, where unemployment is high, poachers have flooded nearby Asian markets with tiger parts. The financially strapped Russian government can devote neither money nor time to protecting the tigers. Like the Florida panther, the Siberian tiger has also been wea-

kened by inbreeding, which increases the possibility of reproductive problems and birth defects.

CHEETAHS. The cheetah is the fastest land animal on Earth, able to sprint at speeds up to seventy miles per hour. Cheetahs occupy grassland, shrubland, and woodland habitats. Their range once extended through most of

TABLE 8.3

Foreign endangered and threatened terrestrial mammal species, March 2006 [CONTINUED]

Status*	Species name	Status*	Species name
T	Tamarin, white-footed (*Saguinus leucopus*)	E	Wallaby, crescent nail-tailed (*Onychogalea lunata*)
E	Tapir, Asian (*Tapirus indicus*)	E	Wallaby, Parma (*Macropus parma*)
E	Tapir, Central American (*Tapirus bairdii*)	E	Wallaby, western hare (*Lagorchestes hirsutus*)
E	Tapir, mountain (*Tapirus pinchaque*)	E	Wallaby, yellow-footed rock (*Petrogale xanthopus*)
E	Tapir, South American (=Brazilian) (*Tapirus terrestris*)	E	Whale, gray (*Eschrichtius robustus*)
T	Tarsier, Philippine (*Tarsius syrichta*)	E	Wolf, maned (*Chrysocyon brachyurus*)
E	Tiger (*Panthera tigris*)	E	Wombat, Queensland hairy-nosed (incl. Barnard's)
E	Tiger, Tasmanian (*Thylacinus cynocephalus*)	E	(*Lasiorhinus krefftii* (formerly *L. barnardi* and *L. gillespiei*))
E	Uakari (all species) (*Cacajao spp.*)		Yak, wild (*Bos mutus* (=*grunniens m.*))
E	Urial (*Ovis musimon ophion*)	T	Zebra, Grevy's (*Equus grevyi*)
E	Vicuna (*Vicugna vicugna*)	T	Zebra, Hartmann's mountain (*Equus zebra hartmannae*)
E	Wallaby, banded hare (*Lagostrophus fasciatus*)	E	Zebra, mountain (*Equus zebra zebra*)
E	Wallaby, brindled nail-tailed (*Onychogalea fraenata*)		

*E=endangered; T=threatened.

SOURCE: "Foreign Listed Species Report as of 03/01/2006," in *Threatenedand Endangered Species System (TESS)*, U.S. Department of the Interior, U.S. Fish and Wildlife Service, March 1, 2006, http://ecos.fws.gov/tess_public/servlet/gov.doi.tess_public.servlets.ForeignListing?listings=0#A (accessed March 1, 2006)

FIGURE 8.10

The Siberian tiger is one of the most endangered species in the world. It now occupies forest habitats in the Amur-Ussuri region of Siberia. (Field Mark Publications.)

Africa as well as southwestern Asia. Currently, cheetahs are found only in a few areas in Iran, North Africa, and sub-Saharan Africa. Cheetahs hunt small prey, particularly Thomson's gazelle. The cheetah has been listed in CITES Appendix I since 1975. In 2006 there were an estimated 12,500 cheetahs in the wild, according to the Cheetah Conservation Fund (http://www.cheetah.org/), a dramatic decrease from approximately 100,000 at the beginning of the twentieth century.

Cheetah populations have declined for many reasons. Much of the species' habitat has been developed for agricultural or ranching use, and many of the cats are shot by farmers who wish to protect their livestock. In addition, because of their declining numbers and loss of habitat, cheetahs are badly inbred, and many individuals are infertile. Cheetahs are also smaller and less aggressive than other predators that share their environment (including lions and leopards) and often have their food

kills stolen or their cubs killed. Conservation biologists have determined that in order to save the cheetah, human assistance in the form of habitat protection, protection from competitor species, and measures to improve the genetic diversity of the species are required.

Elephants

Elephants are the largest land animals on Earth. They are frequently described as the "architects" of the savanna habitats in which they live. Elephants dig water holes, keep forest growth in check, and open up grasslands that support other species, including the livestock of African herders. Elephants are highly intelligent, emotional animals and form socially complex herds. There are two species of elephants, African elephants and Asian elephants, both of which are highly endangered. The African elephant (see Figure 8.11), which sometimes weighs as much as six tons, is the larger species. According to the World Wildlife Fund in "Elephant Ivory Trade," an estimated 500,000 African elephants and between 35,000 and 50,000 Asian elephants remain in the wild as of 2006.

Elephants have huge protruding teeth—tusks—made of ivory. Ivory is valued by humans for several reasons, particularly for use in making jewelry and figurines. Piano keys were also once made almost exclusively of ivory; however, that practice has ceased. The market for ivory has had tragic consequences for African elephants. Their numbers dropped from over ten million individuals in 1900 to only 600,000 in 1989. As a result of this decline, the UN-administered CITES banned worldwide commerce in ivory and other elephant products in 1990. However, like rhinoceros horns, elephant tusks continue to be illegally traded. Numerous elephants are poached each year. Esmond Martin and Tom Milliken in *No Oasis: The Egyptian Ivory Trade in 2005* (June 2005, http://www.traffic.org/news/press-releases/

FIGURE 8.11

Elephants are highly intelligent and social animals. Once on the verge of extinction, elephants have recovered somewhat after a worldwide ban on the ivory trade. (Field Mark Publications.)

TRAFFIC_%20Egypt.pdf) report the price of poached elephant ivory as high as $150 per pound in 2005. The price has risen substantially in recent years, indicating poachers are facing pressure from increased law enforcement.

Despite continued poaching, elephant populations have recovered somewhat since receiving CITES protection. In 1997 Zimbabwe requested that CITES change the listing status of the African elephant in three South African nations—Zimbabwe, Botswana, and Namibia—from Appendix I status (a species in immediate danger of extinction) to Appendix II status (threatened in the absence of trade controls), and include a yearly quota for ivory trade. South Africa has requested a similar downlisting. Kenya, India, and other nations, along with many environmental organizations, opposed the downlisting, in part because they maintained that a reopening of the ivory trade might cause a resurgence in demand and poaching. CITES responded by downlisting the elephant to Appendix II, while simultaneously initiating a program, the Monitoring of Illegal Killing of Elephants (MIKE; 1999, http://www.cites.org/eng/prog/MIKE/index.shtml) to better assess poaching. CITES also allowed a one-time sale of stockpiled ivory from Namibia, Botswana, and Zimbabwe to Japan. This one-time ivory transaction was made in 1999 and grossed approximately $5 million.

At subsequent CITES Conferences, debate continued about authorizing ivory sales and relisting the elephant under CITES Appendix I as immediately endangered. In the end, the opposing factions reached a compromise in which elephants remained listed under Appendix II, and the ban on most ivory sales remained in effect. At the 2002 CITES Conference, CITES conditionally accepted one-time sales by Botswana, Namibia, and South Africa of ivory collected from elephants that died a natural death. However, the sales can occur only after data is collected on poaching and population levels.

In June 2005 TRAFFIC (an organization that monitors worldwide wildlife trade) and the World Wildlife Fund (WWF) issued a joint statement to CITES on the status of ivory trade. The statement notes that illegal ivory sales in Africa and Asia continue to be a problem in several countries, notably Egypt, Mozambique, Angola, and Thailand. However, Ethiopia was reported to have made great progress in reducing ivory trade. In January 2005 Ethiopian officials conducted a major sweep of retail outlets and seized large quantities of ivory products. A few months later undercover TRAFFIC investigators visited the same area and found few ivory products for sale.

Although the ivory trade has always been the largest threat to elephants, conflicts between humans and elephants are an increasing issue. The ranges of many elephant herds now extend outside protected refuges, and elephants frequently come into contact with farmers, eating or otherwise destroying crops. Increasing human settlement in areas inhabited by elephants will likely result in more conflicts over time.

Pandas

Few creatures have engendered more human affection than the giant panda, with its roly-poly character, small ears, and black eye patches on a snow-white face. Giant pandas are highly endangered. According to the National Zoo, there are approximately 1,600 pandas in the wild and about 160 individuals in captivity as of 2006. Pandas are endemic to portions of southwestern China, where they inhabit a few fragmentary areas of high-altitude bamboo forest. Unlike other bear species, to which they are closely related, pandas have a vegetarian diet that consists entirely of bamboo. Pandas also have a sixth digit which functions like a thumb, and which they use to peel tender bamboo leaves from their stalks.

Pandas have become star attractions at many zoos, where they draw scores of visitors. Despite tremendous efforts, pandas have proven notoriously difficult to breed in captivity. The birth of a giant panda cub, named Hua Mei, at the San Diego Zoo in 1999 was a major event, with millions of people following the cub's progress online and in the papers through her first days of life. Hua Mei was the first panda born in captivity outside of China.

The San Diego Zoo pays China $1 million annually for the loan of adult pandas. These funds are used to support panda conservation efforts in China, including the purchase of land for refuges as well as the development of habitat corridors to link protected areas. The agreement also requires that pandas born at the San Diego Zoo will be returned to China after they are three years old. Hua Mei was flown to China in February 2004 to join nearly seventy pandas at the Wolong Giant Panda Protection Research Centre in the Sichuan Province of China. In August 2005 she gave birth to twin cubs after being artificially inseminated.

As of March 2006 zoos in Washington, D.C., Memphis, Tennessee, and Atlanta, Georgia, also have giant pandas on loan from China. In 2000 the National Zoo in Washington, D.C., agreed to pay China $10 million over a ten-year period in exchange for the loan of giant pandas. In July 2005 a male cub was born at the National Zoo. Following a naming contest, the cub was named Tai Shan, which means "peaceful mountain." In August 2005 a female cub was born at the San Diego Zoo, the third cub born there. She was later named Su Lin, which translates to English as "a little bit of something very cute." Su Lin's older brother Mei Sheng was born in August 2003. His name means both "born in the USA" and "beautiful life."

In March 2006 officials from the U.S. zoos keeping giant pandas traveled to China to begin negotiations on new loan contracts for the animals. The zoos hope to reduce the high loan costs they are charged for Chinese pandas. They also hope to be excused from contract stipulations that require the return to China of cubs that reach three years old. U.S. zoo officials believe that the Chinese will be amenable to these new terms because the Chinese breeding program for giant pandas has been so successful.

RED PANDAS. The red panda is also called the lesser panda because it is significantly smaller than the giant panda, with a length of about forty-two inches and a weight of only seven to fourteen pounds. Red pandas are not related to bears—they are actually raccoon relatives. Red pandas are virtually extinct in the wild, mostly because of habitat loss and degradation. Red pandas occupy temperate forests in the foothills of the Himalayas in Nepal, Burma, and southwestern China at altitudes

between 5,000 and 13,000 feet. They are solitary creatures, occupying non-overlapping home ranges of approximately one square mile for females and two square miles for males. Like giant pandas, red pandas eat bamboo, focusing on the tenderest leaves. Because bamboo is not very nutritious, red pandas spend as much as thirteen hours each day eating in order to acquire the nutrients they need. Red pandas have difficulty recovering from population declines because of a slow rate of reproduction. A captive breeding effort for red pandas is underway at zoos across the world to prevent the complete extinction of this species.

Big Game

Most big-game species are members of the Artiodactyla order. This order contains a variety of ungulates (hoofed animals), including antelopes, bison, buffalo, camels, deer, goats, hartebeests, hippos, gazelles, impalas, and sheep. Many of the wild species have been over-hunted for their meat, bones, or horns. Horns are used in traditional Chinese medicine and are popular trophies for big-game hunters. The argali is the largest of the wild sheep and is highly prized for its large curved horns. (See Figure 8.12.)

Big-game species also face threats from domesticated livestock due to competition for habitat and food resources.

Primates

The World Conservation Union (IUCN), in its *2004 IUCN Red List of Threatened Species*, reported that the 296 examined species of primates (excluding humans) are among the most endangered mammals. Since the 1996 IUCN assessment, the number of "critically endangered" primates increased from thirteen to twenty species, and the number of "endangered" primates rose from twenty-nine to forty-eight. Another forty-six primates are considered "vulnerable." Critically endangered primate species included the Roloway monkey (lowland tropical rainforest in Ghana and Cote d'Ivoire), Mentawai macaque (Indonesia), Sclater's black lemur (lowland tropical rainforest, Madagascar), red-handed howling monkey (Brazil), and the black lion tamarin (lowland tropical rainforest, Brazil), among others. Much of the increased endangerment of primate species is due to loss of habitat and hunting.

Countries with large numbers of primate species include Brazil, Indonesia, Democratic Republic of Congo, and Madagascar. Many of the most endangered primate species are found on Madagascar, which has a diverse and unique primate fauna. The majority of Madagascar's primate species are endemic—that is, they are found nowhere else on earth.

FIGURE 8.12

The argali is prized by hunters for its massive horns. (Corbis Corporation.)

Primates are highly threatened partly because they are dependent on large expanses of tropical forests, a habitat under siege worldwide. In regions where tropical forest degradation and conversion have been most intense, such as South and Southeast Asia, Madagascar, and Brazil, as many as 70% of native primate species face extinction.

Habitat loss, especially the fragmentation and conversion of tropical forests for road building and agriculture, contributes to the decline of nearly 90% of all IUCN-listed primates. In Indonesia and Borneo, for example, home to most of the world's 50,000 to 60,000 orangutans (see Figure 8.13), deforestation has shrunk orangutan habitat by over 90%. Logging and extensive burning have caused many orangutans to flee the forests for villages, where they have been killed or captured by humans.

Some threatened primates also face pressures from excessive hunting and poaching. Today, almost all countries have either banned or strictly regulated the trade of primates, but these laws are often hard to enforce. Primates are also used in medical research because of their close biological relationship with humans.

FIGURE 8.13

The orangutan is highly endangered, along with the majority of the world's primate species. (Field Mark Publications.)

Not all relationships between primates and humans are exploitative. People in some regions protect primates from harm by according them sacred status or by making it taboo to hunt or eat them. One of the rarest African monkeys, the Sclater's guenon, survives in three areas of

FIGURE 8.14

The white rhinoceros is native to Africa and can weigh up to 8,000 pounds. (U.S. Fish and Wildlife Service.)

Nigeria in part because residents regard the animal as sacred.

Good news arrived in January 2004 when it was announced that a census led by the International Gorilla Conservation Program found that the highly endangered mountain gorilla had experienced a population rebound, with numbers increasing 17% between 1989 and 2003 in the Virunga forest of Rwanda, Uganda, and the Democratic Republic of Congo. Gorilla populations had plummeted in the 1960s and 1970s due to civil unrest, habitat destruction, and poaching. A total of 380 mountain gorillas were counted in the Virunga forest and an additional 320 were identified in the Bwindi Impenetrable Forest National Park in Uganda, bringing the world total to 700, according to the African Wildlife Foundation (http://www.awf.org/gorillaupdate/).

Rhinoceros

Rhinoceros are among the largest land mammals. They weigh up to 8,000 pounds—as much as fifty average-sized men—and are herbivorous grazers. The name rhinoceros is made up of two Greek words meaning "nose" and "horn," and rhinos are in fact the only animals on Earth that have horns on their noses. Figure 8.14 shows an African white rhinoceros with two horns. The female may be identified by her longer, more slender primary horn.

Rhinoceros have roamed the land for more than forty million years, but in less than a century, humans—their only predators—have reduced populations to dangerously low levels. There are five species of rhinoceros—the black rhino (African), white rhino (African), Sumatran rhino (found in Borneo, Malaysia, and Sumatra), Javan rhino (found in Indonesia and Vietnam), and Indian rhino (found in both India and Nepal). Certain rhino species can be divided into distinct subspecies. For example, the Javan rhino has two subspecies, one found in Vietnam, the other in Indonesia. According to the International Rhino Foundation (IRF; http://www.rhinos-irf.org/rhinoinformation/javanrhino/subspecies/vietnamese.htm), the Vietnamese subspecies consists of only one tiny population of two to seven individuals, and was thought extinct until this tiny population was discovered in 1999. All rhinos are close to extinction.

Hunting has been the primary cause of rhinoceros decline. Rhinoceros horn is highly prized as an aphrodisiac, as well as an ingredient in Chinese medicine (although its potency has never been shown). Rhinos were first listed by CITES in 1976. This banned international trade in the species and their products. In 1992 CITES also started requiring the destruction of horn caches confiscated from poachers. Nonetheless, people continue to buy and consume rhinoceros horn, and many poachers are willing to risk death to acquire it.

INDIAN RHINOS. Conservation efforts have improved the status of some rhino species. The Indian rhinoceros, which was reduced to fewer than 100 individuals in the mid-1970s, has experienced significant population growth in the past twenty-five years. According to the IRF, in 2006 there were approximately 2,400 Indian rhinos in the wild. Population increase resulted from habitat protection, including the designation of several national parks, as well as measures that curbed poaching.

AFRICAN RHINOS. Africa is home to two species of highly imperiled rhinoceros, the black rhino and the white rhino. Both species have a second, smaller horn situated slightly behind the larger main horn. They are threatened primarily by poaching. Wildlife officials in Zimbabwe, Swaziland, and Namibia have gone so far as to sever rhino horns in an effort to curtail poaching. Most experts, however, discourage the practice, as animals use their horns for both digging and defense. In 2006 the IRF reported 3,610 black rhinos in the wild. Of the black rhinoceros subspecies, the western variety is the most severely endangered, with only ten currently found in the wild. The IRF reported 11,330 white rhinos in 2006. African rhino numbers have risen in recent years, primarily due to improved management as well as private sector and community involvement. Captive breeding efforts for the African rhino species have also met with some success, particularly at the San Diego Wild Animal Park, and may aid in the conservation of these species.

CHAPTER 9
BIRDS

Birds belong to the class Aves, which contains dozens of orders. Birds are warm-blooded vertebrates with wings, feathers, and light hollow bones. The vast majority of birds are capable of flight. According to the U.S. Fish and Wildlife Service (FWS), more than 800 species of birds spend all or part of their lives in the United States; more than 9,000 species of birds have been identified around the world.

In addition to taxonomy, birds are broadly classified by their physical characteristics (such as feet or beak structure), eating habits, primary habitats, or migratory habits. For example, raptors or birds of prey have curved beaks and talons well suited for catching prey. This category includes the eagles, vultures, hawks, buzzards, and owls. Perching birds have a unique foot structure with three toes in front and one large flexible toe to the rear. Ducks and geese are known as open-water or swimming birds and have webbed feet. Habitat categories include the sea birds, shore birds, and arboreal (tree-dwelling) birds. Some birds migrate over long distances and others, like turkey and quail, do not migrate at all.

Scientists believe that more than 100 bird species have gone extinct during the course of human history. Bird species have died out because of habitat destruction, hunting and collection, pollution, and predation by non-native species. The extinction rate of bird species is alarming not only because of the irrevocable loss of each species but also because of implications for the health of entire ecosystems.

ENDANGERED AND THREATENED U.S. SPECIES

As of March 2006 there were ninety bird species listed under the Endangered Species Act (ESA) as endangered or threatened in the United States. (See Table 9.1.) The vast majority have an endangered listing, meaning that they are at risk of extinction. Nearly all have recovery plans in place.

The imperiled birds come from many different genera (plural of genus) and represent a variety of habitats. Most are perching birds, sea birds, or shore birds. There are also a handful of other bird types, including woodpeckers and raptors, such as the bald eagle and northern spotted owl.

Just over $103 million was spent on U.S. bird species under the ESA during fiscal year 2004. Table 9.2 shows the ten species with the highest expenditures. The three most expensive species were the red-cockaded woodpecker ($14.1 million), the southwestern willow flycatcher (nearly $12 million), and the bald eagle in the lower forty-eight states ($9.8 million).

Categories of birds found on the list of endangered and threatened species are described below.

Woodpeckers

Woodpeckers belong to the order Piciformes and the family Picidae. They are characterized by their physiology. They have very hard, chisel-like beaks and a unique foot structure with two toes pointing forward and two toes pointing backward. This allows them to take a firm grip on tree trunks and extend horizontally from vertical surfaces. Woodpeckers prefer arboreal habitats, primarily dead trees in old-growth forests. The birds hammer away at the bark on the trees to dig out insects living there. They often form deep cavities in the tree to use as roosting and nesting holes.

RED-COCKADED WOODPECKERS. The red-cockaded woodpecker (*Picoides borealis*) is shown in Figure 9.1. The bird is named for the red patches, or cockades, of feathers found on the heads of the males. This species is found in old pine forests in the southeastern United States, where family groups—consisting of a breeding male and female as well as several helpers—nest within self-dug cavities in pine trees. Tree cavities serve as nesting sites in addition to providing protection from

TABLE 9.1

Endangered and threatened bird species in the United States, March 2006

Common name	Scientific name	Listing status[a]	Recovery plan date	Recovery Plan stage[b]
Akiapola`a (honeycreeper)	*Hemignathus munroi*	E	10/16/2003	RD(1)
Attwater's greater prairie-chicken	*Tympanuchus cupido attwateri*	E	2/8/1993	RF(1)
Audubon's crested caracara	*Polyborus plancus audubonii*	T	5/18/1999	F
Bachman's warbler (=wood)	*Vermivora bachmanii*	E	None	E
Bald eagle	*Haliaeetus leucocephalus*	T	None	—
Black-capped vireo	*Vireo atricapilla*	E	9/30/1991	F
Bridled white-eye	*Zosterops conspicillatus conspicillatus*	E	9/28/1990	F
Brown pelican	*Pelecanus occidentalis*	DM, E	8/1/1980	F
Cactus ferruginous pygmy-owl	*Glaucidium brasilianum cactorum*	E	1/9/2003	D
Cahow	*Pterodroma cahow*	E	None	—
California clapper rail	*Rallus longirostris obsoletus*	E	11/16/1984	F
California condor	*Gymnogyps californianus*	E, EXPN	4/25/1996	RF(3)
California least tern	*Sterna antillarum browni*	E	9/27/1985	RF(1)
Cape Sable seaside sparrow	*Ammodramus maritimus mirabilis*	E	5/18/1999	F
Coastal California gnatcatcher	*Polioptila californica californica*	T	None	E
Crested honeycreeper	*Palmeria dolei*	E	10/16/2003	RD(1)
Eskimo curlew	*Numenius borealis*	E	None	E
Everglade snail kite	*Rostrhamus sociabilis plumbeus*	E	5/18/1999	F
Florida grasshopper sparrow	*Ammodramus savannarum floridanus*	E	5/18/1999	F
Florida scrub jay	*Aphelocoma coerulescens*	T	5/9/1990	F
Golden-cheeked warbler (=wood)	*Dendroica chrysoparia*	E	9/30/1992	F
Guam Micronesian kingfisher	*Halcyon cinnamomina cinnamomina*	E	9/28/1990	F
Guam rail	*Rallus owstoni*	E, EXPN	9/28/1990	F
Hawaii akepa (honeycreeper)	*Loxops coccineus coccineus*	E	10/16/2003	RD(1)
Hawaii creeper	*Oreomystis mana*	E	10/16/2003	RD(1)
Hawaiian (=`alala) crow	*Corvus hawaiiensis*	E	12/18/2003	RD(1)
Hawaiian (=`lo) hawk	*Buteo solitarius*	E	5/9/1984	F
Hawaiian (=koloa) duck	*Anas wyvilliana*	E	8/24/2005	RD(3)
Hawaiian common moorhen	*Gallinula chloropus sandvicensis*	E	8/24/2005	RD(3)
Hawaiian coot	*Fulica americana alai*	E	8/24/2005	RD(3)
Hawaiian dark-rumped petrel	*Pterodroma phaeopygia sandwichensis*	E	4/25/1983	F
Hawaiian goose	*Branta (=nesochen) sandvicensis*	E	9/24/2004	RD(1)
Hawaiian stilt	*Himantopus mexicanus knudseni*	E	8/24/2005	RD(3)
Inyo California towhee	*Pipilo crissalis eremophilus*	T	4/10/1998	F
Ivory-billed woodpecker	*Campephilus principalis*	E	None	E
Kauai akialoa (honeycreeper)	*Hemignathus procerus*	E	10/16/2003	RD(1)
Kauai `o`o (honeyeater)	*Moho braccatus*	E	10/16/2003	RD(1)
Kirtland's warbler (=wood)	*Dendroica kirtlandii*	E	8/11/1978	F
Large Kauai (=kamao) thrush	*Myadestes myadestinus*	E	10/16/2003	RD(1)
Laysan duck	*Anas laysanensis*	E	11/4/2004	RD(1)
Laysan finch (honeycreeper)	*Telespyza cantans*	E	10/4/1984	F
Least Bell's vireo	*Vireo bellii pusillus*	E	5/6/1998	D
Least tern	*Sterna antillarum*	E	9/19/1990	F
Light-footed clapper rail	*Rallus longirostris levipes*	E	6/24/1985	RF(1)
Marbled murrelet	*Brachyramphus marmoratus marmoratus*	T	9/24/1997	F
Mariana (=aga) crow	*Corvus kubaryi*	E	9/28/1990	F
Mariana common moorhen	*Gallinula chloropus guami*	E	9/30/1991	F
Mariana gray swiftlet	*Aerodramus vanikorensis bartschi*	E	9/30/1991	F
Masked bobwhite (quail)	*Colinus virginianus ridgwayi*	E	4/21/1995	RF(2)
Maui akepa (honeycreeper)	*Loxops coccineus ochraceus*	E	10/16/2003	RD(1)
Maui parrotbill (honeycreeper)	*Pseudonestor xanthophrys*	E	10/16/2003	RD(1)
Mexican spotted owl	*Strix occidentalis lucida*	T	10/16/1995	F
Micronesian megapode	*Megapodius laperouse*	E	4/10/1998	F
Mississippi sandhill crane	*Grus canadensis pulla*	E	9/6/1991	RF(3)
Molokai creeper	*Paroreomyza flammea*	E	10/16/2003	RD(1)
Molokai thrush	*Myadestes lanaiensis rutha*	E	10/16/2003	RD(1)
Newell's Townsend's shearwater	*Puffinus auricularis newelli*	T	4/25/1983	F
Nightingale reed warbler (old world warbler)	*Acrocephalus luscinia*	E	4/10/1998	F
Nihoa finch (honeycreeper)	*Telespyza ultima*	E	10/4/1984	F
Nihoa millerbird (old world warbler)	*Acrocephalus familiaris kingi*	E	10/4/1984	F
Northern aplomado falcon	*Falco femoralis septentrionalis*	E	6/8/1990	F
Northern spotted owl	*Strix occidentalis caurina*	T	5/15/1992	D
Nukupu`u (honeycreeper)	*Hemignathus lucidus*	E	10/16/2003	RD(1)
`O`u (honeycreeper)	*Psittirostra psittacea*	E	10/16/2003	RD(1)
Oahu creeper	*Paroreomyza maculata*	E	10/16/2003	RD(1)
Oahu elepaio	*Chasiempis sandwichensis ibidis*	E	10/16/2003	RD(1)
Palila (honeycreeper)	*Loxioides bailleui*	E	6/27/1986	RF(1)
Piping plover	*Charadrius melodus*	E, T	8/1/1994	D
Po`ouli (honeycreeper)	*Melamprosops phaeosoma*	E	10/16/2003	RD(1)
Puerto Rican broad-winged hawk	*Buteo platypterus brunnescens*	E	9/8/1997	F
Puerto Rican nightjar	*Caprimulgus noctitherus*	E	4/19/1984	F

TABLE 9.1

Endangered and threatened bird species in the United States, March 2006 [CONTINUED]

Common name	Scientific name	Listing status[a]	Recovery plan date	Recovery Plan stage[b]
Puerto Rican parrot	*Amazona vittata*	E	4/30/1999	RD(2)
Puerto Rican plain pigeon	*Columba inornata wetmorei*	E	10/14/1982	F
Puerto Rican sharp-shinned hawk	*Accipiter striatus venator*	E	9/8/1997	F
Red-cockaded woodpecker	*Picoides borealis*	E	3/20/2003	RF(2)
Roseate tern	*Sterna dougallii dougallii*	E, T	9/24/1993	F
Rota bridled white-eye	*Zosterops rotensis*	E	None	—
San Clemente loggerhead shrike	*Lanius ludovicianus mearnsi*	E	1/26/1984	F
San Clemente sage sparrow	*Amphispiza belli clementeae*	T	1/26/1984	F
Short-tailed albatross	*Phoebastria (=diomedea) albatrus*	E	10/27/2005	D
Small Kauai (=puaiohi) thrush	*Myadestes palmeri*	E	10/16/2003	RD(1)
Southwestern willow flycatcher	*Empidonax traillii extimus*	E	8/30/2002	F
Spectacled eider	*Somateria fischeri*	T	8/12/1996	F
Steller's eider	*Polysticta stelleri*	T	9/30/2002	F
Western snowy plover	*Charadrius alexandrinus nivosus*	T	5/1/2001	D
White-necked crow	*Corvus leucognaphalus*	E	None	—
Whooping crane	*Grus americana*	E, EXPN	1/11/2005	RD(3)
Wood stork	*Mycteria americana*	E	1/27/1997	RF(1)
Yellow-shouldered blackbird	*Agelaius xanthomus*	E	11/12/1996	RF(1)
Yuma clapper rail	*Rallus longirostris yumanensis*	E	2/4/1983	F

[a]E=endangered, T=threatened, EXPN=experimental population, non-essential.
[b]Recovery plan stages: E=exempt, F=final, D=draft, RD=draft under revision, RF=final revision.

SOURCE: Adapted from "Listed FWS/Joint FWS and NMFS Species and Populations with Recovery Plans (Sorted by Listed Entity)" and "Listed U.S. Species by Taxonomic Group," in *Threatened and Endangered Species System (TESS)*, U.S. Department of the Interior, U.S. Fish and Wildlife Service, March 4, 2006, http://ecos.fws.gov/tess_public/SpeciesRecovery.do?sort=1 and http://ecos.fws.gov/tess_public/SpeciesReport.do?kingdom=V&listingType=L (accessed March 4, 2006)

TABLE 9.2

The ten listed bird entities with the highest expenditures under the Endangered Species Act, fiscal year 2004

Ranking	Common name	Listing*	Expenditure
1	Red-cockaded woodpecker	E	$14,125,085
2	Southwestern willow flycatcher	E	$11,911,824
3	Bald eagle (lower 48 states)	T	$ 9,837,240
4	Northern spotted owl	T	$ 6,980,570
5	Marbled murrelet (California, Oregon, Washington)	T	$ 5,646,695
6	Mexican spotted owl	T	$ 5,276,995
7	Black-capped vireo	E	$ 4,606,463
8	Western snowy plover (Pacific coastal population)	T	$ 4,530,614
9	Golden-cheeked warbler (=wood)	E	$ 4,452,326
10	Piping plover (except Great Lakes watershed)	T	$ 3,489,405

*E=endangered, T=threatened.

SOURCE: Adapted from "Table 1. Reported FY 2004 Expenditures for Endangered and Threatened Species, Not Including Land Acquisition Costs," in *Federal and State Endangered and Threatened Species Expenditures: Fiscal Year 2004*, U.S. Department of the Interior, U.S. Fish and Wildlife Service, January 2005, http://www.fws.gov/endangered/expenditures/reports/FWS%20Endangered%20Species%202004%20Expenditures%20Report.pdf (accessed February 11, 2006)

predators. Because red-cockaded woodpeckers rarely nest in trees less than eighty years old, heavy logging has destroyed much of their former habitat. The red-cockaded woodpecker was first placed on the Endangered Species List in 1970. It is currently found in fragmented populations in the southeastern seaboard westward into Texas. Figure 9.2 shows the historical and current distribution of

FIGURE 9.1

The red cockaded woodpecker

SOURCE: Bob Savannah, artist, "Red Cockaded Woodpeckers," in *Pictures/Graphics, Wildlife Sketches*, U.S. Department of the Interior, U.S. Fish and Wildlife Service, Undated, http://www.fws.gov/pictures/lineart/bobsavannah/redcockadedwoodpeckers.html (accessed February 15, 2006)

FIGURE 9.2

Historic and current distribution of the red-cockaded woodpecker, updated 2002

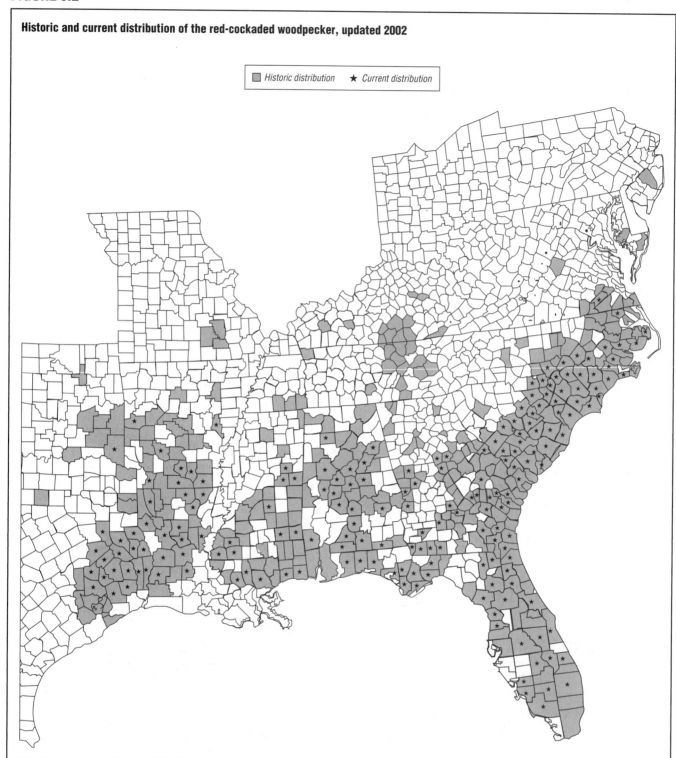

Note: Based on map presented in *Our Living Resources: A Report to the Nation on the Distribution, Abundance, and Health of US Plants, Animals, and Ecosystems*, U.S. Department of the Interior, U.S. Geological Survey, National Biological Service, 1995.

SOURCE: "Map," in *Photos: Red Cockaded Woodpecker: Images*, U.S. Department of the Interior, U.S. Fish and Wildlife Service, Southeast Region, 2002, http://www.fws.gov/southeast/news/2003/rcw/partial_map.jpg (accessed March 6, 2006)

the species in 2002. In 2003 the U.S. Fish and Wildlife Service published an updated recovery plan for the red-cockaded woodpecker and estimated that approximately 14,000 of the birds were in existence at that time.

In March 2001 the Fish and Wildlife Service rescued several red-cockaded woodpeckers from habitat areas in Daniel Boone National Forest in Kentucky. Fifteen woodpeckers in six family groups were relocated to the

Carolina Sandhills National Wildlife Refuge in South Carolina and the Ouachita National Forest in Arkansas. Daniel Boone National Forest had become uninhabitable for the woodpeckers after a 1999 infestation of southern pine beetles. The beetles quickly destroyed 90% of local woodpecker habitat despite efforts by Forest Service officials and volunteers to control the insect's spread. The removal of this red-cockaded woodpecker population from Kentucky means that the species is now absent from the state. The bird is also believed extirpated (wiped out) in Maryland, Missouri, New Jersey, and Tennessee.

In September 2005 the FWS initiated a five-year review of the red-cockaded woodpecker to ensure that the endangered status listing is still appropriate for the species.

IVORY-BILLED WOODPECKERS. The ivory-billed woodpecker (*Campephilus principalis*) is the largest woodpecker species in the United States, with a wingspan up to thirty inches and bodies nearly twenty inches long. The birds have a striking black and white pattern on their bodies and have ivory-colored beaks. The males have brilliant red crests. In the nineteenth century, the species was found throughout the southeastern United States as well as in Cuba. Intense logging and loss of habitat were believed to have driven the birds extinct sometime in the 1940s. Occasional unconfirmed sightings continued to occur over the following decades. John W. Fitzpatrick and his colleagues reported in "Ivory-Billed Woodpecker (*Campephilus Principalis*) Persists in Continental North America" (*Science*, June 3, 2005) that scientists at Cornell University had confirmed sightings and a videotape taken of ivory-billed woodpeckers in the Big Woods region of Arkansas. This area is home to the Cache River National Wildlife Refuge. Conservationists are excited that an apparently lost species has been rediscovered.

Passerines

Just over half of all bird species belong to the order Passeriformes and are called passerines. They are informally known as perching birds or songbirds, although not all passerines are truly songbirds. According to the U.S. Department of Agriculture there are more than sixty families in this order, and they include many well-known species, such as robins, bluebirds, larks, blue jays, mockingbirds, finches, wrens, sparrows, swallows, starlings, cardinals, blackbirds, and crows. More than a third of the U.S. species of endangered and threatened birds are passerine (perching) birds.

SOUTHWESTERN WILLOW FLYCATCHER. The southwestern willow flycatcher (*Empidonax traillii extimus*) is a subspecies of the willow flycatcher. This small bird has a grayish-green back and wings with a pale yellow belly and white-colored throat. It was first listed as endangered in 1995, when less than 600 individuals were believed to

be in existence. The bird is found in portions of Arizona, California, Colorado, New Mexico, Nevada, Texas, and Utah. It migrates to Mexico and Central and South America for the winter. The bird feeds on insects and prefers riparian areas (dense vegetation near rivers or streams) for its habitat. It is endangered primarily due to loss of riparian vegetation. In ranching areas, this vegetation is often stripped by grazing livestock. Another factor in the decline is harm from "brood parasites"— bird species that lay their eggs in the nests of other species. Brown-headed cowbirds are brood parasites that threaten the southwestern willow flycatcher. They lay their eggs in the flycatchers nests, and the unsuspecting flycatchers raise the cowbirds' young as their own.

In 1997 the U.S. Fish and Wildlife Service designated critical habitat for the bird in compliance with a court order resulting from a lawsuit filed against the agency by the Southwest Center for Biological Diversity. The critical habitat covered nearly 600 miles of streams and rivers in California, Arizona, and New Mexico. A recovery plan for the bird was finalized in 2002 that includes six recovery units as shown in Figure 9.3. In 2005 the FWS designated new critical habitat for the southwestern willow flycatcher covering 737 miles of waterways in California, Arizona, Nevada, Utah, and New Mexico. The new designation was made in response to a court order.

THE BLACK-CAPPED VIREO AND GOLDEN-CHEEKED WARBLER. The black-capped vireo and golden-cheeked warbler are among the threatened songbirds listed under the Endangered Species Act. Both species nest in central Texas and other locations in the United States and winter in Mexico and Central America. Both species have declined largely due to loss of habitat caused by land clearing for development and invasion of brown-headed cowbirds. In certain areas, more than half the black-capped vireo nests contain eggs of brood parasites called brown-headed cowbirds. The black-capped vireo was placed on the Endangered Species List in 1987; the golden-cheeked warbler was listed in 1990.

Much of the critical nesting habitat for black-capped vireos and golden-cheeked warblers lies in the Hill Country of central Texas. The Texas Hill Country is characterized by diverse habitats and a high concentration of rare bird species. In the last decade, however, increased water demand by metropolitan areas has caused the local Edwards Aquifer to drop by thirty feet, resulting in a 15% to 45% decrease in available bird habitat. In an effort to balance development with wildlife preservation, the city of Austin, Texas, invited the Nature Conservancy to formulate a plan to protect Hill Country habitats while enabling some development. The result was the Balcones Canyonlands Conservation Plan, which includes a 75,000-acre preserve in the Texas Hill Country.

FIGURE 9.3

Recovery areas for the Southwestern willow flycatcher

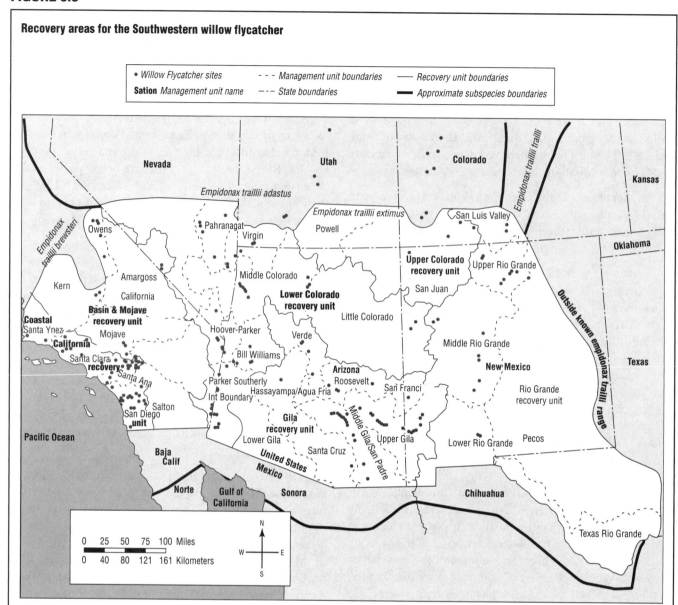

SOURCE: "Figure 4. Recovery and Management Units for the Southwestern Willow Flycatcher," in *Final Recovery Plan, Southwestern Willow Flycatcher (Empidonax traillii extimus)*, U.S. Department of the Interior, U.S. Fish and Wildlife Service, August 2002, http://ecos.fws.gov/docs/recovery_plans/2002/020830c.pdf (accessed March 6, 2006).

Fort Hood, Texas, a heavy artillery training site for the U.S. Army, was designated essential nesting habitat for the golden-cheeked warbler and black-capped vireo in 1993. With the help of the Nature Conservancy, the Army currently manages some 66,000 acres of habitat for these species. Control of brown-headed cowbird populations has been a major part of the conservation efforts. Brown-headed cowbirds parasitize the nests of over 200 species of songbirds, and have caused declines in many of these species. Nest parasitism rates for the black-capped vireo were as high as 90% before control measures were begun. They have been reduced to less than 10%. Many other bird species also use habitat at

Fort Hood, including threatened and endangered species such as the bald eagle, peregrine falcon, and whooping crane.

THE COASTAL CALIFORNIA GNATCATCHER. The coastal California gnatcatcher (*Polioptila californica californica*) is a small, gray and black songbird known for its kitten-like mewing call. Gnatcatchers are nonmigratory, permanent residents of California coastal sage scrub communities, one of the most threatened vegetation types in the nation. In 1995 the U.S. Geological Survey estimated that more than 85% of coastal sage scrub had been destroyed or significantly degraded in Southern California since the time of European settlement.

The Fish and Wildlife Service estimated in 1993 that approximately 2,500 pairs of California gnatcatchers remained in the United States. The plight of the species has emphasized the importance of preserving coastal sage scrub habitat, which supports many other distinctive species as well. The California gnatcatcher was listed as threatened across its entire range in California and Mexico in 1993. In an effort to protect the birds, in 2003 the FWS proposed a critical habitat area of more than 495,000 acres of land covering portions of Ventura, Los Angeles, Orange, Riverside, San Bernardino and San Diego counties.

Hawaiian Honeycreepers

The Hawaiian honeycreepers are a group of songbirds endemic to Hawaii—that is, species in this group are found there and nowhere else on Earth. Hawaiian honeycreepers are believed to have radiated—formed many separate species, each adapted to a particular lifestyle—from a single species that colonized the Hawaiian Islands thousands of years ago. The honeycreepers are named for the characteristic "creeping" behavior some species exhibit as they search for nectar. The Hawaiian honeycreepers are extremely diverse in their diet—different species are seed-eaters, insect-eaters, or nectar-eaters. Species also differ in the shapes of the beaks and in plumage coloration. Hawaiian honeycreepers are found in forest habitats at high elevations. According to Absoluteastronomy.com (http://www.absoluteastronomy.com/reference/hawaiian_honeycreeper) there were some fifty or sixty Hawaiian honeycreeper species originally, but a third of them are already extinct.

Ten species of Hawaiian honeycreepers are currently listed as endangered. Some honeycreeper species are among the most endangered animals on earth, with only a few individuals left. One of the primary factors involved in honeycreeper endangerment is loss of habitat. The Hawaiian Islands are estimated to retain a mere 20% to 30% of their original forest cover. In addition, the introduction of predators that hunt birds or eat their eggs, such as rats, cats, and mongooses, have contributed to the decline of numerous species. The introduction of bird diseases, particularly those spread by introduced mosquitoes, has also decimated honeycreeper populations. The success of mosquitoes in Hawaii has been dependent on another introduced species—pigs. The rooting activity of pigs creates pools of water where mosquitoes lay their eggs. In fact, the greater the number of pigs in a habitat, the more bird disease will be prevalent. Finally, competition with introduced bird species for food and habitat has also been a significant cause of decline.

The Po'ouli is the most endangered Hawaiian honeycreeper and may already be extinct. Along with many other endangered native species, it occupies the Hanawi Natural Reserve Area in Maui, which has been aggressively rehabilitated and cleared of invasive species. The bird was only discovered during the 1970s. At that time less than 200 individuals existed in the wild. By 2004 there were only three Po'ouli birds left. Scientists captured one of the birds, but he died a few months later, apparently of avian malaria. As of March 2006 the remaining two individuals have not been located and may already have died.

In 2003 the U.S. Fish and Wildlife Service published a recovery plan for nineteen endangered Hawaiian forest birds. The agency reports that ten of these species have not been definitely observed in at least a decade and may well be extinct already. Most of these species are native to rain forests at elevations above 4,000 feet on the islands of Hawaii (Big Island), Maui, and Kauai. Major threats to endangered forest species include habitat loss and modification, other human activity, disease, and predation. Of particular importance are nonnative plants, which have converted native plant communities to alien ecosystems unsuitable as habitat.

It is estimated that two-thirds of Hawaii's original bird fauna is already extinct. Of the remaining one-third, a large majority are imperiled. Habitat destruction in Hawaii has been so extensive that all the lowland species now present are nonnative species introduced by humans.

Migratory Songbirds

There are more than 200 species of songbirds known as neotropical migraters. Every year these birds migrate between the United States and tropical areas in Mexico, the Caribbean, and Central and South America. Although some songbirds are appreciated by humans for their beautiful songs and colorful plumage, migratory songbirds also play a vital role in many ecosystems. During spring migration in the Ozarks, for example, dozens of migratory bird species arrive and feed on the insects that inhabit oak trees, thereby helping to control insect populations.

Migratory species are particularly vulnerable because they are dependent on suitable habitat in both their winter and spring ranges. In North America, real estate development has eliminated many forest habitats. Migratory songbird habitats are also jeopardized in Central and South America, where farmers and ranchers have been burning and clearing tropical forests to plant crops and graze livestock. Some countries, including Belize, Costa Rica, Guatemala, and Mexico, have set up preserves for songbirds, but improved forest management is needed to save them.

Raptors (Birds of Prey)

The term raptor is derived from the Latin word *raptores*, which was once the order on the taxonomy

FIGURE 9.4

The bald eagle was once endangered due to habitat destruction and pollution by pesticides, such as DDT. Its populations have recovered with protection and a ban on DDT. (*Field Mark Publications.*)

table to which birds of prey were assigned. Eventually scientists split the birds into three orders as follows:

- Accipitriformes—includes hawks, eagles, and buzzards
- Falconiformes—falcons
- Strigiformes—owls

As shown in Table 9.1 there were less than a dozen raptors listed as endangered or threatened in the United States as of March 2006. Species of note include the bald eagle, northern spotted owl, and California condor.

THE BALD EAGLE. The bald eagle (*Haliaeetus leucocephalus*) is a raptor with special status in the United States. (See Figure 9.4.) A symbol of honor, courage, nobility, and independence (eagles do not fly in flocks), the bald eagle is found only in North America, and its image is engraved on the official seal of the United States of America. There were an estimated 100,000 bald eagles in the country in the late eighteenth century when the nation was founded.

The bald eagle nests over most of the United States and Canada, building its aerie, or nest, in mature conifer forests or on top of rocks or cliffs. Its nest is of such a grand size—sometimes as large as a small car—that a huge rock or tree is necessary to secure it. The birds use the same nest year after year, adding to it each nesting season. It is believed that eagles mate for life. Bald eagles prey primarily on fish, water birds, and turtles.

Bald eagles came dangerously close to extinction in the twentieth century, largely due to the pesticide DDT, which was introduced in 1947. Like other carnivorous species, bald eagles ingested large amounts of DDT by eating prey that had been exposed to it. DDT either prevents birds from laying eggs or causes the eggshells to be so thin they are unable to protect eggs until they hatch. The Bald Eagle Protection Act of 1940, which made it a federal offense to kill bald eagles, helped protect the species. However, numbers continued to dwindle and the bald eagle was listed as endangered in 1967.

Bald eagle populations started to recover with the banning of DDT in 1972. The species also benefited from habitat protection and attempts to clean up water pollution. In 1995 the bald eagle was moved from endangered to threatened status on the Endangered Species List. In 1999 the species was proposed for delisting. A year later all delisting criteria contained in species recovery plans were achieved. However, the FWS has been slow to carry through with the delisting process. In February 2006 the agency reopened the public comment period on the delisting proposal. Public comments were to be accepted until May 2006. The FWS news release announcing the reopening (February 16 2006, http://www.fws.gov/migratorybirds/issues/BaldEagle/Reopening.Comments.06.pdf) notes that there were an estimated 7,066 nesting pairs of bald eagles in the United States at that time.

NORTHERN SPOTTED OWL. The northern spotted owl (*Strix occidentalis caurina*) occupies old-growth forests in the Pacific Northwest, where it nests in the cavities of trees 200 years old or older. It does not seem afraid of humans and in fact appears to be curious about humans and human activity. Its primary prey includes the nocturnal northern flying squirrel, mice, and other rodents and reptiles. According to the Sierra Club, owl pairs may forage across areas as large as 2,200 acres.

Northern spotted owl populations have declined primarily due to habitat loss. Most of the private lands in its range have been heavily logged, leaving only public lands, such as national forests and national parks, for habitat. Because logging has also been permitted in many old-growth national forest areas, the species has lost approximately 90% of its original habitat. In 1990 the U.S. Fish and Wildlife Service placed the northern spotted owl on its list of threatened species. Court battles began over continued logging in national forest habitats. In 1991 a U.S. federal district court ruled in favor of the

Seattle Audubon Society and against the U.S. Forest Service, declaring that the Forest Service was not meeting its obligation to "maintain viable populations." The Forest Service had argued that the FWS was responsible for the management and recovery of this species. However, the court pointed out that the Forest Service had its own distinct obligations to protect species under the Endangered Species Act, and that courts had already reprimanded the FWS for failing to designate critical habitat for the northern spotted owl.

In 1992 the FWS set aside seven million acres as critical habitat for the species and published a recovery plan. A year later the Northwest Forest Plan was established. It reduced logging in thirteen national forests by about 85% to protect northern spotted owl habitats. However, populations of the northern spotted owl continued to decline —this despite the unanticipated discovery of fifty pairs of nesting adults in California's Marin County, just north of the Golden Gate Bridge.

In 2004 the U.S. Fish and Wildlife Service completed a five-year status review of the northern spotted owl. The review was conducted in response to a lawsuit filed by the Western Council of Industrial Workers. The agency concluded that the bird should continue to have a threatened listing under the Endangered Species Act. The FWS found that habitat loss on federal lands has been minimized since the species was originally listed. This success is attributed to the Northwest Forest Plan. However, the agency found that the population of northern spotted owls in Washington, Oregon, and California has continued to decline, and the species faces emerging threats from forest fires, West Nile virus, sudden oak death (a plant disease that has killed hundreds of thousands of trees in California and Oregon), and competition for habitat from barred owls.

In January 2006 the FWS announced its intention to develop a final recovery plan for the northern spotted owl. A draft recovery plan, issued in 1992, was never finalized by the agency. The new recovery plan is expected to address recovery and conservation on non-federal lands and establish delisting criteria. New final designation of critical habit for the species is expected by the end of 2007.

THE CALIFORNIA CONDOR. The California condor (*Gymnogyps californianus*) has a wingspan in excess of nine feet, and is among the continent's most impressive birds. Ten thousand years ago, this species soared over most of North America. However, its range contracted at the end of the Ice Age, and eventually individuals were found only along the Pacific Coast. Like other vulture species, the California condor is a carrion eater, and feeds on the carcasses of deer, sheep, and smaller species such as rodents. Random shooting, egg collection, poisoning, and loss of habitat devastated the condor population. The spe-

FIGURE 9.5

Captively bred condors

Zookeepers use hand puppets that look like adult condors to feed captively bred condor chicks.

SOURCE: "Captively-Bred Condors," in *California Condor*, U.S. Fish and Wildlife Service, August 1998, http://training.fws.gov/library/Pubs/condor.pdf (accessed April 4, 2006)

cies was listed as endangered in 1967. Oliver H. Pattee and Robert Mesta in "California Condors" (http://biology.usgs.gov/s+t/noframe/b162.htm#9944) show that by 1984 only eleven condors remained in the wild. After five of these birds died, the FWS decided to capture the remaining population.

An intense captive breeding program for the California condor was initiated in 1987. (See Figure 9.5.) The first chick hatched in 1988. The breeding program was successful enough that California condors were released into the wild beginning in 1992. Four years later a release took place near the Grand Canyon, providing spectacular opportunities to view the largest bird in North America. The introduced birds in parts of Arizona, Nevada, and Utah were designated a nonessential experimental population. The California condor is listed as endangered in the remainder of Arizona and all of California and Oregon.

In April 2002, for the first time in eighteen years, a condor egg laid in the wild hatched in the wild. The parents of this chick had been captive-bred at the Los Angeles Zoo and the San Diego Wild Animal Park respectively and released into the wild in 1995 at the age of one. Between 2001 and 2005 three wild-born condor chicks died, one from West Nile virus and two from eating trash (fragments of plastic, metal, glass, and fabric). During the summer of 2005 biologists removed a sickly chick from its nest and performed surgery to remove trash from the bird's stomach. The surgery was successful and the chick was expected to be released back to the wild in the spring of 2006.

In September 2005 the U.S. Fish and Wildlife Service announced that 125 condors were known to be living in the wild and 151 were in captivity at the Los Angeles Zoo, San Diego Wild Animal Park, the Oregon Zoo, and the Peregrine Fund's World Center for Birds of Prey in Boise, Idaho.

Water Birds

Water birds live in and around bodies of water. Some prefer marine (ocean) habitats and others are found only near freshwater. Many species inhabit swamps and wetlands. These areas may be inland or intertidal (along the sea coast).

There were more than two dozen water birds listed as endangered or threatened in the United States as of March 2006. They include a variety of species from many different taxonomic orders.

MIGRATORY SHORE BIRDS. Migratory shore birds are found most often in marshes, mudflats, estuaries, and other wetland areas where the sea meets freshwater. This category includes plovers, stilts, snipes, oystercatchers, avocets, shearwaters, and sandpipers. These birds vary greatly in size and color, but nearly all migrate over very long distances. Most of them breed near the North Pole in the spring and spend their winters anywhere from the southern United States to South America. During their annual migrations, the birds stop to rest and feed at specific locations, known as staging areas, in the United States. Major staging areas include Delaware Bay, the Copper River Delta in Alaska, Cheyenne Bottoms in Kansas, San Francisco Bay, and the Great Salt Lake in Utah.

SEA BIRDS. Sea birds spend most of their time out at sea, but nest on land. They are also known as pelagic birds, because pelagic means oceanic (associated with the open seas). Sea bird species include gulls, terns, albatrosses, puffins and penguins, kittiwakes, petrels, murres and murrelets, auks and auklets, and cormorants.

The marbled murrelet (*Brachyramphus marmoratus*) is one of a handful of sea birds listed under the Endangered Species Act. The bird was first listed in 1992 and is designated as threatened in California, Oregon, and Washington. The marbled murrelet is about nine inches long and has a distinctive two-tone pattern of dark and light markings. The species prefers to nest in the trees of old-growth forests along the Pacific Northwest coastline. Logging and other causes of habitat degradation have resulted in population declines.

In 2004 the U.S. Fish and Wildlife Service completed a five-year status review for the marbled murrelet. The agency concluded that the population living in Oregon, Washington, and California did not qualify for a listing as a distinct population segment under the Endangered

FIGURE 9.6

The wood stork is a wading bird

SOURCE: "The Wood Stork Is an Indicator," in *Wood Stork: Everglades National Park*, U.S. Department of the Interior, National Park Service, Everglades National Park, November 17, 1997, http://www.nps.gov/ever/eco/wdstork.htm (accessed March 6, 2006)

Species Act and that the species should retain its listing as threatened. However, the agency has decided to conduct a species-wide review to determine if the listed range of the bird needs to be modified. The status review was performed in response to a lawsuit filed by the American Forest Resources Council and other parties.

WADING BIRDS. Wading birds are unusual birds characterized by long, skinny legs and extended necks and beaks. They wade in the shallow waters of swamps, wetlands, and bays where they feed on aquatic life forms. Wading birds include species of egret, crane, stork, and ibis. As of March 2006 there were two wading birds of note listed under the ESA: the wood stork (*Mycteria americana*) and the whooping crane (*Grus americana*).

The wood stork (see Figure 9.6) weighs only about five pounds, but stands up to three feet tall with a five-foot wing span. At one time tens of thousands of the birds inhabited the southeast coastline. In 1984 the species was listed under the ESA as endangered in Alabama, Florida, Georgia, and South Carolina. A recovery plan for the bird was published in 1999. At that time about 5,000 breeding pairs lived in the wild. Populations have declined in the Everglades in southern Florida, but increased in coastal areas farther north. In a 2005 report the FWS estimated the number of adult wood storks to be 16,000 (http://www.fws.gov/north florida/Species-Accounts/Wood-stork-2005.htm).

Standing five feet tall, the whooping crane (see Figure 9.7) is North America's tallest bird and among the best known endangered species in the United States. Its name comes from its loud and distinctive call, which can be heard for miles. Historically whooping cranes lived

FIGURE 9.7

The whooping crane is highly endangered. Each year whooping cranes migrate from breeding grounds in Canada to wintering grounds in south Texas. (*Field Mark Publications.*)

across the Great Plains and southeast coast of the United States. The birds were once heavily hunted, for meat as well as for their beautiful, long white feathers. In addition, the heavy loss of wetland areas in the United States deprived whooping cranes of much of their original habitat. In 1937 it was discovered that fewer than twenty whooping cranes were left in the wild in two small populations—a migratory population that nested in Canada and wintered on the Texas coast and a nonmigratory population living in Louisiana.

Each year, the migratory whooping cranes fly 2,500 miles from nesting grounds in Wood Buffalo, Canada, to Aransas, Texas, for the winter before returning north in March to breed. Whooping cranes return to the same nesting site each year with the same mate. In 1937 the Aransas Wildlife Refuge was established in south Texas to protect the species' wintering habitat. Conservation efforts for the whooping crane are coordinated with the Canadian government, which manages the birds' breeding areas.

The whooping crane is listed under the ESA as endangered in Colorado, Kansas, Montana, North Dakota, Nebraska, Oklahoma, South Dakota, and Texas. Nonessential experimental populations were designated in 1993 and 2001 in dozens of states from Wyoming to Florida. In 2001 the first introduced cranes in Wisconsin were led to their Florida wintering grounds along the migration route by ultralight aircraft. The birds successfully made the return trip on their own in following years.

In September 2005 the U.S. Geological Survey reported 340 whooping cranes living in the wild and 135 individuals in captive populations.

OTHER BIRDS. Other birds listed under the Endangered Species Act include nonmigratory shore birds, such as the clapper rail and the Guam rail (a flightless bird); swimming birds, including coots, ducks, eiders, and geese; ground-dwelling birds, such as the prairie chicken; and coastal dwellers, such as the brown pelican.

GENERAL THREATS TO U.S. BIRD SPECIES

The U.S. government has long recognized the importance of bird biodiversity and promoted habitat conservation under the Migratory Bird Conservation Act, passed by Congress in 1929. This law established the Migratory Bird Conservation Commission, which works with the Secretary of the Interior to designate and fund avian wildlife refuge areas. The U.S. Fish and Wildlife Service is responsible for acquiring necessary lands through direct purchase, lease, or easement (agreement with landowners). The agency has procured over four million acres of land for bird refuges. Other domestic laws and international conventions from 1990–2001 concerning migratory birds are listed in Table 9.3.

Habitat Loss and Environmental Decline

The driving force behind current declines in many bird species is the destruction, degradation, and fragmentation of habitat due to increasing human population size and the wasteful consumption of resources. The leading cause of habitat destruction in the United States is agricultural development. Large corporate farms cause environmental damage by clearing out native plant species, planting only one or a few crops, and draining wetlands. Natural habitats are also lost to urban sprawl, logging, mining, and road building.

Pesticides

During the latter half of the twentieth century, pesticides and other toxic chemicals were recognized as a major cause of avian mortality and a primary factor in the endangerment of several species, including the bald eagle and peregrine falcon. While the U.S. Environmental Protection Agency regulates the manufacture and use of toxic chemicals nationwide, the Fish and Wildlife Service (under the Federal Insecticide, Fungicide, and Rodenticide Act) is responsible for preventing and punishing the misuse of chemicals that affect wildlife.

Many chemicals harmful to birds, such as DDT and toxaphene, have been banned. Other chemicals, such as endrin, the most toxic of the chlorinated hydrocarbon pesticides, are still legal for some uses. Endrin was responsible for the disappearance of the brown pelican from Louisiana, a population that once numbered 50,000 individuals.

TABLE 9.3

Major international conventions and U.S. legislation devoted to migratory bird conservation, 1990–2001

Year	Authority
1900	Lacey Act (amended 1981)
1913	Weeks-McLean Law (Migratory Bird Conservation Act 1913)
1916	Convention for the Protection of Migratory Birds (Canada)
1918	Migratory Bird Treaty Act
1929	Migratory Bird Conservation Act
1934	Migratory Bird Hunting and Conservation Stamp Act (Duck Stamp Act)
1936	Migratory Bird Convention with Mexico (amended 1972)
1940	Pan American (or Western Hemisphere) Convention
1940	Bald Eagle Protection Act
1956	Waterfowl Depredations Prevention Act
1961	Wetlands Loan Act of 1961 (amended 1969, 1976)
1972	Migratory Bird Convention with Japan
1972	Convention on Wetlands of International Importance especially as waterfowl habitats (RAMSAR)
1973	Endangered Species Act (ESA)
1973	Convention on International Trade in Endangered Species of Wild Fauna and Flora (CITES)
1976	Migratory Bird Convention with the Union of Soviet Socialist Republics
1978	Antarctic Conservation Act
1980	Fish and Wildlife Conservation Act (amended 1988, 1989)
1982	Convention on Conservation of Antarctic Living Marine Resources
1986	Emergency Wetlands Resources Act
1987	Driftnet Impact Monitoring, Assessment, and Control Act of 1987
1989	North American Wetlands Conservation Act (NAWCA)
1990	Coastal Wetlands Planning, Protection and Restoration Act
1992	Wild Bird Conservation Act
2000	Neotropical Migratory Bird Conservation Act
2001	Responsibilities of Federal Agencies to Protect Migratory Birds (executive order 13186)

SOURCE: "Appendix 3. Primary International Conventions and Major Domestic Legislation for the Conservation of Migratory Birds and Their Habitats in the United States," in *A Blueprint for the Future of Migratory Birds: Migratory Bird Program Strategic Plan 2004–2014*, U.S. Department of the Interior, U.S. Fish and Wildlife Service, 2004, http://www.fws.gov/migratorybirds/mbstratplan/MBStratPlanTOC.htm (accessed March 9, 2006)

Oil Spills

Oil spills constitute a major threat to birds. (See Figure 9.8.) One of the worst and most infamous spills in history occurred on March 24, 1989, when the *Exxon Valdez* tanker released eleven million tons of crude oil into Alaska's Prince William Sound. To many Americans, it still exemplifies the disastrous effects oil spills have on wildlife. Thousands of birds died immediately after coming in contact with the oil, either from losing the insulation of their feathers or by ingesting lethal amounts of oil when they tried to clean themselves. Exxon personnel burned untold piles of birds; others were saved in cold storage under orders from the U.S. Fish and Wildlife Service. A complete count was never obtained, but FWS biologists estimated that between 250,000 and 400,000 sea birds died as a result of the accident.

Approximately 40% of the region's entire population of common murres—estimated at 91,000—was eliminated. The yellow-billed loon population was also seriously depleted, as was the population of Kittlitz's murrelet, a species found almost exclusively in Prince William Sound.

FIGURE 9.8

A bird is cleaned of oil after the disastrous *Exxon Valdez* spill in Prince William Sound, Alaska, in 1989. (*AP/Wide World Photos.*)

Other affected bird species included the bald eagle, black oystercatcher, common loon, harlequin duck, marbled murrelet, pigeon guillemot, and the pelagic, red-faced, and double-crested cormorants. Of these, according to the Alaska Center for the Environment ("Lingering Effects of the *Exxon Valdez* Oil Spill," http://www.akcenter.org/oceans/exxon_spill.html), the common loon, the harlequin duck, the pigeon guillemot, and the three species of cormorants had not increased in population size since the spill and were still considered "not recovered" in 2005. In addition, the Kittlitz's murrelet appears to be suffering from continued population decline, and its future prospects appear bleak.

The detergents used to clean up oil spills can also be deadly to waterfowl—detergents destroy feathers, which leads to fatal chills or trauma. Research has shown that even after careful rehabilitation, birds that have been returned to nature after a spill often die in a matter of months. In 1996 Dr. Daniel Anderson, a biologist at the University of California at Davis, found that only 12% to 15% of rehabilitated pelicans survived for two years, compared to the 80% to 90% of pelicans not exposed to oil (Verne G. Kopytoff, "Birds Rescued in Spills Do Poorly, Study Finds," *New York Times*, November 12, 1996). For many ornithologists, these dismal results raise the issue of whether avian rescue efforts are worthwhile. Could money spent on rehabilitation be better used for spill prevention and habitat restoration? Oregon ornithologist Dr. Brian Sharp argued in the same *New York Times* article that the cleanup effort might ease the conscience of the public and of politicians, but in reality, does very little to benefit birds. However, new methods of treating oiled birds and of controlling spills have increased the bird survival rate from 5% to between 60% and 80% for some species. Under the Clean Water Act, the oil industry pays a tax that helps fund cleanups after spills.

Domestic Cats

Studies in the United States and Britain have shown that house cats kill millions of small birds and mammals every year, a death toll that contributes to declines of rare species in some areas. Many cat victims are plentiful urban species, but studies by the U.S. Fish and Wildlife Service have shown that cats also kill hundreds of millions of migratory songbirds annually (http://www.fws.gov/birds/mortality-fact-sheet.pdf). In addition, cats have devastated bird fauna on some islands and are believed to have contributed to the declines of several grassland species in the United States.

Trade in Exotic Birds

Birds are among the most popular pets in American homes. According to the American Pet Products Manufacturers Association in *2005/2006 National Pet Owners Survey* (http://www.appma.org/press_industrytrends.asp), more than 16.6 million birds are kept as pets in the United States. Many of these are common finches, canaries, or parakeets, all of which are raised in captivity in the United States. However, wild birds are owned and traded as well, including numerous species of passerines (song birds) and psittacines (parrots and their relatives).

The most commonly traded passerines include warblers, buntings, weavers, finches, starlings, flycatchers, and sparrows. Passerines are regarded as low-value birds, and few passerines are endangered due to trade.

The 333 species of psittacines, however, are generally rarer, and thus much more valuable, than passerines. The most commonly traded psittacines are macaws, Amazons, cockatoos, lovebirds, lories, and parakeets. In addition to their vivid colors and pleasant songs, many of these birds possess the ability to "talk," which makes them particularly appealing to some owners. Bird dealers have created demand for an ever-increasing variety of birds, including parrots, macaws, cockatoos, parakeets, mynahs, toucans, tanagers, and other tropical species.

Invasive Species—The Case of Guam

Invasive species have damaged bird populations in some parts of the world, particularly those that occupy islands. Guam's unique bird fauna has been all but wiped out by the brown tree snake, an invasive species. According to Earl William Campbell III in "Brown Treesnake Fact Sheet" (U.S. Fish and Wildlife Service, May 3, 2004), the brown tree snake was probably introduced from New Guinea via ship cargo in the late 1940s. The snake population thrived on the island because of the absence of natural enemies and the presence of plentiful prey in the form of forest birds. There are now believed to be as many as fourteen thousand snakes in a single square mile in some forest habitats. Nine bird species have already gone extinct on Guam, including the Guam flycatcher, the Rufus fantail, the white-throated ground dove, and the cardinal honey-eater. Several other Guam bird species are close to extinction. Many of these birds are or were unique to Guam. Measures have been implemented to try to keep this destructive snake from invading other islands, including careful inspection of all cargo arriving from Guam. The removal of the brown tree snake in select habitat areas on Guam (which is a high effort project, requiring the constant trapping of snakes) allowed the reintroduction of one bird, the flightless Guam rail, in 1998. The Guam rail had gone extinct in the wild, but a population is maintained in captivity.

Other particularly destructive invasive species include several associated with humans, including cats, dogs, and rats, which often prey on birds and their eggs.

BACK FROM THE BRINK—SUCCESS STORIES

The Peregrine Falcon

Many falcon species have declined with the spread of humans. Like other predatory species, falcons were often hunted, either for sport or because they were considered a threat to chickens or livestock.

The peregrine falcon is the fastest bird on Earth. It can achieve diving speeds of over 200 miles per hour. Like the bald eagle, much of the species' decline was due to the pesticide DDT. Populations sank to approximately 325 nesting pairs during the 1930s and 1940s. The recovery of this species was made possible by the banning of DDT as well as the establishment of special captive breeding centers on several continents. Between 1974 and 1999 more than 6,000 peregrine falcons were released into the wild. Federal and state agencies contributed to the conservation effort, as did private organizations such as the Peregrine Fund, Santa Cruz Predatory Bird Research Group, and Midwestern Peregrine Falcon Restoration Project.

In 1996 the U.S. Fish and Wildlife Service declared the peregrine falcon officially recovered and began the process to remove the species from the Endangered Species List. The American peregrine falcon was delisted in 1999 across its entire range. In 2003 the FWS conducted a postdelisting survey to monitor the ongoing condition of the species. At that time 3,000 breeding pairs were counted in the United States, Canada, and Mexico. Another survey will be completed in 2006.

Aleutian Canada Goose

The Aleutian Canada goose was first placed on the Endangered Species List in 1966, when there were an estimated 800 individuals. The species had been thought extinct for several decades until a remnant population was discovered in 1962 by FWS biologists on a remote Aleutian island. Deterioration of habitat and the introduction of predators such as Arctic foxes and red foxes were blamed for the animal's decline. According to the Alaska Department of Fish and Game, in April 2006 the goose population had rebounded to 15,000. Conservation efforts included captive breeding, removal of foxes, and relocation and reintroduction of geese to unoccupied islands. The Aleutian Canada goose was officially delisted in 2001.

FOREIGN SPECIES OF ENDANGERED AND THREATENED BIRDS

As of March 2006 there were 181 foreign species of birds listed under the Endangered Species Act as shown in Table 9.4. Categories including several endangered species are the cranes, eagles, owls, parakeets, parrots, pheasants, pigeons, and warblers.

In the World Conservation Union's *2004 Red List of Threatened Species* (2004, http://www.redlist.org) a total of 1,213 bird species were considered threatened out of 9,917 species known and evaluated. Certain groups of birds have declined particularly. All albatross species are considered threatened due largely to deaths from long-line fishing. Many Arctic bird species are threatened by habitat loss due to global warming. Tropical bird species are threatened by large-scale deforestation worldwide. Rapid deforestation in Southeast Asian rainforests has increased the number of threatened doves, parrots, and perching birds. The illegal bird trade has severely harmed many threatened species, particularly in Central and South America.

The largest numbers of endangered birds are found in Indonesia, the Philippines, Brazil, Colombia, China, Peru, India, and Tanzania. Island species are particularly vulnerable to habitat destruction because their ranges are usually very small. In addition, because many island birds evolved in the absence of predators, there are a large number of flightless species—these are highly vulnerable to hunting or predation by introduced species, including humans, cats, dogs, and rats. In fact, the IUCN reports that invasive species represent the single most frequent cause of bird extinctions since 1800.

TABLE 9.4

Foreign endangered and threatened bird species, March 2006

Status*	Species name	Status*	Species name
E	Albatross, Amsterdam (Diomedia amsterdamensis)	E	Macaw, little blue (Cyanopsitta spixii)
E	Alethe, Thyolo (Alethe choloensis)	E	Magpie-robin, Seychelles (thrush) (Copsychus sechellarum)
E	Booby, Abbott's (Papasula (=sula) abbotti)	E	Malimbe, Ibadan (Malimbus ibadanensis)
E	Bristlebird, western (Dasyornis longirostris (=brachypterus l.))	E	Malkoha, red-faced (cuckoo) (Phaenicophaeus pyrrhocephalus)
E	Bristlebird, western rufous (Dasyornis broadbenti littoralis)	E	Megapode, Maleo (Macrocephalon maleo)
E	Bulbul, Mauritius olivaceous (Hypsipetes borbonicus olivaceus)	E	Nuthatch, Algerian (Sitta ledanti)
E	Bullfinch, Sao Miguel (finch) (Pyrrhula pyrrhula murina)	E	Ostrich, Arabian (Struthio camelus syriacus)
T	Bush-shrike, Ulugura (Malaconotus alius)	E	Ostrich, West African (Struthio camelus spatzi)
E	Bushwren, New Zealand (Xenicus longipes)	E	Owl, Anjouan scops (Otus rutilus capnodes)
E	Bustard, great Indian (Ardeotis (=choriotis) nigriceps)	E	Owl, giant scops (Mimizuku (=otus) gurneyi)
E	Condor, Andean (Vultur gryphus)	E	Owl, Madagascar red (Tyto soumagnei)
E	Cotinga, banded (Cotinga maculata)	E	Owl, Seychelles scops (Otus magicus (=insularis) insularis)
E	Cotinga, white-winged (Xipholena atropurpurea)	E	Owlet, Morden's (Otus ireneae)
E	Crane, black-necked (Grus nigricollis)	E	Oystercatcher, Canarian black (Haematopus meadewaldoi)
E	Crane, Cuba sandhill (Grus canadensis nesiotes)	E	Parakeet, blue-throated (=ochre-marked) (Pyrrhura cruentata)
E	Crane, hooded (Grus monacha)	E	Parakeet, Forbes' (Cyanoramphus auriceps forbesi)
E	Crane, Japanese (Grus japonensis)	E	Parakeet, golden (Aratinga guarouba)
E	Crane, Siberian white (Grus leucogeranus)	E	Parakeet, golden-shouldered (Psephotus chrysopterygius)
E	Crane, white-naped (Grus vipio)	E	Parakeet, Mauritius (Psittacula echo)
E	Cuckoo-shrike, Mauritius (Coquus typicus)	E	Parakeet, Norfolk Island (Cyanoramphus cookii (=novaezelandiae c.))
E	Cuckoo-shrike, Reunion (Coquus newtoni)	E	Parakeet, orange-bellied (Neophema chrysogaster)
E	Curassow, razor-billed (Mitu mitu mitu)	E	Parakeet, paradise (Psephotus pulcherrimus)
E	Curassow, red-billed (Crax blumenbachii)	E	Parakeet, scarlet-chested (Neophema splendida)
E	Curassow, Trinidad white-headed (Pipile pipile pipile)	E	Parakeet, turquoise (Neophema pulchella)
E	Dove, cloven-feathered (Drepanoptila holosericea)	E	Parrot, Bahaman or Cuban (Amazona leucocephala)
E	Dove, Grenada gray-fronted (Leptotila rufaxilla wellsi)	E	Parrot, ground (Pezoporus wallicus)
E	Duck, pink-headed (Rhodonessa caryophyllacea)	E	Parrot, imperial (Amazona imperialis)
E	Duck, white-winged wood (Cairina scutulata)	E	Parrot, night (=Australian) (Geopsittacus occidentalis)
E	Eagle, Greenland white-tailed (Haliaeetus albicilla groenlandicus)	E	Parrot, red-browed (Amazona rhodocorytha)
E	Eagle, harpy (Harpia harpyja)	E	Parrot, red-capped (Pionopsitta pileata)
E	Eagle, Madagascar sea (Haliaeetus vociferoides)	E	Parrot, red-necked (Amazona arausiaca)
E	Eagle, Madagascar serpent (Eutriorchis astur)	E	Parrot, red-spectacled (Amazona pretrei pretrei)
E	Eagle, Philippine (Pithecophaga jefferyi)	E	Parrot, red-tailed (Amazona brasiliensis)
E	Eagle, Spanish imperial (Aquila heliaca adalberti)	E	Parrot, Seychelles lesser vasa (Coracopsis nigra barklyi)
E	Egret, Chinese (Egretta eulophotes)	E	Parrot, St. Vincent (Amazona guildingii)
E	Falcon, Eurasian peregrine (Falco peregrinus peregrinus)	E	Parrot, St. Lucia (Amazona versicolor)
E	Flycatcher, Euler's (Empidonax euleri johnstonei)	E	Parrot, thick-billed Mexico (Rhynchopsitta pachyrhyncha)
E	Flycatcher, Seychelles paradise (Terpsiphone corvina)	E	Parrot, vinaceous-breasted (Amazona vinacea)
E	Flycatcher, Tahiti (Pomarea nigra)	E	Penguin, Galapagos (Spheniscus mendiculus)
E	Fody, Mauritius (Foudia rubra)	E	Petrel, Mascarene black (Pterodroma aterrima)
E	Fody, Rodrigues (Foudia flavicans)	E	Pheasant, bar-tailed (Syrmaticus humiae)
E	Fody, Seychelles (weaver-finch) (Foudia sechellarum)	E	Pheasant, Blyth's tragopan (Tragopan blythii)
E	Francolin, Djibouti (Francolinus ochropectus)	E	Pheasant, brown eared (Crossoptilon mantchuricum)
E	Freira (Pterodroma madeira)	E	Pheasant, Cabot's tragopan (Tragopan caboti)
E	Frigatebird, Andrew's (Fregata andrewsi)	E	Pheasant, cheer (Catreus wallichii)
E	Goshawk, Christmas Island (Accipiter fasciatus natalis)	E	Pheasant, Chinese monal (Lophophorus lhuysii)
E	Grackle, slender-billed (Quiscalus palustris)	E	Pheasant, Edward's (Lophura edwardsi)
E	Grasswren, Eyrean (flycatcher) (Amytornis goyderi)	E	Pheasant, Elliot's (Syrmaticus ellioti)
E	Grebe, Alaotra (Tachybaptus rufolavatus)	E	Pheasant, imperial (Lophura imperialis)
E	Grebe, Atitlan (Podilymbus gigas)	E	Pheasant, Mikado (Syrmaticus mikado)
E	Greenshank, Nordmann's (Tringa guttifer)	E	Pheasant, Palawan peacock (Polyplectron emphanum)
E	Guan, horned (Oreophasis derbianus)	E	Pheasant, Sclater's monal (Lophophorus sclateri)
E	Guan, white-winged (Penelope albipennis)	E	Pheasant, Swinhoe's (Lophura swinhoii)
T	Guineafowl, white-breasted (Agelastes meleagrides)	E	Pheasant, western tragopan (Tragopan melanocephalus)
E	Gull, Audouin's (Larus audouinii)	E	Pheasant, white eared (Crossoptilon crossoptilon)
E	Gull, relict (Larus relictus)	E	Pigeon, Azores wood (Columba palumbus azorica)
E	Hawk, Galapagos (Buteo galapagoensis)	E	Pigeon, Chatham Island (Hemiphaga novaeseelandiae chathamensis)
E	Hermit, hook-billed (hummingbird) (Ramphodon (=glaucis) dohrnii)	E	Pigeon, Mindoro imperial (=zone-tailed) (Ducula mindorensis)
E	Honeyeater, helmeted (Lichenostomus melanops cassidix (=meliphaga c.))	E	Pigeon, pink (Columba mayeri)
E	Hornbill, helmeted (Buceros (=rhinoplax) vigil)	T	Pigeon, white-tailed laurel (Columba junoniae)
E	Ibis, Japanese crested (Nipponia nippon)	E	Piping-guan, black-fronted (Pipile jacutinga)
E	Ibis, northern bald (Geronticus eremita)	E	Pitta, Koch's (Pitta kochi)
E	Kagu (Rhynochetos jubatus)	E	Plover, New Zealand shore (Thinornis novaeseelandiae)
E	Kakapo (Strigops habroptilus)	E	Pochard, Madagascar (Aythya innotata)
E	Kestrel, Mauritius (Falco punctatus)	E	Quail, Merriam's Montezuma (Cyrtonyx montezumae merriami)
E	Kestrel, Seychelles (Falco araea)	E	Quetzel, resplendent (Pharomachrus mocinno)
E	Kite, Cuba hook-billed (Chondrohierax uncinatus wilsonii)	E	Rail, Aukland Island (Rallus pectoralis muelleri)
E	Kite, Grenada hook-billed (Chondrohierax uncinatus mirus)	E	Rail, Lord Howe wood (Gallirallus (=tricholimnas) sylvestris)
E	Kokako (wattlebird) (Callaeas cinerea)	E	Rhea, lesser (incl. Darwin's) (Rhea (=pterocnemia) pennata)
E	Lark, Raso (Alauda razae)	E	Robin, Chatham Island (Petroica traversi)
E	Macaw, glaucous (Anodorhynchus glaucus)	T	Robin, dappled mountain (Arcanator orostruthus)
E	Macaw, indigo (Anodorhynchus leari)	E	Robin, scarlet-breasted (flycatcher) (Petroica multicolor multicolor)

TABLE 9.4

Foreign endangered and threatened bird species, March 2006 [CONTINUED]

Status*	Species name	Status*	Species name
E	Rockfowl, grey-necked *(Picathartes oreas)*	T	Vanga, Pollen's *(Xenopirostris polleni)*
E	Rockfowl, white-necked *(Picathartes gymnocephalus)*	T	Vanga, Van Dam's *(Xenopirostris damii)*
E	Roller, long-tailed ground *(Uratelornis chimaera)*	E	Wanderer, plain (=collared-hemipode) *(Pedionomus torquatus)*
E	Scrub-bird, noisy *(Atrichornis clamosus)*	E	Warbler (=wood), Barbados yellow *(Dendroica petechia petechia)*
E	Shama, Cebu black (thrush) *(Copsychus niger cebuensis)*	E	Warbler (=wood), Semper's *(Leucopeza semperi)*
E	Siskin, red *(Carduelis cucullata)*	E	Warbler, Aldabra (old world warbler) *(Nesillas aldabranus)*
E	Sparrowhawk, Anjouan Island *(Accipiter francesii pusillus)*	E	Warbler, Rodrigues (old world warbler) *(Bebrornis rodericanus)*
E	Starling, Ponape mountain *(Aplonis pelzelni)*	E	Warbler, Seychelles (old world warbler) *(Bebrornis sechellensis)*
E	Starling, Rothschild's (myna) *(Leucopsar rothschildi)*	E	Wattle-eye, banded *(Platysteira laticincta)*
E	Stork, oriental white *(Ciconia boyciana (=ciconia b.))*	E	Weaver, Clarke's *(Ploceus golandi)*
E	Sunbird, Marungu (*Nectarinia prigoginei)*	E	Whipbird, western *(Psophodes nigrogularis)*
E	Teal, Campbell Island flightless *(Anas aucklandica nesiotis)*	E	White-eye, Norfolk Island *(Zosterops albogularis)*
E	Thrasher, white-breasted *(Ramphocinclus brachyurus)*	E	White-eye, Ponape greater *(Rukia longirostra)*
E	Thrush, New Zealand (wattlebird) *(Turnagra capensis)*	E	White-eye, Seychelles *(Zosterops modesta)*
E	Thrush, Taita *(Turdus olivaceus helleri)*	E	Woodpecker, imperial *(Campephilus imperialis)*
E	Tinamou, solitary *(Tinamus solitarius)*	E	Woodpecker, Tristam's *(Dryocopus javensis richardsi)*
E	Trembler, Martinique (thrasher) *(Cinclocerthia ruficauda gutturalis)*	E	Wren, Guadeloupe house *(Troglodytes aedon guadeloupensis)*
E	Turaco, Bannerman's *(Tauraco bannermani)*	E	Wren, St. Lucia house *(Troglodytes aedon mesoleucus)*
E	Turtle dove, Seychelles *(Streptopelia picturata rostrata)*		

*E=endangered, T=threatened.

SOURCE: Adapted from "Foreign Listed Species Report as of 03/06/2006," in *Threatened and Endangered Species System (TESS)*, U.S. Department of the Interior, U.S. Fish and Wildlife Service, March 6, 2006, http://ecos.fws.gov/tess_public/servlet/gov.doi.tess_public.servlets.Foreign Listing?listings=0#A (accessed March 6, 2006)

CHAPTER 10
INSECTS AND SPIDERS

Insects are members of the Animalia kingdom and belong to the phylum Arthropoda, along with crustaceans. There are many classes of arthropods, including the insects and arachnids. Both are invertebrates, but insects have six legs, while arachnids have eight legs. The arachnids include spiders, mites, ticks, scorpions, and harvestmen.

Insects are the most diverse group in the animal kingdom. Scientists are not certain of the total number of insect species; estimates range as high as thirty million species. Nearly one million of the species have been described. Insects have not been nearly as thoroughly studied as the vertebrate groups, and so there are likely to be many endangered insects whose desperate state is unknown.

Insects and arachnids, like numerous other species, suffer from diminished habitat as a result of encroaching development, industrialization, changing land use patterns, and invasive species.

THREATENED AND ENDANGERED INSECT SPECIES IN THE UNITED STATES

As of March 2006 there were forty-five U.S. insect species listed under the Endangered Species Act (ESA), as shown in Table 10.1. Predominant species types include butterflies (nineteen species) and beetles (eleven species). The remaining insects are an assortment of types including a dragonfly, a fly, a grasshopper, two ground beetles, two moths, a naucorid (which is pictured in Figure 10.1), three skippers, and four tiger beetles. Most of the listed insects are endangered, and nearly all have recovery plans in place.

According to the U.S. Fish and Wildlife Service (FWS) most of the imperiled insects are found exclusively in one of two states—California (twenty species)

or Texas (seven species). The remainder of the species are scattered across the country.

The FWS reports that $7.5 million was spent under the Endangered Species Act during fiscal year 2004 on imperiled insects. The ten entities with the highest expenditures are shown in Table 10.2. Only three entities accounted for more than half of all money expended on insect species during that year. The Delhi sands flower-loving fly, which is pictured in Figure 10.2, and the valley elderberry longhorn beetle are both found in California. The Karner blue butterfly inhabits Midwestern states.

Butterflies, Skippers, and Moths

Butterflies, skippers, and moths are flying insects that belong to the order Lepidoptera. Scientists believe there could be several hundred thousand species in this order. Skippers have stockier bodies than butterflies, but are also structurally different from moths. They are considered intermediate between butterflies and moths.

Like amphibians, many butterflies and moths are considered indicator species (meaning that their well-being gives scientists a good indication of the general health of their habitat) because they are particularly sensitive to environmental degradation. The decline of these species serves as a warning to human beings about the condition of the environment. Part of the reason butterflies are sensitive to many aspects of the environment is that these species undergo a drastic metamorphosis, or change, from larva to adult as a natural part of their life cycles. Butterfly larvae are generally crawling, herbivorous caterpillars, whereas butterfly adults fly and are nectar-eating. Butterflies can thrive only when intact habitats are available for both caterpillars and adults. Consequently, healthy butterfly populations tend to occur in areas with healthy ecosystems. Because many species are extremely sensitive to changing environmental

TABLE 10.1

Endangered and threatened insect species in the United States, March 2006

Common name	Scientific name	Listing[a]	Recovery plan date	Recovery plan status[b]
Beetle, American burying	*Nicrophorus americanus*	E	9/27/1991	F
Beetle, Coffin Cave mold	*Batrisodes texanus*	E	8/25/1994	F
Beetle, Comal Springs dryopid	*Stygoparnus comalensis*	E	None	—
Beetle, Comal Springs riffle	*Heterelmis comalensis*	E	None	—
Beetle, delta green ground	*Elaphrus viridis*	T	3/7/2006	F
Beetle, Helotes mold	*Batrisodes venyivi*	E	None	—
Beetle, Hungerford's crawling water	*Brychius hungerfordi*	E	8/6/2004	D
Beetle, Kretschmarr Cave mold	*Texamaurops reddelli*	E	8/25/1994	F
Beetle, Mount Hermon June	*Polyphylla barbata*	E	9/28/1998	F
Beetle, Tooth Cave ground	*Rhadine Persephone*	E	8/25/1994	F
Beetle, valley elderberry longhorn	*Desmocerus californicus dimorphus*	T	6/28/1984	F
Butterfly, bay checkerspot	*Euphydryas editha bayensis*	T	9/30/1998	F
Butterfly, Behren's silverspot	*Speyeria zerene behrensii*	E	1/20/2004	D
Butterfly, callippe silverspot	*Speyeria callippe callippe*	E	None	—
Butterfly, El Segundo blue	*Euphilotes battoides allyni*	E	9/28/1998	F
Butterfly, Fender's blue	*Icaricia icarioides fenderi*	E	9/16/2005	U
Butterfly, Karner blue	*Lycaeides melissa samuelis*	E	9/19/2003	F
Butterfly, Lange's metalmark	*Apodemia mormo langei*	E	4/25/1984	RF(1)
Butterfly, lotis blue	*Lycaeides argyrognomon lotis*	E	12/26/1985	F
Butterfly, mission blue	*Icaricia icarioides missionensis*	E	10/10/1984	F
Butterfly, Mitchell's satyr	*Neonympha mitchellii mitchellii*	E	4/2/1998	F
Butterfly, Myrtle's silverspot	*Speyeria zerene myrtleae*	E	9/29/1998	F
Butterfly, Oregon silverspot	*Speyeria zerene hippolyta*	T	8/22/2001	RF(1)
Butterfly, Palos Verdes blue	*Glaucopsyche lygdamus palosverdesensis*	E	1/19/1984	F
Butterfly, Quino checkerspot	*Euphydryas editha quino=E.e. wrighti*	E	9/17/2003	F
Butterfly, Saint Francis' satyr	*Neonympha mitchellii francisci*	E	4/23/1996	F
Butterfly, San Bruno elfin	*Callophrys mossii bayensis*	E	10/10/1984	F
Butterfly, Schaus swallowtail	*Heraclides aristodemus ponceanus*	E	5/18/1999	F
Butterfly, Smith's blue	*Euphilotes enoptes smithi*	E	11/9/1984	F
Butterfly, Uncompahgre fritillary	*Boloria acrocnema*	E	3/17/1994	F
Dragonfly, Hine's emerald	*Somatochlora hineana*	E	9/27/2001	F
Fly, Delhi Sands flower-loving	*Rhaphiomidas terminatus abdominalis*	E	9/14/1997	F
Grasshopper, Zayante band-winged	*Trimerotropis infantilis*	E	9/28/1998	F
Ground beetle, [unnamed]	*Rhadine exilis*	E	None	—
Ground beetle, [unnamed]	*Rhadine infernalis*	E	None	—
Moth, Blackburn's sphinx	*Manduca blackburni*	E	9/28/2005	F
Moth, Kern primrose sphinx	*Euproserpinus euterpe*	T	2/8/1984	F
Naucorid, Ash Meadows	*Ambrysus amargosus*	T	9/28/1990	F
Skipper, Carson wandering	*Pseudocopaeodes eunus obscurus*	E	3/2/2006	D
Skipper, Laguna Mountains	*Pyrgus ruralis lagunae*	E	None	—
Skipper, Pawnee montane	*Hesperia leonardus montana*	T	9/21/1998	F
Tiger beetle, northeastern beach	*Cicindela dorsalis dorsalis*	T	9/29/1994	F
Tiger beetle, Ohlone	*Cicindela ohlone*	E	None	—
Tiger beetle, Puritan	*Cicindela puritana*	T	9/29/1993	F
Tiger beetle, Salt Creek	*Cicindela nevadica lincolniana*	E	None	—

[a]E=endangered; T=threatened.

[b]Recovery plan stages: U=under development, F=final, D=draft, and RF=final revision.

SOURCE: Adapted from "Listed FWS/Joint FWS and NMFS Species and Populations with Recovery Plans (Sorted by Listed Entity)" and "Listed U.S. Species by Taxonomic Group," in *Threatened and Endangered Species System (TESS)*, U.S. Department of the Interior, U.S. Fish and Wildlife Service, March 6, 2006, http://ecos.fws.gov/tess_public/SpeciesRecovery.do?sort=1 and http://ecos.fws.gov/tess_public/SpeciesReport.do?kingdom=I&listingType=L (accessed March 6, 2006)

conditions, moths and butterflies are carefully monitored by scientists and conservationists around the world.

Butterflies and moths have alerted scientists to numerous habitat changes. In southern Florida, for example, the sharp decline of swallowtail butterflies alerted biologists to the harm caused by mosquito sprays, as well as to the fact that pesticides had contaminated the water. In 1996 scientists in Michigan and England reported that during the 1960s darker-colored moths began to predominate over light, white-and-black-flecked moths in polluted areas (B. S. Grant and others, "Parallel Rise and Fall of Melanic Peppered Moths in America and Britain," *Journal of Heredity*, September/October 1996). This was seen in both England and the United States and was probably due to the fact that darker moths were better able to blend into the dingy environment and hide from predators. In both countries, clean air laws were passed and decreases in pollution resulted. Now, in both countries, lighter-colored moths are again predominant. Dr. Douglas Futuyma, a biologist at the State University of New York at Stony Brook, reported that other insect species have shown increases in the proportion of darker-colored individuals in industrialized areas, a phenomenon called "industrial melanism" (Carol Kaesuk Yoon, "Parallel Plots in Classic of Evolution,"

FIGURE 10.1

The ash meadows naucorid

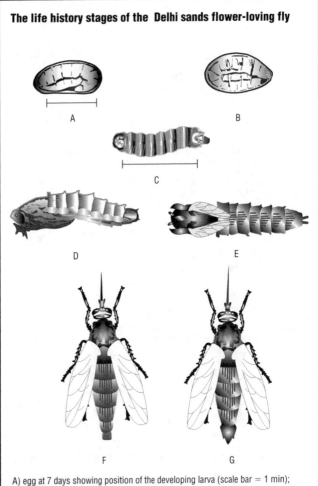

SOURCE: E. Tobin, illustrator, "Ash Meadows Naucorid *Pelecorus shoshone*," in *Planning Update 1: Ash Meadows National Wildlife Refuge*, U.S. Department of the Interior, U.S. Fish and Wildlife Service, http://www.fws.gov/pacific/planning/am_pu1.pdf (accessed March 3, 2006)

TABLE 10.2

The ten listed insect entities with the highest expenditures under the Endangered Species Act, fiscal year 2004

Ranking	Common name	Listing*	Expenditure
1	Delhi Sands flower-loving fly	E	$1,673,466
2	Valley elderberry longhorn beetle	T	$1,513,233
3	Karner blue butterfly	E	$1,085,869
4	American burying beetle	E	$448,459
5	Saint Francis' satyr butterfly	E	$405,700
6	Mission blue butterfly	E	$347,222
7	Hine's emerald dragonfly	E	$312,170
8	Quino checkerspot butterfly	E	$251,444
9	Fender's blue butterfly	E	$248,155
10	Oregon silverspot butterfly	T	$174,682

*E=endangered; T=threatened.

SOURCE: Adapted from "Table 1. Reported FY 2004 Expenditures for Endangered and Threatened Species, Not Including Land Acquisition Costs," in *Federal and State Endangered and Threatened Species Expenditures: Fiscal Year 2004*, U.S. Department of the Interior, U.S. Fish and Wildlife Service, January 2005, http://www.fws.gov/endangered/expenditures/reports/FWS%20Endangered%20Species%202004%20Expenditures%20Report.pdf (accessed February 11, 2006)

FIGURE 10.2

The life history stages of the Delhi sands flower-loving fly

A) egg at 7 days showing position of the developing larva (scale bar = 1 min);
B) egg at 11 days, a few hours before hatching;
C) larva shortly after hatching (scale bar = 5 mm);
D) side view of pupal case;
E) top view of pupal case;
F) adult female;
G) adult male.

SOURCE: "Figure 2. Line Drawings of All Known Life History Stages of the Delhi Sands Flower-Loving Fly," in *Final Recovery Plan for the Delhi Sands Flower-Loving Fly*, U.S. Department of the Interior, U.S. Fish and Wildlife Service, September 14, 1997, http://ecos.fws.gov/docs/recovery_plans/1997/970914.pdf (accessed March 6, 2006)

New York Times, November 12, 1996). In those species, as well, the proportion of dark specimens drops as air quality improves.

In many cases butterflies also help conservationists decide where to locate parks and nature refuges. Generally, the more varieties of butterflies that exist in an area, the more species of other animals and plants will live there too. Unfortunately, many butterfly species are disappearing around the world.

The major threats to butterflies include:

- Habitat destruction
- Mowing of pastures, ditches, and highway rights-of-way
- Collisions with moving automobiles
- Insecticides

KARNER BLUE BUTTERFLY. The Karner blue butterfly was listed as endangered in 1992. Historically it occupied habitats in the eastern United States from Minnesota to Maine as well as Ontario, Canada. However, the species now is found only in portions of Minnesota, Wisconsin, Indiana, Michigan, New York, New Hampshire, and Ohio. Most Karner blue butterfly populations are very small and in danger of extinction.

The caterpillars of the Karner blue butterfly rely for food on a species of lupine that is now found primarily on roadsides, military bases, and some forest areas.

FIGURE 10.3

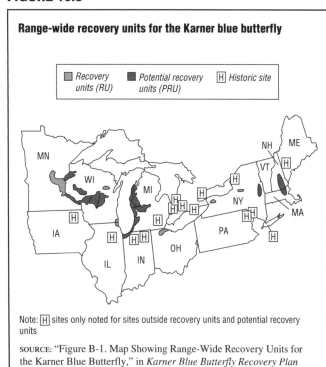

Range-wide recovery units for the Karner blue butterfly

Note: H sites only noted for sites outside recovery units and potential recovery units

SOURCE: "Figure B-1. Map Showing Range-Wide Recovery Units for the Karner Blue Butterfly," in *Karner Blue Butterfly Recovery Plan (Lycaeides Melissa Samuelis)*, U.S. Fish & Wildlife Service, Great Lakes-Big Rivers Regions (Region 3), September 2003, http://ecos.fws .gov/docs/recovery_plans/2003/030919.pdf (accessed April 4, 2006)

The primary reason for endangerment of the Karner blue butterfly is habitat loss due to land development for human use and forest maturation. The U.S. Fish and Wildlife Service published a recovery plan for the species (http://www.fws.gov/midwest/Endangered/insects/kbb/ recplan-fnl-nrel.html) in September 2003. Figure 10.3 shows the recovery units, or populations, of the species, sites for potential recovery units, as well as other sites where the species has historically been found.

BLACKBURN'S SPHINX MOTH. Blackburn's sphinx moth was first listed as an endangered species in February 2000 and is found exclusively in Hawaii. This moth species is threatened by urban development, conversion of land for agricultural use, invasive plant species, trampling of vegetation by nonnative ungulates (hoofed animals), and invasive predators and parasites.

Conservation recommendations in the species recovery plan, which was drawn up by the U.S. Fish and Wildlife Service in October 2003, include habitat conservation and restoration, planting of the moth's host plant in new habitats, and a captive breeding and reintroduction program. The total cost for recovery of the species is estimated at $5.5 million.

Santa Cruz Mountain Insects

California's Santa Cruz Mountains are home to two endangered species—the Zayante band-winged grasshopper and the Ohlone tiger beetle. Factors leading to endangerment include sand mining, urban development, conversion of land to agricultural uses, recreational use (such as hiking, horseback riding, off-road vehicle use, bicycling, and camping), competition with nonnative species, fire suppression, pesticides, logging, and over-collection.

ZAYANTE BAND-WINGED GRASSHOPPER. The tiny Zayante band-winged grasshopper, barely half an inch long, occupies areas containing abundant high-quality silica sand, known as Zayante or Santa Margarita sand. This sand is valuable for making glass and fiberglass products, and several businesses have entered the area in the hope of capitalizing on this. The Zayante band-winged grasshopper joined the ranks of listed endangered species in January 1997. In 2001, as a result of a lawsuit filed by the Center for Biological Diversity, the FWS designated more than 10,000 acres of critical habitat for the grasshopper.

OHLONE TIGER BEETLE. The Ohlone tiger beetle was listed as endangered in October 2001. The species was discovered in 1987 and is found only in Santa Cruz County, California. The Ohlone tiger beetle is a small species, about half an inch long, with spotted metallic-green wings and copper-green legs. Both adults and larvae hunt invertebrate prey. The Ohlone tiger beetle occupies a total of less than twenty acres of remnant native coastal prairie habitat on state land, private land, and property belonging to the University of California at Santa Cruz. The species declined due to habitat loss and habitat fragmentation resulting from urban development, as well as over-collection, pollution from pesticides, and the increasing encroachment of invasive plant species. The petition to list the Ohlone tiger beetle with the FWS was originally made by a private citizen in 1997.

Hine's Emerald Dragonfly

The Hine's emerald dragonfly has been listed as an endangered species since 1995 and is found in federal and state preserves and national forest lands in Illinois, Wisconsin, Michigan, and Missouri. In earlier times, its range extended through portions of Ohio, Alabama, and Indiana as well. The Hine's emerald dragonfly has a metallic-green body and emerald-green eyes. It is considered a biological indicator species because it is extremely sensitive to water pollution. The decline of this dragonfly species has resulted primarily from loss of suitable wetland habitat, such as wet prairies, marshes, sedge meadows, and fens (a type of bog) occurring over dolomite rock. (The lakeside daisy is another species damaged by the decline of these habitats and is listed as threatened.)

Wetland habitats support dragonflies during their aquatic larval period, which lasts some three to four years. Adult dragonflies occupy open areas and forest edges near wetland habitats, where they feed on invertebrate species such as mosquitoes. Hine's emerald dragonflies also serve as prey for a variety of bird and fish species. The recovery plan for the dragonfly includes measures to protect current habitat as well as reintroduction of the species to portions of its former range. Private companies that own land supporting dragonfly populations have aided conservation efforts by monitoring populations and preserving important habitat areas.

THREATENED AND ENDANGERED FOREIGN SPECIES OF INSECTS

As of March 2006 there were only four foreign insects listed under the Endangered Species Act, as follows:

- Luzon peacock swallowtail butterfly (*Papilio chikae*)

- Homerus swallowtail butterfly (*Papilio homerus*)

- Corsican swallowtail butterfly (*Papilio hospiton*)

- Queen Alexandra's birdwing butterfly (*Troides alexandrae*)

All four butterfly species have endangered status.

The World Conservation Union (IUCN) listed 559 species of insects as threatened in its *2004 Red List of Threatened Species*. This number comprises nearly three-fourths of the species evaluated, but less than 1% of described species.

Monarch Butterfly

Among the best-known insect species, the adult monarch butterfly is characterized by orange wings with black veins and white spots at the outer margins. Historically, monarch butterflies migrated by the millions up and down the North American continent on a journey extending 3,000 miles. Over time, monarch butterfly populations have also become established in Australia and on the Pacific islands of Samoa and Tahiti. Other monarch populations have appeared in Hawaii and New Zealand.

For many years, naturalists sought to pinpoint the location where monarchs hibernate in January and February in preparation for their mating season and northward migration in March. In 1975, following an arduous search, a serene monarch hibernation area was located in the high altitude forests of the Michoacán Mountains in Mexico. Mexico declared the impoverished region a protected area. The inhabitants of the area turned the site into an ecotourism attraction in order to generate income for the economy. However, ecotourism not only failed to generate sufficient money to support the people of the area, but also caused severe habitat disruption. The onslaught of tourists affected habitats by introducing excessive noise, tobacco smoke, fire, and pollution. Monarch butterflies are now considered endangered by the

IUCN. The FWS and the Mexican government have since attempted to nurture a self-sustaining economy in the monarch hibernation area by introducing fish breeding and horticulture.

THREATENED AND ENDANGERED ARACHNID SPECIES IN THE UNITED STATES

As of March 2006 there were twelve U.S. species of arachnids listed under the ESA, as shown in Table 10.3. All of the arachnids have endangered status, and six of them have recovery plans in place. The imperiled arachnids fall into four species types, as follows:

- Harvestmen—three species

- Meshweaver—four species

- Pseudoscorpion—one species

- Spider—four species

Ten of the arachnids are cave-dwelling species found only in Texas. The only imperiled arachnids outside of Texas are the Kauai cave wolf spider, which inhabits Hawaii, and the spruce-fir moss spider, which is found in North Carolina and Tennessee.

Table 10.3 also lists the expenditures made under the Endangered Species Act for arachnid species during fiscal year 2004. In total, $1.55 million was spent. The Bone Cave harvestman, a Texas species, accounted for $1.36 million of this total.

Texas Cave Arachnids

Ten of the listed arachnids are found only in underground karst caves in a handful of counties in Texas. (See Figure 10.4.) Karst is a geological term referring to a type of underground terrain resulting when limestone bedrock is exposed to mildly acidic groundwater over a long period of time. Eventually the bedrock becomes a honeycomb of cracks, fissures, holes, and other openings. There are dozens of these karst caves located in Bexar, Travis, and Williamson counties in Texas. In recent decades scientists have discovered unusual invertebrate species living in these caves. The tiny cave dwellers are eyeless and have no pigment (color) to their bodies. Ten of the creatures have been added to the endangered species list. They include two true spiders, one pseudoscorpion, four meshweavers (tiny web-making arachnids), and three harvestmen (commonly known as "daddy longlegs" or "granddaddy longlegs").

The species were listed under the Endangered Species Act after a collection of conservation groups petitioned the U.S. Fish and Wildlife Service in 1992. The creatures were listed as endangered in 2000. In 2003 approximately 1,000 acres were designated as critical habitat for six of the arachnids. In addition, four of the species are included in a recovery plan published in 1994

TABLE 10.3

Endangered and threatened arachnid species in the United States, March 2006 and expenditures for them in fiscal year 2004

Common name	Scientific name	Listing[a]	Recovery plan date	Recovery plan status[b]	Expenditures under ESA in fiscal year 2004
Harvestman, Bee Creek Cave	*Texella reddelli*	E	8/25/94	F	$7,140
Harvestman, Bone Cave	*Texella reyesi*	E	8/25/94	F	$1,361,780
Harvestman, Cokendolpher Cave	*Texella cokendolpheri*	E	None	—	$10,000
Meshweaver, Braken Bat Cave	*Cicurina venii*	E	None	—	$10,160
Meshweaver, Government Canyon Bat Cave	*Cicurina vespera*	E	None	—	$10,160
Meshweaver, Madla's Cave	*Cicurina madla*	E	None	—	60,160
Meshweaver, Robber Baron Cave	*Cicurina baronia*	E	None	—	$10,160
Pseudoscorpion, Tooth Cave	*Tartarocreagris texana*	E	8/25/94	F	$8,660
Spider, Government Canyon Bat Cave	*Neoleptoneta microps*	E	None	—	$10,160
Spider, Kauai cave wolf or pe'e pe'e maka 'ole	*Adelocosa anops*	E	2/9/05	D	$32,101
Spider, spruce-fir moss	*Microhexura montivaga*	E	9/11/98	F	$13,500
Spider, Tooth Cave	*Leptoneta myopica*	E	8/25/94	F	$11,320

[a]E=endangered.
[b]Recovery plan stages: F=final and D=draft.

SOURCE: Adapted from "Listed FWS/Joint FWS and NMFS Species and Populations with Recovery Plans (Sorted by Listed Entity)" and "Listed U.S. Species by Taxonomic Group," in *Threatened and Endangered Species System (TESS)*, U.S. Department of the Interior, U.S. Fish and Wildlife Service, March 6, 2006, http://ecos.fws.gov/tess_public/SpeciesRecovery.do?sort=1 and http://ecos.fws.gov/tess_public/SpeciesReport.do?kingdom=I&listingType=L (accessed March 6, 2006), and adapted from "Table 1. Reported FY 2004 Expenditures for Endangered and Threatened Species, Not Including Land Acquisition Costs," in *Federal and State Endangered and Threatened Species Expenditures: Fiscal Year 2004*, U.S. Department of the Interior, U.S. Fish and Wildlife Service, January 2005, http://www.fws.gov/endangered/expenditures/reports/FWS%20Endangered%20Species%202004%20Expenditures%20Report.pdf (accessed February 11, 2006)

that also covers other imperiled invertebrate species living in the caves.

Kauai Cave Wolf Spider

The Kauai cave wolf spider, ranging from about one-half to three-quarters of an inch in length, is a blind species found only in special caves on the southern part of the island of Kauai in Hawaii. These caves are formed by young lava flows. Unlike most other spiders, which trap their prey in webs, the Kauai cave wolf spider hunts its prey directly. Its prey includes the Kauai cave amphipod, a species that is also highly endangered. The FWS originally listed both species as endangered in January 2000. Female cave wolf spiders lay some fifteen to thirty eggs per clutch, and carry young on their backs after hatching. Cave species are extremely sensitive to changes in temperature and light. In 2005 the Fish and Wildlife Service published a draft recovery plan covering both imperiled invertebrates living in the Kauai cave. The critical habitat established for the species includes fourteen units totaling 272 acres on the southern part of the island.

Spruce-fir Moss Spider

The spruce-fir moss spider is an endangered spider related to the tarantula. It was placed on the Endangered Species List in 1995. Spruce-fir moss spiders live in moss mats found only in the vicinity of Fraser fir trees. Its populations have declined largely due to the introduction in the United States of an invasive European insect species, the balsam-woolly adelgid. The balsam-woolly adelgid infests Fraser fir trees, causing them to die within a time period of two to seven years. With the death of numerous fir trees, other forest trees have also blown over. The resulting increase in light level and temperature causes the moss mats on the forest floor to dry up.

In 2001 the U.S. Fish and Wildlife Service designated critical habitat for the species, including areas in the Great Smoky Mountains National Park and the Pisgah and Cherokee National Forests, as well as a preserve managed by the Nature Conservancy. This designation of critical habitat followed a lawsuit against the agency, which had previously deemed designating critical habitat "not prudent" because it believed the spider would be more vulnerable to collectors.

FIGURE 10.4

A karst cave provides habitat for endangered invertebrates

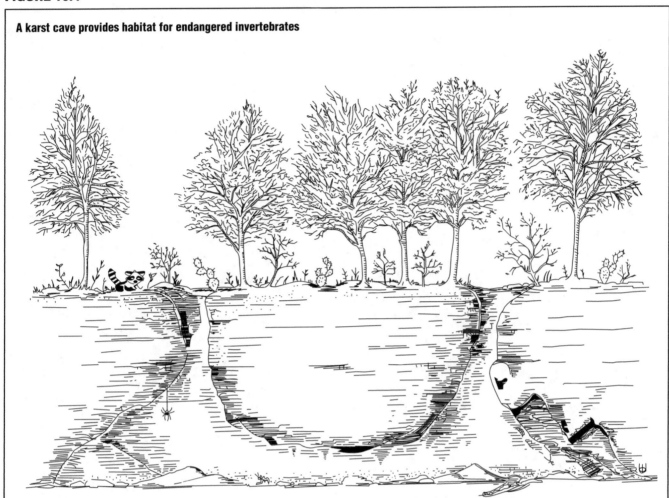

SOURCE: "Front Cover" in *Endangered Karst Invertebrates (Travis and Williamson Counties, Texas) Recovery Plan*, U.S. Department of the Interior, U.S. Fish and Wildlife Service, August 25, 1994, http://ecos.fws.gov/docs/recovery_plans/1994/940825.pdf (accessed March 2, 2006)

CHAPTER 11
PLANTS

Plants belong to the Plantae kingdom. Biologists estimate that there are up to 350,000 species making up this kingdom. In general, there are two types of land-growing plants—vascular and nonvascular. Vascular plants have specially developed organs similar to veins that move liquids through their systems. This category includes the trees, shrubs, flowers, and grasses. Nonvascular plants are mosses, liverworts, and hornworts. The vast majority of plant species on Earth are vascular plants that reproduce through their flowers.

In science, plants are more often identified by their scientific names than are animals. Plant species are so abundant and diverse that many plants have multiple common names. On the other hand, there are plants that have no common names because they are rare or geographically remote. To avoid confusion, this chapter will include the scientific name for any specific common name given.

Many factors contribute to the endangerment of plant species. Numerous species are the victims of habitat loss due to land and agricultural development. Others have declined due to pollution or habitat damage, or as a result of competition with invasive species. Still others have succumbed to introduced or unknown plant diseases. Finally, collectors or dealers often illegally seek rare, showy, or unusual plants, and have depleted populations through over-collection.

The preservation of plant species is important for many reasons. Not only are plants of aesthetic value, they are crucial components of every ecosystem on earth. Plants also serve several functions directly beneficial to humans. First, they provide genetic variation that is used in the breeding of new crop varieties—native plants provide genes that allow for adaptation to local environments, as well as resistance to pests, disease, or drought. In addition, plants are the source of numerous human medicines.

THE AMERICAN CHESTNUT TREE—MAKING A COMEBACK?

During the 1800s the American chestnut (*Castanea dentate*) was the predominant tree of many forests in the eastern United States. Its range extended from Maine to Mississippi, as shown in Figure 11.1. The heaviest concentrations were in the southern Appalachian Mountains where the tree made up more than a third of the overstory trees (the topmost layer of foliage in a forest). Mature trees reached three to five feet in diameter and rose to ninety feet in height with a huge canopy. The species was fast-growing and produced light, durable wood that was extremely popular for firewood and for making furniture, shingles, caskets, telephone poles, railroad ties, and other products. The trees were also valued for their chestnuts and tannin content. Tannin is an extract used in the leather industry.

In 1904 observers in New York City reported that an unknown blight (disease) was killing American chestnut trees at the Bronx Zoo. By 1940 the blight had spread through the entire range of the species, leaving all of the trees dead or dying. The tree structure was not damaged by the disease, so harvesting continued of dead trees for several more decades. Although sprouts would grow from the stumps left behind, they eventually succumbed to the blight. By the 1970s the American chestnut had been virtually eliminated. More than three billion trees had been killed. The culprit was a fungus originally called *Endothia parasitica*, but later renamed *Cryphonectria parasitica*. Scientists believe the disease came into the United States with ornamental chestnut trees imported from Japan or China. The Asian trees could carry the disease, but not succumb to it, because of natural immunity.

During the 1920s frantic efforts began to cross the remaining American chestnut trees with the Asiatic species. Although hybrid trees resulted with some resistance to the blight, they were inferior in quality to the original

FIGURE 11.1

Historical distribution of the American chestnut

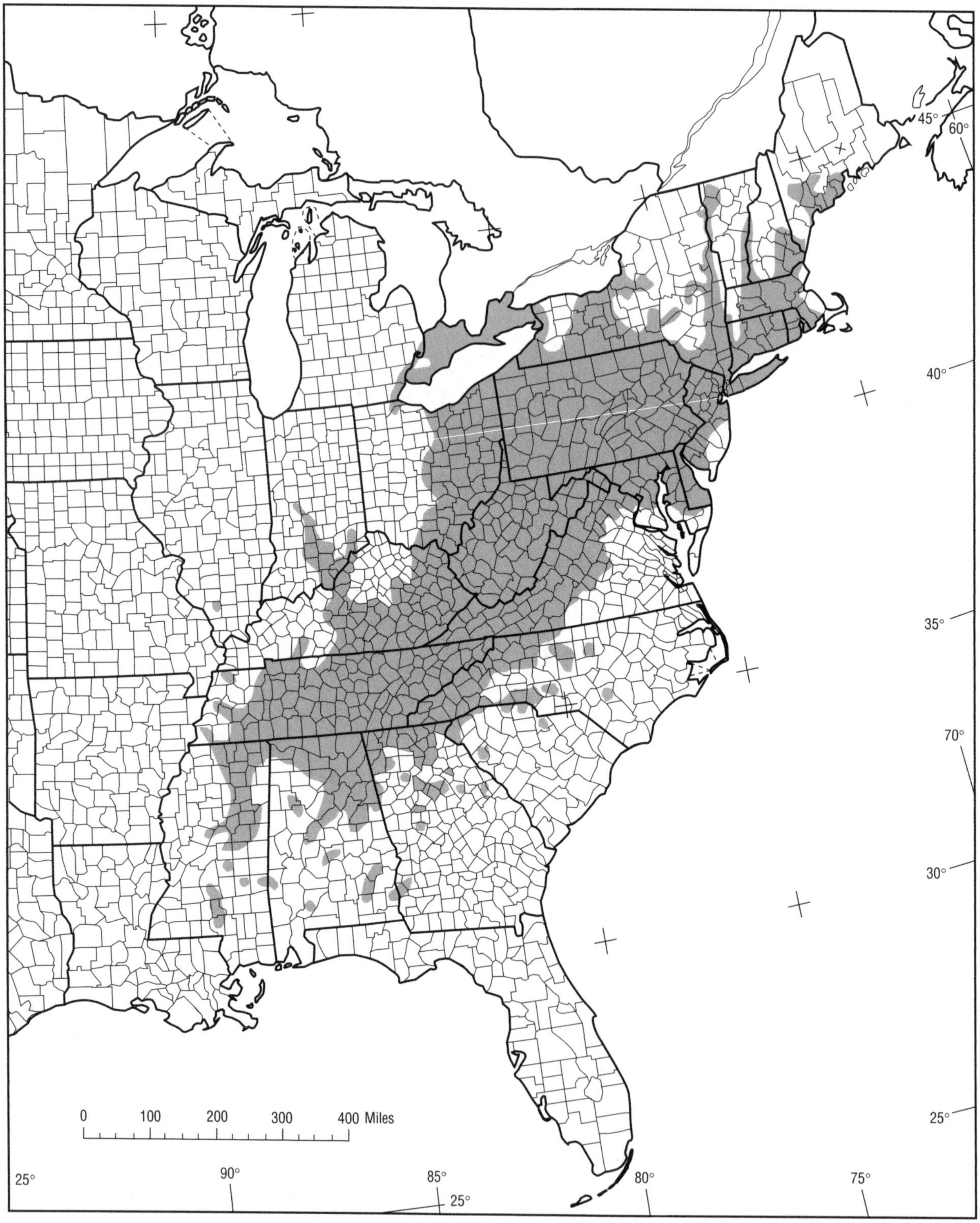

SOURCE: "Figure 1. Natural Range of American Chestnut," in *American Chestnut—An American Wood*, U.S. Department of Agriculture, U.S. Forest Service, February 1973, http://www.fpl.fs.fed.us/documnts/usda/amwood/230chest.pdf#search='American%20chestnut' (accessed March 10, 2006)

American species. Advances in genetic research and forestry techniques led to better hybrids by the 1980s. As of 2006 research continues by two foundations—the American Chestnut Foundation (a nonprofit organization headquartered in Vermont) and the American Chestnut Cooperators' Foundation (ACCF) at Virginia Tech University. The American Chestnut Foundation focuses on crossing naturally blight-resistant Asiatic species with American species. The ACCF produces crosses between American chestnut trees found to have some resistance to the blight in hopes of eventually producing offspring with higher resistance. Both organizations are confident that vigorous blight-resistant American chestnut trees can be developed during the twenty-first century.

PROTECTION OF PLANTS UNDER THE ENDANGERED SPECIES ACT

The Endangered Species Act of 1973 (ESA) protects listed plants from deliberate destruction or vandalism. Plants also receive protection under the consultation requirements of the act—that is, all federal agencies must consult with the U.S. Fish and Wildlife Service (FWS) to determine how best to conserve species as well as to ensure that no issued permits will jeopardize listed species or harm their habitats.

However, many conservationists believe that plants receive less protection than animals under the Endangered Species Act. First, the ESA only protects plants that are found on federal lands. It imposes no restrictions on private landowners whose property is home to endangered plants. Critics also complain that the Fish and Wildlife Service has been slow to list plant species and that damage to plant habitats is not addressed with the same seriousness as for animal species. However, the agency points out that the number of plants listed under the ESA has risen dramatically over the past two decades, as shown in Figure 11.2.

In 2000, in an effort to bolster conservation efforts for plants, the FWS formed an agreement with the Center for Plant Conservation, a national association of botanical gardens and arboreta. The two organizations are cooperating in developing conservation measures to help save North American plant species, particularly those listed as threatened or endangered. Central to the effort is the creation of educational programs aimed at informing the public about the importance of plant species for aesthetic, economic, biological, and medical reasons. The Center for Plant Conservation also aids in developing recovery plans for listed plant species.

THREATENED AND ENDANGERED U.S. PLANT SPECIES

Table 11.1 shows the 745 U.S. plant species listed under the Endangered Species Act as of March 2006. The vast majority of the plants (80%) have endangered status, while the other 20% are threatened. Nearly all of the plants have recovery plans in place. Because several species of imperiled plants are often found in the same ecosystem, many recovery plans cover multiple plant species.

The U.S. Fish and Wildlife Service uses four broad categories for plant types—conifers and cycads, ferns and allies, lichens, and flowering plants. A breakdown of listings by type is as follows:

- Conifers and cycads—three species
- Ferns and allies—twenty-six species
- Lichens—two species
- Flowering plants—714 species

Because the status of most plant species has not been studied in detail, many more plants are probably in danger of extinction than appear on these lists.

Just over $21 million was spent under the Endangered Species Act on threatened and endangered plants during fiscal year 2004. The ten plants with the highest expenditures are listed in Table 11.2. Flowering plants accounted for 97% of the total expenditures. Although plants comprise a slight majority of the total number of species listed under the ESA, they receive far less funding than animal species. Expenditures for plant species during fiscal year 2004 amounted to less than 2% of the total $1.4 billion spent that year.

PLANT TAXONOMY AND CATEGORIZATION

Taxonomy of plant species can be very complicated and is plagued by disagreements among scientists. Historically, plants were categorized by morphology—physical characteristics, such as shape or color of their leaves, fruit, bark, etc. During the 1960s a new classification scheme emerged that groups plants based on their evolutionary similarities—for example, their chemical properties and reproductive mechanisms. This taxonomy is part of the broader science known as phylogenetic systematics, which studies the evolutionary relationships between living organisms. In the future the systematics approach is expected to be used to classify all life forms.

In general, plants are assigned to the same taxonomic levels used to classify animals. This hierarchical structure includes kingdom, phylum, class, order, family, genus, and species. Beneath the species level, plants can be classified as to subspecies, just as in animal taxonomy. There is an additional classification for plants at this level called variety (abbreviated as "var."). Varieties are subgroups with unique differences between them. For example, the invasive species known as kudzu has the scientific name *Pueraria montana*. There are two

FIGURE 11.2

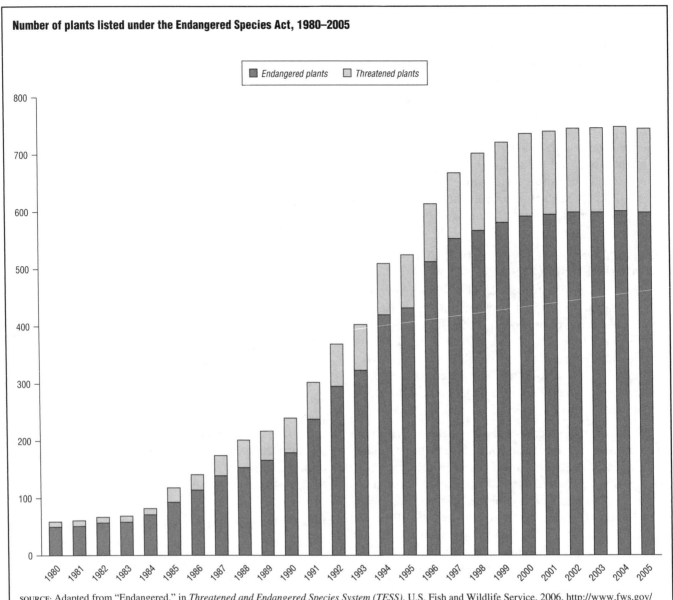

Number of plants listed under the Endangered Species Act, 1980–2005

■ *Endangered plants* ☐ *Threatened plants*

SOURCE: Adapted from "Endangered," in *Threatened and Endangered Species System (TESS)*, U.S. Fish and Wildlife Service, 2006, http://www.fws.gov/endangered/stats/cy%20count_2005.pdf (accessed February 1, 2006) and "Threatened," in *Threatened and Endangered Species System (TESS)*, U.S. Fish and Wildlife Service, 2006, http://www.fws.gov/endangered/stats/cy%20count_2005.pdf (accessed February 1, 2006)

varieties—*Pueraria montana* var. lobata and *Pueraria montana* var. montana. The lobata variety is commonly found in the United States, while the montana variety is not. Note that variety names are not italicized.

Plant taxonomy also includes additional taxa (groups) between kingdom and phylum called subkingdom, superdivision, and division that distinguish between broad categories of plants. The subkingdom level distinguishes between vascular and nonvascular plants. Within vascular plants, there are two superdivisions—seed plants and seedless plants. Seed plants are divided into various divisions, the largest of which is flowering plants.

The categories used by the FWS in Table 11.1 to categorize endangered and threatened plants are division levels or similar groupings.

Conifers and Cycads

Conifers are cone-bearing, woody plants. Most are trees; only a few species are shrubs. Common tree types include pine, cedar, fir, spruce, redwood, and cypress. As shown in Table 11.1, there are only two conifers listed under the Endangered Species Act. The Santa Cruz cypress (*Cupressus abramsiana*) and gowen cypress (*Cupressus goveniana*) are found only in Southern California. Both species are imperiled because they have

TABLE 11.1

Endangered and threatened plant species in the United States, March 2006

Scientific name	Inverted common name	Listing status[a]	Recovery plan date	Recovery plan status[b]
Conifers & cycads				
Cupressus abramsiana	Cypress, Santa Cruz	E	9/26/98	F
Cupressus goveniana ssp. goveniana	Cypress, gowen	T	12/20/04	F
Torreya taxifolia	Torreya, Florida	E	9/9/86	F
Ferns & allies				
Adenophorus periens	Fern, pendant kihi	E	7/10/99	F
Adiantum vivesii	No common name	E	1/17/95	F
Asplenium fragile var. insulare	No common name	E	4/10/98	F
Asplenium scolopendrium var. americanum	Fern, American hart's-tongue	T	9/15/93	F
Ctenitis squamigera	Pauoa	E	4/10/98	F
Cyathea dryopteroides	Fern, elfin tree	E	1/31/91	F
Diellia erecta	Diellia, asplenium-leaved	E	7/10/99	F
Diellia falcata	No common name	E	8/12/95	F
Diellia pallida	No common name	E	9/20/95	F
Diellia unisora	No common name	E	8/12/95	F
Diplazium molokaiense	No common name	E	4/10/98	F
Elaphoglossum serpens	No common name	E	1/17/95	F
Huperzia mannii	Wawa`eiole	E	7/29/97	F
Isoetes louisianensis	Quillwort, Louisiana	E	9/30/96	F
Isoetes melanospora	Quillwort, black spored	E	7/7/93	F
Isoetes tegetiformans	Quillwort, mat-forming	E	7/7/93	F
Lycopodium (=phlegmariurus) nutans	Wawaeìole	E	8/10/98	F
Marsilea villosa	Ihi`ihi	E	4/18/96	F
Polystichum aleuticum	Fern, Aleutian shield	E	9/30/92	F
Polystichum calderonense	No common name	E	1/17/95	F
Pteris lidgatei	No common name	E	4/10/98	F
Tectaria estremerana	No common name	E	1/17/95	F
Thelypteris inabonensis	No common name	E	1/17/95	F
Thelypteris pilosa var. alabamensis	Fern, Alabama streak-sorus	T	10/25/96	F
Thelypteris verecunda	No common name	E	1/17/95	F
Thelypteris yaucoensis	No common name	E	1/17/95	F
Lichens				
Cladonia perforata	Cladonia, Florida perforate	E	5/18/99	F
Gymnoderma lineare	Lichen, rock gnome	E	9/30/97	F
Flowering plants				
Abronia macrocarpa	Sand-verbena, large-fruited	E	9/30/92	F
Abutilon eremitopetalum	No common name	E	9/29/95	F
Abutilon menziesii	Ko`oloa`ula	E	9/29/95	F
Abutilon sandwicense	No common name	E	8/12/95	F
Acaena exigua	Liliwai	E	7/29/97	F
Acanthomintha ilicifolia	Thornmint, San Diego	T	None	—
Acanthomintha obovata ssp. duttonii	Thornmint, San Mateo	E	9/30/98	F
Achyranthes mutica	No common name	E	7/10/99	F
Achyranthes splendens var. rotundata	Chaff-flower, round-leaved	E	10/5/93	D
Aconitum noveboracense	Monkshood, northern wild	T	9/23/83	F
Aeschynomene virginica	Joint-vetch, sensitive	T	9/29/95	F
Agalinis acuta	Gerardia, sandplain	E	9/20/89	F
Agave arizonica	Agave, Arizona	E	None	—
Alectryon macrococcus	Mahoe	E	7/29/97	F
Allium munzii	Onion, Munz's	E	None	—
Alopecurus aequalis var. sonomensis	Alopecurus, Sonoma	E	None	—
Alsinidendron lychnoides	Kuawawaenohu	E	8/23/98	F
Alsinidendron obovatum	No common name	E	8/12/95	F
Alsinidendron trinerve	No common name	E	8/12/95	F
Alsinidendron viscosum	No common name	E	8/23/98	F
Amaranthus brownii	No common name	E	3/31/98	F
Amaranthus pumilus	Amaranth, seabeach	T	11/12/96	F
Ambrosia cheiranthifolia	Ambrosia, south Texas	E	None	—
Ambrosia pumila	Ambrosia, San Diego	E	None	—
Amorpha crenulata	Lead-plant, Crenulate	E	5/18/99	F
Amphianthus pusillus	Amphianthus, little	T	7/7/93	F
Amsinckia grandiflora	Fiddleneck, large-flowered	E	9/29/97	F
Amsonia kearneyana	Blue-star, Kearney's	E	5/24/93	F
Ancistrocactus tobuschii	Cactus, Tobusch fishhook	E	3/18/87	F
Apios priceana	Potato-bean, Price's	T	2/10/93	F
Arabis hoffmannii	Rock-cress, Hoffmann's	E	9/26/2000	F
Arabis mcdonaldiana	Rock-cress, McDonald's	E	2/28/84	F
Arabis perstellata	Rock-cress, Braun's	E	7/22/97	F
Arabis serotina	Rock-cress, shale barren	E	8/15/91	F

TABLE 11.1

Endangered and threatened plant species in the United States, March 2006 [CONTINUED]

Scientific name	Inverted common name	Listing status[a]	Recovery plan date	Recovery plan status[b]
Arctomecon humilis	Bear-poppy, dwarf	E	12/31/85	F
Arctostaphylos confertiflora	Manzanita, Santa Rosa Island	E	9/26/2000	F
Arctostaphylos glandulosa ssp. crassifolia	Manzanita, Del Mar	E	None	—
Arctostaphylos hookeri var. ravenii	Manzanita, Presidio	E	10/6/03	F
Arctostaphylos morroensis	Manzanita, Morro	T	9/28/98	F
Arctostaphylos myrtifolia	Manzanita, Ione	T	None	—
Arctostaphylos pallida	Manzanita, pallid	T	4/7/03	D
Arenaria cumberlandensis	Sandwort, Cumberland	E	6/20/96	F
Arenaria paludicola	Sandwort, Marsh	E	9/28/98	F
Arenaria ursina	Sandwort, Bear Valley	T	None	—
Argemone pleiacantha ssp. pinnatisecta	Poppy, Sacramento prickly	E	8/31/94	F
Argyroxiphium kauense	Silversword, Mauna Loa (=Ka`u)	E	11/21/95	F
Argyroxiphium sandwicense ssp. macrocephalum	`Ahinahina	T	7/29/97	F
Argyroxiphium sandwicense ssp. sandwicense	`Ahinahina	E	9/30/93	F
Aristida chaseae	No common name	E	7/31/95	F
Aristida portoricensis	Pelos del diablo	E	5/16/94	F
Asclepias meadii	Milkweed, Mead's	T	9/22/03	F
Asclepias welshii	Milkweed, Welsh's	T	9/30/92	F
Asimina tetramera	Pawpaw, four-petal	E	5/18/99	F
Astragalus albens	Milk-vetch, Cushenbury	E	9/30/97	D
Astragalus ampullarioides	Milk-vetch, Shivwitz	E	None	—
Astragalus applegatei	Milk-vetch, Applegate's	E	4/10/98	F
Astragalus bibullatus	Ground-plum, Guthrie's (=Pyne's)	E	None	—
Astragalus brauntonii	Milk-vetch, Braunton's	E	9/30/99	F
Astragalus clarianus	Milk-vetch, Clara Hunt's	E	None	—
Astragalus cremnophylax var. cremnophylax	Milk-vetch, Sentry	E	9/14/04	D
Astragalus desereticus	Milk-vetch, Deseret	T	None	—
Astragalus holmgreniorum	Milk-vetch, Holmgren	E	None	—
Astragalus humillimus	Milk-vetch, Mancos	E	12/20/89	F
Astragalus jaegerianus	Milk-vetch, Lane Mountain	E	None	—
Astragalus lentiginosus var. coachellae	Milk-vetch, Coachella Valley	E	None	—
Astragalus lentiginosus var. piscinensis	Milk-vetch, Fish Slough	T	9/30/98	F
Astragalus magdalenae var. peirsonii	Milk-vetch, Peirson's	T	None	—
Astragalus montii	Milk-vetch, heliotrope	T	9/27/95	D
Astragalus osterhoutii	Milk-vetch, Osterhout	E	9/30/92	F
Astragalus phoenix	Milk-vetch, Ash meadows	T	9/28/90	F
Astragalus pycnostachyus var. lanosissimus	Milk-vetch, Ventura Marsh	E	None	—
Astragalus robbinsii var. jesupi	Milk-vetch, Jesup's	E	11/21/89	F
Astragalus tener var. titi	Milk-vetch, coastal dunes	E	12/20/04	F
Astragalus tricarinatus	Milk-vetch, triple-ribbed	E	None	—
Astrophytum asterias	Cactus, star	E	11/6/03	F
Atriplex coronata var. notatior	Crownscale, San Jacinto Valley	E	None	—
Auerodendron pauciflorum	No common name	E	9/29/97	F
Ayenia limitaris	Ayenia, Texas	E	None	—
Baccharis vanessae	Baccharis, Encinitas	T	None	—
Banara vanderbiltii	Palo de ramon	E	3/15/91	F
Baptisia arachnifera	Rattleweed, hairy	E	3/19/84	F
Berberis nevinii	Barberry, Nevin's	E	None	—
Berberis pinnata ssp. insularis	Barberry, island	E	9/26/2000	F
Betula uber	Birch, Virginia round-leaf	T	9/24/90	RF(2)
Bidens micrantha ssp. kalealaha	Ko`oko`olau	E	7/29/97	F
Bidens wiebkei	Ko`oko`olau	E	9/26/96	F
Blennosperma bakeri	Sunshine, Sonoma	E	None	—
Boltonia decurrens	Aster, decurrent false	T	9/28/90	F
Bonamia grandiflora	Bonamia, Florida	T	6/20/96	RF(1)
Bonamia menziesii	No common name	E	7/10/99	F
Brighamia insignis	Olulu	E	9/20/95	F
Brighamia rockii	Pua`ala	E	9/26/96	F
Brodiaea filifolia	Brodiaea, thread-leaved	T	None	—
Brodiaea pallida	Brodiaea, Chinese Camp	T	9/16/05	U
Buxus vahlii	Boxwood, Vahl's	E	4/28/87	F
Caesalpinia kavaiense	Uhiuhi	E	5/6/94	F
Callicarpa ampla	Capa rosa	E	7/31/95	F
Callirhoe scabriuscula	Poppy-mallow, Texas	E	3/29/85	F
Calochortus tiburonensis	Mariposa lily, Tiburon	T	9/30/98	F
Calyptranthes thomasiana	No common name	E	9/30/97	F
Calyptridium pulchellum	Pussypaws, Mariposa	T	9/16/05	U
Calyptronoma rivalis	Manaca, palma de	T	6/25/92	F
Calystegia stebbinsii	Morning-glory, Stebbins'	E	8/30/02	F
Camissonia benitensis	Evening-primrose, San Benito	T	2/2/99	D
Campanula robinsiae	Bellflower, Brooksville	E	6/20/94	F
Canavalia molokaiensis	`Awikiwiki	E	9/26/96	F

TABLE 11.1

Endangered and threatened plant species in the United States, March 2006 [CONTINUED]

Scientific name	Inverted common name	Listing status[a]	Recovery plan date	Recovery plan status[b]
Cardamine micranthera	Bittercress, small-anthered	E	7/10/91	F
Carex albida	Sedge, white	E	None	—
Carex lutea	Sedge, golden	E	None	—
Carex specuicola	Sedge, Navajo	T	9/24/87	F
Castilleja affinis ssp. neglecta	Paintbrush, Tiburon	E	9/30/98	F
Castilleja campestris ssp. succulenta	Owl's-clover, fleshy	T	3/7/06	F
Castilleja cinerea	Paintbrush, ash-grey	T	None	—
Castilleja grisea	Indian paintbrush, San Clemente Island	E	1/26/84	F
Castilleja levisecta	Paintbrush, golden	T	8/23/2000	F
Castilleja mollis	Paintbrush, soft-leaved	E	9/26/2000	F
Catesbaea melanocarpa	No common name	E	8/18/05	F
Caulanthus californicus	Jewelflower, California	E	9/30/98	F
Ceanothus ferrisae	Ceanothus, coyote	E	9/30/98	F
Ceanothus ophiochilus	Ceanothus, Vail Lake	T	None	—
Ceanothus roderickii	Ceanothus, Pine Hill	E	8/30/02	F
Cenchrus agrimonioides	Kamanomano	E	7/10/99	F
Centaurium namophilum	Centaury, spring-loving	T	9/28/90	F
Centaurium sebaeoides	Awiwi	E	8/12/95	F
Cercocarpus traskiae	Mountain-mahogany, Catalina Island	E	9/16/05	U
Cereus eriophorus var. fragrans	Prickly-apple, fragrant	E	5/18/99	F
Chamaecrista glandulosa var. mirabilis	No common name	E	5/12/94	F
Chamaesyce celastroides var. kaenana	`Akoko	E	8/12/95	F
Chamaesyce deltoidea ssp. deltoidea	Spurge, deltoid	E	5/18/99	F
Chamaesyce deppeana	`Akoko	E	8/10/98	F
Chamaesyce garberi	Spurge, Garber's	T	5/18/99	F
Chamaesyce halemanui	No common name	E	9/20/95	F
Chamaesyce herbstii	`Akoko	E	8/10/98	F
Chamaesyce hooveri	Spurge, Hoover's	T	3/7/06	F
Chamaesyce kuwaleana	`Akoko	E	8/12/95	F
Chamaesyce rockii	`Akoko	E	8/10/98	F
Chamaesyce skottsbergii var. kalaeloana	`Akoko, Ewa Plains	E	10/5/93	D
Chionanthus pygmaeus	Fringe-tree, pygmy	E	5/18/99	F
Chlorogalum purpureum	Amole, purple	T	None	—
Chorizanthe howellii	Spineflower, Howell's	E	9/29/98	F
Chorizanthe orcuttiana	Spineflower, Orcutt's	E	None	—
Chorizanthe pungens var. hartwegiana	Spineflower, Ben Lomond	E	9/28/98	F
Chorizanthe pungens var. pungens	Spineflower, Monterey	T	9/29/98	F
Chorizanthe robusta (incl. vars. robusta and hartwegii)	Spineflower, Robust (incl. Scotts Valley)	E	9/28/98	F
Chorizanthe valida	Spineflower, Sonoma	E	9/29/98	F
Chrysopsis floridana	Aster, Florida golden	E	8/29/88	F
Cirsium fontinale var. fontinale	Thistle, fountain	E	9/30/98	F
Cirsium fontinale var. obispoense	Thistle, Chorro Creek bog	E	9/28/98	F
Cirsium hydrophilum var. hydrophilum	Thistle, Suisun	E	None	—
Cirsium loncholepis	Thistle, La Graciosa	E	None	—
Cirsium pitcheri	Thistle, Pitcher's	T	9/20/02	F
Cirsium vinaceum	Thistle, Sacramento Mountains	T	9/27/93	F
Clarkia franciscana	Clarkia, Presidio	E	9/30/98	F
Clarkia imbricata	Clarkia, Vine Hill	E	None	—
Clarkia speciosa ssp. immaculata	Clarkia, Pismo	E	9/28/98	F
Clarkia springvillensis	Clarkia, Springville	T	9/16/05	U
Clematis morefieldii	Leather flower, Morefield's	E	5/3/94	F
Clematis socialis	Leather flower, Alabama	E	12/27/89	F
Clermontia drepanomorpha	`Oha wai	E	5/11/98	F
Clermontia lindseyana	`Oha wai	E	9/26/96	F
Clermontia oblongifolia ssp. brevipes	`Oha wai	E	9/26/96	F
Clermontia oblongifolia ssp. mauiensis	`Oha wai	E	7/29/97	F
Clermontia peleana	`Oha wai	E	9/26/96	F
Clermontia pyrularia	`Oha wai	E	9/26/96	F
Clermontia samuelii	`Oha wai	E	9/19/02	F
Clitoria fragrans	Pigeon wings	T	5/18/99	F
Colubrina oppositifolia	Kauila	E	9/26/96	F
Conradina brevifolia	Rosemary, short-leaved	E	5/18/99	F
Conradina etonia	Rosemary, Etonia	E	9/27/94	F
Conradina glabra	Rosemary, Apalachicola	E	9/27/94	F
Conradina verticillata	Rosemary, Cumberland	T	7/12/96	F
Cordia bellonis	No common name	E	10/1/99	F
Cordylanthus maritimus ssp. maritimus	Bird's-beak, salt marsh	E	12/6/85	F
Cordylanthus mollis ssp. mollis	Bird's-beak, soft	E	None	—
Cordylanthus palmatus	Bird's beak, palmate-bracted	E	9/30/98	F
Cordylanthus tenuis ssp. capillaris	Bird's-beak, Pennell's	E	9/30/98	F
Cornutia obovata	Palo de nigua	E	8/7/92	F
Coryphantha minima	Cactus, Nellie cory	E	9/20/84	F

TABLE 11.1

Endangered and threatened plant species in the United States, March 2006 [CONTINUED]

Scientific name	Inverted common name	Listing status[a]	Recovery plan date	Recovery plan status[b]
Coryphantha ramillosa	Cory cactus, bunched	T	4/13/90	U
Coryphantha robbinsorum	Cactus, Cochise pincushion	T	9/27/93	F
Coryphantha scheeri var. robustispina	Cactus, Pima pineapple	E	9/26/05	U
Coryphantha sneedii var. leei	Cactus, Lee pincushion	T	3/21/86	F
Coryphantha sneedii var. sneedii	Cactus, Sneed pincushion	E	3/21/86	F
Cranichis ricartii	No common name	E	7/15/96	F
Crescentia portoricensis	Higuero de sierra	E	9/23/91	F
Crotalaria avonensis	Harebells, Avon Park	E	5/18/99	F
Cryptantha crassipes	Cat's-eye, Terlingua Creek	E	4/5/94	F
Cucurbita okeechobeensis ssp. okeechobeensis	Gourd, Okeechobee	E	5/18/99	F
Cyanea (=rollandia) crispa	No common name	E	8/10/98	F
Cyanea acuminata	Haha	E	8/10/98	F
Cyanea asarifolia	Haha	E	9/20/95	F
Cyanea copelandii ssp. copelandii	Haha	E	9/26/96	F
Cyanea copelandii ssp. haleakalaensis	Haha	E	9/19/02	F
Cyanea dunbarii	Haha	E	5/20/98	F
Cyanea glabra	Haha	E	9/19/02	F
Cyanea grimesiana ssp. grimesiana	Haha	E	7/10/99	F
Cyanea grimesiana ssp. obatae	Haha	E	8/12/95	F
Cyanea hamatiflora carlsonii	Haha	E	9/26/96	F
Cyanea hamatiflora ssp. hamatiflora	Haha	E	9/19/02	F
Cyanea humboldtiana	Haha	E	8/10/98	F
Cyanea koolauensis	Haha	E	8/10/98	F
Cyanea lobata	Haha	E	7/29/97	F
Cyanea longiflora	Haha	E	8/10/98	F
Cyanea macrostegia ssp. gibsonii	Haha	E	9/29/95	F
Cyanea mannii	Haha	E	9/26/96	F
Cyanea mceldowneyi	Haha	E	7/29/97	F
Cyanea pinnatifida	Haha	E	8/12/95	F
Cyanea platyphylla	Haha	E	5/11/98	F
Cyanea procera	Haha	E	9/26/96	F
Cyanea recta	Haha	T	8/23/98	F
Cyanea remyi	Haha	E	8/23/98	F
Cyanea shipmannii	Haha	E	9/26/96	F
Cyanea stictophylla	Haha	E	9/26/96	F
Cyanea st-johnii	Haha	E	8/10/98	F
Cyanea superba	Haha	E	8/12/95	F
Cyanea truncata	Haha	E	8/10/98	F
Cyanea undulata	Haha	E	5/31/94	F
Cycladenia jonesii (=humilis)	Cycladenia, Jones	T	None	—
Cyperus trachysanthos	Pu`uka`a	E	7/10/99	F
Cyrtandra crenata	Haiwale	E	8/10/98	F
Cyrtandra cyaneoides	Mapele	E	8/23/98	F
Cyrtandra dentata	Ha`iwale	E	8/10/98	F
Cyrtandra giffardii	Ha`iwale	E	9/26/96	F
Cyrtandra limahuliensis	Ha`iwale	T	9/20/95	F
Cyrtandra munroi	Ha`iwale	E	9/29/95	F
Cyrtandra polyantha	Ha`iwale	E	8/10/98	F
Cyrtandra subumbellata	Ha`iwale	E	8/10/98	F
Cyrtandra tintinnabula	Ha`iwale	E	9/26/96	F
Cyrtandra viridiflora	Ha`iwale	E	8/10/98	F
Dalea foliosa	Prairie-clover, leafy	E	9/30/96	F
Daphnopsis hellerana	No common name	E	8/7/92	F
Deeringothamnus pulchellus	Pawpaw, beautiful	E	5/18/99	F
Deeringothamnus rugelii	Pawpaw, Rugel's	E	4/5/88	F
Deinandra (=hemizonia) conjugens	Tarplant, Otay	T	12/28/04	F
Deinandra increscens ssp. villosa	Tarplant, Gaviota	E	None	—
Delissea rhytidosperma	No common name	E	9/20/95	F
Delissea rivularis	Oha	E	8/23/98	F
Delissea subcordata	Oha	E	8/10/98	F
Delissea undulata	No common name	E	9/26/96	F
Delphinium bakeri	Larkspur, Baker's	E	None	—
Delphinium luteum	Larkspur, yellow	E	None	—
Delphinium variegatum ssp. kinkiense	Larkspur, San Clemente Island	E	1/26/84	F
Dicerandra christmanii	Mint, Garrett's	E	5/18/99	F
Dicerandra cornutissima	Mint, longspurred	E	7/1/87	F
Dicerandra frutescens	Mint, scrub	E	5/18/99	F
Dicerandra immaculata	Mint, Lakela's	E	5/18/99	F
Dodecahema leptoceras	Spineflower, slender-horned	E	None	—
Dubautia herbstobatae	Na`ena`e	E	8/12/95	F
Dubautia latifolia	Na`ena`e	E	9/20/95	F
Dubautia pauciflorula	Na`ena`e	E	5/31/94	F

TABLE 11.1

Endangered and threatened plant species in the United States, March 2006 [CONTINUED]

Scientific name	Inverted common name	Listing status[a]	Recovery plan date	Recovery plan status[b]
Dubautia plantaginea ssp. humilis	Naènaè	E	9/19/02	F
Dudleya abramsii ssp. parva	Dudleya, Conejo	T	9/30/99	F
Dudleya cymosa ssp. marcescens	Dudleya, marcescent	T	9/30/99	F
Dudleya cymosa ssp. ovatifolia	Dudleyea, Santa Monica Mountains	T	9/26/2000	F
Dudleya nesiotica	Dudleya, Santa Cruz Island	E	9/30/98	F
Dudleya setchellii	Dudleya, Santa Clara Valley	T	None	—
Dudleya stolonifera	Liveforever, Laguna Beach	E	6/27/85	F
Dudleya traskiae	Liveforever, Santa Barbara Island	E	9/30/99	F
Dudleya verityi	Dudleya, Verity's	T	4/18/95	F
Echinacea laevigata	Coneflower, smooth	E	11/14/89	RF(1)
Echinacea tennesseensis	Coneflower, Tennessee purple	E	4/14/86	F
Echinocactus horizonthalonius var. nicholii	Cactus, Nichol's Turk's head	E	12/8/93	F
Echinocereus chisoensis var. chisoensis	Cactus, Chisos Mountain hedgehog	T	3/28/85	F
Echinocereus fendleri var. kuenzleri	Cactus, Kuenzler hedgehog	E	3/18/87	F
Echinocereus reichenbachii var. albertii	Cactus, black lace	E	9/30/84	TD
Echinocereus triglochidiatus var. arizonicus	Cactus, Arizona hedgehog	E	9/20/84	F
Echinocereus viridiflorus var. davisii	Pitaya, Davis' green	T	4/13/90	F
Echinomastus mariposensis	Cactus, Lloyd's Mariposa	T	9/28/90	F
Enceliopsis nudicaulis var. corrugata	Sunray, Ash Meadows	E	8/10/98	F
Eragrostis fosbergii	Love grass, Fosberg's	E	9/30/98	F
Eremalche kernensis	Mallow, Kern	E	None	—
Eriastrum densifolium ssp. sanctorum	Woolly-star, Santa Ana River	E	9/16/05	U
Erigeron decumbens var. decumbens	Daisy, Willamette	E	8/15/95	F
Erigeron maguirei	Daisy, Maguire	T	9/30/97	D
Erigeron parishii	Daisy, Parish's	T	9/30/88	F
Erigeron rhizomatus	Fleabane, Zuni	T	9/28/98	F
Eriodictyon altissimum	Mountain balm, Indian Knob	E	None	—
Eriodictyon capitatum	Yerba santa, Lompoc	E	None	—
Eriogonum apricum (including var. prostratum)	Buckwheat, Ione (incl. Irish Hill)	E	3/30/84	F
Eriogonum gypsophilum	Wild-buckwheat, gypsum	T	None	—
Eriogonum kennedyi var. austromontanum	Wild-buckwheat, southern mountain	T	6/20/96	RF(1)
Eriogonum longifolium var. gnaphalifolium	Buckwheat, scrub	E	9/30/97	D
Eriogonum ovalifolium var. vineum	Buckwheat, cushenbury	E	9/20/95	F
Eriogonum ovalifolium var. williamsiae	Buckwheat, steamboat	E	11/10/88	F
Eriogonum pelinophilum	Wild-buckwheat, clay-loving	E	9/30/98	F
Eriophyllum latilobum	Sunflower, San Mateo woolly	E	9/3/98	F
Eryngium aristulatum var. parishii	Button-celery, San Diego	E	3/7/06	F
Eryngium constancei	Thistle, Loch Lomond coyote	E	5/18/99	F
Eryngium cuneifolium	Snakeroot	E	4/25/84	RF(1)
Erysimum capitatum var. angustatum	Wallflower, Contra Costa	E	9/29/98	F
Erysimum menziesii	Wallflower, Menzies'	E	9/28/98	F
Erysimum teretifolium	Wallflower, Ben Lomond	E	12/16/87	F
Erythronium propullans	Lily, Minnesota dwarf trout	E	9/11/98	F
Eugenia haematocarpa	Uvillo	E	8/10/98	F
Eugenia koolauensis	Nioi	E	10/6/98	F
Eugenia woodburyana	No common name	E	7/10/99	F
Euphorbia haeleeleana	`Akoko	E	6/22/94	F
Euphorbia telephioides	Spurge, telephus	T	None	—
Eutrema penlandii	Mustard, Penland alpine fen	E	9/20/95	F
Exocarpos luteolus	Heau	E	7/10/99	F
Flueggea neowawraea	Mehamehame	E	5/24/88	F
Frankenia johnstonii	Frankenia, Johnston's	E	8/30/02	F
Fremontodendron californicum ssp. decumbens	Flannelbush, Pine Hill	E	None	—
Fremontodendron mexicanum	Flannelbush, Mexican	E	8/28/03	F
Fritillaria gentneri	Fritillary, Gentner's	E	9/29/95	F
Gahnia lanaiensis	No common name	E	5/18/99	F
Galactia smallii	Milkpea, Small's	E	9/26/2000	F
Galium buxifolium	Bedstraw, island	E	8/30/02	F
Galium californicum ssp. sierrae	Bedstraw, El Dorado	E	9/30/93	F
Gardenia brighamii	Gardenia (=Na`u), Hawaiian	E	8/10/98	F
Gardenia mannii	Nanu	E	None	—
Gaura neomexicana var. coloradensis	Butterfly plant, Colorado	T	7/26/93	F
Geocarpon minimum	No common name	T	7/29/97	F
Geranium arboreum	Geranium, Hawaiian red-flowered	E	7/29/97	F
Geranium multiflorum	Nohoanu	E	10/6/98	F
Gesneria pauciflora	No common name	T	4/28/93	F
Geum radiatum	Avens, spreading	E	9/29/98	F
Gilia tenuiflora ssp. arenaria	Gilia, Monterey	E	9/26/2000	F
Gilia tenuiflora ssp. hoffmannii	Gilia, Hoffmann's slender-flowered	E	4/28/87	F
Goetzea elegans	Goetzea, beautiful	E	7/16/90	F
Gouania hillebrandii	No common name	E	8/12/95	F
Gouania meyenii	No common name	E		

TABLE 11.1

Endangered and threatened plant species in the United States, March 2006 [CONTINUED]

Scientific name	Inverted common name	Listing status[a]	Recovery plan date	Recovery plan status[b]
Gouania vitifolia	No common name	E	8/12/95	F
Grindelia fraxino-pratensis	Gumplant, Ash Meadows	T	9/28/90	F
Hackelia venusta	Stickseed, showy	E	9/21/05	U
Halophila johnsonii	Seagrass, Johnson's	T	10/4/02	F
Haplostachys haplostachya	Honohono	E	9/20/93	D
Harperocallis flava	Beauty, Harper's	E	9/14/83	F
Harrisia portoricensis	Chumbo, Higo	T	11/12/96	F
Hedeoma todsenii	Pennyroyal, Todsen's	E	1/31/01	RF(2)
Hedyotis cookiana	Awiwi	E	9/20/95	F
Hedyotis coriacea	Kio`ele	E	7/29/97	F
Hedyotis degeneri	No common name	E	8/12/95	F
Hedyotis mannii	Pilo	E	9/26/96	F
Hedyotis parvula	No common name	E	8/12/95	F
Hedyotis purpurea var. montana	Bluet, Roan Mountain	E	5/13/96	F
Hedyotis schlechtendahliana var. remyi	Kopa	E	9/19/02	F
Hedyotis st.-johnii	Hedyotis, Na Pali beach	E	9/20/95	F
Helenium virginicum	Sneezeweed, Virginia	T	10/2/2000	D
Helianthemum greenei	Rush-rose, island	T	9/26/2000	F
Helianthus paradoxus	Sunflower, Pecos (=puzzle, =paradox)	T	9/15/05	F
Helianthus schweinitzii	Sunflower, Schweinitz's	E	4/22/94	F
Helonias bullata	Pink, swamp	T	9/30/91	F
Hesperolinon congestum	Dwarf-flax, Marin	T	9/30/98	F
Hesperomannia arborescens	No common name	E	8/10/98	F
Hesperomannia arbuscula	No common name	E	8/12/95	F
Hesperomannia lydgatei	No common name	E	5/31/94	F
Hexastylis naniflora	Heartleaf, dwarf-flowered	T	null	U
Hibiscadelphus distans	Kauai hau kuahiwi	E	6/5/96	F
Hibiscadelphus giffardianus	Hau kuahiwi	E	5/11/98	F
Hibiscadelphus hualalaiensis	Hau kuahiwi	E	5/11/l98	F
Hibiscadelphus woodii	Hau kuahiwi	E	8/23/98	F
Hibiscus arnottianus ssp. immaculatus	Koki`o ke`oke`o	E	9/26/96	F
Hibiscus brackenridgei	Ma`o hau hele, (=native yellow hibiscus)	E	7/10/99	F
Hibiscus clayi	Hibiscus, Clay's	E	9/20/95	F
Hibiscus waimeae ssp. hannerae	Kokiò keòkeò	E	8/23/98	F
Hoffmannseggia tenella	Rush-pea, slender	E	9/13/88	F
Holocarpha macradenia	Tarplant, Santa Cruz	T	None	—
Howellia aquatilis	Howellia, water	T	9/2496	D
Hudsonia montana	Heather, mountain golden	T	9/14/83	F
Hymenoxys herbacea	Daisy, lakeside	T	9/19/90	F
Hymenoxys texana	Dawn-flower, Texas prairie	E	4/13/90	F
Hypericum cumulicola	Hypericum, highlands scrub	E	5/18/99	F
Ilex cookii	Holly, Cook's	E	1/31/91	F
Ilex sintenisii	No common name	E	7/31/95	F
Iliamna corei	Mallow, Peter's Mountain	E	9/28/90	F
Ipomopsis sancti-spiritus	Ipomopsis, Holy Ghost	E	9/26/02	F
Iris lacustris	Iris, dwarf lake	T	None	—
Ischaemum byrone	Ischaemum, Hilo	E	9/26/96	F
Isodendrion hosakae	Aupaka	E	5/23/94	F
Isodendrion laurifolium	Aupaka	E	7/10/99	F
Isodendrion longifolium	Aupaka	T	7/10/99	F
Isodendrion pyrifolium	Kula wahine noho	E	9/26/96	F
Isotria medeoloides	Pogonia, small whorled	T	11/13/92	RF(1)
Ivesia kingii var. eremica	Ivesia, Ash Meadows	T	9/28/90	F
Jacquemontia reclinata	Jacquemontia, beach	E	5/18/99	F
Juglans jamaicensis	Walnut (=Nogal), West Indian	E	12/9/99	F
Justicia cooleyi	Water-willow, Cooley's	E	6/20/94	F
Kanaloa kahoolawensis	Kohe malama malama o kanaloa	E	9/1902	F
Kokia cookei	Koki`o, Cooke's	E	5/27/98	F
Kokia drynarioides	Koki`o	E	5/6/94	F
Kokia kauaiensis	Koki`o	E	8/23/98	F
Labordia cyrtandrae	Kamakahala	E	8/10/98	F
Labordia lydgatei	Kamakahala	E	5/31/94	F
Labordia tinifolia var. lanaiensis	Kamakahala	E	9/19/02	F
Labordia tinifolia var. wahiawaensis	Kamakahala	E	8/23/98	F
Labordia triflora	Kamakahala	E	9/19/02	F
Lasthenia burkei	Goldfields, Burke's	E	None	—
Lasthenia conjugens	Goldfields, Contra Costa	E	3/7/06	F
Layia carnosa	Layia, beach	E	9/29/98	F
Lepanthes eltoroensis	No common name	E	7/15/96	F
Lepidium arbuscula	`Anaunau	E	8/10/98	F
Lepidium barnebyanum	Ridge-cress, Barneby	E	7/23/93	F
Leptocereus grantianus	No common name	E	7/26/95	F

TABLE 11.1

Endangered and threatened plant species in the United States, March 2006 [CONTINUED]

Scientific name	Inverted common name	Listing status[a]	Recovery plan date	Recovery plan status[b]
Lespedeza leptostachya	Bush-clover, prairie	T	10/6/88	F
Lesquerella congesta	Bladderpod, Dudley Bluffs	T	8/13/93	F
Lesquerella filiformis	Bladderpod, Missouri	T	4/7/88	F
Lesquerella kingii ssp. bernardina	Bladderpod, San Bernardino Mountains	E	9/30/97	D
Lesquerella lyrata	Bladderpod, lyrate	T	10/17/96	F
Lesquerella pallida	Bladderpod, white	E	10/16/92	F
Lesquerella perforata	Bladderpod, Spring Creek	E	9/12/05	D
Lesquerella thamnophila	Bladderpod, Zapata	E	8/25/04	F
Lesquerella tumulosa	Bladderpod, kodachrome	E	None	—
Lessingia germanorum (=l.g. var. germanorum)	Lessingia, San Francisco	E	10/6/03	F
Liatris helleri	Blazingstar, Heller's	T	1/28/2000	RF(1)
Liatris ohlingerae	Blazingstar, scrub	E	5/18/99	F
Lilaeopsis schaffneriana var. recurva	Water-umbel, Huachuca	E	None	—
Lilium occidentale	Lily, Western	E	3/31/98	F
Lilium pardalinum ssp. pitkinense	Lily, Pitkin Marsh	E	None	—
Limnanthes floccosa ssp. californica	Meadowfoam, Butte County	E	3/7/06	F
Limnanthes floccosa ssp. grandiflora	Meadowfoam, large-flowered woolly	E	9/21/05	U
Limnanthes vinculans	Meadowfoam, Sebastopol	E	None	—
Lindera melissifolia	Pondberry	E	9/23/93	F
Lipochaeta fauriei	Nehe	E	9/20/95	F
Lipochaeta kamolensis	Nehe	E	7/29/97	F
Lipochaeta lobata var. leptophylla	Nehe	E	8/12/95	F
Lipochaeta micrantha	Nehe	E	9/20/95	F
Lipochaeta tenuifolia	Nehe	E	8/12/95	F
Lipochaeta venosa	No common name	E	5/23/94	F
Lipochaeta waimeaensis	Nehe	E	9/20/95	F
Lithophragma maximum	Woodland-star, San Clemente Island	E	9/16/05	U
Lobelia gaudichaudii ssp. koolauensis	No common name	E	8/10/98	F
Lobelia monostachya	No common name	E	8/10/98	F
Lobelia niihauensis	No common name	E	8/12/95	F
Lobelia oahuensis	No common name	E	8/10/98	F
Lomatium bradshawii	Desert-parsley, Bradshaw's	E	8/13/93	F
Lomatium cookii	Lomatium, Cook's	E	None	—
Lotus dendroideus ssp. traskiae	Broom, San Clemente Island	E	1/26/84	F
Lupinus aridorum	Lupine, scrub	E	6/20/96	RF(1)
Lupinus nipomensis	Lupine, Nipomo Mesa	E	None	—
Lupinus sulphureus (=oreganus) ssp. kincaidii (=var. kincaidii)	Lupine, Kincaid's	T	9/16/05	U
Lupinus tidestromii	Lupine, clover	E	9/29/98	F
Lyonia truncata var. proctorii	No common name	E	7/31/95	F
Lysimachia asperulaefolia	Loosestrife, rough-leaved	E	4/19/95	F
Lysimachia filifolia	No common name	E	9/20/95	F
Lysimachia lydgatei	No common name	E	7/29/97	F
Lysimachia maxima	No common name	E	5/20/98	F
Macbridea alba	Birds-in-a-nest, white	T	6/22/94	F
Malacothamnus clementinus	Bush-mallow, San Clemente Island	E	1/26/84	F
Malacothamnus fasciculatus var. nesioticus	Bush-mallow, Santa Cruz Island	E	9/26/2000	F
Malacothrix indecora	Malacothrix, Santa Cruz Island	E	9/26/2000	F
Malacothrix squalida	Malacothrix, island	E	9/26/2000	F
Manihot walkerae	Manioc, Walker's	E	12/12/93	F
Mariscus fauriei	No common name	E	9/26/96	F
Mariscus pennatiformis	No common name	E	7/10/99	F
Marshallia mohrii	Button, Mohr's Barbara	T	11/26/91	F
Melicope adscendens	Alani	E	7/29/97	F
Melicope balloui	Alani	E	7/29/97	F
Melicope haupuensis	Alani	E	9/20/95	F
Melicope knudsenii	Alani	E	9/20/95	F
Melicope lydgatei	Alani	E	8/10/98	F
Melicope mucronulata	Alani	E	7/29/97	F
Melicope munroi	Alani	E	9/19/02	F
Melicope ovalis	Alani	E	7/29/97	F
Melicope pallida	Alani	E	9/20/95	F
Melicope quadrangularis	Alani	E	9/20/95	F
Melicope reflexa	Alani	E	9/26/96	F
Melicope saint-johnii	Alani	E	8/10/98	F
Melicope zahlbruckneri	Alani	E	5/11/98	F
Mentzelia leucophylla	Blazingstar, Ash Meadows	T	9/28/90	F
Mimulus glabratus var. michiganensis	Monkey-flower, Michigan	E	9/17/97	F
Mirabilis macfarlanei	Four-o'clock, MacFarlane's	T	6/30/2000	RF(1)
Mitracarpus maxwelliae	No common name	E	10/6/98	F
Mitracarpus polycladus	No common name	E	10/6/98	F
Monardella linoides ssp. viminea	Monardella, willowy	E	None	—
Monolopia (=Lembertia) congdonii	Wooly-threads, San Joaquin	E	9/30/98	F

TABLE 11.1

Endangered and threatened plant species in the United States, March 2006 [CONTINUED]

Scientific name	Inverted common name	Listing status[a]	Recovery plan date	Recovery plan status[b]
Munroidendron racemosum	No common name	E	9/20/95	F
Myrcia paganii	No common name	E	9/29/97	F
Myrsine juddii	Kolea	E	8/10/98	F
Myrsine linearifolia	Kolea	T	8/23/98	F
Navarretia fossalis	Navarretia, spreading	T	9/3/98	F
Navarretia leucocephala ssp. pauciflora (=n. pauciflora)	Navarretia, few-flowered	E	3/7/06	F
Navarretia leucocephala ssp. plieantha	Navarretia, many-flowered	E	3/7/06	F
Neostapfia colusana	Grass, Colusa	T	3/7/06	F
Neraudia angulata	No common name	E	8/12/95	F
Neraudia ovata	No common name	E	5/11/98	F
Neraudia sericea	No common name	E	7/10/99	F
Nesogenes rotensis	No common name	E	9/21/05	U
Nitrophila mohavensis	Niterwort, Amargosa	E	9/28/90	F
Nolina brittoniana	Beargrass, Britton's	E	6/20/96	RF(1)
Nothocestrum breviflorum	`Aiea	E	9/26/96	F
Nothocestrum peltatum	`Aiea	E	9/20/95	F
Nototrichium humile	Kulu'i	E	8/12/95	F
Ochrosia kilaueaensis	Holei	E	9/26/96	F
Oenothera avita ssp. eurekensis	Evening-primrose, Eureka Valley	E	12/13/82	F
Oenothera deltoides ssp. howellii	Evening-primrose, Antioch Dunes	E	4/25/84	RF(1)
Opuntia treleasei	Cactus, Bakersfield	E	9/30/98	F
Orcuttia californica	Orcutt grass, California	E	9/3/98	F
Orcuttia inaequalis	Orcutt grass, San Joaquin	T	3/7/06	F
Orcuttia pilosa	Orcutt grass, hairy	E	3/7/06	F
Orcuttia tenuis	Orcutt grass, slender	T	3/7/06	F
Orcuttia viscida	Orcutt grass, Sacramento	E	3/7/06	F
Osmoxylon mariannense	No common name	E	None	—
Ottoschulzia rhodoxylon	Palo de rosa	E	9/20/94	F
Oxypolis canbyi	Dropwort, Canby's	E	4/10/90	F
Oxytheca parishii var. goodmaniana	Oxytheca, cushenbury	E	9/30/97	D
Oxytropis campestris var. chartacea	Locoweed, Fassett's	T	3/29/91	F
Panicum fauriei var. carteri	Panicgrass, Carter's	E	6/4/94	F
Panicum niihauense	Lau`ehu	E	7/10/99	F
Paronychia chartacea	Whitlow-wort, papery	T	5/18/99	F
Parvisedum leiocarpum	Stonecrop, Lake County	E	3/7/06	F
Pedicularis furbishiae	Lousewort, Furbish	E	7/2/91	RF(1)
Pediocactus (=echinocactus,=utahia) sileri	Cactus, Siler pincushion	T	4/14/86	F
Pediocactus bradyi	Cactus, Brady pincushion	E	3/28/85	F
Pediocactus despainii	Cactus, San Rafael	E	10/2/95	D
Pediocactus knowltonii	Cactus, Knowlton	E	3/29/85	F
Pediocactus peeblesianus peeblesianus	Cactus, Peebles Navajo	E	3/30/84	F
Pediocactus winkleri	Cactus, Winkler	T	10/2/95	D
Penstemon haydenii	Penstemon, blowout	E	7/17/92	F
Penstemon penlandii	Beardtongue, Penland	E	9/30/92	F
Pentachaeta bellidiflora	Pentachaeta, white-rayed	E	9/30/98	F
Pentachaeta lyonii	Pentachaeta, Lyon's	E	9/30/99	F
Peperomia wheeleri	Peperomia, Wheeler's	E	11/26/90	F
Peucedanum sandwicense	Makou	T	9/20/95	F
Phacelia argillacea	Phacelia, clay	E	4/12/82	F
Phacelia formosula	Phacelia, North Park	E	3/21/86	F
Phacelia insularis ssp. insularis	Phacelia, island	E	9/26/2000	F
Phlox hirsuta	Phlox, Yreka	E	7/19/04	D
Phlox nivalis ssp. texensis	Phlox, Texas trailing	E	3/28/95	F
Phyllostegia glabra var. lanaiensis	No common name	E	9/29/95	F
Phyllostegia hirsuta	No common name	E	8/10/98	F
Phyllostegia kaalaensis	No common name	E	8/10/98	F
Phyllostegia knudsenii	No common name	E	8/23/98	F
Phyllostegia mannii	No common name	E	9/26/96	F
Phyllostegia mollis	No common name	E	8/12/95	F
Phyllostegia parviflora	No common name	E	7/10/99	F
Phyllostegia racemosa	Kiponapona	E	5/11/98	F
Phyllostegia velutina	No common name	E	5/11/98	F
Phyllostegia waimeae	No common name	E	9/20/95	F
Phyllostegia warshaueri	No common name	E	5/11/98	F
Phyllostegia wawrana	No common name	E	8/23/98	F
Physaria obcordata	Twinpod, Dudley Bluffs	T	8/13/93	F
Pilosocereus robinii	Cactus, Key tree	E	5/18/99	F
Pinguicula ionantha	Butterwort, Godfrey's	T	6/22/94	F
Piperia yadonii	Piperia, Yadon's	E	12/20/04	F
Pityopsis ruthii	Aster, Ruth's golden	E	6/11/92	F
Plagiobothrys hirtus	Popcornflower, rough	E	9/25/03	F
Plagiobothrys strictus	Allocarya, Calistoga	E	None	—

TABLE 11.1

Endangered and threatened plant species in the United States, March 2006 [CONTINUED]

Scientific name	Inverted common name	Listing status[a]	Recovery plan date	Recovery plan status[b]
Plantago hawaiensis	Kuahiwi laukahi	E	9/26/96	F
Plantago princeps	Kuahiwi laukahi	E	7/10/99	F
Platanthera holochila	No common name	E	7/10/99	F
Platanthera leucophaea	Orchid, eastern prairie fringed	T	9/29/99	F
Platanthera praeclara	Orchid, western prairie fringed	T	9/30/96	F
Pleodendron macranthum	Chupacallos	E	9/11/98	F
Pleomele hawaiiensis	Hala pepe	E	5/11/98	F
Poa atropurpurea	Bluegrass, San Bernardino	E	9/16/05	U
Poa mannii	Bluegrass, Mann's	E	9/20/95	F
Poa napensis	Bluegrass, Napa	E	None	—
Poa sandvicensis	Bluegrass, Hawaiian	E	9/20/95	F
Poa siphonoglossa	No common name	E	9/20/95	F
Pogogyne abramsii	Mesa-mint, San Diego	E	9/3/98	F
Pogogyne nudiuscula	Mesa-mint, Otay	E	9/3/98	F
Polygala lewtonii	Polygala, Lewton's	E	5/18/99	F
Polygala smallii	Polygala, tiny	E	5/18/99	F
Polygonella basiramia	Wireweed	E	5/18/99	F
Polygonella myriophylla	Sandlace	E	5/18/99	F
Polygonum hickmanii	Polygonum, Scotts Valley	E	None	—
Portulaca sclerocarpa	Po`e	E	9/26/96	F
Potamogeton clystocarpus	Pondweed, Little Aguja (=Creek)	E	6/20/94	F
Potentilla hickmanii	Potentilla, Hickman's	E	12/20/04	F
Primula maguirei	Primrose, Maguire	T	9/27/90	F
Pritchardia affinis	Lo`ulu	E	9/26/96	F
Pritchardia aylmer-robinsonii	Wahane	E	N/A	E
Pritchardia kaalae	Lo`ulu	E	8/10/98	F
Pritchardia munroi	Lo`ulu	E	9/26/96	F
Pritchardia napaliensis	Lo`ulu	E	8/23/98	F
Pritchardia remota	Lo`ulu	E	3/31/98	F
Pritchardia schattaueri	Lo`ulu	E	5/11/98	F
Pritchardia viscosa	Lo`ulu	E	8/23/98	F
Prunus geniculata	Plum, scrub	E	6/20/96	RF(1)
Pseudobahia bahiifolia	Sunburst, Hartweg's golden	E	9/16/05	U
Pseudobahia peirsonii	Sunburst, San Joaquin adobe	T	9/16/05	U
Pteralyxia kauaiensis	Kaulu	E	9/20/95	F
Ptilimnium nodosum	Harperella	E	3/5/91	F
Purshia (=cowania) subintegra	Cliff-rose, Arizona	E	6/16/95	F
Quercus hinckleyi	Oak, Hinckley	T	9/30/92	F
Ranunculus aestivalis (=acriformis)	Buttercup, autumn	E	9/16/91	F
Remya kauaiensis	No common name	E	9/20/95	F
Remya mauiensis	Remya, Maui	E	7/29/97	F
Remya montgomeryi	No common name	E	9/20/95	F
Rhododendron chapmanii	Rhododendron, Chapman	E	9/8/83	F
Rhus michauxii	Sumac, Michaux's	E	4/30/93	F
Rhynchospora knieskernii	Beaked-rush, Knieskern's	T	9/29/93	F
Ribes echinellum	Gooseberry, Miccosukee	T	N/A	E
Rorippa gambellii	Watercress, Gambel's	E	9/28/98	F
Sagittaria fasciculata	Arrowhead, bunched	E	9/8/83	F
Sagittaria secundifolia	Water-plantain, Kral's	T	8/12/91	F
Sanicula mariversa	No common name	E	8/12/95	F
Sanicula purpurea	No common name	E	7/10/99	F
Santalum freycinetianum var. lanaiense	Sandalwood, Lanai (=`iliahi)	E	9/29/95	F
Sarracenia oreophila	Pitcher-plant, green	E	12/12/94	RF(2)
Sarracenia rubra alabamensis	Pitcher-plant, Alabama canebrake	E	10/8/92	F
Sarracenia rubra ssp. jonesii	Pitcher-plant, mountain sweet	E	8/13/90	F
Scaevola coriacea	Naupaka, dwarf	E	7/29/97	F
Schiedea adamantis	Schiedea, Diamond Head	E	2/2/94	F
Schiedea apokremnos	Ma`oli`oli	E	9/20/95	F
Schiedea haleakalensis	No common name	E	7/29/97	F
Schiedea helleri	No common name	E	8/23/98	F
Schiedea hookeri	No common name	E	7/10/99	F
Schiedea kaalae	No common name	E	8/12/95	F
Schiedea kauaiensis	No common name	E	8/23/98	F
Schiedea kealiae	Ma`oli`oli	E	8/10/98	F
Schiedea lydgatei	No common name	E	9/26/96	F
Schiedea membranacea	No common name	E	8/23/98	F
Schiedea nuttallii	No common name	E	7/10/99	F
Schiedea sarmentosa	No common name	E	5/20/98	F
Schiedea spergulina var. leiopoda	No common name	E	9/20/95	F
Schiedea spergulina var. spergulina	No common name	T	9/20/95	F
Schiedea stellarioides	Laulihilihi	E	8/23/98	F
Schiedea verticillata	No common name	E	3/31/98	F

TABLE 11.1

Endangered and threatened plant species in the United States, March 2006 [CONTINUED]

Scientific name	Inverted common name	Listing status[a]	Recovery plan date	Recovery plan status[b]
Schoenocrambe argillacea	Reed-mustard, clay	T	9/14/94	F
Schoenocrambe barnebyi	Reed-mustard, Barneby	E	9/14/94	F
Schoenocrambe suffrutescens	Reed-mustard, shrubby	E	9/14/94	F
Schoepfia arenaria	No common name	T	1/10/92	F
Schwalbea americana	Chaffseed, American	E	9/29/95	F
Scirpus ancistrochaetus	Bulrush, Northeastern	E	8/25/93	F
Sclerocactus glaucus	Cactus, Uinta Basin hookless	T	9/27/90	F
Sclerocactus mesae-verdae	Cactus, Mesa Verde	T	3/30/84	F
Sclerocactus wrightiae	Cactus, Wright fishhook	E	12/24/85	F
Scutellaria floridana	Skullcap, Florida	T	6/22/94	F
Scutellaria montana	Skullcap, large-flowered	T	5/15/96	F
Sedum integrifolium ssp. leedyi	Roseroot, Leedy's	T	9/25/98	F
Senecio franciscanus	Groundsel, San Francisco Peaks	T	7/21/87	F
Senecio layneae	Butterweed, Layne's	T	8/30/02	F
Serianthes nelsonii	Iagu, Hayun (=(Guam), Tronkon guafi (Rota))	E	2/2/94	F
Sesbania tomentosa	Ohai	E	7/10/99	F
Sibara filifolia	Rockcress, Santa Cruz Island	E	9/16/05	U
Sicyos alba	`Anunu	E	5/11/98	F
Sidalcea keckii	Checker-mallow, Keck's	E	9/16/05	U
Sidalcea nelsoniana	Checker-mallow, Nelson's	T	9/30/93	F
Sidalcea oregana ssp. valida	Checker-mallow, Kenwood Marsh	E	None	—
Sidalcea oregana var. calva	Checkermallow, Wenatchee Mountains	E	9/30/04	F
Sidalcea pedata	Checker-mallow, pedate	E	7/31/98	F
Silene alexandri	No common name	E	9/26/96	F
Silene hawaiiensis	No common name	T	9/26/96	F
Silene lanceolata	No common name	E	9/26/96	F
Silene perlmanii	No common name	E	8/12/95	F
Silene polypetala	Campion, fringed	E	10/1/96	D
Silene spaldingii	Catchfly, Spalding's	T	9/21/05	U
Sisyrinchium dichotomum	Irisette, white	E	4/10/95	F
Solanum drymophilum	Erubia	E	7/9/92	F
Solanum incompletum	Popolo ku mai	E	7/10/99	F
Solanum sandwicense	`Aiakeakua, popolo	E	9/20/95	F
Solidago albopilosa	Goldenrod, white-haired	T	9/28/93	F
Solidago houghtonii	Goldenrod, Houghton's	T	9/17/97	F
Solidago shortii	Goldenrod, Short's	E	5/25/88	F
Solidago spithamaea	Goldenrod, Blue Ridge	T	10/28/87	F
Spermolepis hawaiiensis	No common name	E	7/10/99	F
Spigelia gentianoides	Pinkroot, gentian	E	None	—
Spiraea virginiana	Spiraea, Virginia	T	11/13/92	F
Spiranthes delitescens	Ladies'-tresses, Canelo Hills	E	None	—
Spiranthes diluvialis	Ladies'-tresses, Ute	T	9/21/95	D
Spiranthes parksii	Ladies'-tresses, Navasota	E	9/21/84	F
Stahlia monosperma	Cobana negra	T	11/1/96	F
Stenogyne angustifolia var. angustifolia	No common name	E	9/20/93	D
Stenogyne bifida	No common name	E	9/26/96	F
Stenogyne campanulata	No common name	E	9/20/95	F
Stenogyne kanehoana	No common name	E	8/12/95	F
Stephanomeria malheurensis	Wire-lettuce, Malheur	E	3/21/91	F
Streptanthus albidus ssp. albidus	Jewelflower, Metcalf Canyon	E	9/30/98	F
Streptanthus niger	Jewelflower, Tiburon	E	9/30/98	F
Styrax portoricensis	Palo de jazmin	E	7/31/95	F
Styrax texanus	Snowbells, Texas	E	7/31/87	F
Suaeda californica	Seablite, California	E	None	—
Swallenia alexandrae	Grass, Eureka Dune	E	12/13/82	F
Taraxacum californicum	Taraxacum, California	E	9/16/05	U
Ternstroemia luquillensis	Palo colorado	E	7/31/95	F
Ternstroemia subsessilis	No common name	E	7/31/95	F
Tetramolopium arenarium	No common name	E	9/26/96	F
Tetramolopium capillare	Pamakani	E	7/29/97	F
Tetramolopium filiforme	No common name	E	8/12/95	F
Tetramolopium lepidotum ssp. lepidotum	No common name	E	8/12/95	F
Tetramolopium remyi	No common name	E	9/29/95	F
Tetramolopium rockii	No common name	T	9/26/96	F
Tetraplasandra gymnocarpa	`ohe`ohe	E	8/10/98	F
Thalictrum cooleyi	Meadowrue, Cooley's	E	4/21/94	F
Thelypodium howellii spectabilis	Thelypody, Howell's spectacular	T	6/3/02	F
Thelypodium stenopetalum	Mustard, slender-petaled	E	7/31/98	F
Thlaspi californicum	Penny-cress, Kneeland Prairie	E	8/14/03	F
Thymophylla tephroleuca	Dogweed, ashy	E	7/29/88	F
Thysanocarpus conchuliferus	Fringepod, Santa Cruz Island	E	9/26/2000	F
Townsendia aprica	Townsendia, Last Chance	T	8/20/93	F

TABLE 11.1

Endangered and threatened plant species in the United States, March 2006 [CONTINUED]

Scientific name	Inverted common name	Listing status[a]	Recovery plan date	Recovery plan status[b]
Trematolobelia singularis	No common name	E	8/10/98	F
Trichilia triacantha	Bariaco	E	8/20/91	F
Trichostema austromontanum ssp. compactum	Bluecurls, Hidden Lake	T	9/16/05	U
Trifolium amoenum	Clover, showy Indian	E	None	—
Trifolium stoloniferum	Clover, running buffalo	E	8/12/05	RD(1)
Trifolium trichocalyx	Clover, Monterey	E	12/20/04	F
Trillium persistens	Trillium, persistent	E	3/27/84	F
Trillium reliquum	Trillium, relict	E	1/31/91	F
Tuctoria greenei	Tuctoria, Greene's	E	3/7/06	F
Tuctoria mucronata	Grass, Solano	E	9/11/85	F
Urera kaalae	Opuhe	E	8/12/95	F
Verbena californica	Vervain, Red Hills	T	9/16/05	U
Verbesina dissita	Crownbeard, big-leaved	T	None	—
Vernonia proctorii	No common name	E	7/31/95	F
Vicia menziesii	Vetch, Hawaiian	E	5/18/84	F
Vigna o-wahuensis	No common name	E	7/10/99	F
Viola chamissoniana ssp. chamissoniana	Pamakani	E	8/12/95	F
Viola helenae	No common name	E	5/31/94	F
Viola kauaiensis var. wahiawaensis	Nani wai`ale`ale	E	8/23/98	F
Viola lanaiensis	No common name	E	9/29/95	F
Viola oahuensis	No common name	E	8/10/98	F
Warea amplexifolia	Warea, wide-leaf	E	2/17/93	F
Warea carteri	Mustard, Carter's	E	5/18/99	F
Wilkesia hobdyi	Iliau, dwarf	E	9/20/95	F
Xylosma crenatum	No common name	E	9/20/95	F
Xyris tennesseensis	Grass, Tennessee yellow-eyed	E	6/24/94	F
Yermo xanthocephalus	Yellowhead, desert	T	None	—
Zanthoxylum dipetalum var. tomentosum	A`e	E	5/11/98	F
Zanthoxylum hawaiiense	A`e	E	9/26/96	F
Zanthoxylum thomasianum	Prickly-ash, St. Thomas	E	4/5/88	RF(1)
Zizania texana	Wild-rice, Texas	E	2/14/96	F
Ziziphus celata	Ziziphus, Florida	E	5/18/99	F

[a]E=endangered, T=threatened.
[b]Recovery plan stages: E=exempt, U=under development, F=final, D=draft, TD=technical draft, RD=draft under revision, RF=final revision, O=other.

SOURCE: Adapted from "Flowering Plants Species Report" and "Non-Flowering Species Report" and "Listed FWS/Joint FWS and NMFS Species and Populations with Recovery Plans (Sorted by Listed Entity)," in *Threatened and Endangered Species System (TESS)*, U.S. Department of the Interior, U.S. Fish and Wildlife Service, March 6, 2006, http://ecos.fws.gov/tess_public/StartTESS.do (accessed March 6, 2006)

limited range of distribution and are threatened by alteration and loss of habitat.

Cycads are unusual plants often mistaken for palms or ferns. They have thick, soft trunks and large, leaf-like crowns. Cycads are found in tropical or semitropical regions. Their rarity makes them popular with collectors. The Florida torreya (*Torreya taxifolia*) is the only cycad listed under the ESA. This scrubby tree is extremely rare and is found only on the bluffs along the Apalachicola River in the panhandle of Florida. An unknown disease virtually wiped out the species in the wild during the 1950s.

Ferns and Allies

Ferns are an abundant and diverse plant group. There are up to 20,000 species of ferns, and they are associated mostly with tropical and subtropical regions. In general these plants are characterized by stems with long protruding "leaves" called fronds. Fern allies are plants with similar life cycles to ferns, but without their stem or leaf structure. Examples of fern allies include the club mosses and horsetails.

There are twenty-six fern and allied species listed under the ESA. Nearly all are endangered. Geographical locations with large numbers of imperiled ferns include Hawaii (twelve species) and Puerto Rico (eight species). The remaining species are found primarily in the Southeast, with the exception of the Aleutian shield fern (*Polystichum aleuticum*), which is native to Alaska.

Lichens

Lichens are not truly plants. Scientists place them in the fungi kingdom, instead of the plant kingdom. Lichens are plantlike life-forms composed of two separate organisms—a fungus and an alga. Biologists believe there are up to 4,000 lichen species in the United States. They are found in many different habitats and grow extremely slowly. Some lichens look like moss, while others appear more like traditional plants with a leafy or blade structure. Lichens do not have a "skin" to protect them from the atmosphere. They are highly sensitive to air contaminants and have disappeared from many urban areas, presumably because of air pollution. Lichens are most predominant in undisturbed forests, bogs, and wetlands,

TABLE 11.2

The ten listed plant entities with the highest expenditures under the Endangered Species Act, fiscal year 2004

Common name	Scientific name	Listing status*	Expenditure
Peirson's milk-vetch	*Astragalus magdalenae var. peirsonii*	T	$1,069,717
Pondberry	*Lindera melissifolia*	E	$827,115
Nelson's checker-mallow	*Sidalcea nelsoniiana*	T	$621,980
Gentner's fritillary	*Fritillaria gentneri*	E	$427,440
Texas wild-rice	*Zizania texana*	E	$417,660
Mauna Loa (=Ka`u) silversword	*Argyroxiphium kauense*	E	$360,152
Ute ladies'-tresses	*Spiranthes diluvialis*	T	$303,810
Western prairie fringed orchid	*Platanthera praeclara*	T	$292,639
Seabeach amaranth	*Amaranthus pumilus*	T	$283,384
Kincaid's lupine	*Lupinus sulphureus (=oreganus) ssp. kincaidii (=var.kincaidii)*	T	$276,068

*E=endangered; T=threatened.

SOURCE: Adapted from "Table 1. Reported FY 2004 Expenditures for Endangered and Threatened Species, Not Including Land Acquisition Costs," in *Federal and State Endangered and Threatened Species Expenditures: Fiscal Year 2004*, U.S. Department of the Interior, U.S. Fish and Wildlife Service, January 2005, http://www.fws.gov/endangered/expenditures/reports/FWS%20Endangered%20Species%202004%20Expenditures%20Report.pdf (accessed February 11, 2006)

FIGURE 11.3

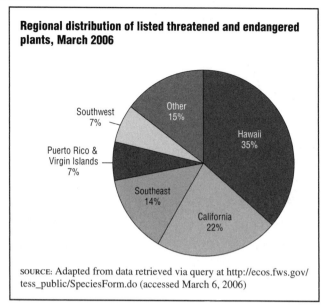

Regional distribution of listed threatened and endangered plants, March 2006

SOURCE: Adapted from data retrieved via query at http://ecos.fws.gov/tess_public/SpeciesForm.do (accessed March 6, 2006)

particularly in California, Hawaii, Florida, the Pacific Northwest, and the Appalachians. They are commonly found on rocky outcroppings. Lichens provide a foodstuff for some animals and are used by some bird species in nest building.

As of March 2006 there were two lichen species listed under the ESA—rock gnome lichen (*Gymnoderma lineare*) and Florida perforate cladonia (*Cladonia perforata*). Both are classified as endangered. During the 1970s rock gnome lichen was virtually wiped out in the Great Smoky Mountains National Park in Tennessee due to zealous collecting by scientists. Florida perforate cladonia is found only in rosemary scrub habitats in portions of Florida. It is endangered due to loss or degradation of those habitats.

Flowering Plants

Flowering plants are vascular plants with flowers—clusters of specialized leaves that participate in reproduction. The flowers of some species are large and colorful, while others are extremely small and barely noticeable to humans. Biologists estimate that 80% to 90% of all plants on Earth are flowering plants.

As shown in Table 11.1, there are more than 700 flowering plants listed as endangered or threatened under the ESA. They come from a wide variety of taxonomic groups and are found in many different habitats. The five largest families represented are as follows:

- Asteraceae (asters, daisies, and sunflowers)—eighty-six species

- Campanulaceae (bellflowers)—forty-nine species

- Fabaceae (legumes and pulses)—forty-nine species

- Lamiaceae (mints)—thirty-five species

- Brassicaceae (mustard and cabbage)—thirty-four species

GEOGRAPHICAL BREAKDOWN OF PLANTS

Most threatened and endangered plant species in the United States are concentrated in specific areas of the country. Figure 11.3 shows a breakdown of listed plants by predominant region as of March 2006. More than one-third of all listings occur in Hawaii. California is home to nearly one-fourth of all listed plants. Together these two states account for more than half of all plants listed under the Endangered Species Act. One other specific region, the Southeast, is notable for its contingent (14%) of threatened and endangered plants. The majority of the imperiled plants in this region are found in Florida. The southwestern United States and Puerto Rico are each home to 7% of listed plants. The remaining 15% of imperiled plants are scattered across other regions of the country.

Hawaiian Plants

Figure 11.4 shows the eight major islands comprising the state of Hawaii. The island of Oahu is home to the state's capital, Honolulu. However, Oahu is not the largest of the islands. That distinction goes to the island labeled "Hawaii," which is commonly called "the big island." In the following discussion, the term Hawaii refers to the entire state.

FIGURE 11.4

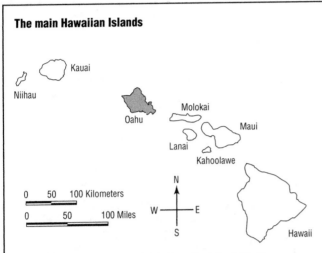

The main Hawaiian Islands

Kauai

Niihau

Molokai

Oahu

Maui

Lanai

Kahoolawe

0   50   100 Kilometers

0   50   100 Miles

N
W — E
S

Hawaii

SOURCE: "Figure 1. Map of the Main Hawaiian Islands," in *Recovery Plan for the Oahu Plants*, U.S. Department of the Interior, U.S. Fish and Wildlife Service, August 10, 1998, http://ecos.fws.gov/docs/recovery_plans/1998/980810.pdf (accessed March 7, 2006)

Because of its isolation from continental land masses, many of the species found in Hawaii exist nowhere else in the world. An estimated 90% of Hawaiian plant species are in fact endemic. Because of large-scale deforestation and habitat destruction on the islands, Hawaii is home to more threatened and endangered plants than any other state in the nation. The U.S. Fish and Wildlife Service (2006, http://www.fws.gov/pacificislands/wesa/endspindex.html) reports that in 2006 there are 273 listed species in Hawaii. Hawaiian plants have suffered from the introduction of invasive predators such as cows, pigs, and insects, as well as the loss of critical pollinators with the decline of numerous species of native birds and insects. According to Marie M. Bruegemann in "A Plan for Hawaiian Plants and Their Ecosytems" (*Endangered Species Bulletin*, July–December 2003), 100 of Hawaii's 1,500 known plant species are believed to have become extinct since the islands were colonized by humans.

The U.S. Fish and Wildlife Service has developed more than a dozen recovery plans for imperiled Hawaiian plants. Many of the plans cover multiple species found in the same ecosystem or habitat types. Examples include:

- Oahu plants—sixty-six species
- Kauai plant cluster—thirty-seven species
- Waianae plant cluster—thirty-one species
- Multi-island plants—twenty-six species
- Big Island plant cluster—twenty-two species

In 2003 the FWS designated over 208,000 acres of critical habitat on the Big Island as habitat for forty-one listed plant species. The area designated was 52% smaller than originally anticipated because it excluded a large tract of U.S. Army land as well as private land held by the Queen Liliuokalani Trust and others. The U.S. Army land was excluded because of national security concerns and also because the Army agreed to voluntarily cooperate with the FWS regarding activity that affects endangered species. The Queen Liliuokalani Trust land was excluded because the trust vowed to discontinue its current efforts on behalf of endangered species if its lands were included in the critical habitat designation. Finally, land near the cities of Kailua and Kona, for which housing development was planned, was excluded from critical habitat designation because the economic and social costs of inclusion were too great.

Designation of critical habitat in Hawaii was completed after a successful lawsuit brought against the Fish and Wildlife Service by Earthjustice, the Conservation Council for Hawaii, the Sierra Club, and the Hawaii Botanical Society.

Californian Plants

As shown in Figure 11.3 California is home to 22% of threatened and endangered plant species in the United States. More than 160 imperiled plants are found there, including several types of checker-mallow, dudleya, evening primrose, grass, jewelflower, larkspur, manzanita, milk-vetch, paintbrush, rock-cress, spineflower, and thistle.

MILK-VETCH. Milk-vetch is an herbaceous perennial flowering plant found in various parts of the world. It received its common name during the 1500s thanks to a belief among European farmers that the plant increased the milk yield of goats. As of March 2006 there were ten species of milk-vetch listed as threatened or endangered in California, the most listings for any single plant type in that state. These species are as follows:

- Braunton's milk-vetch (*Astragalus brauntonii*)
- Clara Hunt's milk-vetch (*Astragalus clarianus*)
- Coachella Valley milk-vetch (*Astragalus lentiginosus* var. coachellae)
- Coastal dunes milk-vetch (*Astragalus tener* var. titi)
- Cushenbury milk-vetch (*Astragalus albens*)
- Fish Slough milk-vetch (*Astragalus lentiginosus* var. piscinensis)
- Lane Mountain milk-vetch (*Astragalus jaegerianus*)
- Peirson's milk-vetch (*Astragalus magdalenae* var. peirsonii)
- Triple-ribbed milk-vetch (*Astragalus tricarinatus*)
- Ventura Marsh milk-vetch (*Astragalus pycnostachyus* var. lanosissimus)

FIGURE 11.5

Location of the Imperial Sand Dunes Recreation Area

Socio-economics area

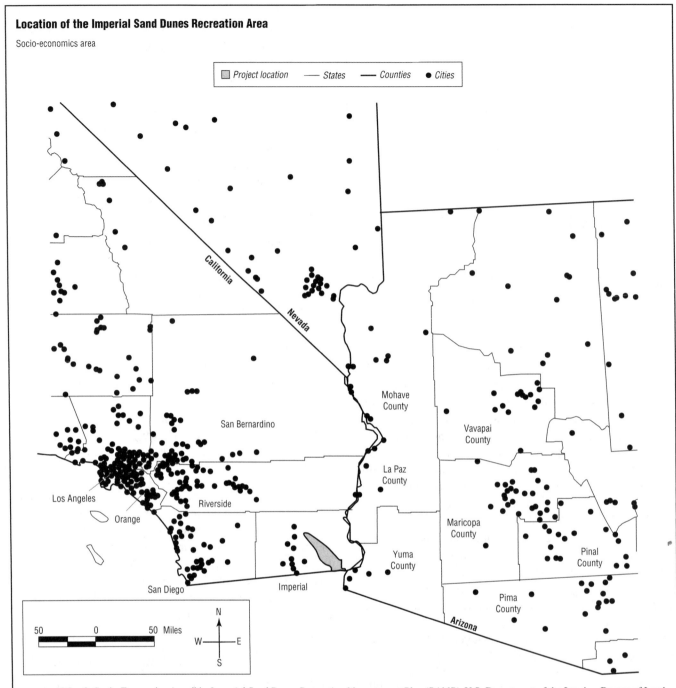

SOURCE: "Map 2. Socio-Economics Area," in *Imperial Sand Dunes Recreation Management Plan (RAMP)*, U.S. Department of the Interior, Bureau of Land Management, May 2003, http://www.blm.gov/ca/elcentro/ImperialSandDunes/isdra_feis.html (accessed March 10, 2006)

Peirson's milk-vetch is a plant with a long history of litigation and controversy in California. It is found in only one small area of Imperial County in the southern part of the state. (See Figure 11.5.) This area is the Imperial Sand Dunes Recreation Area (ISDRA) managed by the Bureau of Land Management under the U.S. Department of the Interior. ISDRA has a remote and barren landscape dominated by huge rolling sand dunes—the Algodones Dunes, the largest sand dune

fields in North America. ISDRA covers 185,000 acres and is a popular destination for off-highway vehicle (OHV) riders, receiving more than one million visitors annually.

In 1998 Peirson's milk-vetch was designated a threatened species by the U.S. Fish and Wildlife Service because of the threat of destruction by OHVs and other recreational activities at Imperial Sand Dunes Recreation

Area. The agency decided not to designate critical habitat at that time, fearing the remaining plants would be subject to deliberate vandalism. The Bureau of Land Management was sued by conservation groups and accused of not consulting with the FWS about the threats to the Peirson's milk-vetch before establishing a management plan for the Recreation Area. In 2000, in response to that lawsuit, the Bureau of Land Management closed more than a third of the ISDRA to off-highway vehicle use.

In October 2001 a petition to delist the species was submitted on behalf of the American Sand Association, San Diego Off-Road Coalition, and Off-Road Business Association. A month later two lawsuits were filed against the Fish and Wildlife Service by conservation organizations challenging the agency's decision not to designate critical habitat for the species. Under court order, the FWS proposed critical habitat in 2003. Meanwhile the delisting petition submitted in 2001 triggered a status review.

In 2004 the FWS issued a final designation of critical habitat for Peirson's milk-vetch that encompassed nearly 22,000 acres of Imperial Sand Dunes Recreation Area. This was less than half of the acreage originally proposed. The reduction was made after an economic analysis revealed that closure of ISDRA areas to off-road vehicle use would have a negative impact on local businesses. That same year the agency completed the status review triggered by the 2001 delisting proposal and found that the species should remain listed as threatened. In July 2005 the original petitioners and additional OHV and motorcycle associations submitted a new petition to delist Peirson's milk-vetch. This petition also triggered a status review, which was expected to be completed in late 2006. In a public statement, the U.S. Fish and Wildlife Service noted that the new petition contains data indicating that the species is more abundant and widespread than originally believed.

As of spring 2006 portions of the ISDRA remained under temporary closure to off-highway vehicle riders due to ongoing litigation against the Bureau of Land Management regarding management of the Recreation Area.

LOS ANGELES BASIN MOUNTAIN PLANTS. Numerous species of threatened and endangered plants have reached their precarious state due to urbanization and other human activity. Figure 11.6 shows the species distribution of six threatened and endangered plant species found in the mountains surrounding the Los Angeles basin:

- Braunton's milk-vetch (*Astragalus brauntonii*)
- Marcescent dudleya (*Dudleya cymosa ssp. marcescens*)
- Santa Monica Mountains dudleya (*Dudleya cymosa ssp. ovatifolia*)
- Conejo dudleya (*Dudleya abramsii ssp. parva*)
- Verity's dudleya (*Dudleya verityi*)
- Lyon's pentachaeta (*Pentachaeata lyonii*)

The recovery plan for these species cites threats including "urban development, recreational activities, alteration of fire cycles through fire suppression and pre-suppression (fuel modification) activities, over-collecting, habitat fragmentation and degradation, and competition from invasive weeds." Some species are currently so reduced in number that extinction due to random events is also a threat.

Floridian Plants

As shown in Figure 11.3, the southeastern states contain 14% of the threatened and endangered plant species listed under the ESA as of March 2006. Approximately half of these listed plants are found only in Florida. They include multiple species of mint, pawpaw, rosemary, and spurge.

Many of Florida's imperiled plants are found in the southern part of the state—the only subtropical ecological habitat in the continental United States. Figure 3.2 in Chapter 3 shows a map of the south Florida ecosystem, including its national parks, national preserves, and numerous national wildlife refuges. The Fish and Wildlife Service maintains a field office in this area in Vero Beach, Florida. The majority of native plant species located in the bottom half of the south Florida ecosystem originated from the tropics.

In 1999 the FWS published the *South Florida Multi-Species Recovery Plan* (MSRP) covering sixty-six species, including dozens of plant species. In 2004 an implementation schedule for many of the species in the plan was issued, which divided the ecosystem into ecological communities as follows:

- Florida scrub/scrubby flatwoods/scrubby high pine—nineteen plant species
- Pine rocklands—five plant species
- Beach dune/coastal strand—one plant species
- Tropical hardwood hammock—one plant species
- Mesic and hydric pine flatwoods—one plant species
- Freshwater marsh/wet prairie—one plant species

The recovery and restoration tasks outlined in the MSRP are to be implemented through creation of a team of federal, state, and local governmental agencies; Native American tribal governments; academic representatives; industry representatives; and members of the private sector. The schedule prioritizes the plan's recovery actions

FIGURE 11.6

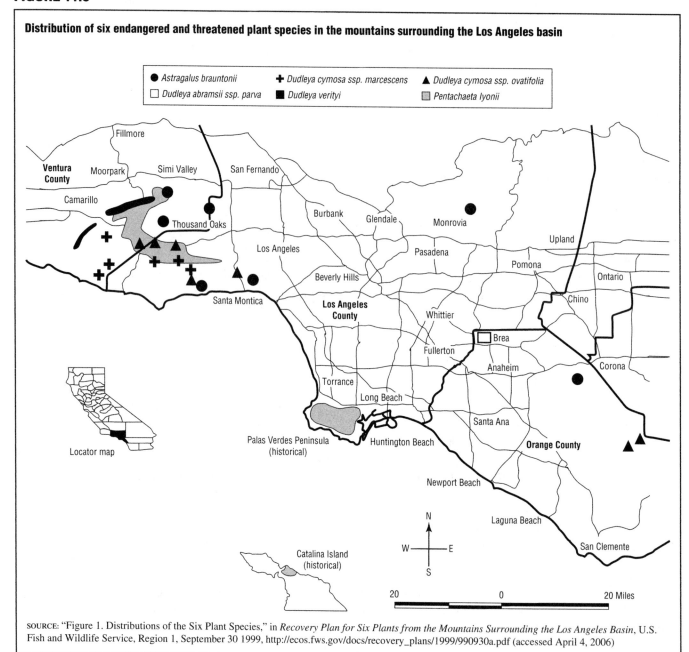

Distribution of six endangered and threatened plant species in the mountains surrounding the Los Angeles basin

SOURCE: "Figure 1. Distributions of the Six Plant Species," in *Recovery Plan for Six Plants from the Mountains Surrounding the Los Angeles Basin*, U.S. Fish and Wildlife Service, Region 1, September 30 1999, http://ecos.fws.gov/docs/recovery_plans/1999/990930a.pdf (accessed April 4, 2006)

and estimates costs on an annual basis for implementing the actions in each ecological community.

The *South Florida Multi-Species Recovery Plan* is considered a landmark plan, because it was one of the first recovery plans to focus on an ecosystem approach to recovery, rather than a species-by-species approach.

THREATENED AND ENDANGERED FOREIGN SPECIES OF PLANTS

As of March 2006 the U.S. Fish and Wildlife Service listed only three foreign species of plants as threatened or endangered as follows:

- Guatemalan pinabete fir (*Abies guatemalensis*)—Threatened

- Chilean false larch (*Fitzroya cupressoides*)—Threatened

- Coast Rican jatropha (*Jatropha costaricensis*)—Endangered

The *1997 IUCN Red List of Threatened Plants* from the World Conservation Union (IUCN) was the first global assessment of plants, and was the result of over twenty years of study by botanists, conservation organizations, botanical gardens, and museums around the world. It revealed that 12.5%—one of every eight—of the world's plant species are in danger of extinction. In the United States, the figure is even higher, with 29% of the nation's 16,000 plant species threatened.

The IUCN also reported that the vast majority of plants at risk are extremely limited geographically; most are not found outside of their home nations, making these species particularly vulnerable to extinction. Many plant species known to have medicinal value are threatened, including many species in the yew family, a source of cancer-fighting compounds. The IUCN notes that the loss of each species causes a loss of genetic material that could be used to produce stronger, healthier crops for human and animal consumption.

The *2004 IUCN Red List of Threatened Species* currently lists 8,321 species of threatened plants. This is 70% of the 11,824 plants that have been examined. However, only 4% of plant species have been studied in sufficient detail to assess their status, and the actual number of threatened species is likely to be much higher.

The majority of IUCN-listed species are flowering plants, a diverse and well-studied group. In 2004 the IUCN reported that 7,796 flowering plants were threatened. Other IUCN-listed species include eighty true mosses, 140 ferns and allies, and 305 cycads. Habitat loss accounts at least in part for the threatened status of the vast majority of IUCN-listed plants.

IMPORTANT NAMES AND ADDRESSES

**Alaska Fisheries Science Center
National Oceanic and
Atmospheric Administration**
7600 Sand Point Way NE, Building 4
Seattle, WA 98115
(206) 526-4000
FAX: (206) 526-4004
URL: http://www.afsc.noaa.gov

AmphibiaWeb
U.C. Berkeley 3101 Valley Life Sciences
Building #3160
Berkeley, CA 94720
URL: http://amphibiaweb.org

**Biological Resources Division
U.S. Geological Survey**
12201 Sunrise Valley Dr., MS 300
Reston, VA 20192
(703) 648-4050
URL: http://biology.usgs.gov/

BirdLife International
Wellbrook Court
Girton Rd.
Cambridge CB3 ONA
United Kingdom
(44-0) 1223 277 318
E-mail: birdlife@birdlife.org
URL: http://www.birdlife.org

**Center for Plant
Conservation (CPC)**
P.O. Box 299
St. Louis, MO 63166
(314) 577-9450
E-mail: cpc@mobot.org
URL: http://
www.centerforplantconservation.org

**Earth System Research Laboratory
National Oceanic and Atmospheric
Administration**
325 Broadway R/GMD1
Boulder, CO 80305-3328
URL: http://www.cmdl.noaa.gov/

Environmental Defense
257 Park Ave. S
New York, NY 10010
(212) 505-2100
FAX: (212) 505-2375
E-mail:
members@environmentaldefense.org
URL: http://
www.environmentaldefense.org/home.cfm

Florida Panther Society, Inc.
P.O. Box 358683
Gainesville, FL 32635-8683
(386) 397-2945
E-mail: karenhill@panthersociety.org
URL: http://www.panthersociety.org

**Goddard Institute for Space Studies
National Aeronautics and Space
Administration**
2880 Broadway
New York, NY 10025
(212) 678-5500
URL: http://www.giss.nasa.gov/

Government Accountability Office (GAO)
441 G St. NW
Washington, DC 20548
(202) 512-3000
E-mail: webmaster@gao.gov
URL: http://www.gao.gov

Greenpeace U.S.A.
702 H St. NW, Suite 300
Washington, DC 20001
1-800-326-0959
URL: http://www.greenpeace.org/usa/

Land Trust Alliance
1331 H St. NW, Suite 400
Washington, DC 20005-4734
(202) 638-4725
URL: http://www.lta.org/

National Audubon Society
700 Broadway
New York, NY 10003

(212) 979-3000
FAX: (212) 979-3188
URL: http://www.audubon.org

**National Forest Service U.S. Department
of Agriculture**
1400 Independence Ave. SW
Washington, DC 20250-0003
(202) 205-8333
E-mail: webmaster@fs.fed.us
URL: http://www.fs.fed.us

**National Marine Fisheries Service
(NMFS) National Oceanic and
Atmospheric Administration**
1315 East West Highway, 9th Floor
Silver Spring, MD 20910
(301) 713-2379
FAX: (301) 713-2385
URL: http://www.nmfs.noaa.gov

**National Marine Mammal Laboratory
National Oceanic and Atmospheric
Administration**
7600 Sand Point Way NE F/AKC3
Seattle, WA 98115-6349
(206) 526-4045
FAX: (206) 526-6615
URL: http://nmml.afsc.noaa.gov

National Park Service
1849 C St. NW
Washington, DC 20240
(202) 208-6843
URL: http://www.nps.gov/

**National Research Council The National
Academies**
500 Fifth St. NW
Washington, DC 20001
(202) 334-2000
URL: http://www.nas.edu/nrc/

National Wildlife Federation
11100 Wildlife Center Dr.
Reston, VA 20190-5362

1-800-822-9919
URL: http://www.nwf.org

National Wildlife Health Center
U.S. Geological Survey
6006 Schroeder Rd.
Madison, WI 53711-6223
(608) 270-2400
FAX: (608) 270-2415
E-mail: NWHCweb@usgs.gov
URL: http://www.nwhc.usgs.gov

Natural Resources Defense Council
40 West 20th St.
New York, NY 10011
(212) 727-2700
FAX: (212) 727-1773
E-mail: nrdcinfo@nrdc.org
URL: http://www.nrdc.org

Nature Conservancy
4245 North Fairfax Dr., Suite 100
Arlington, VA 22203-1606
(703) 841-53001-800-628-6860
URL: http://nature.org

Northeast Fisheries Science Center
National Oceanic and Atmospheric
Administration
166 Water St.
Woods Hole, MA 02543-1026
(508) 495-2000
FAX: (508) 495-2258
URL: http://www.nefsc.noaa.gov

Northwest Fisheries Science Center
National Oceanic and Atmospheric
Administration
2725 Montlake Blvd. E
Seattle, WA 98112-2097
(206) 860-3200
FAX: (206) 860-3217
URL: http://www.nwfsc.noaa.gov

Sierra Club
85 Second St., 2nd Floor
San Francisco, CA 94105-3441
(415) 977-5500
FAX: (415) 977-5799

E-mail: information@sierraclub.org
URL: http://www.sierraclub.org

TRAFFIC International
219a Huntingdon Rd.
Cambridge CB3 0DL
United Kingdom
(44) 1223 277427
FAX:(44) 1223 277237
E-mail: traffic@trafficint.org
URL: http://www.traffic.org

TRAFFIC North America—Regional
Office
1250 24th St. NW
Washington, DC 20037
(202) 293-4800
FAX: (202)775-8287
E-mail: tna@wwfus.org
URL: http://www.traffic.org

United Nations Environment Programme
United Nations Ave., Gigiri
P.O. Box 30552
Nairobi 00100
Kenya
(254-2) 7621234
FAX: (254-2) 7624489/90
E-mail: unepinfo@unep.org
URL: http://www.unep.org

U.S. Bureau of Land Management
1849 C St., Room 406-LS
Washington, DC 20240
(202) 452-5125
FAX: (202) 452-5124
URL: http://www.blm.gov

U.S. Bureau of Reclamation
1849 C St. NW
Washington, DC 20240-0001
(202) 513-0575
URL: http://www.usbr.gov/

U.S. Environmental Protection Agency
Office of Water
1200 Pennsylvania Ave. NW
Washington, DC 20460

(202) 566-0430
URL: http://epa.gov/waterscience

U.S. Fish and Wildlife Service—Division
of Endangered Species
United States Department of
the Interior
4401 North Fairfax Dr., Rm. 420
Arlington, VA 22203
URL: http://www.fws.gov/endangered

Western Ecological Research
Center—U.S. Geological Survey
3020 State University Dr. E
Modoc Hall, Room 3006
Sacramento, CA 95819
(916) 278-9485
FAX: (916) 278-9475
URL: http://www.werc.usgs.gov

The Wilderness Society
1615 M St. NW
Washington, DC 20036
1-800-843-9453
E-mail: member@tws.org
URL: http://www.wilderness.org

World Conservation Union (IUCN)
Rue Mauverney 28
Gland 1196
Switzerland
41 (22) 999-0000
FAX: 41 (22) 999-0002
E-mail: webmaster@iucn.org
URL: http://www.iucn.org

World Wildlife Fund (WWF)
1250 24th St. NW
Washington, DC 20090-7180
(202) 293-4800
URL: http://www.worldwildlife.org

Worldwatch Institute
1776 Massachusetts Ave. NW
Washington, DC 20036-1904
(202) 452-1999
FAX: (202) 296-7365
E-mail: worldwatch@worldwatch.org
URL: http://www.worldwatch.org

RESOURCES

A first source of information on endangered species is the U.S. Fish and Wildlife Service (FWS), an agency of the U.S. Department of the Interior. The Fish and Wildlife Service oversees the Endangered Species List. Their comprehensive Web site (http://www.fws.gov/endangered/) includes news stories on threatened and endangered species, information about laws protecting endangered species, regional contacts for endangered species programs, and a searchable database called the Threatened and Endangered Species System (TESS) with information on all listed species (http://ecos.fws.gov/tess_public/StartTESS.do). Each listed species has an information page that provides details regarding the status of the species (whether it is listed as threatened or endangered and in what geographic area), *Federal Register* documents pertaining to listing, information on habitat conservation plans and National Wildlife Refuges pertinent to the species, and, for many species, links to descriptions of biology and natural history. Particularly informative are the recovery plans published for a large number of listed species. These detail the background research on the natural history of endangered species and also list measures that should be adopted to aid in conservation.

The Fish and Wildlife Service also maintains updated tables of the number of threatened and endangered species by taxonomic group, as well as lists of U.S. threatened and endangered species. The agency publishes the bimonthly *Endangered Species Bulletin* (available online at http://endangered.fws.gov/bulletin.html), which provides information on new listings, delistings, and reclassifications, in addition to news articles on endangered species. Finally, the FWS prints an annual report on expenditures made under the Endangered Species Act. These reports are available at the Web site http://www.fws.gov/endangered/pubs/expenditurereports.html.

The National Marine Fisheries Service (NMFS) is responsible for the oversight of threatened and endangered marine animals and anadromous fish. Valuable information is available at the agency's Web site (http://www.nmfs.noaa.gov). The NMFS is a division of the National Oceanic and Atmospheric Administration (NOAA), which also operates the National Marine Mammal Laboratory at the Alaska Fisheries Science Center (http://nmml.afsc.noaa.gov), the Northeast Fisheries Science Center (http://nefsc.noaa.gov) and the Northwest Fisheries Science Center (http://www.nwfsc.noaa.gov).

The United States Geological Survey (USGS) performs research on many imperiled animal species. Data sheets on individual species are available from the USGS National Wildlife Health Center at http://www.nwhc.usgs.gov. Other important USGS centers include the Western Ecological Research Center (http://www.werc.usgs.gov), the Northern Prairie Wildlife Research Center (http://www.npwrc.usgs.gov), the Nonindigenous Aquatic Species (NAS) information resource at the Center for Aquatic Resource Studies (http://nas.er.usgs.gov), the Biological Resources Division (http://biology.usgs.gov), and the Center for Biological Informatics, which maintains the National Biological Information Infrastructure (NBII) at http://www.nbii.gov.

Information on federal lands and endangered species management can be found at the National Wildlife Refuge Web site (http://refuges.fws.gov), the National Park System Web site (http://www.nps.gov), and the National Forest Service Web site (http://www.fs.fed.us/). National Wildlife Refuge brochures are available at http://library.fws.gov/refuges/index.html.

Endangered Ecosystems of the United States—A Preliminary Assessment of Loss and Degradation, a 1995 publication from the National Biological Service, remains the most up-iresto-iresdate assessment of U.S. ecosystems. Information on water quality in the United States is available at the Web site of the Environmental Protection Agency, http://www.epa.gov/water. Information on wetlands can be found at the Fish and Wildlife Service's "National Wetlands Inventory" page at http://www.nwi.fws.gov.

Data and information related to global warming are available from the National Aeronautics and Space Administration's Goddard Institute for Space Studies at http://data.giss.nasa.gov and at NOAA (National Oceanic and Atmospheric Administration)/ESRL (Earth System Research Laboratory) Global Monitoring Division (http://www.cmdl.noaa.gov).

Other federal agencies that proved useful for this book were the U.S. Commission on Ocean Policy, which published the 2004 report *An Ocean Blueprint for the 21st Century, Final Report* (available at http://www.oceancommission.gov) and the U.S. Army Corps of Engineers, which maintains a database of the nation's dams at the Web site http://crunch.tec.army.mil/nid/webpages/nid.cfm. The U.S. Department of the Interior operates the National Atlas of the United States, an online mapping tool and information source available at http://nationalatlas.gov. The U.S. Government Accountability Office (GAO) publishes a number of reports assessing the policies and effectiveness of the Endangered Species Program. GAO reports are available at http://www.gao.gov.

The World Conservation Union (IUCN) has news articles on a wide array of worldwide conservation issues at its Web site (http://www.iucn.org). Information from the *2004 IUCN Red List of Threatened Species* is also available online at http://www.redlist.org. This site includes an extensive database of information on IUCN-listed threatened species. Species information available includes Red List endangerment category, the year the species was assessed, the countries in which the species is found, a list of the habitat types the species occupies, major threats to continued existence, and current population trends. Brief descriptions of ecology and natural history and of conservation measures for protecting listed species are also available. Searches can also be performed by taxonomic group, Red List categories, country, region, or habitat.

The Convention on International Trade in Endangered Species of Wild Fauna and Flora (CITES) has information on international trade in endangered species at http://www.cites.org. This includes a species database of protected fauna and flora in the three CITES appendices, as well as information on the history and aims of the convention and its current programs.

Numerous private organizations are dedicated to the conservation of listed species and their ecosystems. Readers with interest in a particular endangered species are advised to conduct Internet searches to locate these groups. The Save the Manatee Club (http://www.savethemanatee.org), which focuses on West Indian manatees, and the Save Our Springs Alliance (http://www.sosalliance.org), which focuses on protection of the endangered Barton Springs salamander, are only two of many examples.

The World Conservation Union's *1997 IUCN Red-List of Threatened Plants* is a valuable resource on threatened plant species.

BirdLife International (http://www.birdlife.net) provides diverse resources on global bird conservation. It is an association of nongovernmental conservation organizations that has over two million members worldwide.

AmphibiaWeb (http://amphibiaweb.org) provides detailed information on global amphibian declines. It maintains a watch list of recently extinct and declining species, discusses potential causes of amphibian declines and deformities, and also provides detailed information on amphibian biology and conservation. AmphibiaWeb also sponsors a discussion board where readers can submit questions regarding amphibians.

TRAFFIC (http://www.traffic.org) was originally founded to help implement the CITES treaty but now addresses diverse issues in wildlife trade. It is a joint wildlife trade monitoring organization of the World Wildlife Fund (WWF) and the World Conservation Union (IUCN). The TRAFFIC Web site contains articles on current topics related to wildlife trade. In addition, TRAFFIC also publishes several periodicals and report series on wildlife trade, including the *TRAFFIC Bulletin*, TRAFFIC Online Report Series, and *Species in Danger Series*. These publications are available online at http://www.traffic.org/publications/index.html.

The International Whaling Commission has a Web site at http://www.iwcoffice.org/. Information on whaling regulations, whale sanctuaries, and other issues associated with whales and whaling can be accessed there.

The Gallup Organization provided information related to public polls conducted in recent years concerning environmental issues.

Information Plus sincerely thanks all of the organizations listed above for the valuable information they provide.

INDEX

golden-cheeked warblers, 139–140
Habitat Conservation Plans, 29
horned lizards, 109
insects, 151
Kemp's ridley sea turtles, 108
whooping cranes, 145
Texas blind salamanders, 101*f*
Texas cougars, 120, 121
This Land is Our Land (Pombo), 27
Thomas, Chris D., 11
Threatened, Endangered and Sensitive
Species Program, 38
Threatened and Endangered Species
System (TESS), 183
Threatened species, 3, 4
Three Gorges Dam, *52*
Tidal wetlands, 34, 36
Tigers, 125–127, *128*, 128*t*
Toads
description of, 99
endangered and threatened
(foreign), 102*t*
endangered and threatened (U.S.),
100*t*, 101–102
golden, 103
horny, 109
Tongass National Forest, 31
Torreya taxifolia. See Florida torreya
Tortoises, desert, 108–109, *109*
Trade
in animal species, 12
international, 46–47
pet, 147
TRAFFIC, 129, 184
Trawlers, 62, 107
Treaties. *See* Legislation and treaties
Tree snails, Oahu, 96
Trematodes, 104
Tropical forests, 30, 32–33
Trout, bull, 82, 85, 86(*f*6.2)
Tuataras, 111
Tuna bycatch, 62, 65, 71–72
Turbidity, water, 57
Turtle excluder devices (TEDs),
107–108, 108*f*
Turtles
endangered and threatened (foreign),
110*t*, 111
endangered and threatened (U.S.),
105–108, 106*t*
excluder devices, 107–108, 108*f*
nesting, 107
sea, 105–108, 107*f*, 108*f*
Tusks, 128–129
Twain, Mark, 101–102

U

Ultraviolet (UV) radiation, 103, 104(*f*7.2)
UNEP (United Nations Environmental
Program), 46
United Nations
Food and Agricultural Organization, 33
Global Biodiversity Outlook 2, 3
United Nations Convention on Biological
Diversity, 47
United Nations Environmental Program
(UNEP), 46
Urbanization, 10
Urodela, 99
U.S. Army Corp of Engineers
Missouri River spring rise issue, 50
National Inventory of Dams, 49
Snake River dam removal, 52
U.S. Commission on Ocean Policy, 59
U.S. Fish and Wildlife Service (FWS)
bats, 113–114
beluga sturgeon program, 91
budget expenditures, 23–24, 24*f*, 24*t*
endangered marine mammals,
66–67, 66*t*
Endangered Species Act litigation, 23
gray wolf status, 117
information resources, 183
Marine Mammal Protection Act
and, 65
Missouri River spring rise issue, 50
northern spotted owl policy, 5–6, 8,
142–143
pallid sturgeon recovery plan, 82, 84–85
*Recovery Plan for the California Red-
legged Frog*, 101–102
role of, 3
sea otter program, 76
Utah prairie dog penalties, 124
U.S. Forest Service. *See* National Forest
Service
U.S. Geologic Survey
Arctic National Wildlife Refuge, 43
freshwater fish survey, 82
information resources, 183
North American Reporting Center for
Amphibian Malformations
(NARCAM), 104
sea otter population study, 76
water supply data, 49
Utah prairie dogs, 123–124, 124*f*, 125*f*
Utah valvata snails, 96

V

Vernal pool fairy shrimp, 96–97
Vietnam War herbicides, 36
Vireos, black-capped, 139–140

W

Wading water birds, 144–145, 144*f*,
145*f*
Warblers, golden-cheeked, 139–140
Washington State
Canada lynx, 120
pygmy rabbit program, 123
Water birds, 144–145
migratory shore, 144
sea, 144
wading, 144–145, 144*f*, 145*f*
Water ecosystem. *See* Aquatic
environments
Water management
Everglades, 34
freshwater diversions, 53
Klamath Basin, 53
Missouri River spring rise issue, 50
See also Dams
Water pollution
air pollution and, 57–58
amphibian declines, 103
threat of, 53–57
Water supply, global, 49
Water turbidity, 57
Watersnakes, Lake Erie, 109
West Indian manatees, 77
Western Council of Industrial
Workers, 143
Wetlands, 33–36
Whales, 67–71, *67*
baleen, 68, 68*f*
blue, 1, *2f*
endangered and threatened, 68, 71*t*
northern right, 68, 69, 70–71
sei, 68
ship strikes of, 69, 70(*f*5.3),
70(*f*5.4)
White rhinoceros, 132, 132*f*, 133
Whooping cranes, 144–145, 145*f*
Wilderness Act, 41
Wilderness Preservation System
Areas, 41
Wildlife Conservation Society, 125
Wilson, E. O., 27
Wolf spiders, Kauai cave, 156
Wolves, 116–117, 118*f*, *119*
gray, 117, 118*f*, 119(*f*8.4)
red, 117, *119*
Wood storks, 144, 144*f*
Woodpeckers, 135, 137–139, 137*f*
ivory-billed, 139
red-cockaded, 135, 137–139, 137*f*, 138*f*
World Commission on Protected
Areas, 48

World Conservation Union, 111
  birds, 148
  establishment of, 3
  fish, 89, 91
  information resources, 184
  invasive species effects, 12–13
  longline fishing, 62
  plants, 178–179
  primates, 130
  reptiles, 111
World Commission on Protected
  Areas, 48
  *See also IUCN Red List of Threatened
  Species*
World Trade Organization (WTO), 108
World Wildlife Fund
  elephant ivory trade, 128, 129
  establishment of, 15
  saimaa seals, 72
WTO (World Trade Organization), 108

Y

Yangtze River dam, 52–53, 52*f*
Yellowstone National Park, 4, 116

Z

Zayante band-winged grasshoppers, 154
Zebra mussels, 93, 95*f*
Zoo breeding programs. *See* Captive
  breeding programs